INDEPENDENCE
AND AFTER

By Jawaharlal Nehru

TOWARD FREEDOM

GLIMPSES OF WORLD HISTORY

THE UNITY OF INDIA

THE DISCOVERY OF INDIA

NEHRU ON GANDHI

VISIT TO AMERICA

INDEPENDENCE AND AFTER

JAWAHARLAL NEHRU

INDEPENDENCE AND AFTER

A Collection of Speeches
1946-1949

THE JOHN DAY COMPANY   NEW YORK

AMERICAN EDITION, JULY, 1950

SECOND IMPRESSION

LITHOGRAPHED IN THE UNITED STATES OF AMERICA
FROM THE ORIGINAL EDITION PUBLISHED BY THE
PUBLICATIONS DIVISION, MINISTRY OF INFORMATION
AND BROADCASTING, GOVERNMENT OF INDIA, DELHI.

Publisher's Note

THE following speeches, barring four, cover the period of a little over a year and a half immediately following the attainment of independence by India. They are grouped according to topic and arranged in chronological order.

The wide range of Jawaharlal Nehru's interests, however, has inevitably swelled not only the number of the sections, but also the section called "Miscellaneous." For this reason no single principle has determined the selection of the speeches. Some of them, notably on Kashmir, give a connected historical narrative; others bring out important matters of policy; yet others breathe sentiments which have inspired India and will inspire readers abroad. The unique personality of the speaker has given them all a basic unity. His insistence on moral values, disarming candor and spontaneous sincerity have invested the spoken word with lasting significance.

At the same time, the variety and versatility of his interests and his alert awareness of facts and tendencies have imparted to the Prime Minister's speeches an immediacy of purpose. They may rightly be regarded as "the abstracts and brief chronicles of our time." They underline the stress of events and crises which his great country has had to face since the dawn of freedom and is still having to face. Political slavery has ended, but the promised land is yet far. "This generation," as the Prime Minister has said, "is sentenced to hard labor"; for years to come only toil and tears are to be the portion of India before she can complete the noble mansion of her greatness.

Dangers and difficulties overcome and glories achieved also find a place in these speeches. The Prime Minister never tires of insisting that there is always a hope and a promise as long as his people do not forget what their great leader, Mahatma Gandhi, taught them: as long as they relate ends to means, this ancient nation is bound to come into its own and take its proper place in the comity of nations.

The speeches in this selection were all delivered in English except one; "The Last Journey" has been translated from Hindustani in which it was originally made.

CONTENTS

Contents (*contd.*)

ON INDEPENDENCE

A TRYST WITH DESTINY

LONG years ago we made a tryst with destiny, and now the time comes when we shall redeem our pledge, not wholly or in full measure, but very substantially. At the stroke of the midnight hour, when the world sleeps, India will awake to life and freedom. A moment comes, which comes but rarely in history, when we step out from the old to the new, when an age ends, and when the soul of a nation, long suppressed, finds utterance. It is fitting that at this solemn moment we take the pledge of dedication to the service of India and her people and to the still larger cause of humanity.

At the dawn of history India started on her unending quest, and trackless centuries are filled with her striving and the grandeur of her success and her failures. Through good and ill fortune alike she has never lost sight of that quest or forgotten the ideals which gave her strength. We end today a period of ill fortune and India discovers herself again. The achievement we celebrate today is but a step, an opening of opportunity, to the greater triumphs and achievements that await us. Are we brave enough and wise enough to grasp this opportunity and accept the challenge of the future?

Freedom and power bring responsibility. That responsibility rests upon this Assembly, a sovereign body representing the sovereign people of India. Before the birth of freedom we have endured all the pains of labour and our hearts are heavy with the memory of this sorrow. Some of those pains continue even now. Nevertheless, the past is over and it is the future that beckons to us now.

That future is not one of ease or resting but of incessant striving so that we may fulfil the pledges we have so often taken and the one we shall take today. The service of India means the service of the millions who suffer. It means the ending of poverty and ignorance and disease and inequality of opportunity. The ambition of the greatest man of our generation has been to wipe every tear from every eye. That may be beyond us, but as long as there are tears and suffering, so long our work will not be over.

A speech delivered at the Constituent Assembly, New Delhi, August 14, 1947.

And so we have to labour and to work, and work hard, to give reality to our dreams. Those dreams are for India, but they are also for the world, for all the nations and peoples are too closely knit together today for any one of them to imagine that it can live apart. Peace has been said to be indivisible ; so is freedom, so is prosperity now, and so also is disaster in this One World that can no longer be split into isolated fragments.

To the people of India, whose representatives we are, we make an appeal to join us with faith and confidence in this great adventure. This is no time for petty and destructive criticism, no time for ill-will or blaming others. We have to build the noble mansion of free India where all her children may dwell.

I beg to move, Sir,

"That it be resolved that :

(1) After the last stroke of midnight, all members of the Constituent Assembly present on this occasion, do take the following pledge :

'At this solemn moment when the people of India, through suffering and sacrifice, have secured freedom, I, ..., a member of the Constituent Assembly of India, do dedicate myself in all humility to the service of India and her people to the end that this ancient land attain her rightful place in the world and make her full and willing contribution to the promotion of world peace and the welfare of mankind ;'

(2) Members who are not present on this occasion do take the pledge (with such verbal changes as the President may prescribe) at the time they next attend a session of the Assembly."

ANNIVERSARY OF OUR
INDEPENDENCE

THE 15th of August came and we rejoiced at our achievement in spite of the pain of partition. We looked forward to the sun of freedom and the opportunity that freedom brings. But though the sun rose it was hidden from us by dark clouds, and for us it remained a twilight hour. It has been a long twilight and the brightness of the day is still to come. For freedom is not a mere matter of political decision or new constitutions, not even a matter of what is more important, that is, economic policy. It is of the mind and heart and if the mind narrows itself and is befogged and the heart is full of bitterness and hatred, then freedom is absent.

Another August 15th has come and it is a solemn day for us in spite of all that has happened. The year has considerable achievement to its credit and we have gone forward some distance along our long journey. But the year is also full of unhappiness and humiliation and of a betrayal of the spirit that has been the redeeming feature of India. This year has seen the triumph of evil in the assassination of the Father of the Nation, and what greater shame and sorrow could there have been for anyone of us than this?

We celebrate this solemn day as we should, but our celebration cannot be one of vainglory and pious platitudes. It must be one of heart-searching and a fresh dedication to our cause. Let us think not so much of what we have done, but of what we have left undone and what we have done wrongly. Let us think of the millions of refugees who, deprived of all they possessed, are still homeless wanderers. Let us think of the masses of India who continue to suffer and who have looked to us with hope and waited patiently for a betterment of their unhappy lot. Let us think also of the mighty resources of India which, if harnessed and utilized for the common good, can change the face of India and make her great and prosperous. To this great task let us address ourselves with all the strength in us. But above all let us remember the great lessons that Mahatma Gandhi taught us and the ideals that he

A message from New Delhi, August 15, 1948.

held aloft for us. If we forget those lessons and ideals we betray our cause and our country.

So on this anniversary of our Independence we dedicate ourselves anew to the great cause of free India and her people. May we prove worthy! JAI HIND.

FIRST SERVANT OF THE
INDIAN PEOPLE

FELLOW countrymen, it has been my privilege to serve India and
the cause of India's freedom for many years. Today I address
you for the first time officially as the First Servant of the Indian
people, pledged to their service and their betterment. I am here
because you willed it so and I remain here so long as you choose
to honour me with your confidence.

We are a free and sovereign people today and we have rid
ourselves of the burden of the past. We look at the world with
clear and friendly eyes and at the future with faith and
confidence.

The burden of foreign domination is done away with, but
freedom brings its own responsibilities and burdens, and they
can only be shouldered in the spirit of a free people, self-
disciplined, and determined to preserve and enlarge that
freedom.

We have achieved much ; we have to achieve much more.
Let us then address ourselves to our new tasks with the determination and adherence to high principles which our great leader
has taught us. Gandhiji is fortunately with us to guide and inspire
and ever to point out to us the path of high endeavour. He taught
us long ago that ideals and objectives can never be divorced
from the methods adopted to realize them ; that worthy ends
can only be achieved through worthy means. If we aim at the
big things of life, if we dream of India as a great nation giving
her age-old message of peace and freedom to others, then we
have to be big ourselves and worthy children of Mother India.
The eyes of the world are upon us watching this birth of freedom
in the East and wondering what it means.

Our first and immediate objective must be to put an end to
all internal strife and violence, which disfigure and degrade us
and injure the cause of freedom. They come in the way of consideration of the great economic problems of the masses of the
people which so urgently demand attention.

Our long subjection and the World War and its aftermath

A talk broadcast from New Delhi, August 15, 1947.

have made us inherit an accumulation of vital problems, and today our people lack food and clothing and other necessaries, and we are caught in a spiral of inflation and rising prices. We cannot solve these problems suddenly, but we cannot also delay their solution. So we must plan wisely so that the burdens on the masses may grow less and their standards of living go up. We wish ill to none, but it must be clearly understood that the interests of our long-suffering masses must come first and every entrenched interest that comes in their way must yield to them. We have to change rapidly our antiquated land tenure system, and we have also to promote industrialization on a large and balanced scale, so as to add to the wealth of the country, and thus to the national dividend which can be equitably distributed.

Production today is the first priority, and every attempt to hamper or lessen production is injuring the nation, and more especially harmful to our labouring masses. But production by itself is not enough, for this may lead to an even greater concentration of wealth in a few hands, which comes in the way of progress and which, in the context of today, produces instability and conflict. Therefore, fair and equitable distribution is essential for any solution of the problem.

The Government of India have in hand at present several vast schemes for developing river valleys by controlling the flow of rivers, building dams and reservoirs and irrigation works and developing hydro-electric power. These will lead to greater food production and to the growth of industry and to all-round development. These schemes are thus basic to all planning and we intend to complete them as rapidly as possible so that the masses may profit.

All this requires peaceful conditions and the co-operation of all concerned, and hard and continuous work. Let us then address ourselves to these great and worthy tasks and forget our mutual wrangling and conflicts. There is a time for quarrelling and there is a time for co-operative endeavour. There is a time for work and there is a time for play. Today, there is no time for quarrelling or overmuch play, unless we prove false to our country and our people. Today, we must co-operate with one another and work together, and work with right goodwill.

I should like to address a few words to our Services, civil and military. The old distinctions and differences are gone and today we are all free sons and daughters of India, proud of our country's freedom and joining together in our service of her. Our common allegiance is to India. In the difficult days ahead our Services and our experts have a vital role to play and we invite them to do so as comrades in the service of India. JAI HIND.

THE APPOINTED DAY

THE Appointed Day has come—the day appointed by destiny, and India stands forth again after long slumber and struggle, awake, vital, free and independent. The past clings on to us still in some measure and we have to do much before we redeem the pledges we have so often taken. Yet the turning point is past, history begins anew for us, the history which we shall live and act and others will write about.

It is a fateful moment for us in India, for all Asia and for the world. A new star rises, the star of freedom in the East, a new hope comes into being, a vision long cherished materializes. May the star never set and that hope never be betrayed!

We rejoice in that freedom, even though clouds surround us, and many of our people are sorrow-stricken and difficult problems encompass us. But freedom brings responsibilities and burdens and we have to face them in the spirit of a free and disciplined people.

On this day our first thoughts go to the architect of this freedom, the Father of our Nation, who, embodying the old spirit of India, held aloft the torch of freedom and lighted up the darkness that surrounded us. We have often been unworthy followers of his and have strayed from his message, but not only we but succeeding generations will remember this message and bear the imprint in their hearts of this great son of India, magnificent in his faith and strength and courage and humility. We shall never allow that torch of freedom to be blown out, however high the wind or stormy the tempest.

Our next thoughts must be of the unknown volunteers and soldiers of freedom who, without praise or reward, have served India even unto death.

We think also of our brothers and sisters who have been cut off from us by political boundaries and who unhappily cannot share at present in the freedom that has come. They are of us and will remain of us whatever may happen, and we shall be sharers in their good and ill fortune alike.

The future beckons to us. Whither do we go and what shall

A message to the Press from New Delhi, August 15, 1947.

be our endeavour? To bring freedom and opportunity to the common man, to the peasants and workers of India ; to fight and end poverty and ignorance and disease ; to build up a prosperous, democratic and progressive nation, and to create social, economic and political institutions which will ensure justice and fullness of life to every man and woman.

We have hard work ahead. There is no resting for any one of us till we redeem our pledge in full, till we make all the people of India what destiny intended them to be. We are citizens of a great country, on the verge of bold advance, and we have to live up to that high standard. All of us, to whatever religion we may belong, are equally the children of India with equal rights, privileges and obligations. We cannot encourage communalism or narrow-mindedness, for no nation can be great whose people are narrow in thought or in action.

To the nations and peoples of the world we send greetings and pledge ourselves to co-operate with them in furthering peace, freedom and democracy.

And to India, our much-loved motherland, the ancient, the eternal and the ever-new, we pay our reverent homage and we bind ourselves afresh to her service. JAI HIND.

FREE INDIA IS ONE YEAR OLD

FELLOW countrymen, comrades and friends, a year ago on this very day and at this very hour I broadcast to you from this place. Free India is one year old today. But what trials and tribulations she has passed through during this infancy of her freedom! She has survived, in spite of all the peril and disaster that might well have overwhelmed a more mature and well established nation. We have reason to be thankful for this achievement and for the many other achievements that stand to the credit of our people. Let us not belittle our record or forget the courage, the hard work and the sacrifice with which our people have faced and overcome many of these perils during this fateful year.

But let us also not forget where we have failed or where we have erred. For our failures and errors have been many. Some of these are obvious enough, but the real failure has been a failure of the spirit and a falling away from the high standards set by the Father of our Nation, under whose wise guidance we had struggled and marched for over a quarter of a century. He taught us that worthy ends could only be achieved through worthy means, that ideals and objectives could never be divorced from the methods adopted to realize them. He had told us to cast out fear, for fear is not only ignoble but is also the parent of hatred and violence.

Many of us forgot this lesson and fear gripped us, fear not of some distant adversary, but fear of one another, and evil deeds followed in its train.

The Master who guided us and inspired us is no more. We have to shoulder the burden ourselves now and the first question that we have to put to ourselves is this: Do we stand by his teaching and message or do we stray into new paths? I want to tell you that this year of hard trial has convinced me more than ever that if India is to prosper and grow in stature, as she must and will, it will be through adherence to that message and teaching. I know I am feeble and have often proved unworthy of India to whose service I had pledged myself so often. But

A talk broadcast from New Delhi, August 15, 1948.

however unworthy we may be of India, we have still something of the strength that the Master gave us. That strength comes not only from him, but from his message, and so today I pledge myself anew to the service of the Motherland and of the ideals that Gandhiji placed before us.

All of us talk of India and all of us demand many things from India. What do we give her in return? We can take nothing from her beyond what we give her. India will ultimately give us what we give her of love and service and productive and creative work. India will be what we are: our thoughts and action will shape her. Born of her fruitful womb, we are children of hers, little bits of the India of today, and yet we are also the parents of the India of tomorrow. If we are big, so will India be, and if we grow little minded and narrow in outlook, so also will India be.

Our troubles during the past year were largely the result of this narrowness in outlook and pettiness in action which is so foreign to India's great cultural inheritance. Communalism threatened to crush the free spirit in us, the communalism of the Muslim, of the Hindu and of the Sikh. Provincialism came in the way of that larger unity which is so essential to India's greatness and progress. The spirit of faction spread and made us forget the big things that we had stood for.

We have to find ourselves again and go back to the free India of our dreams. We have to rediscover the old values and place them in the new setting of a free India. For freedom brings responsibility and can only be sustained by self-discipline, hard work, and the spirit of a free people.

So let us be rid of everything that limits us and degrades us. Let us cast out fear and communalism and provincialism. Let us build up a free and democratic India, where the interest of the masses of our people has always the first place to which all other interests must submit.

Freedom has no meaning unless it brings relief to these masses from their many burdens. Democracy means tolerance, tolerance not merely of those who agree with us, but of those who do not agree with us. With the coming of freedom our patterns of behaviour must change also so as to fit in with this freedom.

There is conflict and there are rumours of greater conflict in India and all over the world. We have to be ready for every emergency and contingency. When the nation is in peril, the first duty of every citizen is to give his or her service to the nation without fear or expectation of reward. But today I do not wish to speak of conflicts and wars but rather of peace and co-operation and I want to say to all the nations of the world, including our neighbour country, that we stand for peace and friendship with them. The only war that we want to fight with all our might is the war against poverty and all its unhappy brood.

All the world suffers from the after-effects of the World War, and inflation and rising prices and unemployment oppress the people. In India we have all these and, in addition, the care of vast numbers of our brothers and sisters who have suffered untold hardship and have been driven away from their homes to seek a new life elsewhere.

It is this war we have to fight, the war against economic crisis and to rehabilitate the disinherited. In this war there is no hatred or violence but only service of our country and our people. In this war every Indian can be a soldier. This is no time for individuals or groups to think of a narrow self-interest forgetting the larger good. This is no time for wrangling or the spirit of faction.

And so I appeal to all my countrymen and countrywomen who have the love of India in their hearts and the passion to raise her masses, to cast aside the barriers that separate them and to join together in this historic and magnificent task worthy of a great people.

To all those in our Services, civil and military, I would appeal for a single-minded devotion to the cause of India and for integrity, hard work, efficiency and impartiality. He who fails in this at this critical hour, fails in his duty to India and her people.

To the youth of the country I would make a special appeal for they are the leaders of tomorrow and on them will be cast the burden of upholding India's honour and freedom.

My generation is a passing one and soon we shall hand over the bright torch of India, which embodies her great and eternal spirit, to younger hands and stronger arms. May they hold it aloft, undimmed and untarnished, so that its light reaches every home and brings faith and courage and well-being to our masses. JAI HIND.

ON MAHATMA GANDHI

THE LIGHT HAS GONE OUT

FRIENDS and comrades, the light has gone out of our lives and there is darkness everywhere. I do not know what to tell you and how to say it. Our beloved leader, Bapu as we called him, the Father of the Nation, is no more. Perhaps I am wrong to say that. Nevertheless, we will not see him again as we have seen him for these many years. We will not run to him for advice and seek solace from him, and that is a terrible blow, not to me only, but to millions and millions in this country. And it is a little difficult to soften the blow by any other advice that I or anyone else can give you.

The light has gone out, I said, and yet I was wrong. For the light that shone in this country was no ordinary light. The light that has illumined this country for these many many years will illumine this country for many more years, and a thousand years later, that light will still be seen in this country and the world will see it and it will give solace to innumerable hearts. For that light represented something more than the immediate present , it represented the living, the eternal truths, reminding us of the right path, drawing us from error, taking this ancient country to freedom.

All this has happened when there was so much more for him to do. We could never think that he was unnecessary or that he had done his task. But now, particularly, when we are faced with so many difficulties, his not being with us is a blow most terrible to bear.

A madman has put an end to his life, for I can only call him mad who did it, and yet there has been enough of poison spread in this country during the past years and months, and this poison has had an effect on people's minds. We must face this poison, we must root out this poison, and we must face all the perils that encompass us, and face them not madly or badly, but rather in the way that our beloved teacher taught us to face them.

The first thing to remember now is that none of us dare misbehave because he is angry. We have to behave like strong

A talk broadcast from New Delhi on the evening of January 30, 1948.

and determined people, determined to face all the perils that surround us, determined to carry out the mandate that our great teacher and our great leader has given us, remembering always that if, as I believe, his spirit looks upon us and sees us, nothing would displease his soul so much as to see that we have indulged in any small behaviour or any violence.

So we must not do that. But that does not mean that we should be weak, but rather that we should, in strength and in unity, face all the troubles that are in front of us. We must hold together and all our petty troubles and difficulties and conflicts must be ended in the face of this great disaster. A great disaster is a symbol to us to remember all the big things of life and forget the small things of which we have thought too much. In his death he has reminded us of the big things of life, that living truth, and if we remember that, then it will be well with India.....

It was proposed by some friends that Mahatmaji's body should be embalmed for a few days to enable millions of people to pay their last homage to him. But it was his wish, repeatedly expressed, that no such thing should happen, that this should not be done, that he was entirely opposed to any embalming of his body, and so we decided that we must follow his wishes in this matter, however much others might have wished otherwise.

And so the cremation will take place on Saturday in Delhi city by the side of the Jumna river. On Saturday forenoon, about 11.30, the bier will be taken out at Birla House and it will follow a prescribed route and go to the Jumna river. The cremation will take place there at about 4 P.M. The place and route will be announced by radio and the Press.

People in Delhi who wish to pay their last homage should gather along this route. I will not advise too many of them to come to Birla House, but rather to gather on both sides of this long route from Birla House to the Jumna river. And I trust that they will remain there in silence without any demonstrations. That is the best way and the most fitting way to pay homage to this great soul. Also, Saturday should be a day of fasting and prayer for all of us.

Those who live elsewhere out of Delhi and in other parts of India will no doubt also take such part as they can in this last homage. For them also, let this be a day of fasting and prayer. And at the appointed time for cremation, that is 4 P.M. on

Saturday afternoon, people should go to the river or to the sea and offer prayers there. And while we pray, the greatest prayer that we can offer is to take a pledge to dedicate ourselves to the truth, and to the cause for which this great countryman of ours lived and for which he has died. That is the best prayer that we can offer him and his memory. That is the best prayer that we can offer to India and ourselves. JAI HIND.

A GLORY HAS DEPARTED

SIR, may I associate myself with what you have said? It is customary in this House to pay some tribute to the eminent departed, to say some words of praise and condolence. I am not quite sure in my own mind if it is exactly fitting for me or for any others of this House to say much on this occasion, for I have a sense of utter shame both as an individual and as the head of the Government of India that we should have failed to protect the greatest treasure that we possessed. It is our failure, as it has been our failure in the many months past, to give protection to many an innocent man, woman and child ; it may be that the burden and the task was too great for us or for any government. Nevertheless, it is a failure. And today the fact that this mighty person whom we honoured and loved beyond measure has gone because we could not give him adequate protection is a shame for all of us. It is a shame to me as an Indian that an Indian should have raised his hand against him, it is a shame to me as a Hindu that a Hindu should have done this deed and done it to the greatest Indian of the day and the greatest Hindu of the age.

We praise people in well-chosen words and we have some kind of a measure for greatness. How shall we praise him and how shall we measure him, because he was not of the common clay that all of us are made of? He came, lived a fairly long span of life and has passed away. No words of praise of ours in this House are needed, for he has had greater praise in his life than any living man in history. And during these two or three days since his death he has had the homage of the world ; what can we add to that? How can we praise him, how can we who have been children of his, and perhaps more intimately his children than the children of his body, for we have all been in some greater or smaller measure the children of his spirit, unworthy as we were?

A glory has departed and the sun that warmed and brightened our lives has set and we shiver in the cold and dark. Yet, he

A statement made before the Constituent Assembly (Legislative), New Delhi, February 2, 1948.

would not have us feel this way. After all, that glory that we saw for all these years, that man with the divine fire, changed us also—and such as we are, we have been moulded by him during these years ; and out of that divine fire many of us also took a small spark which strengthened and made us work to some extent on the lines that he fashioned. And so if we praise him, our words seem rather small and if we praise him, to some extent we also praise ourselves. Great men and eminent men have monuments in bronze and marble set up for them, but this man of divine fire managed in his life-time to become enshrined in millions and millions of hearts so that all of us became somewhat of the stuff that he was made of, though to an infinitely lesser degree. He spread out in this way all over India not in palaces only, or in select places or in assemblies but in every hamlet and hut of the lowly and those who suffer. He lives in the hearts of millions and he will live for immemorial ages.

What then can we say about him except to feel humble on this occasion? To praise him we are not worthy—to praise him whom we could not follow adequately and sufficiently. It is almost doing him an injustice just to pass him by with words when he demanded work and labour and sacrifice from us ; in a large measure he made this country, during the last thirty years or more, attain to heights of sacrifice which in that particular domain have never been equalled elsewhere. He succeeded in that. Yet ultimately things happened which no doubt made him suffer tremendously though his tender face never lost its smile and he never spoke a harsh word to anyone. Yet, he must have suffered—suffered for the failing of this generation whom he had trained, suffered because we went away from the path that he had shown us. And ultimately the hand of a child of his—for he after all is as much a child of his as any other Indian—a hand of that child of his struck him down.

Long ages afterwards history will judge of this period that we have passed through. It will judge of the successes and the failures—we are too near it to be proper judges and to understand what has happened and what has not happened. All we know is that there was a glory and that it is no more ; all we know is that for the moment there is darkness, not so dark certainly because when we look into our hearts we still find the living flame which he lighted there. And if those living flames exist, there will not be darkness in this land and we shall be able, with our effort, remembering him and following his path, to illumine this land again, small as we are, but still with the fire that he instilled into us.

He was perhaps the greatest symbol of the India of the past, and may I say, of the India of the future, that we could have had. We stand on this perilous edge of the present between that past and the future to be and we face all manner of perils and the greatest peril is sometimes the lack of faith which comes to us, the sense of frustration that comes to us, the sinking of the heart and of the spirit that comes to us when we see ideals go overboard, when we see the great things that we talked about somehow pass into empty words and life taking a different course. Yet, I do believe that perhaps this period will pass soon enough.

Great as this man of God was in his life, he has been great in his death and I have not the shadow of a doubt that by his death he has served the great cause as he served it throughout his life. We mourn him ; we shall always mourn him, because we are human and cannot forget our beloved Master. But I know that he would not like us to mourn him. No tears came to his eyes when his dearest and closest passed away—only a firm resolve to persevere, to serve the great cause that he had chosen. So he would chide us if we merely mourn. That is a poor way of doing homage to him. The only way is to express our determination, to pledge ourselves anew, to conduct ourselves in a befitting manner and to dedicate ourselves to the great task which he undertook and which he accomplished to such a large extent. So we have to work, we have to labour, we have to sacrifice and thus prove, to some extent at least, worthy followers of his.

It is clear, as you said, Sir, that this happening, this tragedy, is not merely the isolated act of a madman. This comes out of a certain atmosphere of violence and hatred that has prevailed in this country for many months and years and more especially in the past few months. That atmosphere envelops us and surrounds us and if we are to serve the cause he put before us we have to face this atmosphere, to combat it, to struggle against it and root out the evil of hatred and violence.

So far as this Government is concerned, I trust they will spare no means, spare no effort to tackle it, because if we do not do that, if we, in our weakness or for any other reason that we may consider adequate, do not take effective means to stop this violence, to stop this spreading of hatred by word of mouth or writing or act, then indeed we are not worthy of being in this Government ; we are certainly not worthy of being his followers and we are not worthy of even saying words of praise for this great soul who has departed. So on this occasion or any other when we think of this great Master who has gone, let us always think of him in terms of work and labour and sacrifice, in terms of fighting evil wherever we see it, in terms of holding to the truth as he put it before us, and if we do so, however unworthy we may be, we shall at least have done our duty and paid proper homage to his spirit.

He has gone, and all over India there is a feeling of having been left desolate and forlorn. All of us sense that feeling, and I do not know when we shall be able to get rid of it, and yet together with that feeling there is also a feeling of proud thankfulness that it has been given to us of this generation to be associated with this mighty person. In ages to come, centuries and maybe millenia after us, people will think of this generation when this man of God trod on earth and will think of us who, however small, could also follow his path and tread the holy ground where his feet had been. Let us be worthy of him.

THE LAST JOURNEY

THE last journey has ended. The final pilgrimage has been made. For over fifty years Mahatma Gandhi wandered all over our great country, from the Himalayas and the North Western Frontier and the Brahmaputra in the North East to Kanya Kumari (Cape Comorin) in the far South. He visited every part and corner of this country, not as a mere tourist or visitor for the sake of amusement, but in order to understand and serve the Indian people. Perhaps no other Indian in history has travelled so much in India or got to know the common people so well and served them so abundantly. And now his journey in this world is over, though we have still to continue for a while. Many people are moved to grief, and this is proper and natural. But why should we grieve? Do we grieve for him or for something else? In his life as in his death there has been a radiance which will illumine our country for ages to come. Why then should we grieve for him? Let us grieve rather for ourselves, for our own weaknesses, for the ill-will in our hearts, for our dissensions and for our conflicts. Remember that it was to remove all these that Mahatmaji gave his life. Remember that during the past few months it was on this that he concentrated his vast energy and service. If we honour him, do we honour his name only or do we honour what he stood for, his advice and teachings, and more especially what he died for?

Let us, standing here on the banks of the Ganga, search our own hearts and ask ourselves the question: how far have we followed the path shown to us by Gandhiji and how far have we tried to live in peace and co-operation with others? If even now we follow the right path, it will be well with us and well with our country.

Our country gave birth to a mighty soul and he shone like a beacon not only for India but for the whole world. And yet he was done to death by one of our own brothers and compatriots.

Translation of a speech in Hindustani delivered on February 12, 1948, to a crowd of over a million people who assembled on the banks to watch the immersion of Mahatma Gandhi's ashes in the holy waters of the Ganges at the confluence of the sacred rivers, the Ganges and the Jumna, at Allahabad.

How did this happen? You might think that it was an act of madness, but that does not explain this tragedy. It could only occur because the seed for it was sown in the poison of hatred and enmity that spread throughout the country and affected so many of our people. Out of that seed grew this poisonous plant. It is the duty of all of us to fight this poison of hatred and ill-will. If we have learnt anything from Gandhiji, we must bear no ill-will or enmity towards any person. The individual is not our enemy. It is the poison within him that we fight and which we must put an end to. We are weak and feeble, but Gandhiji's strength passed to us also to some extent. In his reflected glory we also gained in stature. The splendour and the strength were his and the path he showed was also his. We stumbled often enough and fell down in our attempts to follow that path and serve our people as he wanted us to serve them.

Our pillar of strength is no more. But why do we say that? His image is enshrined in the hearts of the million men and women who are present here today, and hundreds of millions of our countrymen, who are not present here, will also never forget him. Future generations of our people, who have not seen him or heard him, will also have that image in their hearts because that image is now a part of India's inheritance and history. Thirty or forty years ago began in India what is called the Gandhi Age. It has come to an end today. And yet I am wrong, for it has not ended. Perhaps it has really begun now, although somewhat differently. Thus far we have been leaning on him for advice and support, from now onwards we have to stand on our own feet and to rely on ourselves. May his memory inspire us and his teachings light our path. Remember his ever recurring message: "Root out fear from your hearts, and malice, put an end to violence and internecine conflict, keep your country free."

He brought us to freedom and the world marvelled at the way he did it. But at the very moment of gaining our freedom we forgot the lesson of the Master. A wave of frenzy and fanaticism overtook our people and we disgraced the fair name of India. Many of our youth were misled and took to wrong paths. Are we to drive them away and crush them? They are our own people and we have to win them over and mould them and train them to right thought and action.

The communal poison, which has brought disaster upon us, will put an end to our freedom also if we are not vigilant and if we do not take action in time. It was to awaken us to this impending danger that Gandhiji undertook his last fast two or three weeks ago. His self-crucifixion roused the nation's conscience and we pledged before him to behave better. It was only then that he broke his fast.

Gandhiji used to observe silence for one day in every week. Now that voice is silenced for ever and there is unending silence. And yet that voice resounds in our ears and in our hearts, and it will resound in the minds and hearts of our people and even beyond the borders of India, in the long ages to come. For that voice is the voice of truth, and though truth may occasionally be suppressed it can never be put down. Violence for him was the opposite of truth and therefore he preached to us against violence not only of the hand but of the mind and heart. If we do not give up this internecine violence and have the utmost forbearance and friendliness for others, we are doomed as a nation. The path of violence is perilous and freedom seldom exists for long where there is violence. Our talk of Swarajya and the people's freedom is meaningless, if we have internal violence and conflict.

I see a large number of soldiers of the Indian Army in this audience. It is their proud privilege and duty to defend the integrity and honour of this country of ours. They can only do so if they stand together and function together. If they were to fall out amongst themselves, what would their strength be worth and how could they then serve their country?

Democracy demands discipline, tolerance and mutual regard. Freedom demands respect for the freedom of others. In a democracy changes are made by mutual discussion and persuasion and not by violent means. If a government has no popular support, another government which commands that popular support takes its place. It is only small groups who know that they cannot get sufficient popular support that resort to methods of violence, imagining in their folly that they can gain their ends in this way. This is not only utterly wrong but it is also utterly foolish. For the reaction to the violence of the minority, which seeks to coerce the majority, is to provoke the majority into violence against them.

This great tragedy has happened because many persons, including some in high places, have poisoned the atmosphere of this country of ours. It is the duty of the Government as well as

the people to root out this poison. We have had our lesson at a
terrible cost. Is there anyone amongst us now who will not pledge
himself after Gandhiji's death to fulfil his mission—a mission
for which the greatest man of our country, the greatest man in
the world, has laid down his life?

You and I and all of us will go back from these sands of our
noble river, the Ganga. We shall feel sad and lonely. We shall
never see Gandhiji again. We used to run to him for advice and
guidance whenever we were confronted with any great problem
or when we felt ill at ease or in doubt. There is none to advise
us now or to share our burdens. It is not I alone or a few of us
who looked up to him for help. Thousands and hundreds of
thousands of our countrymen considered him their intimate
friend and counsellor. All of us felt that we were his children.
Rightly he was called the Father of our Nation and in millions
of homes today there is mourning as on the passing away of a
beloved father.

We shall go away from this river bank sad and lonely. But
we shall also think with pride of the high and unique privilege
that has been ours to have had for our chief and leader and
friend this mighty person, who carried us to great heights on
the way to freedom and truth. And the way of struggle that he
taught us was also the way of truth. Remember also that the path
he showed us was one of fighting for the good and against evil
and not the way of sitting quietly on the peaks of the Himalayas.
And so we have to fight on and not seek escape or rest. We have
to do our duty and fulfil the pledges we have given him. Let us
tread the path of truth and Dharma. Let us make India a great
country in which goodwill and harmony prevail and every man
and woman, irrespective of faith and belief, can live in dignity
and freedom.

How often we have shouted, "Mahatma Gandhi ki Jai".
By shouting this slogan we thought we had done our duty.
Gandhiji always felt pained to hear this shouting, for he knew
what little it meant and how often it just took the place of action
or even of thought. "Mahatma Gandhi ki Jai"—"Victory to
Mahatma Gandhi", what victory could we wish him or give him?
He was the Victorious One in life and in death. It is you and
I and this unfortunate country who have to struggle for victory.

Throughout his life he thought of India in terms of the poor
and the oppressed and the downtrodden. To raise them and free

them was the mission of his life. He adopted their ways of life and dress so that no one in the country might feel lowly. Victory to him was the growth of freedom of these people.

What kind of triumph did Gandhiji wish for us? Not the triumph for which most people and countries strive through violence, fraud, treachery and evil means. That kind of victory is not stable. For the foundations of a lasting victory can only be laid on the rock of truth. Gandhiji gave us a new method of struggle and political warfare and a new kind of diplomacy. He demonstrated the efficacy of truth and goodwill and non-violence in politics. He taught us to respect and co-operate with every Indian as a man and as a fellow-citizen, irrespective of his political belief or religious creed. We all belong to Mother India and have to live and die here. We are all equal partners in the freedom that we have won. Everyone of our three or four hundred million people must have an equal right to the opportunities and blessings that free India has to offer. It was not a few privileged persons that Gandhiji strove and died for. We have to strive for the same ideal and in the same way. Then only shall we be worthy to say, " Mahatma Gandhi ki Jai ".

THE GREATEST INDIAN

Two weeks have passed since India and the world learnt of that tragedy which will shame India for ages to come. Two weeks of sorrow and searching of heart, and strong and dormant emotions rising in a flood, and of tears from millions of eyes. Would that those tears had washed away our weakness and littleness and made us a little worthy of the Master for whom we sorrowed! Two weeks of homage and tribute from every corner of the globe, from kings and potentates and those in high authority to the common man everywhere who instinctively looked to him as a friend, a comrade and a champion.

The flood of emotion will tone down gradually as all such emotions do, though none of us can ever be the same as we were before, for he has entered into the very texture of our lives and minds.

People talk of memorials to him in statues of bronze or marble or pillars and thus they mock him and belie his message. What tribute shall we pay to him that he would have appreciated? He has shown us the way to live and the way to die and if we have not understood that lesson, it would be better that we raised no memorial to him, for the only fit memorial is to follow reverently in the path he showed us and to do our duty in life and in death.

He was a Hindu and an Indian, the greatest in many generations, and he was proud of being a Hindu and an Indian. To him India was dear because she had represented throughout the ages certain immutable truths. But though he was intensely religious and came to be called the Father of the Nation which he had liberated, yet no narrow religious or national bonds confined his spirit. And so he became the great internationalist, believing in the essential unity of man, the underlying unity of all religions, and the needs of humanity, and more specially devoting himself to the service of the poor, the distressed and the oppressed millions everywhere.

His death brought more tributes than has been paid at the passing of any other human being in history. Perhaps what

---

A talk broadcast from New Delhi, February 14, 1948.

would have pleased him best was the spontaneous tributes that came from the people of Pakistan. On the morrow of the tragedy, all of us forgot for a while the bitterness that had crept in, the estrangement and conflict of these past months, and Gandhiji stood out as the beloved champion and leader of the people of India, of India as it was before partition cut up this living nation.

What was his great power over the mind and heart of man due to? Ages to come will judge and we are too near him to assess the many facets of his extraordinarily rich personality. But even we realize that his dominating passion was truth. That truth led him to proclaim without ceasing that good ends can never be attained by evil methods, that the end itself is distorted if the method pursued is bad. That truth led him to confess publicly whenever he thought he had made a mistake—Himalayan errors he called some of his own mistakes. That truth led him to fight evil and untruth wherever he found them regardless of the consequences. That truth made the service of the poor and the dispossessed the passion of his life, for where there is inequality and discrimination and suppression, there is injustice and evil and untruth. And thus he became the beloved of all those who have suffered from social and political evils, and the great representative of humanity as it should be. Because of that truth in him, wherever he sat became a temple and where he trod was hallowed ground.

His physical body has left us and we shall never see him again or hear his gentle voice or run to him for counsel. But his imperishable memory and immortal message remain with us. How can we honour them and live up to them?

He was the great unifier in India, who taught us not only a bare tolerance of others but of a willing acceptance of them as our friends and comrades in common undertakings. He taught us to rise above our little selves and prejudices and see the good in others. His last few months and his very death symbolize to us this message of large-hearted tolerance and unity. A little before he died we pledged ourselves to this before him. We must keep that pledge and remember that India is a common home to all those who live here, to whatever religion they may belong. They are equal sharers in our great inheritance and they have equal rights and obligations. Ours is a composite nation, as all great nations must necessarily be. Any narrowness in outlook, any attempt to confine the bounds of this great nation, will be a

betrayal of his final lesson to us and will surely lead to disaster
and to the loss of that freedom for which he laboured and which
he gained for us in large measure.

Equally important is the service of the common man in India
who has suffered so much in the past. His claims must be paramount and everything that comes in the way of his betterment
must have second place. Not merely from moral and humanitarian grounds but also from the point of view of political com-
monsense, has it become essential to raise the standard of the
common man and to give him full opportunity of progress. A
social structure which denies him this opportunity stands self-
condemned and must be changed.

Gandhiji has gone though his flaming spirit envelops us.
The burden is upon us now and the immediate need is that we
should endeavour to the utmost of our ability to discharge that
burden. We have to hold together and fight the terrible poison
of communalism that has killed the greatest man of our age. We
must root this out not in any spirit of ill-will to misguided individuals but in militant opposition to the evil itself wherever it may
be. That evil has not ended by the killing of Gandhiji. It was
an even more shameful thing for some people to celebrate this
killing in various ways. Those who did so or feel that way have
forfeited their rights to be called Indians.

I have said that we must all hold together in this hour of
crisis for our nation and must avoid public controversy as far as
possible and lay stress on the points of agreement on essential
matters. I would make a special appeal to the Press to help in
this urgent task and to avoid personal or other criticisms which
encourage fissiparous tendencies in the country. I would appeal
more especially to the millions of my colleagues and comrades in
the Congress who have followed, often haltingly enough, the
leadership of Mahatma Gandhi.

It has distressed me beyond measure to read in newspapers
and otherwise learn of whisperings about vital differences
between Sardar Patel and myself. Of course, there have been for
many years past differences between us, temperamental and
other, in regard to many problems. But India at least should
know that these differences have been overshadowed by fundamental agreements about the most important aspects of our
public life and that we have co-operated together for a quarter
of a century or more in great undertakings. We have been sharers

in joy and sorrow alike. Is it likely that at this crisis in our national destiny either of us should be petty-minded and think of anything but the national good? May I pay my tribute of respect and admiration to Sardar Patel not only for his life-long service to the nation but also for the great work he has done since he and I have served together in the Government of India? He has been a brave captain of our people in war and peace, stout-hearted when others might have wavered, and a great organizer. It has been my privilege to have been associated with him for these many years and my affection for him and appreciation of his great qualities have grown with the passing of time.

Recently certain reports have appeared in the public press which were unauthorized and which led people to believe that I had used strong language to criticize my old friend and colleague, Jayaprakash Narayan. These reports were incorrect. I should like to say that I have deeply regretted some of the policies pursued by the Socialist Party in India and I think that they have been led by the stress of events or emotion into wrong action and wrong statement. But I have never had any doubt about the ability and integrity of Jayaprakash Narayan whom I value as a friend and I am sure that a time will come when he will play a very important part in shaping India's destiny. Unfortunately the Socialist Party has adopted rather negative policies for a long time and has often ignored wider considerations which must be given priority.

I plead therefore for tolerance and co-operation in our public life and a joining together of all the forces which want to make India a great and progressive nation. I plead for an all-out effort against the poison of communalism and narrow provincialism. I plead for a cessation of industrial conflict and a joint endeavour of all concerned to build up India. In these great tasks I pledge myself and I earnestly trust that it may be given to us of this generation to realize somewhat the dreams that Gandhiji had. Thus will we honour his memory and erect a worthy memorial for him.

THE MOST SUITABLE MEMORIAL

EVERY part of India is naturally desirous of erecting some memorial to Mahatma Gandhi. Provincial Governments, State Governments, Municipalities and Local Boards, other public bodies and private individuals are all eager to erect their own memorials. Proposals have been made for all kinds of structures from temples to statues. In a recent statement Sardar Patel said that he deplored with all the emphasis at his command the many attempts that were being made to raise temples or erect memorials which would savour of idolatry. This would surely have displeased Gandhiji and indeed he had often expressed his views on such matters in forcible language.

It seems obvious that the most suitable memorial is to follow his great teachings and to organize work in order to further his constructive ideas in the development of the nation.

Nevertheless, it is perhaps inevitable that some statues might be put up. If so, the greatest care should be taken that only real works of art are permitted. Unfortunately the standard in India of such statuary has been low and most people are satisfied with anything that bears a remote resemblance to the person concerned. Our cities and public places are full of structures which cannot by any stretch of the imagination be called artistic or pleasing to the sight. I have been shocked on many occasions at seeing these totally inadequate efforts. I should like to warn most earnestly those who are thinking in terms of having statues not to take any hasty decisions and to await a full consideration of this question by the National Memorial Committee under the chairmanship of the Congress President.

There is another matter to which I should like to draw public attention. All over India there is a tendency to name roads, squares and public buildings after Gandhiji. This is a very cheap form of memorial, and a certain satisfaction is gained without expense or exertion. Almost, it seems to me that this is exploiting his name, and a showing off that we honour him without any effort on our part. Even more undesirable is to change famous and historical names which have had a distinction of their own.

A statement made in New Delhi, February 25, 1948.

If these tendencies are not checked we shall have thousands of roads and parks and squares named after Gandhiji. That will not contribute either to convenience or to the glory of the Father of the Nation. Only confusion will result as well as a certain drab uniformity. Most of us will then live in Gandhi Roads, in Gandhinagars or Gandhigrams.

THE FATHER OF THE NATION

FRIENDS and comrades, what shall I say to you on this day which is specially dedicated to the memory of him whom we call the Father of the Nation? I shall not speak to you today as Prime Minister of India but as Jawaharlal, a pilgrim like you in India's long journey to freedom and one whose high privilege it was to learn the service of India and of truth at the feet of the Master. Nor will I say much to you about the problems of the day, which fill our minds and demand our continuous attention. Rather I would like to speak about those basic things which Gandhiji taught us and without which life would be superficial and empty.

He taught us the love of truth and straight dealing not only in our individual lives but also in public affairs and in the intercourse of nations. He taught us the dignity of man and of man's labour. He repeated the old lesson that, out of hatred and violence, nothing but hatred and violence and destruction can result. And so he taught us the way of fearlessness, of unity, of tolerance and of peace.

How far have we lived up to this teaching? Not very far, I fear. And yet we learned much and under his guidance we achieved our country's freedom by peaceful methods. But at the very moment of deliverance we became forgetful and strayed into evil ways, causing infinite pain to that great heart which throbbed continuously for India and for the great truths that India has embodied through ages past.

What of today? When we remember him and praise him, and sometimes childishly talk of putting up statues to him, do we give thought to the great message for which he lived and died? I fear all of us are still very far from living up to that message. But I do believe that the great forces that he set in motion are working silently but powerfully to move India in the direction of his wishes. There are other forces also, forces of disruption and untruth and violence and narrow-mindedness, which work in the opposite direction. Between the two there is unceasing conflict, as between the forces of good and evil there is conflict all over the world. If we honour the memory of

A talk broadcast from New Delhi on the occasion of the anniversary of Mahatma Gandhi's birthday, October 2, 1948.

Gandhiji, we must do so actively by working ceaselessly for the causes he represented.

I am proud of my country, proud of my national inheritance, proud of many things, but I speak to you not in pride but with all humility. For events have humbled me and often shamed me and the dream of India that I have had has sometimes grown dim. I have loved India and sought to serve her not because of her geographical magnitude, not even because she was great in the past, but because of my faith in her today and my belief that she will stand for truth and freedom and the higher things of life.

Do you want India to stand for these great aims and ideals which Gandhiji placed before us? If so, then you will have to think and act in accordance with them and not allow yourself to be carried away by the passion of the moment or by thoughts of petty advantage. You will have to root out every tendency that weakens the nation, whether it is communalism, separatism, religious bigotry, provincialism or class arrogance.

We have said repeatedly that we will not tolerate any communalism in this country and that we are building a free secular State, where every religion and belief has full freedom and equal honour, where every citizen has equal liberty and equal opportunity. In spite of this, some people still talk in the language of communalism and separatism. I want to tell you that I am entirely opposed to this and I expect you likewise to oppose it with all your might, if you have faith in Gandhiji's teaching.

Another evil is that of provincialism and of that we see a great deal today running riot and forgetting the larger issues. That also has to be opposed and combated.

Some people have recently called India an aggressor nation. I can only say that they spoke in ignorance. If India took to the ways of aggression against any other nation, there would be no place left for me and for many of my colleagues in the Government of India. If we indulged in aggression, we should be false to all that we have stood for and all that Gandhiji taught us.

Our neighbour country, Pakistan, has exhibited a strange fever during the past weeks. I have been astonished to read its newspapers and the public utterances of its leaders, utterances which have no relation to fact but foster wild fears and fantasies.

If the people of Pakistan have to read this literature of hatred and fear from day to day, I am not surprised that they should form a picture of India in their minds which is completely divorced from reality. I deeply regret this, for as I have said before, I cannot think of the people of Pakistan as strangers. They have been our countrymen, and neither they nor we can rid ourselves of the past or forget our close kinship, however much momentary passions may seem to divide us. I would like to utter, in all earnestness and friendship, a note of warning to those who are carrying on an unscrupulous propaganda against India in Pakistan. They are doing an ill service to their own country and to their own people.

I can assure the people of Pakistan that India has no aggressive designs against any country, least of all against Pakistan. We want Pakistan to live in peace and to progress and to have the closest ties with us. There never will be aggression from our side.

But there has been aggression of a brutal and unforgivable kind, aggression against the people of Kashmir and against the Indian Union. We met that aggression as any self-respecting country was bound to meet it. Memories are short and it is well to remember what happened a little more than eleven months ago in Kashmir. Pakistan denied its complicity and, even in the face of incontrovertible facts, continued to deny it. It built up its case in the Security Council of the United Nations on this denial and now it has had to admit that its armies are operating in Kashmir which is Indian Union territory. History offers few parallels of a case built up so greatly on a complete denial of truth. The United Nations Commission proposed a truce. We accepted it. Pakistan in its pride and arrogance rejected it.

I want to tell you as well as the people of Pakistan, and now I speak to you as the Prime Minister of India that on no account, and whatever happens, are we going to submit to this aggression. We shall fight it to the utmost, for it involves not only the freedom of Kashmir but also the honour of the Indian people and respect for the law of nations.

Many things have happened in India during the past year or more which have deeply pained me because they were evil and a falling away from the teachings of the Master. But I have no regret for what we did and are doing in Kashmir and Hyderabad. Indeed, if we had not done what we did and are doing in

Kashmir and Hyderabad, there would have been infinitely greater trouble and violence and misery. I would have been ashamed of India if she had not run to the rescue of Kashmir, or gone to the aid of the people of Hyderabad who were being crushed by an unscrupulous clique.

Whatever may happen in other countries, let us remain calm and let us try to remain true to Gandhiji's teachings. If we keep faith with him, we shall keep faith with ourselves and with India, and all will be well with this country so dear to us.   JAI HIND.

A YEAR AGO

FRIENDS and comrades, a year ago I spoke to you from here, a year ago to the day and the hour, and announced to you that the light that had illumined our lives had gone out and darkness enveloped us. And now I address you again after you and I have shouldered the burden of this fateful year.

That light had not gone out, for it shines more brightly than ever, and the message of our beloved leader rings in our ears. And yet often many of us, led away by passion and prejudice, close our eyes to this light and our ears to that message.

Let us today open our eyes and ears and hearts and think of him with all reverence, and think, above all, of what he stood for, and what he wanted us to do.

This evening many of us over India, in city and town and village, have heard the message of Gandhiji repeated and we have pledged ourselves anew to work in its light. At no time was this message more necessary than in the distracted and disintegrating world of today. Again and again this world has tried to solve its problems by methods of violence and hatred. Again and again it has failed and faced disaster. It is time we learnt the lesson from our own bitter experience.

That lesson is that we cannot ignore moral values except at peril to ourselves : that not by conflict and hatred shall we put an end to the ills of India and the world, but by peaceful methods and co-operation and disinterested service of freedom and truth ; that we must promote unity and goodwill among all the people of India, and endeavour to abolish class distinctions and those based on birth or caste or religion. Even to those who may think ill of us we have to stretch out the hand of friendship and win their goodwill.

To the nations of the world we say : we have no quarrel with any of you, we seek only your friendly co-operation in the great task of ensuring freedom and well-being to all the peoples of the world ; we seek no domination or advantage over others, but we shall guard our own freedom at all costs and with all the

A talk broadcast from New Delhi on the first anniversary of Mahatma Gandhi's death, January 30, 1949.

strength in us. Our voice may be feeble today but the message it conveys is no feeble message. It has the strength of truth in it and it will prevail.

With this thought and pledge let us pay homage to our Master and beloved leader who has left us, and yet is so much with us. May we prove worthy of him and his message, and of India, our dear Motherland, to whose service we have dedicated ourselves again this day. JAI HIND.

ON COMMUNALISM

THIS UNHAPPY LAND OF THE
FIVE RIVERS

On the 15th and 16th August, India celebrated the coming of independence; not only India but Indians wherever they happened to be in this wide world. I have received thousands of messages of greetings from abroad. They have come from representatives of great nations, from famous men and from Indians from every remote corner of the world. While I have been deeply moved by these messages from the leaders of other countries welcoming India into the fellowship of free nations, nothing has affected me more than the very touching messages from our countrymen overseas. Cut away from their Motherland they have hungered for India's freedom even more perhaps than we have, and the coming of this freedom has been a tremendous event in their lives. May the New India always remember her children abroad who look to her with such pride and affection and give them all the succour she can.

Nearly the whole of India celebrated the coming of independence, but not so the unhappy land of the five rivers. In the Punjab, both in the east and the west, there was disaster and sorrow. There was murder and arson and looting in many places and streams of refugees poured out from one place to another.

One of the first tasks of our Government was to think of the Punjab and so I hurried thither on the morning of the 17th, accompanied by my colleague, Sardar Baldev Singh, the Defence Minister, and Mr. Liaquat Ali Khan, the Prime Minister of Pakistan, and some of his colleagues. I want to tell you what we found there and what we did there. There have been wild rumours enough and people's minds all over India are naturally agitated, because whatever happens, the people of the Punjab, whether they live to the east or to the west, are our own kith and kin and anything that affects them affects us.

You must remember that till the 15th August there was a different regime in the Punjab as a whole. The province was governed under section 93 of the Government of India Act. The change over took place on the 15th and the new Provincial

A talk broadcast from New Delhi, August 19, 1947.

Governments thus are only four days old. So also are the new
Central Governments. These Governments, Central or Provincial,
are directly responsible only since the 15th August. The Provincial Governments of East and West Punjab had to face a terrible
crisis in the very hour of their birth, even before they had settled
down to work or had proper offices functioning.

The story of disastrous happenings in the Punjab takes us
back many months to March of this year. One disaster has
followed another, each producing its reaction elsewhere. I am not
going to narrate the story, nor am I going to apportion blame.
There has been sufficient murder and arson and crime of all
descriptions in many parts of the Punjab, and this fair province,
so rich in promise, has suffered untold agony during these months.
It would serve little purpose to go into this long story. We begin
our new life from the 15th August.

Mr. Liaquat Ali Khan, Sardar Baldev Singh and I went to
Ambala first and held a Conference there with Ministers of East
and West Punjab and various civil and military officers. We met
also the leaders of various communities, notably the Akali Sikh
leaders, Master Tara Singh and Giani Kartar Singh. We went
then to Lahore and had a first-hand account of occurrences there
and then to Amritsar.

In both Amritsar and Lahore we heard a ghastly tale and we
saw thousands of refugees, Hindu, Muslim and Sikh. There were
some fires still burning in the city and reports of recent outrages
reached us. We were all unanimously of opinion that we must
deal firmly with the situation as we found it and not enter into
acrimonious debate about the past, and that the situation
demanded that crime must be put an end to immediately at
whatever cost.

The alternative was complete chaos and ruin for the land and
for every community. Anti-social elements were abroad, defying
all authority and destroying the very structure of society. Unless
these elements were suppressed, to whatever community they
belonged, there was no freedom or even security for any person ;
and so, all of us who were present, whether we belonged to the
two Central or the two Provincial Governments, or whether we
were leading members of the various communities, pledged
ourselves to do our utmost to put an end to this orgy of murder
and arson.

We have taken effective steps to this end, effective not only from the administrative and military point of view, but, what is even more important, from the point of view of a popular approach to all our people. We have established high level committees of the two Provincial Governments of the Punjab and liaison officers between the civil and the military authorities, so that there should be the fullest amount of co-operation between the two Provincial Governments and the military forces. We have pledged the Central Governments to help in this task. Popular leaders have assured us of their fullest co-operation.

I am convinced that we shall deal with this situation effectively and that fairly soon security will return to the Punjab, but that requires the utmost effort and constant vigilance from all concerned, whether they are Government officers or others. Each one of us who cares for his country must help in this business of restoring peace and security.

In the past we have unfortunately had communal troubles on a large scale. They are not going to be tolerated in the future. So far as the Government of India are concerned, they will deal with any communal outbreak with the greatest firmness. They will treat every Indian on an equal basis and try to secure for him all the rights which he shares with others.

Our State is not a communal state, but a democratic state in which every citizen has equal rights. The Government is determined to protect these rights.

I have been assured by Mr. Liaquat Ali Khan that this is also the policy of the Pakistan Government.

We have made arrangements for the transport of refugees from Lahore to Amritsar or Amritsar to Lahore. They will be carried by railway trains and motor lorries and we hope that very soon most of those who so want will be carried to their destinations. We are further making arrangements for their proper accommodation and food. The Government of India have sanctioned today a sum of Rs. 5 lakhs to the East Punjab Government for the care of refugees. They have sanctioned a further sum of Rs. 5 lakhs for the help of refugees who have come to Delhi and elsewhere. Our Refugee Commissioner, Mr. Chandra, is proceeding immediately to Amritsar.

We are appointing a Deputy High Commissioner in Lahore to look after our interests there, and, more especially, to look after the refugees who wish to come to East Punjab. We hope to provide a number of tents to the East Punjab Government for accommodating the refugees. In every way that is possible to us we shall help the unfortunate sufferers in the Punjab. So far as Eastern Punjab is concerned, it is our direct responsibility and we shall act accordingly.

While we shall give every help to those who wish to come to East Punjab, we would not like to encourage mass migration of peoples across the new borders, for this will involve tremendous misery for all concerned. We hope that very soon peace and order will be established and people will have security to carry on their avocations.

While we have done all this, ultimately the future depends on the co-operation we receive from the people. It is with confident expectation of this co-operation that we are proceeding and declaring with conviction that we shall settle this Punjab problem soon. We can make no progress there or elsewhere in India if these horrible disturbances continue. I appeal, therefore, to all people concerned to face this task with firmness and courage and thus to demonstrate how free India can handle a difficult situation.

The Punjab problem is one of first priority with us and I propose to go there again soon, or whenever needed. Because we seek the co-operation of the people, we must also take them into our confidence. I have, therefore, spoken to you today and I propose to do so again whenever necessity arises. Meanwhile, I hope that people will not give credence to wild rumours which spread so easily and influence people's opinions. The reality has been bad enough, but rumour makes it worse.

To those who have suffered during these dark days in the Punjab, our deepest sympathy goes out. Many have lost their lives, many others have lost everything else that they possessed. We cannot restore the dead, but those who are alive must certainly receive aid from the State now, which should later rehabilitate them.

DANGEROUS ALLIANCE OF RELIGION AND POLITICS

SIR, before this debate proceeds any further I should like to indicate the attitude of the Government in regard to this Resolution. The Government welcome this Resolution and desire to say that they wish to do everything in their power to achieve the objective which lies behind this Resolution. After the eloquent speech of the Honourable Mover, I need not say much about the desirability of this Resolution ; as a matter of fact, it is an inevitable policy which an independent country must adopt. There might have been in the past various reasons which came in the way of such policy being given effect to, although I think that even in the past those of us who accepted any measure of communalism erred and acted unwisely, and we have suffered greatly for our unwisdom. However, in the past, conditions were different ; but when a country is functioning independently there is no alternative except to follow this. The only alternative is civil conflict. We have seen as a matter of fact how far communalism in politics has led us ; all of us remember the grave dangers through which we have passed and the terrible consequences we have seen. In any event now there is no other alternative ; and we must have it clearly in our minds and in the mind of the country that the alliance of religion and politics in the shape of communalism is a most dangerous alliance, and it yields the most abnormal kind of illegitimate brood.

A speech delivered at the Constituent Assembly (Legislative), New Delhi, April 3, 1948.

This speech was made during debate on the following Resolution moved by Mr. Ananthasayanam Ayyangar, member of the Constituent Assembly:

" Whereas it is essential for the proper functioning of democracy and the growth of national unity and solidarity that communalism should be eliminated from Indian life, this Assembly is of opinion that no communal organization which by its constitution or by the exercise of discretionary power vested in any of its officers or organs, admits to or excludes from its membership persons on grounds of religion, race and caste, or any of them, should be permitted to engage in any activities other than those essential for the *bona fide* religious and cultural needs of the community, and that all steps, legislative and administrative, necessary to prevent such activities should be taken."

The Resolution as amended (the amendment being accepted by the Prime Minister towards the end of his speech) was passed by the House.

We have talked a great deal about politics being allied to ethics ; that is something which, I hope, we shall always stand for. During the last quarter of a century or more Mahatma Gandhi taught us to place politics on an ethical level. How far we succeeded it is for the world to judge and for future generations to decide. But it was something at least that we placed that great ideal before us and tried in our own weak and halting way to give effect to it. But the combination of politics and of religion in the narrowest sense of the word, resulting in communal politics is—there can be no doubt—a most dangerous combination and must be put an end to. It is clear, as has been pointed out by the Honourable Mover, that this combination is harmful to the country as a whole ; it is harmful to the majority, but probably it is most harmful to any minority that seeks to have some advantage from it. I think even the past history of India will show that. But in any event a minority in an independent State which seeks to isolate and separate itself does some injury to the cause of the country, and most of all it injures its own interests, because inevitably it puts a barrier between itself and the others, a barrier not on the religious plane but on the political plane—sometimes even to some extent on the economic plane ; and it can never really exercise the influence which it legitimately ought to aspire to exercise, if it functions in that way.

Now the future Constitution of India is being hammered out in the Constituent Assembly and no doubt it will give shape to it in the course of the next two or three months and finalise it, and any Resolution that we may pass is not going to alter that Constitution as it is finally adapted. But after all the constitution-making body is more or less this body—there is not much difference. And if this House thinks in terms of this Resolution, I have no doubt that the constitution-making body will also think in terms of this Resolution. Further, from such evidence as we have of the working of that constitution-making body, it has already gone a long way in terms of this Resolution. It has put aside many of the dangerous features of our old constitution which led to communalism. Whether other features will remain or not I cannot obviously guarantee. But as far as I am concerned, I think the less we have of any form of communalism, the better it is for our Constitution and for the practical working of our Government.

Now, Sir, so far as this Resolution is concerned, as I said, we

warmly welcome the objective underlying it and the spirit behind
it. But this Resolution mentions administrative and legislative
measures to be taken to give effect to it. Exactly what those
administrative and legislative measures might be, it is impossible
to say straight off ; it will require the closest scrutiny, certainly
the legislative part of it. And presumably the right course for
the Government will be—if this Resolution is passed, as I feel sure
it will be—to consider this matter and see what administrative
and—more specially—what legislative measures are necessary to
gain this end ; and then later when this House meets again for
another session, to consider any recommendations in that respect
so far as legislative measures are concerned.

Meanwhile, no doubt our new Constitution will have taken
shape also and it will help us then to consider those legislative
measures in terms of that new Constitution. But we need not wait
till then. The point, so far as the Government is concerned, is that
we should function as closely as possible in accordance with the
spirit of this Resolution. Further, the purpose of this Resolution,
I take it, is also to give a lead to the country in this matter, so
that the country may realize as clearly as possible that the only
right way for us to act is to do away with communalism in
its political aspect in every shape and form. That we accept. Now
there are at the present moment, as some Members may later
point out, in the draft Constitution that has been proposed, certain definite communal elements. For instance, I believe that
there is a proposal that although there should be joint and common electorates, still there might be some reservation of seats for
minorities or for the scheduled castes on, more or less, I take it,
the population basis. Now what the final decision will be about
that I cannot say. I hope personally that the less reservation there
is the better, and I think that is so mostly even more from the
point of view of the group or the minority that might have that
reservation than from the point of view of any other group or
majority.

There is another aspect of this matter which must be
remembered. We talk about democracy and unity and all that
and I hope we shall rapidly have more and more democracy and
more and more unity in this country. A democracy is not purely
a political affair. The nineteenth century conception of democracy, that is, each person having a vote, was a good enough
conception in those days, but it was incomplete and people think

in terms of a larger and deeper democracy today. After all there is no equality between the pauper who has a vote and the millionaire who has a vote. There are a hundred ways of exercising influence for the millionaire which the pauper has not got. After all there is no equality between the person who has tremendous educational advantages and the person who has had none. So educationally, economically and otherwise, people differ greatly. People will, I suppose, differ to some extent. All human beings are not equal in the sense of ability or capacity. But the whole point is that people should have equality of opportunity and that they should be able to go as far as they can go.

Now it is patent in India today that there are huge differences between certain groups, classes and individuals. There is a big hiatus between those at the top and those at the bottom. If we are to have democracy it becomes necessary and essential for us not merely to bridge that gap but to lessen it very greatly: in fact to bring them closer together as far as opportunities are concerned, as far ultimately as general living conditions are concerned and in so far as the necessities of life are concerned, leaving out for the moment luxuries and the rest, though ultimately there seems to me to be no particular reason why any particular group or class should be favoured even in regard to the luxuries of life. But that is perhaps a rather distant picture. Now, because there are such great differences in India, it becomes incumbent upon us, not only for humanitarian reasons but from the standpoint of the fulfilment of democracy to raise up those people who are low down in the social and economic scale and to bring to them every possible opportunity of growth and progress. That has been the generally accepted policy of this country and it is the accepted policy of this Government. Now in pursuance of that policy, a certain reservation of seats was granted, for instance, to the scheduled castes, and various scholarships and educational amenities, etc., have been granted and no doubt will be granted still more, not only to the scheduled castes but also to other backward groups in the country. For there are the tribal people and others who require every help. It is no good for us to say that we have given a vote to the member of a tribal folk and we have done our duty by him ; having for hundreds and thousands of years not done our duty by him, by giving him a vote we consider ourselves absolved of all further duty. Therefore, we have to think always in terms of raising the level of all those who have been denied opportunities in the past. I do not personally think myself that the best way to do that is on the political plane by the reservation of seats and the rest. I think the best way, and the more basic and fundamental way, is to advance them rapidly in the economic and educational spheres and then they will stand on their own feet.

There is a great danger, whether you deal with an individual, group or community, of giving certain props to that community which give it a false sense of strength which does not belong to it. The props are external to it, and when they are removed suddenly make the community weak. A nation ultimately ought to stand on its own feet. So long as it relies on some external prop, it is not strong. It is weak. So these external props, as I might call them—that is, reservation of seats and the rest—may possibly be helpful occasionally in the case of the backward groups, but they produce a false sense of the political relation, a false sense of strength, and ultimately, therefore, they are not so nearly as important as real educational, cultural and economic advance, which gives them inner strength to face any difficulty or any opponent. However, I can conceive that in the present context of affairs in regard to these unfortunate countrymen of ours who have not had these opportunities in the past, special attempts should be made, of course, in the educational and economic field and even in the political field to see that they have a proper place till they find their own legs to stand upon without any external aid.

So I accept this Resolution on behalf of the Government, but in accepting it I should like to make it perfectly clear again that as far as the implementation of it is concerned, more especially in regard to the legislative aspect of it, it will have to be very carefully considered and will ultimately have to come before this House.

I have no objection on behalf of the Government to accept the addition of the words " social and educational " which are mentioned in one of the amendments to this Resolution. It would read :

> " . . . should be permitted to engage in any activities other than those essential for the *bona fide* religious, cultural, social and educational needs of the community. . ."

ON KASHMIR

WHO IS RESPONSIBLE?

I WANT to speak to you to-night about Kashmir, not about the beauty of that famous valley, but about the horror which it has had to face recently. We have passed through very critical days and the burden of taking vital and far-reaching decisions has fallen upon us. We have taken those decisions and I want to tell you about them.

The neighbouring Government, using language which is not the language of Governments or even of responsible people, has accused the Government of India of fraud in regard to the accession of Kashmir to the Indian Union. I cannot emulate that language nor have I any desire to do so, for I speak for a responsible Government and a responsible people. I agree that there has been fraud and violence in Kashmir but the question is: Who is responsible for it? Already considerable parts of the Jammu and Kashmir State have been overrun by raiders from outside, well-armed and well-equipped, and they have sacked and looted the towns and villages and put many of the inhabitants to the sword. Frightfulness suddenly descended upon this lovely and peaceful country and the beautiful city of Srinagar was on the verge of destruction.

I want to say at once that every step that we have taken in regard to Kashmir has been taken after the fullest thought and consideration of the consequences and I am convinced that what we have done was the right thing. Not to have taken those steps would have been a betrayal of a trust and cowardly submission to the law of the sword with its accompaniment of arson, rape and slaughter.

For some weeks past we had received reports of infiltration of raiding bands into the State territory of Jammu province. Also of a concentration of armed men near the border of Kashmir with the North West Frontier Province. We were naturally concerned about this not only because of our close ties with Kashmir and her people but also because Kashmir is a frontier territory adjoining great nations and therefore we were bound to take an interest in the developments there. But we were anxious not to interfere

A talk broadcast from New Delhi, November 2, 1947.

and we took no step whatever to intervene even though a part of the Jammu province was overrun by these raiders.

It has been stated that there were raids from the Jammu side across the Pakistan border and that there was communal trouble in Jammu, and Muslims were killed and driven away. In the past we have not hesitated to condemn evil whoever might have committed it, whether Hindus or Sikhs or Muslims, and so if Hindus or Sikhs or any functionaries of the State misbehaved in the Jammu province, certainly we condemn them and regret their deeds.

But I have before me a detailed list of 95 villages in the Jammu province which have been destroyed by the raiders from Pakistan. Bhimbar, a considerable town, had also been sacked and destroyed. Other towns are besieged and a considerable part of Poonch and Mirpur areas is in the possession of the raiders. Does this indicate that aggression took place from the Kashmir side on to West Punjab or does it not show that there has been continuous organized aggression from West Punjab into the Kashmir State? These raiders possess the latest type of modern arms. It is reported that they have used flame-throwers, and a disabled tank has been discovered with them.

About this time we were asked by the Kashmir State to provide them with arms. We took no urgent steps about it and although sanction was given by our States and Defence Ministries, actually no arms were sent.

On the night of the 24th October I learnt of another raid, this time from the Abbottabad-Mansara Road which enters Kashmir near Muzzafarabad. We were told that armed and well-equipped persons in over one hundred lorries had broken in, had sacked Muzzafarabad and killed many persons there, including the District Magistrate, and were proceeding along the Jhelum Valley road towards Srinagar. The State forces were spread out in small numbers all over the State and they could not stop this armed and well-organized raid. The civil population, Hindu and Muslim, fled before the raiders.

It was on the night of the 24th that for the first time a request was made to us on behalf of the Kashmir State for accession and military help. On the morning of the 25th we considered this in the Defence Committee but no decision was taken about sending troops in view of the obvious difficulties of the undertaking. On the morning of the 26th we again considered this matter. The situation was even more critical then. The raiders had sacked several towns and had destroyed the great power house at Mahora which supplies electricity to the whole of Kashmir. They were on the point of entering the valley. The fate of Srinagar and the whole of Kashmir hung in the balance.

We received urgent messages for aid not only from the Maharaja's Government but from representatives of the people, notably that great leader of Kashmir, Sheikh Mohammed Abdullah, the President of the National Conference. Both the Kashmir Government and the National Conference pressed us to accept the accession of Kashmir to the Indian Union. We decided to accept this accession and to send troops by air, but we made a condition that the accession would have to be considered by the people of Kashmir later when peace and order were established. We were anxious not to finalise anything in a moment of crisis and without the fullest opportunity being given to the people of Kashmir to have their say. It was for them ultimately to decide.

And here let me make clear that it has been our policy all along that where there is a dispute about the accession of a State to either Dominion, the decision must be made by the people of that State. It was in accordance with this policy that we added a proviso to the Instrument of Accession of Kashmir.

We decided to send troops on the afternoon of the 26th October. Srinagar was in peril and the situation was urgent and critical. Our staff worked hard day and night and at daybreak on the 27th our troops went by air. They were small in numbers to begin with but immediately on arrival they rushed into action to stop the invader. Their gallant Commander, a brave officer of our Army, was killed the next day.

Since then troops and equipment have been flown over daily, and I should like to express my high appreciation and the appreciation of my Government for the fine work which our staff have done, as well as the pilots and the air crews who have thrown themselves into this adventure heart and soul. The air lines have co-operated with us fully and to them also I am grateful. Our young men have shown how they can rise to the occasion in a moment of crisis to serve their country.

Srinagar was in peril and the invader was almost on its doorstep. There was no administration left there, no troops, no police. Light and power had failed and there were a vast number of refugees there and yet Srinagar functioned without obvious panic and the shops were opened and people went about the streets. To what was this miracle due? Sheikh Abdullah and his colleagues of the National Conference and their unarmed volunteers, Muslim and Hindu and Sikh, took charge of the situation, kept order and prevented panic. It was a wonderful piece of work that they did at a moment when the nerves of most people might have failed them. They did so because of the strength of their organization, but even more so, because they were determined to protect their country from the ruthless invader who was destroying their country and trying to compel them by terrorism to join Pakistan. Whatever the future may hold, the people of the valley of Kashmir have exhibited during these past few days remarkable courage, capacity for organization and unity.

It would be well if this lesson were understood by the whole of India which has been poisoned by communal strife. Under the inspiration of a great leader, Sheikh Abdullah, the people of the valley, Muslim and Hindu and Sikh, were brought together for the defence of their common country against the invader. Our troops could have done little without this popular support and co-operation.

The Maharaja of Kashmir deserves to be congratulated on his decision to make Sheikh Abdullah the head of the administration at this critical juncture. That was a wise step which other rulers might well follow, making their people trustees and defenders of freedom.

It must be remembered, therefore, that the struggle in Kashmir is a struggle of the people of Kashmir under popular leadership against the invader. Our troops are there to help in this struggle, and as soon as Kashmir is free from the invader, our troops will have no further necessity to remain there and the fate of Kashmir will be left in the hands of the people of Kashmir.

We have passed through days of peril not only for Kashmir but for the whole of India. That peril is less now but it is by no means over and many other dangers confront us. We have to be very vigilant and well prepared for whatever may happen. The first step in this preparation is to put an end completely to every manner of communal strife in India and to stand up as a united nation to face every danger which might threaten our freedom. External danger can only be faced effectively when there is internal peace and order and an organized nation.

We talk about the invaders and raiders in Kashmir and yet

these men are fully armed and well-trained and have competent leadership. All of these have come across from Pakistan territory. We have a right to ask the Pakistan Government how and why these people could come across the Frontier Province or West Punjab and how they have been armed so effectively. Is this not a violation of International Law and an unfriendly act towards a neighbour country? Is the Pakistan Government too weak to prevent armies marching across its territory to invade another country or is it willing that this should happen? There is no other alternative.

We have asked the Pakistan Government repeatedly to stop these raiders from coming and to withdraw those who have come. It should be easy for them to stop them, for the roads into Kashmir are very few and have to pass over bridges. We on our part have no intention of using our troops in Kashmir when the danger of invasion is passed.

We have declared that the fate of Kashmir is ultimately to be decided by the people. That pledge we have given, and the Maharaja has supported it, not only to the people of Kashmir but to the world. We will not and cannot back out of it. We are prepared when peace and law and order have been established to have a referendum held under international auspices like the United Nations. We want it to be a fair and just reference to the people and we shall accept their verdict. I can imagine no fairer and juster offer.

Meanwhile, we have given our word to the people of Kashmir to protect them against the invader and we shall keep our pledge.

KASHMIR HAS GONE THROUGH FIRE

I AM glad to have this opportunity of explaining to the House the course of events that have led to our intervention in Kashmir with the aid of armed forces, and the attitude of the Government of India to the grave problems that have arisen in that State.

The House is aware that on the lapse of Crown Paramountcy on the 15th August, this year, Kashmir did not accede to either Dominion. We were of course vitally interested in the decision that the State would take. Kashmir, because of her geographical position with her frontiers with three countries, namely, the Soviet Union, China and Afghanistan, is intimately connected with the security and international contacts of India. Economically also Kashmir is intimately related to India. The caravan trade routes from Central Asia to India pass through the Kashmir State.

Nevertheless, we did not put the slightest pressure on the State to accede to the Indian Dominion, because we realized that Kashmir was in a very difficult position. We did not want a mere accession from the top but an association in accordance with the will of her people. Indeed, we did not encourage any rapid decision. Even in regard to a standstill agreement, no speedy steps were taken by us, although Kashmir had entered into a standstill agreement with Pakistan soon after the 15th August.

We learnt later that serious external pressure was being applied on Kashmir by the Pakistan authorities refusing to send to Kashmir supplies vital to the needs of the people, such as food-grains, salt, sugar and petrol. Thus an attempt was being made to strangle Kashmir economically and force her to accede to Pakistan. This pressure was serious, because it was not easy for Kashmir to obtain these essential supplies from India on account of the difficulty of communications.

In September, news reached us that tribesmen of the North West Frontier Province were being collected and sent to the Kashmir border. In the beginning of October events took a grave turn. Armed bands moved into the Jammu province from the

A statement made in the Constituent Assembly (Legislative), New Delhi, November 25, 1947.

neighbouring districts of West Punjab, committed serious acts of depredation on the local inhabitants, burnt villages and towns and put a large number of people to death. Refugees from these areas poured into Jammu.

On the Jammu side of the border the local inhabitants, who are chiefly Hindu and Rajput, took retaliatory measures and drove out the Muslims living in those border villages. In these border conflicts a very large number of villages were destroyed or burnt by both parties on either side of the frontier.

The raiders from West Punjab into the Jammu province increased in number and spread out over that province. The Kashmir State Army which had to meet these raids at numerous points soon found itself broken into small fragments and gradually ceased to be a fighting force. The raiders were highly organized, had competent officers and modern arms. They succeeded in occupying a considerable part of the Jammu province, more especially in the Poonch area. The town of Poonch, Mirpur, Kotli and some other places held out.

About this time the State authorities asked us to supply them with arms and ammunition. We agreed to do so in the normal course. But in fact no supply was made till events took a more serious turn. Even at this stage no mention was made of accession to India.

The leader of the popular organization in Kashmir, Sheikh Mohammed Abdullah, President of the Kashmir National Conference, was released from prison during this period and we discussed the situation in Kashmir with him as well as with the representatives of the Maharaja of Kashmir. We made it clear to both of them that while we would welcome the accession of Kashmir we did not want any hurried or forced accession and we would rather wait for the people to decide. Sheikh Abdullah was himself of this opinion.

On the 24th October we heard that large armed bands consisting both of tribesmen from the Frontier and ex-servicemen had broken through Muzzafarabad and were marching to Srinagar. These raiders had crossed Pakistan territory and they were equipped with Bren guns, machine guns, mortars and flame-throwers and had at their disposal a large number of transport vehicles. They moved rapidly down the valley, sacking and burning and looting all along the way. We gave earnest consider-

ation to this situation in our Defence Committee on the 25th and
26th October. The position on the morning of the 26th was that
the raiders were marching towards Srinagar and there was no
military detachment capable of stopping them. They had been
stopped for two days near Uri by the State forces under a gallant
commander who resisted this advance to the point of death. These
two days thus gained were very valuable.

We were asked at this stage both on behalf of the Maharaja
and Sheikh Abdullah to accept the accession of the State to the
Indian Union and to intervene with the armed forces of the
Union. An immediate decision was necessary, and in fact it is
now clear that if we had delayed the decision even by 24 hours,
Srinagar would have fallen and would have suffered the tragic
fate that befell Muzzafarabad, Baramula and other places. It
was clear to us that we could not possibly accept under any
circumstances the ruin of Kashmir by brutal and irresponsible
raiders. This would have been a surrender to frightfulness and
fanaticism of the worst type and it would have had the most
serious consequences all over India. To intervene at this stage was
no easy matter and was full of risks and danger. Yet we decided
to face this risk and intervene because any other course would
have meant ruin to Kashmir and greater danger to India.

In accepting the accession, however, we made it perfectly clear
to the Maharaja that his Government must be carried on in
future according to the popular will and that Sheikh Abdullah
should be charged with the formation of an interim government
on the new model adopted in Mysore. Sheikh Abdullah, in our
opinion, had undoubtedly the support of the large majority of
the people of Kashmir, Muslims, Hindus and Sikhs. Further,
we made it clear that as soon as law and order had been restored
in Kashmir and her soil cleared of the invaders, the question of
the State's accession should be settled by reference to the people.

I shall not detain the House by dealing with the course of the
military campaign that followed. The facts are well-known and
redound to the credit of our military organization, our troops
and our airmen. It must be remembered also that our operations
have been very largely based on air transport in difficult
circumstances. Our civil airlines and their aircrews functioned
with remarkable success.

One fact, however, which contributed to our success, at least as
much as the military operations, was the maintenance, under

the leadership of Sheikh Abdullah, of the civil administration and the morale of the civilian population. The civilian population, completely unarmed, with the enemy within a few miles of the city, behaved in a manner which showed extraordinary courage and coolness. They did so, because they had a great leader and because Hindus, Muslims and Sikhs all joined together under him to throw back the enemy and to save Kashmir, their common heritage. This fact is one of the most remarkable events of recent times in India and one from which the rest of the country may well take a profitable lesson. It was certainly a factor of the most vital importance in the saving of Srinagar.

The present position is that our troops have relieved Poonch and are within 8 miles of Kotli. The terrain in which they are fighting is difficult and mountainous and the roads and approaches have been destroyed by the raiders. Progress is, therefore, slow. In the Poonch area occupied by the raiders several massacres of the non-Muslim inhabitants have taken place involving large numbers of persons.

I should like to say here that certain events happened near Jammu early in November which I regret very deeply. The Muslim convoys of evacuees were being taken away from Jammu when they were attacked by non-Muslim refugees and others and a large number of casualties were inflicted. The troops escorting them did not play a creditable role. I might add that none of our troops were present or had anything to do with this. We have issued the most stringent orders to our troops to protect the people, to act with impartiality and indeed to make friends with the local population. I am glad to say that they have carried out these instructions.

The House is aware that the Pakistan Government have protested emphatically against our action in Kashmir. In doing so they have used language which is not becoming in any government and have alleged fraud and conspiracy on our part. I need only say that I am completely convinced that every action that the Government of India have taken in regard to Kashmir has been straight and above board and I can defend it at any time before the world. We have indeed been over-scrupulous in this matter so that nothing may be done in the passion of the moment which might be wrong. The behaviour of our army has all along been good and worthy of our traditions.

I cannot say this of the Pakistan Government. Their case is

that the genesis of the trouble was the extensive killing of Muslims in Eastern Punjab and Kashmir and that the raid on Kashmir was a spontaneous reaction to this on the part of the tribesmen. I think this is completely untrue. I regret deeply that in parts of the Jammu province Muslims were killed and driven out. This of course has had nothing to do with our Government or our forces. But this mutual killing has been a very tragic feature during these past months in the Punjab, and Jammu was powerfully affected by this. We have sufficient evidence in our possession to demonstrate that the whole business of the Kashmir raids both in the Jammu province and in Kashmir proper was deliberately organized by high officials of the Pakistan Government. They helped the tribesmen and ex-servicemen to collect, they supplied them with the implements of war, with lorries, with petrol and with officers. They are continuing to do so. Indeed, their high officials openly declare so. It is obvious that no large body of men could cross Pakistan territory in armed groups without the goodwill, connivance and active help of the authorities there. It is impossible to escape the conclusion that the raids on Kashmir were carefully planned and well organized by the Pakistan authorities with the deliberate object of seizing the State by force and then declaring accession to Pakistan. This was an act of hostility not only to Kashmir but to the Indian Union. It is only necessary to see the semi-official organs of the Muslim League and the Pakistan Government to find out the attitude of that Government. If we had allowed this scheme to succeed, we would have been guilty of the betrayal of the people of Kashmir and of a grave dereliction of duty to India. The results of these on the communal and political situation all over India would have been disastrous.

The Pakistan Government have proposed a simultaneous withdrawal of our forces and the raiders from Kashmir. This was a strange proposal and could only mean that the raiders were there at the instance of the Pakistan Government. We cannot treat with freebooters who have murdered large numbers of people and tried to ruin Kashmir. They are not a State, although a State may be behind them. We have gone to Kashmir to protect the people and as soon as this duty is discharged our forces need not remain there and we shall withdraw our forces. We cannot desert the people of Kashmir till the danger is passed. If the Pakistan Government are sincere, they can stop the entry of these raiders and thus accelerate the return of peace and order. After that let the people of Kashmir decide and we shall accept their decision. But if this armed conflict continues, no opportunity is given to the people to decide by peaceful means, and the decision gradually takes shape through the sacrifice and power of the people in this conflict.

In order to establish our *bona fides*, we have suggested that when the people are given the chance to decide their future, this should be done under the supervision of an impartial tribunal such as the United Nations Organization.

The issue in Kashmir is whether violence and naked force should decide the future or the will of the people. The raiders encouraged by Pakistan have sought to enforce by the sword accession to Pakistan against the obvious wishes of large numbers of the people in Kashmir. We cannot permit the success of this method to achieve political ends. It is a tragedy that Pakistan should ally itself to such methods instead of devoting itself to the urgent tasks of economic and social reconstruction.

Kashmir has gone through fire and I am sure that the House would like me to communicate their sympathy to the people of Kashmir for the tribulations they have been going through in recent weeks. This fair land, which Nature has made so lovely, has been desecrated by people who have indulged in murder, arson, loot and foul attacks on women and children. The people have suffered greatly from shortage of the most vital necessities of life and yet, under the inspiring lead of Sheikh Abdullah, they have stood together in the hour of calamity and showed to the rest of India an example of what communal unity can achieve. Whatever the future may hold, this chapter in the history of Kashmir will be worth reading and we shall never regret that in their hour of distress we have been able to be of assistance to this gallant people. Kashmir and India have been bound together in many ways from ages past. These last few weeks have forged a new link which no one can sunder.

FACTS RELATING TO KASHMIR

As is well known now, the Government of India has made a reference to the Security Council of the UNO in regard to the invasion of Kashmir by persons coming from or through Pakistan.

The Government desires to take the Press and the public into full confidence in so far as it can, having regard to diplomatic decorum and propriety. It has waited thus far because it would have been proper for the Security Council to consider the matter first before any publicity was given to it, but, in view of references being made to this subject by the Foreign Minister of Pakistan and by others, it is desirable to state the facts briefly.

I have previously, on several occasions, placed before the country the facts relating to Kashmir ever since we sent our troops there on October 27, 1947. Our troops succeeded in saving the valley of Kashmir and the city of Srinagar and drove back the enemy to Uri along the Jhelum Valley road.

Since then, fighting has taken place on a large front along almost the entire border of the Kashmir State and Pakistan. Very large numbers of armed men, in battle formation and fully equipped with modern arms, have entered Kashmir State territory at many places, and still larger concentrations of these men have been made along the border on the Pakistan side.

These border areas of Pakistan have become the base of operations for these invaders and, from the security of these bases, large numbers come across and raid, burn and loot on Kashmir State territory which is Indian Dominion territory.

The Government of India would have been justified, in self-defence, to strike at these bases, and thus put an end to the sources of supply of these invaders. It has, however, scrupulously avoided doing so, so as to limit the field of operations and in the hope that the Pakistan Government will cease aiding and abetting these invaders.

During the last two months, repeated requests have been made to the Pakistan Government to prevent the use of its territory for aggression on India. It has not only not done so, but it

A statement made at a Press Conference, New Delhi, January 2, 1948.

is an established fact that these invaders, among whom are a large number of Pakistan nationals, have been helped in every way by the Pakistan Government.

They are allowed transit through Pakistan territory by motor transport and railway trains, supplied petrol, food and accommodation ; and the arms they possess are manifestly the arms of the Pakistan Army. Pakistan Army personnel have also been captured by our troops in the operations in Kashmir.

Not only has the Pakistan Government not taken effective steps to prevent this invasion, but it has refused even to call upon the invaders to desist from their active aggression.

The Government of India cannot tolerate the use of a friendly and neighbouring country as a base for the invasion of Indian territory but, in its desire to avoid any action, unless it is compelled by circumstances to take it, it has decided to refer this matter to the Security Council of the UNO.

On December 22, 1947, a formal request was made in writing to the Prime Minister of Pakistan. In this letter, the acts of aggression of Pakistan and the forms of aid given by Pakistan to the invaders were briefly stated and the Government of Pakistan was asked to call upon Pakistan nationals to cease participating in the attack on the Jammu and Kashmir State and to deny to the invaders: (1) all access to and use of Pakistan territory for operations against the Kashmir State ; (2) all military and other supplies ; (3) all other kinds of aid that might tend to prolong the present struggle.

The Government of India expressed its earnest desire again to live on terms of friendship with Pakistan and hoped that its request would be acceded to promptly and without reserve. It pointed out, however, that, failing such response, it would be compelled to take such action, with due regard to its rights and obligations as a member of the UNO, as it might consider necessary to protect its own interests and those of the Government and people of Jammu and Kashmir State.

As no reply was received to this formal request, two reminders were sent. Ultimately, on December 30, a formal reference was made to the Security Council of the UNO through the representative of the Government of India with UNO. On December 31, a copy of this reference was sent by telegram to the Pakistan Government.

This reference stated the facts of the case and pointed out that they indisputably pointed to the following conclusions:

(a) that the invaders are allowed transit across Pakistan territory ;

(b) that they are allowed to use Pakistan territory as a base of operations ;

(c) that they include Pakistan nationals ;

(d) that they draw much of their military equipment, transport and supplies (including petrol) from Pakistan ; and

(e) that Pakistan officers are training, guiding and otherwise helping them.

There was no source other than Pakistan from which such quantities of modern military equipment, training and guidance could have been obtained. The Government of India requested the Security Council, therefore, to ask the Government of Pakistan:

(1) to prevent Pakistan Government personnel, military and civil, participating in or assisting the invasion of the Jammu and Kashmir State ;

(2) to call upon other Pakistan nationals to desist from taking any part in the fighting in the Jammu and Kashmir State ;

(3) to deny to the invaders: (a) access to and use of its territory for operations against Kashmir ; (b) military and other supplies ; (c) all other kinds of aid that might tend to prolong the present struggle.

The reference to the Security Council is thus limited to the matters mentioned above. There is an urgency about these matters, for the first step that must be taken is to put a stop to the fighting and this can only be done if the invaders withdraw. It must be remembered that all the fighting has taken place on Indian Union territory and it is the inherent right of the Government of India to drive back any invaders on its territory. Till the Kashmir State is free of the invaders, no other matter can be considered.

The Government of India deeply regrets that this serious crisis has arisen. It is not of its seeking, and it has been thrust upon it by invading armies from outside who have committed acts of barbarism against the inhabitants of the Kashmir State and destroyed and burnt a large number of villages and some towns. No Government can tolerate such an invasion.

In its desire, however, to avoid any act which might lead to further complications, it has shown the greatest forbearance and made repeated appeals to the Pakistan Government. Those appeals have been in vain, and hence it decided to refer this particular question to the Security Council. It has naturally reserved to itself freedom to take such action in self-defence as the situation may require.

The Foreign Minister of Pakistan, in a recent Press interview, has brought a large number of charges against the Government of India. I shall not go into these charges except to repudiate them utterly. What has happened during the past year is well known and we are prepared to stand the test of the closest scrutiny. Apparently all this variety of charges has been brought to cover up the Kashmir issue in a forest of other matters which have nothing to do with it.

It is completely untrue to say that the Government of India has tried to undo the partition or to strangle Pakistan. The mere fact of our agreeing to what everybody recognizes to be very generous financial terms is evidence of our desire to help Pakistan and to have friendly relations with it.

It is completely untrue that we have repudiated these financial agreements ; we stand by them and shall honour them, but it is true that we have pointed out to Pakistan that we cannot make these payments at present when the money we give might be utilized for warlike operations against India.

The Kashmir issue stands by itself. If the methods of invasion of friendly territory by a barbarous foe are encouraged and submitted to, there is no future either for India or for Pakistan and therefore this has to be and will be resisted by us to the utmost, and the Kashmir State will have to be freed completely. Even from the narrowest viewpoint of self-interest, the Government of Pakistan should realize that the encouragement of such an invasion is perilous to its own future, because, once the forces of unbridled violence are let loose, they endanger the whole security of any State.

It must be remembered that in Kashmir there is no communal issue as such. Large numbers of Kashmiris, Muslims, Hindus and Sikhs are fighting the invaders. It is a national issue for them to preserve their freedom, and we have gone there to support them. We have pledged our honour to them and we shall stand by our pledge.

I would appeal to the Press for restraint in dealing with this issue at this critical stage and to avoid publishing unauthorized

matter. We shall try to give full information to the Press whenever it is possible. The publication of unauthorized stories is likely
to do harm to the State and to the cause we represent.

PLEDGE TO KASHMIR

THE Government's decision in regard to the payment of the cash balances to Pakistan has been taken after the most careful thought and after consultation with Gandhiji. I should like to make it clear that this does not mean any change in our unanimous view about the strength and validity of the Government's position as set out in various statements made by distinguished colleagues of mine. Nor do we accept the facts or arguments advanced in the latest statement of the Finance Minister of Pakistan.

We have come to this decision in the hope that this generous gesture, in accord with India's high ideals and Gandhiji's noble standards, will convince the world of our earnest desire for peace and goodwill. We earnestly trust also that this will go a long way towards producing a situation which will induce Gandhiji to break his fast. That fast, of course, had nothing to do with this particular matter, and we have thought of it because of our desire to help in every way in easing the present tension.

Six months ago we witnessed a miracle in Calcutta where ill-will changed overnight into goodwill, through the alchemy of a similar fast. The alchemist who worked this change was described by our Governor-General as the one-man boundary

A statement from New Delhi, January 15, 1948.

India very generously agreed to allocate Rs. 75 crores to Pakistan out of the cash balances to help the latter to make a start. It was felt that the Arbitral Tribunal should not have allocated so big an amount to Pakistan, and it was hoped that this generosity on the part of the Indian Union would have reciprocal response. The Deputy Prime Minister, Sardar Patel, made it clear that this financial deal was linked with the overall settlement of all outstanding issues. But in the meantime, in Kashmir Pakistan waged virtually an undeclared war against India ; and lest the Rs. 55 crores (Rs. 20 crores having already been paid out of the 75 crores) should be spent against India in Kashmir, it was withheld pending the settlement of the Kashmir issue. It became another cause of bitterness between India and Pakistan. When Mahatmaji began his fast on January 13 and appealed to the nation to remove ill-will, prejudice, and passion which poisoned the relations between India and Pakistan, the Government of India decided to pay the amount due, namely, Rs. 55 crores to Pakistan immediately as a gesture of goodwill to that State and as their contribution " to the non-violent and noble effort made by Gandhiji." On January 18, Mahatma Gandhi terminated his fast in response to the pledge given by the citizens of Delhi through the peace committees that they would banish communalism from their hearts and from the country.

force which succeeded when the boundary force of 50,000 men in West Punjab did not succeed in keeping the peace. This unarmed knight of non-violence is functioning again. May the same alchemy work again in India and elsewhere!

We have sought to remove one major cause of dispute and argument between India and Pakistan and we hope that other problems will also be resolved. But let it be remembered that the people of Kashmir are suffering from a brutal and unprovoked invasion, and we have pledged ourselves to help them to gain their freedom. To that pledge we shall hold and we shall do our utmost to redeem it. We seek their freedom not for any gain to us, but to prevent the ravishing of a fair country and a peaceful people.

THE SWEEP OF HISTORY

SIR, I crave your leave and the indulgence of the House to make a statement on Kashmir. I would beg the House to bear with me for a while, because there is a great deal to say, however briefly I might say it,—not that I am going to make any sensational disclosures, there is nothing very secret about what I am going to say and the facts have appeared in the public Press and in other places frequently enough during the last few months. Nevertheless, it is right that I should place before the House some kind of a consecutive account of what has happened. In order to lessen my task and to help Members of the House, we have prepared a White Paper on Kashmir which will be distributed to members. This White Paper does not bring matters right up-to-date. It is practically up to the period of the reference to the Security Council. It is not an absolutely complete paper in the sense that every telegram and every letter is included, but, on the whole, most of the messages that passed between us and the Government of Pakistan, or connected messages have been given in this White Paper.

Now, before I speak on this particular Kashmir issue, I should like by your leave to say a few words on a wider issue of which the Kashmir issue is a part. We have been living through strenuous days ; we have been passing through a period of dynamic history in India. Much has happened during the past six months, much that was good and much that was very bad. But, perhaps, when the history of India comes to be written, when much of the horror of today has been forgotten, one of the biggest things that will be mentioned will be the change that has come over India and that is coming over India in regard to the Indian States. We see something very remarkable happening. It is perhaps difficult for us who live in the middle of this change to appreciate the bigness of what has happened. But it is the upsetting in a very curious way—a peaceful way—of a structure that has endured in India for the past 130 or 140 years, more or less ever since the beginning of the nineteenth century.

We see the sweep of history suddenly coming, the big broom

A statement made in the Constituent Assembly (Legislative), New Delhi, March 5, 1948.

of history, and changing this 130 year old structure and putting something else in its place. We cannot definitely and absolutely say what the final and precise outcome of all this will be, though the picture is clearing up fairly rapidly. It would almost appear that there is the hand of destiny at work. What is happening is nothing that we did not expect. In fact, many of us for many years past have had certain objectives in regard to the Indian States and we have worked for them both through our political and other organizations in India, through the people of the States, through the people of the provinces and otherwise. And, on the whole, what is happening today is in line with the objectives we had laid down. So it is not surprising. Yet, may I confess to you, Sir, that even I who have been rather intimately connected with the States peoples' movement for many years, if I had been asked six months ago what the course of developments would be in the next six months since then, I would have hesitated to say that such rapid changes would take place. Many factors have gone to bring about these rapid changes. Ultimately, I suppose, they are the forces of history working,—the unleashing of all manner of forces which had been repressed for so long. For we had during these 130 years a strange phenomenon. The British Government had constructed a State structure in the course of a quarter of a century in the early days of the nineteenth century. Whether it fitted in, in reality, with conditions then existing in India or not, it is a little difficult to say what would have happened minus the British Government. Anyhow, the dominant power of the British created this system, no doubt for their own advantage as they thought fit. That system continued, not because of any inherent strength, as is obvious today, but because of the continuance of that dominant power, of the paramount power as it was called. All manner of changes were going on in India and in the outside world and yet the Indian States structure continued. Many of us said that it was rather archaic, it was out of date, it had to change and must change and so on. But now that the protecting hand of a foreign Government has been removed, the repressions also are removed. The forces that had been kept in check suddenly began to function and we see them in action,—in rapid action. The forces are there of course ; they have not been curbed by any of us, but I think in the manner of dealing with this situation,—an intricate and difficult situation —this House will agree with me that we owe a debt of gratitude to my friend and colleague, the Deputy Prime Minister.

So it is in this mighty context of a changing India in regard to the States that we have to view any particular aspect of it. We saw unfortunately six months back the partition of India, the splitting up of India, a part of India going out of India. Immediately after that process of cutting off, another process started, or rather we have always had these two processes—the process of integrating India. We have seen this process of integrating India going on in regard to the States, and not only in regard to the States but, to some extent, even in regard to the provinces, but much more so in regard to the States. So these two things have gone on together—a process of cutting away and a process of integration—and in the balance it is difficult to say how far we have gained and how far we have lost. It is difficult to say also how far this process of integration will go and whither it will take us ultimately. Nevertheless, it is interesting for us living through this rather strange and dynamic period of India's history, to look at it in some perspective, not as actors in the drama but rather as historians looking back on what has happened. The historian who looks back will no doubt consider this integration of the States into India as one of the dominant phases of India's history.

Well, Sir, the process is taking various shapes. There has been an actual merger of a large number of small States with India ; there has been a bringing together of a number of States into Unions of States which form units of the Union of India and a certain number of major States remain as separate entities. But what is equally important—and if I may say so, even more important—is not this integration externally but the inner integration, that is, the growth of democratic institutions and responsible government in the States, because that brings about a real integration, not at the top level of government but at the level of the people. Both these processes have gone on and both these processes, may I remind the House, are in line with the objectives for which we have laboured for many years.

Now, it is in this context of changes in the States system that I would like this House to consider the particular case of Kashmir, although it stands apart and many other factors come into play. Today in India two States stand quite apart from the rest in regard to these processes. These States are Hyderabad and Kashmir. I am not going at this moment to say anything about Hyderabad. In regard to Kashmir, it stands apart for many reasons, partly because it has got entangled in external politics, that is to say, it has got entangled in the relations between India and Pakistan and so the two essentially State issues there are somewhat submerged. It is an odd thing that it should get so entangled. That it got entangled is not odd, but the manner of its entanglement, because the Government of Pakistan have assured us time and again that they have nothing to do with the recent events in Kashmir, raids and invasions, etc.—they go on repeating that ; nevertheless, they seek to profit by those events. They seek political advantages out of those events, so that while disclaiming all responsibility for what has happened they do want to share in whatever they might get out of it. Anyhow, the Kashmir problem stands apart.

But for the moment, leaving out this external implication of the Kashmir problem, if you consider it, it is essentially the same problem, that is to say, a problem of the growth of the freedom of the people and the growth also of a new integration. Now, we have been aiming, the Government of India and the States Ministry, at the growth of this inner freedom of the people of all the States. If many of the States have agreed to merge with India or come into closer contact with her, it is not because the States Ministry took a big stick and threatened them with consequences. It is because of those forces, arising from the people, and other forces, and fundamentally the sudden withdrawal of an external force which had kept the States together, or rather the States system together, the might of the British Government and the sanctions behind it. That disappearing, immediately the structure began to collapse and it is an astonishing thing—this sudden collapse of a structure which seemed so solid just a few months or a year ago—not surprising to those who knew the facts, but undoubtedly surprising to those people who take a superficial view of things. So essentially we have been aiming at the freedom of the people, knowing and realizing that ultimately it will be for the people of the States to decide what their future will be. We are not going to compel them. We do not propose to compel them, and indeed we cannot compel them in the context of the world today in any State. There are other compulsions, the compulsions of geography. That is true ; one cannot ignore it. There are many other compulsions. And naturally in considering the problem, we, that is, the Government of India, have always to consider the interests of India as a whole, the interests of

India in regard to security, defence, etc., but apart from that, we do not wish to exercise any other compulsion in the slightest, over the growth of freedom. In fact, we want to encourage it in the people of the States. We know well that if there is that growth of freedom and freedom of decision by the people of the States, then it will be a powerful factor in bringing them nearer to our people, because we hope that whatever constitution we may adopt in India, it will be based completely on the will of the people.

Now, may I say a few words before I go on to the Kashmir issue and that is this: in this matter I feel a slight difficulty, because the matter is being or going to be discussed again in the Security Council of the United Nations and I would not like to say anything which might be construed, shall I say, into putting difficulties in the way of coming to a settlement either in the Security Council or elsewhere. Because we earnestly desire a settlement, we earnestly desire that these great forces should be allowed to function normally and to achieve their results ; any other result will be an artificial result. We cannot impose a result—certainly Pakistan cannot impose a result. Ultimately there is no doubt in my mind that in Kashmir as elsewhere, the people of Kashmir will decide finally, and all that we wish is that they should have freedom of decision without any external compulsion.

Now, there is one other factor which I should like to put before the House in regard to Kashmir. We have become too used in India, unfortunately, to thinking of every problem or many problems in terms of communalism, of Hindu versus Muslim or Hindu and Sikh versus Muslim and so on. That has been an unfortunate legacy of ours, and the extent to which it took us cannot be forgotten by us nor the tragedies that it has led to. We are trying, I hope, to get rid of the spirit of communalism, in India at least. We hope to put an end to it, not suddenly perhaps, but certainly fairly rapidly.

Now, in this context of communal conflict the case of Kashmir stands apart, because Kashmir is not a case of communal conflict ; it may be a case of political conflict, if you like ; it may be a case of any other conflict, but it is essentially not a case of communal conflict. Therefore, this struggle in Kashmir, although it has brought great suffering in its train to the people of Kashmir and placed a burden on the Government of India and the people of India, nevertheless it stands out as a sign of hope that

there we see a certain co-operation, combination and co-
ordination of certain elements, Hindu and Muslim and Sikh and
others on an equal level, and for a political fight for their own
freedom. I wish to stress this because it is continually being said
by our opponents and critics on the other side that this is a communal affair and that we are there to support the Hindus or
the Sikh minorities as against the Muslim masses of Kashmir.
Nothing can be more fantastically untrue. We could not for an
instant send our armies and we would not be there if we were not
supported by very large sections of the population, which means
the Muslims of Kashmir. We would not have gone there in spite
of the invitation of the Maharaja of Kashmir, if that invitation
had not been backed by the representatives of the people of
Kashmir and may I say to the House that in spite of our armies
having functioned with great gallantry, even our armies could not
have succeeded except with the help and co-operation of the
people of Kashmir. Now, we are blamed by people outside,
beyond the borders of India, for going to Kashmir to support an
autocratic monarch. The House will remember that one of the
conditions that we made at that critical moment, when we had
to decide whether to send the Indian Army or not, whether to
accept accession or not, one of the conditions was that there must
be a popular government there, not as a goal and an ideal,
but immediately. It was an immediate thing and it was given
effect to immediately in so far as it could be given effect to. So
it is strange that this charge should be brought against us. Look
at this charge in another context. Those people, men and women
of Kashmir, who are with us and who are fighting for their
freedom and liberty there, they are not newcomers in the struggle
for freedom ; for the greater part of a generation, they have
fought for the freedom of Kashmir, in Kashmir ; they have
suffered for it and some of us have deemed it a privilege to be
associated with them in this fight for the freedom of Kashmir
against autocratic rule. These people are with us today. Who are
their opponents, who are against them in Kashmir or elsewhere?
What has been their record in the past ten, twenty years in regard
to the freedom of Kashmir? It is an interesting speculation and an
interesting inquiry, because these gentlemen who talk about the
autocracy of the Ruler of Kashmir, who talk about autocracy
there, what did they do during these last ten, twenty years? They
never fought for the freedom of the people of Kashmir ; most of

them supported that autocracy ; most of them opposed the free-dom movement in Kashmir. Now, because of entirely different reasons, they have become the champions of the freedom of Kashmir. And what is the type of freedom they have brought into Kashmir today? The freedom so-called that they have brought into Kashmir is the license to loot and murder and burn that love-ly country and to abduct and carry away the beautiful women of the Jammu and Kashmir State ; and not only carry them away, but place some of them in the open market place for sale! So let us have this background before us when we consider this Kashmir story. It is a stirring background of events and many of us have been distressed at the strangely narrow view that people in the Security Council have taken on this matter. I do not desire to enter into the details of what happened or did not happen in the Security Council, but I do feel that this background must be appreciated. It is not a Hindu-Muslim question in Kashmir ; it is not a question certainly of our standing for any autocracy or any-thing. We have already, during the last fifteen or twenty years, shown where we stand in regard to the States people and their rulers. In regard to Kashmir, more particularly, we have shown by our actions from the very first day we went there, from October last until today, and I shall have something more to say about it before I finish as to how we feel about the freedom of Kashmir.

Now, Sir, I shall go into some slight detail about the events in Kashmir.

The House will recall the statement I made on Kashmir on the 25th November, 1947. In that statement I recounted briefly the course of events in the Jammu and Kashmir State up to that day, the part played by the Government of Pakistan in these events, and our own objectives.

Our complaint against Pakistan was that it had incited and aid-ed tribesmen from outside and its own nationals to wage war on the Jammu and Kashmir State. The month of December showed an intensification of military pressure on the State. Nearly 19,000 raiders had been reinforced in the Uri area. 15,000 raiders were operating against the western and south-western borders of the State. Incursions by the raiders into the State territory, involving murder, arson, loot and the abduction of women were continuing. The booty was being collected and carried to tribal areas to serve as an inducement to the tribesmen to swell the ranks of the raiders. In addition to those actively participating in the raids, a large number of tribesmen and others, estimated at 100,000, had been collected in different places in the districts of West Punjab bordering upon the Jammu and Kashmir State, and many of them were receiving military training under Pakistan nationals, including officers of the Pakistan Army. They were being looked after in Pakistan territory, fed, clothed, armed and otherwise equipped and transported to the territory of the Jammu and Kashmir State with the help, direct and indirect, of Pakistan officials, both military and civil. The equipment of the invaders included modern weapons, such as mortars and medium machine guns ; the men wore the battle dress of regular soldiers, fought in regular battle formation and used the tactics of modern warfare. Man-packed wireless sets were in regular use and even Mark ' V ' mines were being employed.

More than once, the Government of India had asked the Pakistan Government to deny facilities to the invaders, facilities which constituted an act of aggression and hostility against India, but without any satisfactory response. On the 22nd December, I handed personally to the Prime Minister of Pakistan in New Delhi, a letter in which the various forms of aid were briefly recited, and his Government were asked to put an end to such aid, promptly and without reservation.

As no reply to this letter was received for some days I sent a reminder by telegram on the 26th December. On the 31st December the Government of India instructed their Ambassador in Washington to convey a message to the Chairman of the Security Council of the United Nations. This message was a reference to the Security Council under Article 35 of the Charter of the United Nations. On that same day, the full text of the message was sent to the Prime Minister of Pakistan by telegram.

On the 1st January, I received a reply from the Prime Minister of Pakistan to my letter, dated 22nd December. The contents of this letter revealed no helpful approach to a solution of the Kashmir problem. They consisted only of a series of fantastic charges against India, e.g., a determination to crush Pakistan, organized genocide of Muslims in India, and the procurement of the accession of Kashmir by force and fraud. This letter, even if it had been received earlier, could not have modified our decision to request the Security Council of the United Nations to ask the Government of Pakistan:

(1) to prevent Pakistan Government personnel, military or

civil, from participating and assisting the invasion of the Jammu and Kashmir State ;

(2) to call upon other Pakistan nationals to desist from taking part in the fighting in the Jammu and Kashmir State ;

(3) to deny to the raiders (a) access to and use of its territory for operations against Kashmir ; (b) military and other supplies ; (c) all other kinds of aid that might tend to prolong the present struggle.

The House will remember the circumstances in which we had sent our forces to Kashmir. Kashmir State territory, that is, after accession, Indian Dominion territory, was being invaded to the accompaniment of murder, arson, loot and the abduction of women. The whole countryside was being ruined. Fresh raiders were continually coming from Pakistan territory into the Kashmir State. All the fighting was taking place in Indian Dominion territory. The invaders had their principal bases across the border in Pakistan, received supplies and reinforcements from them, and could go back there to rest and recuperate in safety. Our troops had strict orders not to enter Pakistan territory. The normal course to prevent raids on Indian territory would have been to deny the use of any bases to them in Pakistan. Since Pakistan was unwilling to co-operate with us in this manner, the alternatives left to us were to send our armed forces across Pakistan territory to deal effectively with the invaders, or to request the United Nations to ask Pakistan to do so. Any resort to the first course would have involved armed conflict with Pakistan. We were anxious to avoid this and to try every available method to find a peaceful solution. Therefore, the only course left open to us was to make a reference to the Security Council.

I shall not take up the time of the House with a detailed account of the proceedings of the Security Council ; these have been fairly fully reported in the Press. I must confess that I have been surprised and distressed at the fact that the reference we made has not even been properly considered thus far and other matters have been given precedence. If the facts we stated in our reference were correct, as we claim they were, then certain consequences naturally followed from them, both in law and from the point of view of establishing peace and order.

On behalf of Pakistan, there was a repetition of the fantastic charges against India which had been made previously in the letter of the Prime Minister of Pakistan to which I have referred.

Pakistan refused to act at once, to deny assistance in men and material to our enemies in Jammu and Kashmir, to prevent further incursions through Pakistan into the State, and to ask the tribesmen and Pakistanis now in the State to withdraw unless a previous agreement had been reached and announced to the effect that the Indian Armed Forces would be withdrawn completely from the Jammu and Kashmir State, and the administration of the State would be replaced by another administration. There were some other matters in dispute also but the principal ones were the two I have mentioned above.

In effect, Pakistan not only admitted that they were aiding the raiders but made it clear that they would continue to do so till certain political objectives of theirs were achieved by them. This was a proposal to which the Government of India could not agree. For such an agreement would have been a betrayal not only of the people of Kashmir to whom they had pledged their word, but also a surrender to methods of violence and aggression which would have had disastrous consequences both for India and Pakistan. It was impossible for us to withdraw our forces without grave danger to the State and without handing over the people of the State who trusted in us to an unscrupulous and cruel invader who had already brought so much misery to the State and its people. Nor could we share the responsibility of protecting the people of Kashmir with any other outside force. It was equally impossibe for us to agree to the replacement of Sheikh Abdullah's administration by any other. The Government of Jammu and Kashmir is now no longer an autocratic government ; it is a government representing the largest popular party in the State and is under a leader who, during these many months of unparalleled stress, has sustained the morale of his people, maintained an effective administration over the greater part of the State, and, generally, has inspired effective resistance to the brutal attempts of the invaders to overrun and destroy Kashmir. There is no alternative administration possible in Kashmir, unless that administration rested on coercion. If Sheikh Abdullah as not there by the will of the people, he could not have survived, much less could he have accomplished what he has done during these difficult months. It is for him to choose any national of Kashmir to assist him in his Government and it would be improper for us to interfere with his discretion in this matter.

I regret greatly that the representative of Pakistan before the

Security Council should have made many statements and charges against India which have no foundation in fact. A great deal has happened in India and Pakistan during the last six months or more which has brought shame on all of us and I am prepared to admit at any stage and at any time the errors of our own people, for I do not think that it is good for the individual or the nation to lapse from truth. That is the lesson our Master taught us and we shall hold on to it to the best of our ability. Many horrible things have happened in India and Pakistan during these past months and while we hold strong views as to the initial responsibility for all the frightfulness that has occurred, all of us, in a greater or lesser degree, have a certain responsibility for it. But so far as the events in Kashmir are concerned, I am convinced in my mind that every action that the Government of India has taken has been straight and above board and inevitable in the circumstances. Our going there at the end of October was thrust upon us by the course of events. Not to have rushed to the rescue of the people of Kashmir, when they were in dire peril, would have been an eternal disgrace, a gross betrayal and a deep injury. We feel deeply about this matter and it is not merely a question of political advantage or disadvantage. It has been and is a moral issue with us, apart from other aspects of the case, and because of this, at every stage and at every step, I consulted Mahatma Gandhi and had his approval. In the confusion of a welter of charges and exaggerated statements, the basic facts are apt to be forgotten. I should like to know from anyone who studies our record in Kashmir since that fateful day when the raiders swooped down at Muzzafarabad and started their career of rapine and arson, I should like to know what major step we took that was morally or otherwise wrong.

The role of the Indian Army in this conflict, which I repeat was not our own seeking, has been conspicuous for its discipline, impartiality, endurance and gallantry. They have extended their protection to every section of the people of the State. To suggest that they should be withdrawn before complete order is restored is to suggest something which is neither practicable nor reasonable and which is further a reflection on the exemplary record of our forces in Kashmir. We are in Kashmir and our forces are there because, legally, we are on unassailable ground. But even apart from law, the moral case of the Indian Union in Kashmir is equally unassailable. If we had not gone there and if our armed forces had not been rushed at great peril into Kashmir, that lovely country would now have been sacked, destroyed and ruined and its men and women who have been noted for ages past for their intelligence and their cultural traditions would have been crushed under the heel of a barbarian invader. No Government in India could tolerate such a happening so long as it had the strength to resist it with all its might, and if such a fate befell Kashmir, what freedom or security would we have in the rest of India?

We have only two objectives in the Jammu and Kashmir State; to ensure the freedom and the progress of the people there, and to prevent anything happening that might endanger the security of India. We have nothing else to gain from Kashmir, though Kashmir may profit much by our assistance. If those two objectives are assured to us, we are content.

Our making a reference on this issue to the Security Council of the United Nations was an act of faith, because we believe in the progressive realization of world order and a world government. In spite of many shocks, we have adhered to the ideals represented by the United Nations and its Charter. But those very ideals teach us also certain duties and responsibilities to our own people and to those who put their trust in us. To betray these people would be to betray the basic ideals for which the United Nations stand or should stand. Even at the moment of accession we went out of our way to make a unilateral declaration that we would abide by the will of the people of Kashmir as declared in a plebiscite or referendum. We insisted further that the Government of Kashmir must immediately become a popular government. We have adhered to that position throughout and we are prepared to have a plebiscite, with every protection for fair voting, and to abide by the decision of the people of Kashmir.

Our delegation has gone back to Lake Success after full discussions with us. They have gone back with a clear appreciation of the position of the Government of India and of Indian opinion and fortified with the knowledge that they have our full support. I should like to express my gratitude to Shri Gopalaswami Ayyangar and his colleagues for the ability and firmness with which they presented our case before the Security Council. Sheikh Abdullah has not gone back because his work lies with his people at this grave juncture. He has to assume a heavier responsibility. I feel confident that he will discharge this new responsibility with that strength and vision which have endeared him to Muslims, Hindus and Sikhs in Kashmir. His place in the delegation has been taken by Shri Girja Shankar Bajpai, Secretary-General of the Ministry of External Affairs, who has been a tower of strength to me during these difficult months.

I shall not say much about the military situation in Jammu and Kashmir. We have had our moments of anxiety but at no time have I had any doubt about our capacity to meet the enemy and defeat him. Our officers and men are in high spirit, ready to meet any challenge. We have good reason to be proud of our officers and men, both of the Army and the Air Force. In particular, I should like to pay a tribute to Brigadier Usman, whose leadership and success have been in keeping with the highest traditions of India's army.

The representative of Pakistan before the Security Council has brought in many charges against us which have little bearing on the Kashmir issue. He has talked of what he called our aggression in Junagadh and genocide and of much else. I do not wish to take up the time of the House in dealing with these matters. We wish to conceal nothing and if the Security Council desires an investigation we shall welcome it.

Now, I should like to inform the House that today the Maharaja of Kashmir is issuing a proclamation and I shall briefly place the contents of that proclamation before the House, or I might as well read the whole proclamation:

PROCLAMATION OF HIS HIGHNESS MAHARAJA HARI SINGH INDAR MAHINDAR BAHADUR OF JAMMU AND KASHMIR, THIS FIFTH DAY OF MARCH, ONE THOUSAND NINE HUNDRED AND FORTY-EIGHT

In accordance with the traditions of my dynasty I have, from time to time, provided for increasing association of my people with the administration of the State with the object of realizing the goal of full responsible government at as early a date as possible. In pursuance of that object I have, by the Jammu and Kashmir Constitution Act of 1896 (XIV of 1896), established a constitutional government with a Council of Ministers, a legislature with a majority of elected members and an independent judiciary ;

I have noted with gratification and pride the progress so far made and the legitimate desire of my people for the immediate establishment of a fully democratic constitution based on adult franchise with a hereditary Ruler from my dynasty as the constitutional head of an executive responsible to the legislature ;

I have already appointed the popular leader of my people, Sheikh Mohammed Abdullah, as the Head of the Emergency Administration ;

It is now my desire to replace the Emergency Administration by a popular Interim Government and to provide for its powers, duties and functions, pending the framing of a fully democratic Constitution ;

I accordingly HEREBY ORDAIN as follows:

1. My Council of Ministers shall consist of the Prime Minister and such other Ministers as may be appointed on the advice of the Prime Minister. I have by Royal Warrant appointed Sheikh Mohammed Abdullah as the Prime Minister with effect from the 1st day of March, 1948.

2. The Prime Minister and other Ministers shall function as a Cabinet and act on the principle of joint responsibility. A Dewan appointed by me shall also be a member of the Cabinet.

3. I take this opportunity of giving once again a solemn assurance that all sections of my people will have opportunities of service, both civil and military, solely on the basis of their merits and irrespective of creed or community.

4. My Council of Ministers shall take appropriate steps, as soon as the restoration of normal conditions has been completed, to convene a National Assembly based upon adult suffrage, having due regard to the principle that the number of representatives from each voting area should, as far as practicable, be proportionate to the population of that area.

5. The constitution to be framed by the National Assembly shall provide adequate safeguards for the minorities and contain appropriate provisions guaranteeing freedom of conscience, freedom of speech and freedom of assembly.

6. The National Assembly shall, as soon as the work of framing the new constitution is completed, submit it through the Council of Ministers for my acceptance.

7. In conclusion I repeat the hope that the formation of a popular Interim Government and the inauguration, in the near future, of a fully democratic Constitution will ensure the contentment, happiness and the moral and material advancement of my beloved people.

I am placing this Proclamation on the table of the House.

I should like to congratulate His Highness the Maharaja of Jammu and Kashmir on the decision that he has taken. But the burden now lies on Sheikh Abdullah and his colleagues and the people of Kashmir. I have no doubt as to how they will discharge their burden, because they are not newcomers and we have seen them functioning in the face of all manner of difficulties during the last few months. So I look forward with a certain measure of assurance to the future of Kashmir in spite of all difficulties.

I am, Sir, also placing a copy of the White Paper on the table of the House.

INDIA HAS NOTHING TO CONCEAL

I HAVE seen in the Press reports of a statement said to have been made by the Prime Minister of Pakistan, Mr. Liaquat Ali Khan, on my letter to the President of the Security Council, dated 5th June, 1948. I do not propose to enter into the merits of Pakistan's charges against India of genocide and non-implementation of agreements with Pakistan or against the accession of Junagadh to India. Our views have been repeatedly stated before the Security Council and also in statements made by me and some of my colleagues. We regard the accusations of genocide and non-implementation of agreements as baseless. That we have protested against the Security Council's decision to include these charges within the scope of the functions of the Council's Commission is certainly not due, as alleged by the Prime Minister of Pakistan, to a desire to conceal anything. Because India has nothing to conceal is no reason why India should acquiesce in an investigation by an outside body in something which, in our view, is outside the competence of that body and which has no foundation in fact.

The Prime Minister of Pakistan has also attributed India's decision to refer the Kashmir dispute to the Security Council to a desire to gain time in which to force a military decision. A reference to India's complaint to the Security Council will show that, contrary to what Mr. Liaquat Ali Khan has suggested, India has all along insisted on the urgency of action by the Council on her complaint against Pakistan. If such action has not been taken, the fault is not India's. In referring the Kashmir dispute to the Security Council, India never intended to sacrifice her freedom of military action to rid the State of Jammu and Kashmir of all invaders and to restore peace. She has both the right and the obligation to do so in respect of a State which has acceded to her. It is strange that Mr. Liaquat Ali Khan should complain of India's action in using her resources to achieve this legitimate and humane object.

Once more allegations have ben made of atrocities by Indian troops against "defenceless old men, women and children in

A statement from New Delhi, June 10, 1948.

areas occupied by them." I most emphatically repudiate this unfounded charge. The purpose of these accusations, often repeated
but without any vestige of truth, can only be to divert the attention of the world from the barbarous atrocities which the raiders
whom Pakistan has so actively been aiding and abetting have
been committing on innocent civilians, regardless of creed, sex or
age, in the areas which they have occupied or into which they
have penetrated. Such crimes against humanity can never be
concealed. Baramula, Bhimbar, Mirpur and Rajauri, to cite only
a few instances, will always proclaim the infamy of their cruel
assailants.

Mr. Liaquat Ali Khan has complained of Indian troops violat-
ing Pakistan's frontiers and Indian airmen bombing villages well
within Pakistan's boundaries. Every complaint of the violation by
our troops of Pakistan's frontiers that could be investigated has
been enquired into. Most of these complaints have, on enquiry,
proved to be baseless. As is well known, the raiders, when forced
to retire from State territory, often flee into Pakistan. Our troops
chase them up to the frontier of the State ; this is their duty as
well as their right. As regards our airmen also, every complaint
of Pakistan has been carefully investigated. In the particular
case of Garhi Habibullah, which the Pakistan Prime Minister
has quoted, a double investigation was made to establish the facts
and the regret of the Government of India has already been
communicated to the Government of Pakistan for the incident.
The history of two world wars shows how impossible it is to avoid
damage to neutrals through *bona fide* mistakes of observation.
No aggression against Pakistan was intended.

Mr. Liaquat Ali Khan has referred to " the exemplary
patience " shown by the Government of Pakistan " in the face
of provocations." He has conveniently forgotten the continuous
and continuing provocation to which the Government of India
have been subjected ever since the invasion, last October, by
tribesmen of the valley of Kashmir, itself inspired by Pakistan,
in the shape of every kind of aid given by Pakistan to the
aggressor. More recently, Pakistan troops have been opposing
Indian troops on the Uri front in strength. It is idle, in the
circumstances, either to speak of the Pakistan Government's
" anxiety to maintain peaceful and friendly relations with India "
or to suggest that Indian action in Kashmir constitutes " grave
threat to the security of Pakistan " or a campaign of " murder

and destruction " against the Muslims of Jammu and Kashmir.

Far from seeking to murder and destroy Muslims in the State, Indian forces have been used to protect them against ruthless marauders whom Pakistan has let loose. An Interim Government, representative of the people, headed by a Muslim who has for years been the most outstanding leader of popular and progressive forces in Jammu and Kashmir, and composed of a majority of Muslims, has been formed in the State. On the question of accession, India has repeatedly affirmed that the freely declared will of the people of Jammu and Kashmir shall prevail. Though, short of a declaration of war, Pakistan has done everything to help the invaders of and the insurgents within the State, the Government of India have acted with unexampled restraint in the interests of peace. They still desire to live on the friendliest possible terms with the neighbour State of Pakistan. The fulfilment of that desire, however, is more likely to be defeated than achieved by the kind of statement which Mr. Liaquat Ali Khan is reported to have made yesterday.

THE STORY OF KASHMIR GOES ON

SIR, I crave your leave to place certain papers on the table of the House and to make a statement thereon. These papers relate to the United Nations Commission on Kashmir which has been in India and in Pakistan for about two months now. The Honourable Members of the House must have read in this morning's papers some correspondence which has passed between this Commission and the Government of India; a Resolution passed by the Commission some three weeks ago; the Government of India's reply thereto and some indication of Pakistan's reply. The full set of papers has not been published in the Press yet and, in fact, we received them only this morning by special courier from Karachi. No doubt these papers will be published in the newspapers. Meanwhile, I shall place on the table of the House some of these papers; and the rest I hope to place there in the course of the day, as soon as they are typed.

Now, the House knows that this Commission has been here for the last two months or more and the House will have seen from this published correspondence what their resolution was and our response to it. In fact they will have seen that we accepted certain conditions for a truce and cease-fire. Pakistan, however, has rejected them. Now, I do not wish at this stage to say very much more about this matter, partly because I should like to go through those papers more carefully than I have had time to do this morning when they came, partly because the Commission is considering what further steps they may or may not take and it will not perhaps be quite proper for me to say anything which might embarrass the Commission.

As the House perhaps knows, it was the desire of the Commission that we postpone the publication of papers and any statements in this House till today. We have been anxious right from the beginning of these consultations with the Commission to take this House and the country into our confidence, because we wished to take no steps in such a vital and important matter

A speech delivered at the Constituent Assembly (Legislative), New Delhi, September 7, 1948.

without the full knowledge and consent of this House, but inevitably in the circumstances, it became difficult for us, much as we wanted to do so, to make statements in this House when the Commission was engaged in these delicate negotiations, and so at their request we had to postpone such publication from time to time. Ultimately, they issued their statement yesterday at 4 p.m. in Karachi. Now, although I do not wish to say much on this subject, there are certain facts to which I should like to draw the attention of the House. The facts themselves are very well known, not only in this House, but all over the country. Nevertheless, sometimes known and established facts are denied and it does make a difference when those facts are admitted.

The present story and tragedy of Kashmir began over ten months ago. Late in October last year there was an invasion of Kashmir by people coming across or from Pakistan territory, and the Government of India were faced with a very difficult problem, calling for a decision as difficult as any Government has had to make, and we had to make that decision within a few hours. We made that decision and since then we have followed that decision. It became clear to us then, and that fact has become abundantly clear to all the world that wants to know it, that this invasion was not only encouraged and patronized but actively supported by the Pakistan Government. Later it became clear that apart from supporting others, there was active participation of the Pakistan army in it. Now, throughout these ten months the Pakistan Government have denied that fact, they denied it aggressively, loudly and persistently. We stated it before the Security Council of the United Nations.

In fact, we went to the Security Council with the very simple plea that the peace of Kashmir had been disturbed by these raiders coming across the Pakistan territory and we stated our case as moderately as possible, although we could have stated it much more forcefully. We said that it was inevitable that people coming from Pakistan could only come with the assistance and goodwill of Pakistan and, therefore, we requested the Security Council to ask Pakistan not to assist them and not to permit them to come in this way. It was, if I may say so, a very moderate request, couched in moderate language. Pakistan denied that fact and during the long discussions before the Security Council they not only went on denying it, but expressed a great deal of irritation and anger that anyone should have made such a charge against them. Well, I do not want to go into this long history of denial by them, but the point is that today, on their own admission, their denial was false. Now, that is an important matter.

It is important from the point of view not only of practical politics and the situation we have to face today, it is important also from the point of view of the standards of morality, good behaviour and decency that should subsist between nations. Now, I know very well that the standard of public morality and international morality is unfortunately not very high in this world. Nevertheless, certain appearances have to be kept up, certain decencies have to be maintained and some standards have to be observed. I do submit to this House and to the country that the story of these ten months and more and the way the Pakistan Government have reacted to all that has been said about them in the course of these ten months is so extraordinary as to be hardly creditable for a nation. Even till yesterday, as far as the world is concerned, even till 4 p.m. yesterday, there was no admission by Pakistan that they were participating in any way in those Kashmir operations. Of course, we knew. We have the most definite and positive evidence to that effect and ultimately you cannot hide large armies. Nevertheless, till 4 p.m. yesterday, when those papers were issued to the public, there was no public admission. In fact, there was a continual denial in the course of the last few weeks, while this large Pakistan Army was active in Kashmir, battling with the Indian forces in Indian Union territory.

Please remember that all the fighting that has taken place in the last ten months has been in Kashmir, has been in Indian territory ; there has been no fighting, there has been no incursion, there has been no Indian Army anywhere on Pakistan territory. That is a fundamental and basic fact, which apart from any other enquiry and any other facts would lead one to the conclusion that if any outsiders are fighting in Indian Union territory, those outsiders are the aggressors. Why are they there? During the last six weeks or so, again we pointed out in the most explicit language to the Pakistan Government and to the Prime Minister of Pakistan this presence of Pakistan troops in the Kashmir State.

Again, there was either a denial or an evasion of the issue. It was an extraordinary thing to me. I do not claim to be in any way different from others of my kind. My standards, I hope, are not lower than those of others. It has been a shock to me that any country, any responsible Minister of a Government should make statements which are patently and obviously false and try to mislead the world by that means. You will remember that before the Security Council at Lake Success, there were prolonged arguments on this issue. The Foreign Minister of the Pakistan Government, who was the Chief Delegate of their Government there, placed the case for Pakistan before the Security Council.

How does that case stand now, I would beg you and the country and the world to consider, because the whole cas was based on one fundamental fact, that is, the denial of Pakistan's complicity in Kashmir. They denied throughout that they had actively participated in it. If this fact is proved, as it is proved out of their very mouths today, to have been false, then what happens to that whole case so laboriously built up by the Pakistan Government before the Security Council? What happens to the charge that we brought against them which was never considered by the Security Council at all, much to our regret and amazement? So the fundamental thing for us to remember is this, that a fact which was denied for ten months and more has at last been publicly admitted by the Pakistan Government. They have, of course, admitted in their own way. I shall now read out some passages from their letter to the Commission. They say:

> "India was steadily building its armed forces in Jammu and Kashmir. This building up process did not cease on the 21st April, 1948, but was continued and intensified. The Indian Army mounted a big offensive in the beginning of April, thereby causing a material change in the situation. This offensive action has continued ever since. The publicly declared intention of the Government of India was to secure a military decision in Jammu and Kashmir, thus presenting the United Nations Organization with a *fait accompli*. This situation not only put in jeopardy the entire population of the areas under the Azad Kashmir Government, and led to a big influx of refugees into Pakistan, but also constituted a direct threat to Pakistan's security. It was this which compelled the Government of Pakistan to move their troops into certain defensive positions."

Observe here, too, they do not say clearly that the defensive positions happened to be in another country.

Quite apart from their decision in regard to cease-fire and other proposals, the country which participates in aggression against a neighbouring country, maybe in the name of defence or its own security, denies it for many months and then, in fact, when it finds that its guilt is proved, when it cannot hide it any more, then grudgingly admits it and gives some reason for it—how shall we consider the politics of that country from any international or national or moral point of view? Observe that, according to this statement, they took this action in April last, four months or four and a half months ago. If they felt that their security was imperilled, or that something was happening which endangered them and that they had to send their troops, what then should they have done? Obviously, they should have informed the Government of India, and informed the United Nations Organization that this was happening and that there had been, as they say, a material change in the situation, and therefore they were compelled to take this or that action.

I cannot conceive of any country in the wide world which would not have done so. Quite apart from motives, this is the obvious and inevitable thing to do. They sent this army, according to them, in April last or thereabout and there is no intimation to us into whose territory they were coming, and there was no intimation to the United Nations Organization which was seized of this question, and was, as a matter of fact, then thinking of sending out a Commission to India. You will remember that in the very early stages of the Security Council's activities, an appeal was made to India and Pakistan in regard to these military operations and in regard to avoiding any situation arising between India and Pakistan. That appeal was repeated. In the few lines I have read to you from Pakistan's reply, they accused India of mounting an offensive. We are trying to push out the invader from Indian Union territory. It has been our declared policy, which we have repeated before the United Nations Security Council, which in fact was inevitable for us and would have been for any other country with any grain of self-respect.

On the other hand, what did the Pakistan Government do? We have, right from the beginning taken whatever step we have taken, in the limelight ; there has been no hiding about it. The House has been greatly interested in this matter of Kashmir. The Indian public has taken the greatest interest in it and, rightly, the burden of it has fallen on our Government. It has been a heavy burden. I shall be frank and tell you why it has been heavy on me and more especially on my Government: not because military operations were involved, although that is always a burden, but rather it has been a burden since we wanted to be sure that at no time we acted against the principles we had so long proclaimed.

May I take the House into my confidence? In the early stages, towards the end of October and in November, and indeed subsequently, I was so exercised over Kashmir and if anything had happened or was likely to have happened to Kashmir, which, according to me, might have been disastrous for Kashmir, I would have been heart-broken. I was intensely interested, apart from the larger reasons which the Government have, for emotional and personal reasons ; I do not want to hide this: I am interested in Kashmir. Nevertheless, I tried to keep down the personal and emotional aspect and consider it from the larger viewpoint of India's good and Kashmir's good. I tried to consider the question from the point of view of not straying or drifting from the high principles which we had proclaimed in the past.

When this question first came up, I sought guidance, as I often did in other matters, from Mahatmaji and I went to him repeatedly and put to him my difficulties. The House knows that that apostle of non-violence was not a suitable guide in military matters—and he said so—but he undoubtedly always was a guide on the moral issue. And so I put my difficulties and my Government's difficulties before him ; and though it is not proper for me to drag in his name at this juncture in order to lessen my own responsibility or my Government's responsibility on this issue, which is complete, I, nevertheless, mention this matter merely to show how the moral aspect of this question has always troubled me. And more especially, when I saw in India all manner of things happening, which had happened in previous months and had brought India's name into disrepute, I was greatly troubled and worried and was anxious that we should keep straight or as straight as we possibly could.

Now, this has been my attitude and on several occasions I had proclaimed it publicly. And apart from rhetoric and vague insinuations, I should like to know from anybody—friend or enemy, from that day in the last week of October, when we took the fateful decision to send our troops by air to Kashmir till today, what it is we have done in Kashmir which from any point of view and from any standard is wrong.

I want an answer to that question. Individuals may have erred here and there ; but I say that the Government of India and the Indian army as a whole have done something which was inevitable, and each step that we have taken has been an inevitable step which, if we had not taken it, would have brought disgrace to us. That is how I have ventured to look at this question of Kashmir. And when I find that on the other side the whole case that has been built up on what I venture to say—using strong language—is falsehood and deceit, am I wrong? That is what I ask this House and the country and the world to consider.

Now, therefore, this is the first fact to remember ; that all this case built up by Pakistan before the Security Council crumbles by this admission of theirs and by the proven fact that large armies of theirs are active in Kashmir, and no doubt similar armies —if you like—and others connected with them have operated in Kashmir on Indian Union territory during these ten months or so. Every subsequent proceeding should be viewed from that aspect.

Now, we come to the present, and I must add one more thing. This has been an aggression ; and if it is called— as according to their own admission it must be called—an aggression, then certain consequences ought to follow. Now, my difficulty has been that in considering any question if you lose yourself in a forest of intricate detail sometimes you lose sight of the wood for the trees. There have been long discussions over the Kashmir issue and every aspect and phase and the past and present history have been considered. But what has been the major point? I repeat that, because I think the fundamental factor is the aggression of Pakistan on Indian Union territory ; secondly, the denial of the fact of that aggression ; thirdly, the present admission of the fact. These are the governing factors of that situation. And the argument has gone on for so long, because these governing factors were slurred over and were not emphasized. We emphasized them, of course, and the problem was discussed in intricate detail.

Now, if you start from a wrong premise in an argument, obviously your whole argument goes wrong and you land yourself in difficulties. If you try to solve a problem without analyzing or stating the nature of the problem, how are you to solve it? And that has been the fundamental difficulty in this Kashmir business :

the fundamental issue has been slurred over and by-passed and passed over. Therefore, we have been dealing with other matters which cannot yield a solution. Now, the basic factor is revealed by the very admission of the Pakistan Government.

Now, coming to this proposal of the United Nations Commission in India in regard to cease-fire and truce, etc., I shall not discuss it much, because I do not wish at this moment to say anything which might embarrass that Commission. But certain papers are before you. I need hardly say that the proposal they made was not welcomed by us with joy and enthusiasm ; there were many matters in it which went against the grain. But we tried to look at the matter as coolly and dispassionately as possible with a view to establishing peace in the harried State of Kashmir, to avoiding needless suffering and shedding of blood ; and we agreed to that cease-fire proposal after the Commission had been good enough to elucidate certain points which we. had placed before them. We did not place too many points before them but only certain simple obvious points relating to the security of Kashmir. We placed these before them and they were good enough to tell us that that was their meaning. Thereupon we accepted the cease-fire proposal, accepted many things in it which we did not like, because we felt that both in the interest of peace and of international order, it was a good thing for us to go a few steps forward even though some of the steps might be unwilling ones. We did so in order to bring about this peace and to show that we were prepared to go as far as possible to meet the wishes of an international organization like the United Nations. The original proposal of the United Nations was given to us on the 14th August. The 15th was our Independence Day. Immediately after, on the 16th, we met the members of the Commission and discussed the matter with them to find out exactly what they meant and told them exactly what we meant ; and within four days, i.e. on the 20th August we sent them our reply. We did not want to delay matters as they were anxious that they should not be delayed.

The Pakistan Government had also received these proposals at the same time, on the 14th August, at 3 or 4 p.m. They also had the same amount of time. But even after the return of the Commission to Pakistan—and some members of the Commission went in between to Karachi—they were not ready with their reply. And, in fact, it was by the pressure of events or the pressure of the Commission that ultimately they gave some kind of a reply yesterday. Meanwhile, they sent long letters seeking elucidation. I am sorry I have not yet read the reply wholly because I received it just a little before coming here. But I have read the significant parts of it, and in effect it is a rejection of those proposals.

Now, the Commission told us that these proposals stood as a whole and while they were prepared to discuss any matter gladly it was difficult—in fact, it was not possible for them to accept conditional acceptances, because if we made some conditions and Pakistan naturally made other conditions, what exactly was accepted and by whom? So they said that these proposals were to be accepted as they were, and if there were conditions attached to them, it was not an acceptance but a rejection. Now, therefore, what the Pakistan Government have done is tantamount to rejection. It is for the Commission to decide and to say what they are going to do. It is not for me to advise them. So we arrive at a curious state of affairs, that the country which was the aggressor nation according to its own showing, now even rejects and refuses a proposal for a cease-fire, or puts forward conditions which are tantamount to such a refusal.

Now, certain international consequences should follow from all this. What consequences follow? In a somewhat narrow sphere. all those officers and individuals who are participating in this aggressive war against India in Kashmir territory—there are, of course, Pakistani nationals and others there too—are participating not only in an aggressive war, but in a war after the refusal of a United Nations Commission proposal for a cease-fire. Their position is worthy of consideration.

That is all that I wish to say on the Kashmir issue. Naturally the story of Kashmir goes on. It has been a saga during these ten months or so, and there has been a great deal of suffering and blood and tears involved in it. There have been high moments also. But for us in India, and for the Government of India, it has been a period of trial and difficulty from many points of view ; still, at no time have we considered that we were wrong or that we had taken a step which we could not fully justify. It is in that faith that we are going to continue, and may I say that in all these consultations with the United Nations Commission and in other matters affecting Kashmir, we have kept in close touch with the Kashmir Government under Sheikh Abdullah and consulted him in all the steps that we have taken? That was natural and it is inevitable in the circumstances that we should march together in full consultation with each other. Proceeding on that basis, we shall go ahead, whether in the military sphere or in other spheres, and I am quite convinced that, if we adhere to the right course and do not stray from it, even from the opportunist point of view of some present advantage, we shall win through, and any country that bases its case on an essential falsehood cannot gain its ends.

ON HYDERABAD

THIS QUESTION OF HYDERABAD

I SHALL now address the House, Sir, on an entirely different topic, unrelated completely, but it is difficult really to separate things in the organic life of a country. So one thing affects another. But in effect what I am going to say now in regard to Hyderabad is something which stands apart from what I have said about Kashmir and does not bear any relation to it.

For over a year now, we have been making earnest attempts to come to a peaceful and satisfactory settlement with the Government of Hyderabad. In November last, our efforts led to a Stand-Still Agreement for a year. We hoped that this would soon be followed up by a final and satisfactory settlement. In our view, this settlement could only be based on the establishment of responsible government in the State and accession to India. That accession meant, of course, that the State would be an autonomous unit in the Indian Union enjoying the same powers and privileges as other autonomous units. What we offered Hyderabad was, in fact, an honourable partnership in the great brotherhood of the Indian Union.

Popular responsible government in Hyderabad or in any other State or province of India has long been our objective and we are glad to say that it is very near fulfilment all over India, except for the State of Hyderabad. It was inconceivable to us that, in the modern age, and in the heart of India which is pulsating with a new freedom, there should be a territory deprived of this freedom and indefinitely under autocratic rule.

As for accession, it was equally clear to us that a territory like Hyderabad, surrounded on all sides by the Indian Union and with no outlet to the rest of the world, must necessarily be part of that Indian Union. Historically and culturally, it had to be a part, but geographic and economic reasons were even more peremptory in this matter and they could not be ignored, whatever the wishes of particular individuals or groups of individuals. Any other relationship between Hyderabad and the rest of India would have involved continuing suspicion and, therefore, an ever-

A statement made at the Constituent Assembly (Legislative), New Delhi, September 7, 1948.

present fear of conflict. A State does not become independent by merely declaring itself to be so. Independence connotes certain relationships with independent States and recognition by them. India could never agree to Hyderabad having independent relations with any other Power for that would endanger her own security. Historically, Hyderabad has at no time been independent. Practically, in the circumstances of today, it cannot be independent.

Further, in conformity with the principles that we have repeatedly proclaimed, we were agreeable that the future of Hyderabad should be determined after a reference to its people, provided that such a reference was made under free conditions. It cannot possibly be made under the conditions of terror which prevail in Hyderabad today.

Our repeated attempts at a settlement, which came near to success on one or two occasions, ended unfortunately in failure. The reasons for this were obvious to us ; there were sinister forces at work in the Hyderabad State which were determined not to allow any agreement with the Indian Union. These forces, led by completely irresponsible persons, have progressively gained in strength and now completely control the Government. The resources of the State were and are being mobilized for war in every way. The State army has been increased and irregular armies have been allowed to grow up rapidly. Arms and ammunition were smuggled in from abroad ; this process, in which a number of foreign adventurers have been taking a prominent part, is continuing. No country, situated as India is, would have tolerated these warlike preparations by a State in its very heart. Nevertheless, the present Government of India patiently continued negotiations in the hope that they would lead to some settlement. The only other step they took was to prevent, in so far as they could, the flow of warlike material into Hyderabad.

The private armies that grew up in Hyderabad, notably the Razakars, have become more and more aggressive and brutal within the State and sometimes across its borders, in India. I do not propose to give a full account of this here as full particulars are available partly in the White Paper on Hyderabad which the Deputy Prime Minister presented to the House earlier during the session, and partly in other published documents. The growing terrorism and frightfulness inside the Hyderabad State against all those, Muslims and non-Muslims, who are opposed to the

Razakars and their allies, both official and non-official, has produced a very grave situation and has had its repercussions on the bordering areas of the Union and in India generally. At the present moment, our immediate and most anxious preoccupation is this mounting wave of violence and anarchy inside the Hyderabad State.

A full account of Razakar activities will take long. I shall mention only some recent incidents and a few figures. The inhabitants of a village inside the State, which, under the spirited leadership of its headman, had offered stout resistance to these gangsters, were, when resistance became impossible owing to the exhaustion of ammunition, put to the sword and the village itself burnt. The brave headman was decapitated and his head carried about on a pole. In another village, men, women and children were collected in one spot and shot dead by the Razakars and the Nizam's police.

A large party of villagers, fleeing in bullock carts to some haven of safety in India, was brutally attacked ; the men were beaten up and the women abducted.

A train was held up, the passengers looted and a number of coaches burnt. The House is aware of the attacks on our troops seeking to enter our enclaves within Hyderabad State territory and of Razakar incursions into our own villages along the border.

According to reports received yesterday, Razakars and a unit of the regular Hyderabad army with armoured cars went into action against Indian troops on Indian territory. They were repulsed ; one armoured car was destroyed and one officer and 85 other ranks taken prisoner. The incident further illustrates the mounting aggression against India.

Since this provocative campaign of violence started, according to information which has so far reached us, over 70 villages have been attacked inside the State, about 150 incursions have occurred into our territory, hundreds of persons have been killed, a large number injured and many women raped or abducted, 12 trains attacked, property worth over a crore of rupees looted. Hundreds of thousands have fled from the State in order to seek refuge in the neighbouring provinces of India.

The House will agree that no civilized Government can permit such atrocities to continue to be perpetrated with impunity within the geographical heart of India ; for this affects not only the security, honour, life and property of the law-abiding inhabitants of Hyderabad, but also the internal peace and order of India. We cannot have a campaign of murder, arson, rape and loot going on in Hyderabad without rousing communal passion in India and jeopardising the peace of the Dominion. Let the House consider what our predecessors in the Government of India would have done in these circumstances. For far less, they would have intervened drastically ; the lapse of the Paramountcy of the British Crown cannot alter the organic inter-relation of Hyderabad and the Power whose responsibility for the security of India as a whole is, and should continue to be unquestioned, or the mutual obligations of the one to the other. We have been patient and forbearing in the hope that good sense would prevail and a peaceful solution be found. This hope has proved to be vain and not only is peace inside the State or on its borders nowhere in sight, but peace elsewhere in India is seriously threatened.

We have been criticized for having been too patient and too forbearing. That criticism may have some justification. But we have tried to act on the principle that no effort should he spared at any time to avoid conflict and to secure a settlement by peaceful methods. Except in the last resort, any other course would be a sad contradiction of the ideals and principles to which we have repeatedly pledged ourselves from the beginning to the termination of our struggle for freedom from foreign rule. But we cannot blind ourselves to cruel facts or shirk the hard responsibilities that such facts might impose. At the present moment, let me repeat the issue that compels immediate priority is that of security of life and honour. in Hyderabad and the stoppage of the brutal terrorism that persists in that State. Other issues may well be taken up later, for indeed peace and order are essential for the consideration of other questions.

The Hyderabad Government have demonstrated both their unwillingness and their incapacity to put down the terrorism that has made the life of the law-abiding citizens of the State so extremely insecure that large numbers of them are fleeing to the neighbouring provinces and States. We feel that internal security in Hyderabad will not be assured at this stage unless our troops are stationed at Secunderabad as they used to be until India withdrew them early this year. In reply to a recent letter from the Nizam, His Excellency the Governor-General made this suggestion to His Exalted Highness who has replied that no such action is necessary as conditions in Hyderabad are entirely normal. This, of course, is contrary to all known facts and we have now asked the Nizam for the last time to disband the Razakars immediately and, as suggested by His Excellency the Governor-General, to facilitate the return of our troops to Secunderabad, in such strength as may be necessary to restore law and order in the Hyderabad State. If they are so stationed, there will be a sense of security in the people and the terrorist activities of private armies will cease.

May I add a few more words? First of all, I should like to state to this House and place before this country that we have tried to look upon the question of Hyderabad as far as possible entirely away from the communal point of view and I should like the country to look upon it in this non-communal way. I know, as I have just stated, that communal passions have been roused. But it should be the business of all of us, to whatever religion or community we may belong, to lift this question away from the communal plane and to consider it from other, and, I think more valid and more basic points of view.

We wish to send our troops to Secunderabad to ensure security in Hyderabad, the security of all the people there, whether they are Hindus or Muslims, or they belong to any other religion or group. If subsequently freedom comes to Hyderabad, it must come to all equally and not to a particular group. Therefore, I would like to lay stress on this and I would like those organs of public opinion which can influence the public so much at any time, and more especially during times of stress and strain, always to lay stress on this non-communal aspect. Also, whatever steps we may have to take in the nature of police action or other, our instructions are going to be definite and clear that any kind of communal trouble from any side will be most sternly dealt with.

There has been, as I mentioned to this House, a large migration from Hyderabad of terror-stricken people. I do not know how many have come out, but in the Central Provinces even now there are large camps of tens of thousands—probably several hundred thousand people may have come out in the course of the last two months. Now, if I may give advice—although the giving of this advice means the assumption of a certain responsibility—I would give this advice and take the risk that people should not migrate from Hyderabad or from any part, wherever they may be.

(AN HONOURABLE MEMBER: AND GET BUTCHERED!)

Somebody said 'get butchered.' I can only speak in my own terms. If I were there I would not migrate, whatever happened— butchery or no butchery. I think that when we have to face a serious situation, nothing can be worse than running away from it: and especially in the present instance I see no benefit in regard to that matter. Because the person who runs away exposes himself to that very danger more than a person who sits or stands quietly, normally speaking. Of course I am not considering exceptional cases and some things may happen here and there. But my general point is this, that we may be on the eve of grave happenings in this country, and because of that our Government has paid the greatest and the deepest attention to these matters. We have discussed them, not only amongst ourselves, but with our advisers: we have considered various possible consequences, for every action has to be judged from their possible consequences. We cannot just take an action in the air. That is what we have done. And having done that, we have come to certain conclusions which I am placing before you. At any time I would have advised the country to be calm and poised and I refuse to be panicky and refuse to run away from a difficult situation. At this time particularly, I do call upon everybody with all the earnestness that lies in me that we should maintain peace and calm and face any situation that may arise not only in a calm and collected and disciplined way, but also always remembering the fundamental principles and lessons that our Master placed before us.

WE ARE MEN OF PEACE

COMRADES and friends, I am going to speak to you about Hyderabad. You know already the swift developments that have taken place there in the course of the last five days. You know that the action that our Government undertook in Hyderabad has achieved its object. Our troops are in Secunderabad cantonment. The Razakars, who did so much mischief during the past few months, have been banned and are being disbanded. New problems now face us and we shall have to deal with them wisely, keeping in view the well-being of all the people of India, including Hyderabad.

It is natural that we should rejoice at this swift termination of this action that we undertook after prolonged and painful thought and much deliberation. As I have repeatedly said, we are men of peace, hating war and the last thing we desire is to come into armed conflict with anyone. Nevertheless, circumstances, which you know well, compelled us to take this action in Hyderabad. Fortunately, it was brief and we return with relief to the paths of peace again.

We rejoice at the splendid way in which the officers and men of our armed forces have carried out this work, like true soldiers, with skill, expedition and forbearance, strictly observing all codes of honour. What has pleased me most during these past six days is the splendid response of our people, both Muslim and non-Muslim, to the call of restraint and discipline and the test of unity. It is a remarkable thing, and one which is full of good augury for the future, that not a single communal incident occurred in the whole length and breadth of this great country. I am deeply grateful for this. I should also like to congratulate the people of Hyderabad, who, during these days of trial, kept calm and helped the cause of peace. Many persons warned us of the risks and dangers that we faced and of the communal trouble that might besmirch our land. But our people have falsified these prophets and demonstrated that when crisis faced them, they could face it with courage, dignity and calm.

Let this be an example and a pledge for the future. Hence-

A talk on Hyderabad broadcast from New Delhi, September 18, 1948.

forth let there be no talk or hint of communal antagonism. We must bury the false doctrine and the ignoble urges that have given rise to this antagonism and build firmly the united India for which we laboured for long in the past, and in which every Indian, to whatever religion he may belong, has equal rights and opportunities.

We rejoice today and rightly, but let us remember that a great nation and a great people do not lose their balance whether in adversity or in success. We have faced many adversities and overcome them. We have to face success also without getting intoxicated by it.

We must take this opportunity to consolidate our real gains—the gains in unity, goodwill, and mutual forbearance. I should like at this moment to appeal to the people of Pakistan, our countrymen till yesterday and still as near to us, to cast aside their fear and suspicion and to join us in the works of peace.

To the people of Hyderabad, both Muslim and non-Muslim, I should like to send my greetings. It has been a sorrow to us that there should have been armed conflict among the people of this country. Happily that is over. An evil course was followed by the ruling clique in Hyderabad and that led to this unfortunate conflict. I am glad that His Exalted Highness the Nizam realized that he had acted wrongly and been misled and that he wisely retraced his steps. He is to be congratulated on acting rightly even at this late hour. Much misery and complication of issues might have been avoided if this right action had been taken a little earlier.

But I do not wish to speak of the past now and I do not wish anyone to harbour ill-will any more. We have stated clearly that the future of Hyderabad will be determined in accordance with the wishes of her people. We shall stand by that declaration. That future, I am convinced, lies in the closest association with India. History, geography and cultural traditions bear witness to this fact.

For the present our Military Commander will be in charge of Hyderabad, for much work has to be done before normality is restored. He has been charged by us to interfere as little as possible with the normal life of the people of the State, in town and village alike, which must go on as before.

As soon as this immediate task is over, other arrangements will be made, and later steps will be taken for the election of a

Constituent Assembly, which will determine the constitutional structure of Hyderabad.

I would repeat that we do not consider, as we have not considered in the past, Hyderabad as something different or alien from us. Her people, whether Hindu or Muslim, are our kith and kin and sharers with us in the great heritage of India. JAI HIND.

ON EDUCATION

THE UNIVERSITIES HAVE MUCH
TO TEACH

I HAVE come back after a long while to my home town of Allahabad to which I have almost become a stranger. During these past fifteen months I have lived in New Delhi, next door to Old Delhi City. What do these two cities convey to us, what pictures and thoughts do they bring to our minds? When I think of them, the long vista of India's history stretches out before me, not so much the succession of kings and emperors, but rather that of the inner life of a nation, its cultural activities in many fields, its spiritual adventures and its voyages in the realms of thought and action. The life of a nation, and more especially of a nation like India, is lived principally in the villages. Nevertheless, it is the cities that represent the highest cultural achievements of the age, as they also do sometimes the more unpleasant aspects of human life. So these cities remind me of the cultural growth of India, of that inner strength and balance which come from long ages of civilization and culture. We have been very proud of this inheritance of ours in India, and rightly so. And yet, where do we stand today?

It is well that we put this question to ourselves in this ancient city of Allahabad and in this seat of learning. The universities have much to teach in the modern world and their scope of activity ever enlarges. I am myself a devotee of science and believe that the world will ultimately be saved, if it is to be saved, by the method and approach of science. But whatever path of learning we may pursue, and however profitable it might seem to us, there is a certain basis and foundation without which the house of learning is built on shifting sands. It is for a university to realize and to lay stress on this essential basis and foundation, those standards of thought and action, which make an individual and a nation. Above all this is necessary today, during this extremely rapid phase of transition, when old values have almost left us and we have adopted no new ones. Freedom came to us, our long-sought freedom, and it came with a minimum of violence. But imme-

A speech delivered at the Special Convocation of the Allahabad University, December 13, 1947.

diately after, we had to wade through oceans of blood and tears. Worse than the blood and tears was the shame and disgrace that accompanied them. Where were our values and standards then, where was our old culture, our humanism and spirituality and all that India has stood for in the past? Suddenly darkness descended upon this land and madness seized the people. Fear and hatred blinded our minds and all the restraints which civilization imposes were swept away. Horror piled on horror and a sudden emptiness seized us at the brute savagery of human beings. The lights seemed all to go out ; not all, for a few still flickered in the raging tempest. We sorrowed for the dead and the dying and for those whose suffering was greater than death. We sorrowed even more for India, our common mother, for whose freedom we had laboured these long years.

The lights seemed to go out. But one bright flame continued to burn and shed its light on the surrounding gloom. And looking at that pure flame, strength and hope returned to us and we felt that whatever momentary disaster might overwhelm our people, there was the spirit of India, strong and unsullied, rising above the turmoil of the present and not caring for the petty exigencies of the day. How many of you realize what it has meant to India to have the presence of Mahatma Gandhi during these months? We all know of his magnificent services to India and to freedom during the past half century and more. But no service could have been greater than the one he has performed during the past four months when in a dissolving world he has been like a rock of purpose and a lighthouse of truth, and his firm low voice has risen above the clamours of the multitude, pointing to the path of rightful endeavour.

And because of this bright flame we could not lose faith in India and her people. And yet the surrounding gloom was in itself a menace. Why should we relapse into this gloom when the sun of freedom had arisen? It is necessary for all of us, and more especially young men and young women in the universities, to pause and think for a while on these basic matters, for the future of India is taking shape in the present, and the future is going to be what millions of young men and women want it to be. There is today a narrowness and intolerance and insensitiveness and lack of awareness which rather frighten me. We have recently passed through a great world war. That war has not brought peace and freedom, but it should teach us many lessons. It brought the downfall of what had been called Fascism and Nazism. Both of these creeds were narrow and overbearing and based on hatred and violence. I watched their growth in their respective countries as well as elsewhere. They brought a certain prestige to their people for a while, but they also killed the spirit and destroyed all values and standards of thought and behaviour. They ended by ruining the nations they sought to exalt.

I see something very similar to that flourishing in India today. It talks in the name of nationalism, sometimes of religion and culture, and yet it is the very opposite of nationalism, of true morality and of real culture. If there was any doubt of this, the past few months have shown us the real picture. For some years we have had to contend against the policy of hatred and violence and narrow communalism on the part of a section of the community. Now, that section has succeeded in forming a State carved out of certain parts of India. Muslim communalism, which had been such a danger and obstruction to Indian freedom, now calls itself a State. It has ceased to be a living force in India proper today, because its strength is concentrated in other parts. But it has resulted in degrading other sections of the community who seek to copy it and sometimes even to improve upon it. We have now to face this reaction in India and the cry is raised for a communal State, even though the words used may be different. And not only a communal State is demanded, but in all fields of political and cultural activity the same narrowing and strangling demand is put forward.

If we look back at India's long history we find that our forefathers made wonderful progress whenever they looked out on the world with clear and fearless eyes and kept the windows of their minds open to give and to receive. And, in later periods, when they grew narrow in outlook and shrank from outside influences, India suffered a setback, politically and culturally. What a magnificent inheritance we have, though we have abused it often enough. India has been and is a vital nation, in spite of all the misery and suffering she has experienced. That vitality in the realm of constructive and creative effort spread to many parts of the Asian world and elsewhere and brought splendid conquests in its train. Those conquests were not so much of the sword, but of the mind and heart which bring healing and which endure when the men of the sword and their work are forgotten. But that very vitality, if not rightly and creatively directed, may turn inward and destroy and degrade.

Even during the brief span of our lives we have seen these two forces at play in India and the world at large—the forces of constructive and creative effort and the forces of destruction. Which will triumph in the end? And on which side do we stand? That is a vital question for each one of us and, more especially, for those from whom the leaders of the nation will be drawn, and on whom the burden of tomorrow will fall. We dare not sit on the fence and refuse to face the issue. We dare not allow our minds to be befuddled by passion and hatred when clear thought and effective action are necessary.

What kind of India are we working for, and what kind of world? Are hatred and violence and fear and communalism and narrow provincialism to mould our future? Surely not, if there has been any truth in us and in our professions. Here in this city of Allahabad, dear to me not only because of my close association with it, but also because of its part in India's history, my boyhood and youth were spent in dreaming dreams and seeing visions of India's future. Was there any real substance in those dreams or were they merely the fancies of a fevered brain? Some small part of those dreams has come true, but not in the manner I had imagined, and so much still remains. Instead of a feeling of triumph at achievement, there is an emptiness and distress at the sorrow that surrounds us, and we have to wipe the tears from a million eyes.

A university stands for humanism, for tolerance, for reason, for progress, for the adventure of ideas and for the search for truth. It stands for the onward march of the human race towards even higher objectives. If the universities discharge their duty adequately, then it is well with the nation and the people. But if the temple of learning itself becomes a home of narrow bigotry and petty objectives, how then will the nation prosper or a people grow in stature?

A vast responsibility, therefore, rests on our universities and educational institutions and those who guide their destinies. They have to keep their lights burning and must not stray from the right path even when passion convulses the multitude and blinds many amongst those whose duty it is to set an example to others. We are not going to reach our goal through crookedness or flirting with evil in the hope that it may lead to good.

The right end can never be fully achieved through wrong means.

Let us be clear about our national objective. We aim at a strong free and democratic India where every citizen has an equal place and full opportunity of growth and service, where present-day inequalities in wealth and status have ceased to be, where our vital impulses are directed to creative and co-operative endeavour. In such an India communalism, separatism, isolation, untouchability, bigotry, and exploitation of man by man have no place, and while religion is free, it is not allowed to interfere with the political and economic aspects of a nation's life. If that is so, then all this business of Hindu and Muslim and Christian and Sikh must cease in so far as our political life is concerned and we must build a united but composite nation where both individual and national freedom are secure.

We have passed through grievous trials. We have survived them but at a terrible cost, and the legacy they have left in tortured minds and stunted souls will pursue us for a long time. Our trials are not over. Let us prepare ourselves for them in the spirit of free and disciplined men and women, stout of heart and purpose, who will not stray from the right path or forget our ideals and objectives. We have to start this work of healing and we have to build and create. The wounded body and spirit of India call upon all of us to dedicate ourselves to this great task. May we be worthy of the task and of India!

EDUCATION IS MEANT TO FREE
THE SPIRIT OF MAN

I HAVE come back to Aligarh and to this University after a long interval. We have been separated not only by a distance of time, but also by a distance of spirit and outlook. I do not quite know where you, or for the matter of that most of us, stand today, for we have gone through convulsions and heart-breaks which have no doubt created in many of us doubts and disillusionment. While the present is full of uncertainty, the future is even more shrouded and difficult to pierce. Nevertheless, we have to face this present and try to mould the future. We have to see, each one of us, where we stand and what we stand for. Without a stout anchor of faith in the future we will drift in the present and life itself would have no objective worth striving for.

I have accepted the invitation of your Vice-Chancellor with pleasure, for I wanted to meet all of you and to probe somewhat into your minds and to let you have a glimpse of my own mind. We have to understand one another, and if we cannot agree about everything, we must at least agree to differ, and know where we agree and where we differ.

For every sensitive human being in India the last six months have brought pain and sorrow, and what is worst of all, a humiliation of the spirit. It has been bad enough for those who are old in years and experienced, but I often wonder how the young feel who, at the threshold of their lives, have seen and experienced catastrophe and disaster. They will, no doubt, survive it, for youth is resilient ; but it may well be that they will carry the mark of it for the rest of their days. Perhaps if we are wise and strong enough to think and act rightly even now, we may succeed in erasing that mark.

For my part I wish to say that, in spite of everything, I have a firm faith in India's future. Indeed, if I did not have it, it would not have been possible for me to work effectively. Although many of my old dreams have been shattered by recent events, yet the basic objective still holds and I see no reason to change

---

A speech delivered at the Annual Convocation of the Muslim University at Aligarh (U.P.), January 24, 1948.

it. That objective is to build up a free India of high ideals and noble endeavour where there is equality of opportunity for all and where many variegated streams of thought and culture meet together to form a mighty river of progress and advancement for her people.

I am proud of India, not only because of her ancient magnificent heritage, but also because of her remarkable capacity to add to it by keeping the doors and windows of her mind and spirit open to fresh and invigorating winds from distant lands. India's strength has been twofold ; her own innate culture which flowered through the ages, and her capacity to draw from other sources and thus add to her own. She was far too strong to be submerged by outside streams, and she was too wise to isolate herself from them, and so there is a continuing synthesis in India's real history, and the many political changes which have taken place have had little effect on the growth of this variegated and yet essentially unified culture.

I have said that I am proud of our inheritance and our ancestors who gave an intellectual and cultural pre-eminence to India. How do you feel about this past? Do you feel that you are also sharers in it and inheritors of it and, therefore, proud of something that belongs to you as much as to me? Or do you feel alien to it and pass it by without understanding it or feeling that strange thrill which comes from the realization that we are the trustees and inheritors of this vast treasure? I ask you these questions, because in recent years many forces have been at play diverting people's minds into wrong channels and trying to pervert the course of history. You are Muslims and I am a Hindu. We may adhere to different religious faiths or even to none ; but that does not take away from that cultural inheritance that is yours as well as mine. The past holds us together ; why should the present or the future divide us in spirit?

Political changes produce certain results, but the essential changes are in the spirit and outlook of a nation. What has troubled me very greatly during these past months and years is not the political changes, but rather the creeping sense of a change of spirit which has created enormous barriers between us. The attempt to change the spirit of India was a reversal of the historic process through which we had been passing for long ages past and it is because we tried to reverse the current of history that disaster overwhelmed us. We cannot easily play about with geography or with the powerful trends which make history. And it is infinitely worse if we make hatred and violence the springs of action.

Pakistan has come into being, rather unnaturally I think. Nevertheless, it represents the urges of a large number of persons. I believe that this development has been a throw-back, but we accepted it in good faith. I want you to understand clearly what our present view is. We have been charged with desiring to strangle and crush Pakistan and to force it into a reunion with India. That charge, as many others, is based on fear and a complete misunderstanding of our attitude. I believe that, for a variety of reasons, it is inevitable that India and Pakistan should draw closer to one another, or else they will come into conflict. There is no middle way, for we have known each other too long to be indifferent neighbours. I believe indeed that in the present context of the world India must develop a closer union with many other neighbouring countries. But all this does not mean any desire to strangle or compel Pakistan. Compulsion there can never be, and an attempt to disrupt Pakistan would recoil to India's disadvantage. If we had wanted to break Pakistan, why did we agree to the partition? It was easier to prevent it then than to try to do so now after all that has happened. There is no going back in history. As a matter of fact it is to India's advantage that Pakistan should be a secure and prosperous State with which we can develop close and friendly relations. If today by any chance I were offered the reunion of India and Pakistan, I would decline it for obvious reasons. I do not want to carry the burden of Pakistan's great problems. I have enough of my own. Any closer association must come out of a normal process and in a friendly way which does not end Pakistan as a State, but makes it an equal part of a larger union in which several countries might be associated.

I have spoken of Pakistan, because that subject must be in your minds and you would like to know what our attitude towards it is. Your minds are probably in a fluid state at present, not knowing which way to look and what to do. All of us have to be clear about our basic allegiance to certain ideas. Do we believe in a national State which includes people of all religions and shades of opinion and is essentially secular as a State, or do we believe in the religious, theocratic conception of a State which considers people of other faiths as something beyond the pale? That is an odd question to ask, for the idea of a religious or theocratic State was given up by the world some centuries ago and has no place in the mind of the modern man. And yet the question has to be put in India today, for many of us have tried to jump back to a past age. I have no doubt that whatever our individual answers may be, it is not possible for us to go back to a conception that the world has outlived and that is completely out of tune with modern conceptions. As far as India is concerned, I can speak with some certainty. We shall proceed on secular and national lines in keeping with the powerful trends towards internationalism. Whatever confusion the present may contain, in the future, India will be a land, as in the past, of many faiths equally honoured and respected, but of one national outlook, not, I hope, a narrow nationalism living in its own shell, but rather the tolerant creative nationalism which, believing in itself and the genius of its people, takes full part in the establishment of an international order. The only ultimate aim we can have is that of One World. That seems a far cry today with warring groups and preparations for and shouting of World War Number Three. Yet despite all this shouting, that is the only aim that we can keep in view, for the alternative to world co-operation is world disaster.

We must cultivate this broad outlook and not be led away by the narrowness of others into becoming narrow in spirit and outlook ourselves. We have had enough of what has been called communalism in this country and we have tasted of its bitter and poisonous fruit. It is time that we put an end to it. For my part I do not like the intrusion of this communal spirit anywhere, and least of all in educational institutions. Education is meant to free the spirit of man and not to imprison it in set frames. I do not like this university being called the Muslim University just as I do not like the Benares University to be called the Hindu University. This does not mean that a university should not specialize in particular cultural subjects and studies. I think it is right that this University should lay special stress on certain aspects of Islamic thought and culture.

I want you to think about those problems and come to your own conclusions. These conclusions cannot be forced upon you except to some extent, of course, by the compulsion of events which none of us can ignore. Do not think that you are outsiders here, for you are as much flesh and blood of India as anyone else, and you have every right to share in what India has to offer. But those who seek rights must share in the obligations also. Indeed, if the duties and obligations are accepted, then rights flow of themselves. I invite you as free citizens of free India to play your role in the building up of this great country and to be sharers, in common with others, in the triumphs and setbacks alike that may come our way. The present with all its unhappiness and misery will pass. It is the future that counts, more especially to the young, and it is that future that beckons to you. How will you answer that call?

A TIME FOR WORK

YOUR Excellency, Mr. Premier, Vice-Chancellor, members of the University and friends,

You have had a great deal of eloquence today and you have seen many eminent persons, and I am not quite sure if it is not an imposition on you to have to listen to another address. Yesterday, I am told, you listened to a very eloquent address from Dr. Radhakrishnan. I had the misfortune not to be present. And the giving of too many addresses and, perhaps, of too much good advice may not be good for the giver or to the listener. Nevertheless, I have to perform a function and a duty and I suppose it is your function and duty at present to listen to me.

I have to thank you, the University, for the honour you have conferred upon me. I should say frankly that I have had so much honour and love from my people that a little addition to it should not make much difference. That is true. You have showered so much affection on me that I doubt if anyone else could have had such a privilege at any time. And, while it has naturally warmed my heart and affected me greatly, it has also made me feel very embarrassed and sometimes a little frightened. So, although the grant of a Doctorate by the Lucknow University, may, if you will permit me to say so, make no great difference to me, the invitation coming from Lucknow, from this University and from my dear friend and colleague, the Vice-Chancellor, did make a difference, and I appreciated it and my heart warmed inside me. And I wanted to come here and I did come here. Because, however much I might be tied up in other work and in other places, I can never forget that the days, perhaps, of my most intense activity were passed round about Lucknow or Allahabad, or other parts of this province. A great part of my days of work, of activity, as well as of enforced inactivity, were passed in Lucknow and Allahabad. So, sitting in New Delhi, I have often a feeling of nostalgia for those old places, which are associated with those old days. And I come here from time to time, much too rarely, and I see old faces and I think again of those old

An address given at Lucknow at the Special (Silver Jubilee) Convocation of Lucknow University, January 28, 1949.

days. And I find those old faces somewhat changed, and then it strikes me that I too have changed greatly. So I am happy to be here among friends and to thank you not merely for this additional honour you have done me, but all the great honour you have done me for years past, in the love that you have given me.

I have been wondering what I should speak to you about. I can hardly give you advice, but whether you call it advice or not, I do wish to tell you of something that I have in my mind, something that troubles me often enough and that, I think, should trouble each one of you, because we live through difficult and stirring times. And it is up to each one of us, whatever his station in life, whatever his job, to think of himself in terms of these big problems that we have to face and think of his own duty towards them, what he has to do and what he has not to do. When I see these great problems of India; when I see the tremendous affection and the confidence that the people of India have placed in me, I am often filled with a sense of my own inadequacy. How can anyone be adequate enough to deal with such problems? Problems have to be dealt with ; if not by one person then by some other, but how can anyone be adequate enough to receive this great confidence and affection? I feel that. Yet in regard to one matter my faith has never wavered, and that is in the adequacy of India. And because I have that faith in me (it does not very much matter after all, I think, whether I am individually or personally adequate or not, so long as I put all the strength and energy that is in me in my task and in my duty, that is as much as I can do, that is as much as you can do)—and so because of that faith and that assurance I carry on, though sometimes there is a certain weariness of spirit and sometimes a little sorrow that the wild dreams that many of us had somehow do not take shape as we wanted them to take shape. Somehow when work is to be done, solid work, great work calling upon us to do it, our attention is distracted by petty conflicts, by all kinds of wrong things being done. When the young generation on whose shoulders the great task of carrying India a stage further on her long journey is going to fall,—when the young generation behaves in a manner which is incomprehensible to me, it amazes me and they talk of taking part in politics, and this or that. I am amazed that when the whole of India is shouting for work, shouting for labour, shouting for building up, they think in other directions, they work in other directions and they talk in a language that I do not understand. Then I think, and I wonder, "Am I cut off from this younger generation? Am I right or are they right"? Who is wrong and who is right, I do not know. Perhaps I may be wrong. Anyhow, I can only work according to my own lights.

This is a time when work is required, when labour is required, peace is required, co-operative effort is required, when all the concentrated energies that the nation possesses are required to be put to the great task of the nation. What are we doing? No doubt many of us are working to that end, many of us are trying our utmost to that end. No doubt the nation is advancing and progressing. Nevertheless, when I look around me, I see not an atmosphere of work, not a psychology of things being done, but only talk, only criticism and running down and finding fault, petty factions and the like. I see them in all grades, above and below, the younger generation and the older generation, everywhere. And then, as I said, a slight feeling of uneasiness comes over me at the thought of my age, because, after all, I may have only a few more years to live and the only ambition that I have is that to the end of my days I should work my hardest and then when I have done my job I should be thrown on the scrap heap. When I have done my job, there is no need to bother about me further. It is the job and the work that count, not thinking and shouting about people who have done their job and gone. So I shall go on doing my job as best I can.

But what then? When those of my colleagues and I, who have, for good or ill, played an important part on the Indian stage, all over India or in this province, during the past twenty or thirty years or more, when we go, others will take our places, of course, because a nation goes on and on and on. A nation does not die. Men and women come and go, but the nation goes on. It has something of the eternal about it. And India certainly is that type of a nation which has something of eternity behind it, in its ideas and in its growth, and even in its decay. So we shall pass, and the burden that we have carried, adequately or not, will fall on other shoulders. What are those shoulders? Have I come here to praise you or to listen to your praises? We have done that frequently enough—you have praised me, and maybe I have praised you. It is not good enough. Let us not waste our time in mutual praises and embracings when work has to be done.

There is a time for work and there is a time for play, just as there is a time for laughter and there is a time for tears. And today is the time for work in this nation. For, this generation of ours, if I may say so, is condemned to hard labour. You cannot get out of it, however you may want to. We are all condemned to hard labour. But, then, it makes all the difference what kind of labour we do, in what spirit we approach it. If it is labour, good work, then that is an uplifting thing, an exhilarating thing, a strengthening thing. It does not matter how hard you work. People come and tell me, do not work so hard, you do not sleep enough. As if that counts! What counts is something entirely different. No man ever died of hard work, if he is working in a good cause, if his spirit is in it, but people do die of ennui and other things. So you and I have got to work. What kind of work? What is your conception of work?

Today people seem to imagine that work lies in marching up and down the streets and calling it a demonstration ; or stopping work, whether it is in a factory or a school, or somewhere else, calling it a *hartal ;* or some other kind of demonstrative activity. Now, maybe that has its uses sometimes, no doubt it has. But I do tell you, and I tell you in all sincerity, that I can imagine no greater crime to India than the kind of thing that is going on today. I am not joking with you. I have a few more years of activity and I want to see India great and strong, a flourishing State, not only doing its duty to its own people, but to the wide world. And when I see our young men behaving as they do, when I see young men and hysterical young women misbehaving, I am angry, I tell you. Is all the work we have done just going to be lost because some hysterical people talk nonsense in this way, and behave in a nonsensical manner? What is happening here—is that your idea of liberty and democracy and freedom? I am amazed at this business. I want to be frank with you about it. This is not the way we are going to build up our nation. Have you any idea of what the difficulties before our country are? We who are in the Government may make mistakes, an infinite number of mistakes. I do not mind walking out of the Government, as I am quite sure the U.P. Government do not mind walking out too. Have you any idea of the burden of those whom you have put in the seats of authority? Criticize them by all means. But the hardest sentence you can give to any individual today in India is to put him in a seat of authority.

But what are the problems? You have to face them, think of them, not only in relation to India but the wide world, the world in a peculiar frame of mind. It is an astonishing spectacle that you see in this world today. You see fine upsurges of the spirit, fine constructive efforts, great men all over the world, probably more men of goodwill all over the world than ever in the history of the world previously. At the same time you see evil forces at work, you see disruptive forces, warlike forces, all kinds of things working. There is conflict between all these things and I do not know and you do not know what the result of this conflict will be. But I do know this, that in this business as long as we have life and strength, we will have evil forces in India and elsewhere. We stand for the good forces, for the forces that free the human spirit and not suppress it.

What is the problem? You seek to answer that problem, you in your debating societies or in your demonstrations. But have you even formulated the problem, have you even framed the question? Too many people seek an answer without knowing what the question is. It is an odd thing. But the fact remains that we are talking about answers and answer without knowing what the question is, without trying to understand the question or the problem that is before the world.

Well, the world is a big place. Nevertheless, you cannot isolate the problem of India from the world problem. You cannot isolate the problem of the U.P. or Lucknow from the larger problem. Therefore, you must have at least some vague conception of this wide problem.

And if I may say so at this great moment of transition in human history, if you want to understand any problem you will have to understand it in the sweep of history, of the past, to see how it has developed, what the roots of it are. It is not good enough for you and me to shout out a few slogans now and call that the understanding of a problem, or the solution of a problem. Slogans may be good, because they do sometimes concentrate an idea in a few words ; slogans may be used. But to think that a slogan is a problem or an answer to a problem is just to delude oneself.

I should like to tell you what I think about the many aspects of the world problems, of India's problems, and problems we have to face, because I have to wrestle with these problems all the while knowing my own inadequacy. Nevertheless.

I have to wrestle, because it is my job to do so. So I am continually thinking about them, worrying about them, talking about them, discussing them and my mind is muddled with their various aspects, and I want to share those aspects with you if I have the time. I want to tell you about them, because I do believe, in this country, if you have to get on in a democratic way and there is no other way of getting on—we must share our difficulties with one another, we must understand one another, we must give our ideas to one another and point out objections or difficulties to one another. Therefore, I should like to share all this with you, but life is too short for me and I cannot be here, there and everywhere. But some indication at least I want to place before you.

Look at this problem. Just for a moment, forget India, look at the broad aspects of this problem in the sweep of history. Where have we arrived? I do not go too far back, but say a hundred and fifty years ago or so, we saw the beginnings of the industrial revolution in the western world, and it progressed for a hundred years or more. It was based on a certain development, a new form of capitalist structure of society, industrial capitalism. Now, what did industrial capitalism seek to do, what did it aim at? It aimed at the greater production of wealth, greater production. Before that, the world was very poor, production was limited. It had stabilized itself at the poverty level. Industrial capitalism sought to increase the wealth of the world by a new means of production. It has in it the seed of certain difficulties and contradictions. How are we to escape them? Industrial capitalism for a variety of reasons progressed and solved the problems it had set itself. Remember that capitalism has been one of the greatest successes of the past. It solved the problem of production. But in solving it, it produced other contradictions and other difficulties. When people shout slogans, this and that, without understanding that a certain phase is good for one age, yet it may be evil for another, they do not show any understanding. They only show a blurring of the mind. Now, you are not going to solve the problems of today by blurring your minds in that way. Now, what happened was that the problem of production was solved in theory, in practice only in some countries, in theory all over the world. But essentially as you solve the problem of production immediately a different problem raises its head, that is the problem of distribution of what is produced. So a conflict arose and that conflict did not come to a head for a long time because this industrial capitalism, in a sense, only grew up in a certain sector of the world, certain parts of Europe and America, and they had the rest of the world to play with, to expand, to exploit, if you like. So they kept a certain balance, because they could spread out in this way. Otherwise the crisis would have come much sooner in the western world. But gradually crisis came to the western world, a big crisis led to the first world war thirty or forty years ago. It was the first world war that upset the more or less stabilized, or what appeared to be stabilized, economy of the world. Since then, after the first world war, there has been no settling down and tnere is going to be no settling down perhaps for a long time to come, till a large number of adjustments are made. And essentially, the question of settling down is not only the growth of production, a tremendous growth of production in all those countries where there is this production and where there has been this development but also the solution of the problem of equitable distribution.

Now, I am purposely not using terms which have definite connotations in your minds, socialism, capitalism, communism and the like. We should try to think what the problem is and not to get lost in vague terms which may have a hundred meanings.

So you have a second world war following the first because of this maladjustment and lack of adjustment. And I do not know, you may even have a third war, although the odd thing is that these wars do not help to solve the problem but make it infinitely more difficult. I refer to a third possible war. I do not personally think that it will take place in the very near future, that is, shall I say, in two or three years, I do not see any possibility of war, any probability of war. Do not be afraid that war is next door. Nevertheless, nobody can say that war is outlawed, or outmoded or will not take place.

Now, just keep a picture in your minds of what this business of war means, a new war. If there is a war, there can be little doubt that that war would mean the most tremendous destruction on the widest scale, infinitely more than in any past war. It will mean, apart from the destruction of humanity, of cities, what the human race built up through the ages, it will mean the limiting of food production, to take one thing. Ever since the last war, food has been a big problem in the world. As you know, in India, it has been our major problem. If there is another war, food production will be so limited that there probably will be death by starvation by the million all over the world. People think rather lightly of war. The next world war is going to be the greatest disaster that humanity has ever experienced, and do not imagine that India or any part of the world is going to escape that disaster. Some may have more of it, some may have less ; but it just does not matter who is going to be the winner in the war, because destruction will be a common factor, tremendous loss will be a common factor all over the world. The winner in that war will face a ruined world, not a pleasant thing to face.

So we have these problems. If we think that we can solve these problems by war,—I personally think that that is not going to be done—it is a mistaken notion. Of course, the world solves its problems, each generation solves its problems, just as each individual solves his problems, if not in life, then by dying ; the problem is solved with death. So the problems of the world will also be solved, maybe by millions dying, or something equivalent, but that is not the normal way to seek a solution.

So in solving these problems, on the one hand, if we see the tide of war and growing violence, we find that it does not solve the problem, but it confuses it and makes that very solution infinitely more difficult. On the other hand, there must be a solution of the problem. If we do not find one, then other problems will overwhelm us. How are we to proceed about it?

If people think that we are going to remain static and things will adjust themselves, then they are wrong. They are completely wrong in their analysis, if they think that thereby we are bound to solve them, and solve them in a way which avoids a major catastrophe.

Now, having said this, I want to take your minds back in another direction. All these changes that the development of science has brought about in the world have meant the addition of a tremendous deal of knowledge, a vast quantity of it, which very few people, if any, can wholly grasp. It is too much for the human mind to grasp. I do not know, some prodigies may grasp it, but for normally intelligent people, it is too much. The whole field of human knowledge only is vast. Take the field of scientific knowledge, take only the field of a particular branch of science —so much of it that an individual has to specialize in it if he is to be good in that branch—he becomes an authority in his subject, but perhaps not knowing much about other departments of life. Thus it is probably the case with a highly specialized individual, scientist or technician, that he may be ignorant of many important aspects of life, he may, in other words, be a bad citizen, although he is a very good scientist. He may be a good citizen too. With the growth of science, of industrial civilization, there is such a tremendous fund of knowledge, not easy to grasp, that specialization has grown. With the growth of specialization, the synthetic view of human life, what might be called, a philosopher's view of human life, and all its problems have receded into the background. And our politicians too. They may be specialized persons who win elections or who deal with the immediate problems of the day. They have neither the time nor the leisure to consider these problems in their broader aspects. How are we to get over this difficulty? I do not know. I put this before you.

Take a country like the United States of America which is, technologically speaking, the most advanced country, and therefore from the point of view of material resources, the most powerful country. It can produce wealth that is power. But I do feel, looking at it, that this very growth has made it very difficult for the people of the United States—individuals apart, of course,—the average person to be anything but a specialist in his own domain. He is very good ; take an American engineer, an American doctor ; he is so good that he has not the time to be good at anything else. It is a good thing to understand America, because America is the highest development of a certain type towards which the world has been going. Others have also gone that way, but not quite so far.

Now, in India, we are bound to be industrialized, we are trying to be industrialized, we want to be industrialized, we must be industrialized,—greater wealth, greater production,—all that is true. But, are we going just to create a number of specialized agencies and specialists, and thus think that we are solving the problem? We have to create specialists, but we must have the understanding of this problem not only in its wide context today but rather in the wide sweep of history.

Then, perhaps, at least we will try to understand it; then later, we can try to answer it. Obviously, a complicated problem like this is not going to be answered by a slogan or by a demonstration in the streets of Lucknow. I am merely giving you ideas to think about because the problem can be discussed *ad infinitum,* without coming to an end. But I just want you to realize how complex and difficult this problem is, which stretches back both in extent and in time, in its context today and in history. Now, having some rough idea of the world we live in, of all these conflicts, come back to India.

In India, a year and a half ago, we attained political independence. In a sense, politically speaking, our goal is achieved. And the test of it is this—it is not even some law that ensures your constitution, though that is a semblance of the freedom that you may have—can you and your Government do this or that, are you at liberty to do anything domestically, in the foreign sphere, or not? I think it is perfectly clear that there is nothing to stop or impede us, in war or peace, to do what we want, except something which every country has to face, that is, the fact and circumstances in which we live. That we cannot help. There are plenty of countries which I can name here, which are a hundred per cent independent in theory and a hundred per cent not independent in practice, because they are too weak to do what they like, because politically or economically or in some other ways they are dependent on some other country's good wishes.

Now, normally speaking, we would have had to face a multitude of problems that had accumulated during the past 150 years of British rule, because British rule being an imposition from outside prevented the normal adjustment of social relations, the normal solution of problems which otherwise would have taken place, either peacefully or by violence. Something would have happened. But this imposition from outside prevented the process of adjustment that goes on in a country from time to time. The result is that as soon as British domination goes, all these problems suddenly rise up and demand solution, whether it is the States problem or any other. And we have to face them. At the same time, all this occurs when the world is trying to recover from the effects of a tremendous world war. We have all the problems of that world war in the financial and economic spheres. Just then, at the minute of independence, India is partitioned, a living thing is cut into two, with tremendous loss of blood and loss of all manner of things. Everything is cut up, our army, our postal services, telegraph services, telephone services, irrigation services; all governmental machinery is suddenly cut in two. It is an astounding performance, and the consequence of it was, quite apart from the other consequences that followed, migration and killing and the rest of it on a tremendous scale. Now, we have a refugee problem of vast dimensions, six million people of all classes to be looked after—middle class people, working-class people, business people, people who have never done any work all their lives. Just look at all these problems. When you sit down and criticize the Government of India or the Government of the United Provinces, just try to think these problems.

Yesterday, when I was coming from the aerodrome, a number of refugees tried to stop my car. I understand they wanted to meet us today. I shall probably meet them. But when these refugees, with whom all of us sympathize, when they say that they have not received this help or that help, have you ever tried to think how many have been settled out of the six million—sixty lakhs—of refugees? Try to think of the job that we have done. I tell you, it is an amazing job that we have done in regard to refugee settlement. I tell you, it is one of the biggest jobs in history that we have done. But what you hear all the time is what we have not done. I do not mind. I want to listen to what we have not done so that we may not forget it. We may be kept reminded of it. That is all right. But try to conceive of what has been achieved and what is being achieved in that sphere of national life, and not think always of the lack of achievement only. Try to think of the problems first, that this Government had to face, all those that I pointed out to you, and then see what the achievement is and then see what the lack of achievement is, and let us try our hardest. And then speak of both the achievement and the lack of achievement.

After all, you must understand, in a democratic country especially, you cannot expect the government just to pass laws and do everything for you. It is an astonishing thing how you and I and most of us have not got rid of the habit of mind which we developed under British rule. We have not got rid of the habit of action that we developed under British rule. This business of walking up and down with half a dozen banners might have been a suitable thing under British rule. It is—I will not say it is never suitable—it is seldom suitable today. I am talking about the habit of mind which the British Government tried to inculcate, talking about themselves as a *ma bap* Government; that is, the Government is to do everything, the people are merely to send in petitions to some Government official and he will graciously pass orders on them. That is not the way that a democratic government functions.

A government which deals with vital social problems has to function very differently from a government which is essentially a police state. A police state has only to keep the peace, to collect revenue, more or less, and do a few other little jobs. Today, we have to tackle intricate social, economic problems. Those problems cannot be tackled by a *fireman* or *ukase* or a decree from the Government. There must be right laws. I agree that Government activity must be right and ought to be right. But in such economic matters governmental activity goes only thus far. It is the activity of the people, it is the temper of the people, and the co-operation that the people in general give that will solve these problems this way or that. And I tell you that the best of our laws or activities of the Government can be, if not nullified, lessened greatly in effect if there is no will to work in the people or to co-operate to that end. And I tell you also that even an enfeebled government, even a bad political government can yield greater results in the country if people co-operate to that end.

So the essential thing is, how to develop that psychology of work and co-operation among the people. And today, if we are suffering from anything in India, it is the absence of that right psychology. Whether it is in the worker, whether it is in the owner of the factory or whether it is in the younger generation, it is entirely a wrong psychology. It is the psychology of thinking that they can achieve ends by strikes and demonstrations and the rest. And I am sorry to say that people who ought to know better are somehow taken in by it, somehow encourage this kind of thing. Now, I tell you that I consider nothing more dangerous for India's present and India's future than the continuance of this psychology.

I have infinite faith in India's future, and if I did not have that faith, perhaps I could not have worked as I have done. But having that infinite faith I want to tell you that we have to face pretty hard problems today. Let us not deceive one another. We have to face very difficult problems, and we have to lift ourselves up, almost rise up, rise up from our boot straps in many ways. You are not going to get gold and money and silver from other countries. We have to produce it ourselves. How do you produce it, by *hartals* and the like? How are you

going to increase wages and salaries and the rest, as we want to?
Where is the money to come from? Where does the money come
from? It comes from taxation, your pockets and nobody else's.
It is a very simple proposition. Sit down and think it out. You
make demands. It just amazes me when a number of students
come to me and talk casually that they thought they ought to
have been members of the University Commission in order to
place their demands before them. They are always talking about
demands. Now, there is such a thing as India also having some
demands upon you. You seem to have forgotten that. And I think
it is about time that you remembered the demands upon you in
terms of your gratitude, of your duty and work and hard labour.
There are too few people in India who think of this and work
hard to that end. Everybody has demands, everybody has objections, everybody has criticisms and everybody thinks that possibly
if his demands were met everything would be all right, forgetting
that the meeting of his demands means making somebody else
give up his demands, because demands clash.

Think of all these problems. It is a fantastic thing that I see.
Obviously, we have inherited a certain structure, a certain
political structure, administrative structure, judicial structure,
economic structure and the rest ; we have to change that. Now,
how are we going to change that? There can be two ways of
changing. One is : smash it to little bits and build anew, break it
up, if you like, get a clean slate and write upon it. As a matter of
fact, there is no clean slate in life ; there never has been, there
never will be. You can never get rid of the past completely.
Nevertheless, you can have a more or less clean slate. You can
have something that follows from the destruction of the existing
apparatus of government or economic, social set-up or structure.
If we decide that it is essential for the progress of the nation that
we should smash up the structure that we have, well, let us set
about doing it and smashing it up understanding the consequences
of it. Because I do not personally agree with that, I want you to
realize that one must be clear about it ; we are neither trying to
smash up and build anew, right from the bottom up, nor are we
going to change as rapidly as we can, as rapidly as we are capable
of, the existing structure and bring it nearer to what we think
is the right one. We have to choose between the two, because the
adoption of a middle course is fatal. You do not completely smash
it up, so you never start building again ; and you do not allow

the changing process to go on. Neither takes place, except a continuous deterioration and a gradual drifting towards collapse. Now,
this business of breaking up, smashing it and starting anew—
some people say that—the consequences of that of course are:
if you succeed, first of all, it means an enormous conflict, because
some resist, some do not. It means a continuous conflict, not an
immediate smashing up as we might like. A slow smashing up
takes a mighty long time and prevents other things being done.

It means, if you succeed in smashing up, then you perhaps
have a clean slate, but a completely clean slate, as I said, is
impossible. The smashing up process also enfeebles the nation
in every sense, from the military, from economic, from the financial point of view. Therefore, suddenly, India at a critical phase of
her young existence as a free country, is enfeebled. I do not know
what the consequences might be. As a person responsible for the
State of India, I dare not enfeeble my nation and give a chance
to evil-minded countries and evil-minded forces to come in and
play havoc in this country. I may hereby imperil my freedom.
Freedom will be imperilled, not only politically, from the military
point of view, but from the economic point of view. If we are
enfeebled and helpless and in a starving condition, and we cannot
do anything, what are we to do about it? We may take out our
processions and shout out our slogans. How are we to feed these
millions who have no food and who gradually arrive at so low
a level, that they are too weak really to stand up to the
world.

That, I tell you, is an almost inevitable consequence, the
immediate consequence, whatever the final emergence may be ;
the inevitable consequence of any process which aims at smashing
up the present structure completely is the enfeebling of the nation,
the imperilling of our freedom, and evil forces, evil countries
taking advantage of it and exploiting the situation for their own
profit and advantage. I do not want that to happen. During this
smashing up process, this generation, and when I say this generation, I do not mean my generation but the younger generation,
the generation of the young men and young women who have
taken their degrees and will be citizens tomorrow or the day after,
I repeat that this generation will be a ruined generation if this
smashing up takes place. As I just said, we are condemned to
hard labour. That is true. But you can have no conception of what
you will be condemned to if you start smashing up the apparatus

in India today. It is possible that at the end of this generation,
out of the inner strength of India something else will grow.

But, for the moment, you must give up that idea. Therefore, if
you give up the idea, then you have to be wary, then you have
to avoid all actions that lead to a deterioration of the situation
and towards smashing up the present. Smash up the evil, certainly. Fight the evil. Therefore, you have to proceed on
lines not of smashing up the structure, but of changing it as
rapidly as you can.

I wish to put another aspect of it and that is in terms of
violence and non-violence, peaceful methods and violent methods.
That is a good test, because if you employ peaceful methods, I
do not think you are likely to go very wrong, even though you
may employ them for wrong purposes, you are safe and you apply
your own brake. The peaceful method is itself a brake on too much
wrong action. If you have to employ the violent method, however
much a violent method might be justified against a foreign enemy
and against a foreign dominating nation in a country, that is
another argument ; as a matter of fact, even against the foreigner
we employed peaceful methods on the whole. But the use of
violent methods on a democratic issue, not against a foreigner,
but against some of yourselves, is a most dangerous thing. I am
not prepared for the moment to discuss the philosophy or theory
or rule it out from every country. But I do say in India as she is
situated today, the use of methods of violence is the greatest act
of treason that any Indian can be guilty of. We have a strong
unifying force, but at the same time we have all kinds of disruptive and fissiparous tendencies among us. We have fought
communalism, and we have suffered from communalism. We
have provincialism, and we have so many " isms " and separating
tendencies. And now, if in this field, violence comes in any shape
or form and people take to violent methods, then the result is,
of course, that violence is smashed and quickly stopped, as indeed
every government must suppress violence. No government can
take risks with violence. And I tell you from such accounts that I
have heard, the United Provinces Government has been too weak
in dealing with the situation here. There has been a lot of shouting
about what happened. If I had been in charge, I would have
taken stronger action against those who have been misbehaving
in the streets of Lucknow. What is this business of young men
and young women going and attacking the police and slapping

them and throwing bombs and playing about with lathis? Are our young men and women degraded to this level of vulgarity and indiscipline and lack of understanding that they behave in this way? And they call that freedom! That is not my conception of freedom, that has never been my conception of freedom. If you are going to act like this, well, you do an ill turn to your country and your city and your nation. It is an astounding thing, the things I hear of what has been done, and I am surprised that intelligent young men and women do not see the folly of it, not only the folly, but the criminality of it. Are we turning ourselves into a lot of hysterical persons of no understanding, and shouting slogans without understanding what they mean? Is this the idea of freedom? I want you to think about it. Where are we going? Because no government in the wide world can tolerate this kind of thing, one government may go and another government take its place, but if the government has violence done before its eyes, it must suppress that violence, and it will suppress it so long as that government has anything to do with administration. Let there be no doubt about it, whether men, women or children, whoever does it, women will be picked up, boys will be picked up, you simply cannot allow it. I have to congratulate the police of Lucknow (and I want to say this publicly too) on the way they have behaved here and the restraint they have shown. So come to me and talk to me and ask me what you are to do, if you are slapped in the face, should you turn the other cheek as Christ said? Well, if we could all do this, the world would be a different place to live in. But obviously, the police force is not supposed to turn the other cheek when it is slapped. So please understand these enormous problems that we have to face here, problems that require hard work.

Now, take another thing. There is a certain definite quantity of money available in the Government of India or in the provincial Government. We want it to go far. We cannot spend the same money twice over or three or four times over. Demands of all kinds come. Maybe, we spend it wrongly some times, but it cannot be spent twice. You simply cannot produce money where there is none. You can produce money by hard work. Therefore, the problem becomes one of hard work and proper distribution. All these problems, all these aspects, have to be gone into; I want you, even as students, to think about them with all the data before you, to bring out all the facts before you. Nevertheless, you can have and you do have the main things to consider, and your professors can help you. Then prepare yourselves for the burden that you will have to shoulder tomorrow. Students come to me and say, are we to take part in politics or not? I say, of course, always. But what is politics? It is an astounding conception of politics to go up and down the street in a procession. You just cannot get out of the habit of the days of British rule. When a crisis comes in the life of a country, as the great war came in the life of the western countries, well, almost every student above a certain age, whether at Oxford or Cambridge or London, or other Universities volunteered or was conscripted, and had to go to the war. He had to leave his college, had to fight for his country and for his people, whether it was an Englishman, or Frenchman, or German, they were all conscripted to fight for the life of their country. Now, for India fighting for freedom I can conceive a crisis coming, and the colleges closing and the students going out and all that, but that is during a period of crisis and peril for the nation's freedom. If that pattern of behaviour becomes continual, a sort of picture for people to copy, well, of course, whatever good that activity may result in, those people who indulge in it are not training themselves for any future activity of any value. Obviously not, because India is going to be run by a large number of trained people in future and ultimately, as everywhere else, by a relatively small number of A class men in technology and science. Ultimately, a country's standing in the world is obviously judged not by the number of people it has, crores and crores, it is by the number of top-ranking men and women it has, who show results, who can give a proper lead, and also by the number of other eminent men it has to carry on the work of a large country. It is a certain quality that counts in the end, not quantity, although quantity also is necessary in a certain measure. Do you realize that out of you are going to come or ought to come those top-ranking men and women? But if education is looked upon as a time for demonstration—unless as I said the nation is in peril and everything has to be set aside,—then you do not get prepared for the future. And then, the problem that I have to face comes up before me. I tell you it is my biggest headache to find A-1 persons in India, and a sufficient number of them. They are very, very few.

Mind you, when I say that, I know that there is the best and the most excellent material in India, and what we have is very fine. I want to tell you of the three branches of which I have had some personal experience. I have had a lot to do with the Indian Army, and the Navy and the Air Force. And it is my opinion, and it has been confirmed by expert foreign opinion, that the young Indian officer in our defence services is first class, first class not merely in discipline, but in the quality of his mind. It is important that the quality of mind should be there. For warfare has ceased now to be merely a thing of gymnastics and drill, it is the quality of the mind that counts in this business, and we have been told by very eminent judges of this that they have been surprised at the quality of the mind of the young Indian officer. Now, this is a comfort. I did not mention other qualities like courage and daring ; they are very good, they are very necessary. But after all, it is the quality of the mind that counts even with courage and daring.

Take another thing. I am also dealing with the Department of Scientific Research in the Government of India and to some extent indirectly and rarely directly, I come across and I hear about young scientists. My own impression is, and again this has been confirmed by expert opinion, that we have a very fine band of young scientists of the first quality, and, further, that if there is opportunity in our laboratories and universities, for further teaching and proper direction, we would have many more of these first-rate people ; that is, the quality is there, it has to be developed. Given the chance, on the one side there is this quality, potential quality becoming actual ; on the other, the diversion of people's minds to activities which prevent them from developing such qualities as they may have. Now, this is very important, and this tussle is going on in the mind of India.

I want you, therefore, to look at this problem in its entirety and see not merely what is just right or just wrong, but where you must throw your entire weight.

Finally, I want to put yet another aspect of this problem, although it has many facets and aspects, and it is, if I may say so, the moral aspect. It is my belief and conviction that these world problems today are not going to be solved just by financial or economic means or purely by what I might call political means. At the back of them lies a tremendous conflict of the spirit which is reflected in other conflicts, economic or political, and whether it is solved today or tomorrow, unless this conflict of the spirit is solved there is going to be no peace in any country. And it is well for us to remember this at all times and especially today.

The day after tomorrow is the first anniversary of the death of Mahatma Gandhi. A year has passed since he died. It has been a hard year for all of us and for the country, and yet I suppose his death has made us think of some of the things he stood for, even more than his life. And I believe that fundamentally what he stood for, unless we understand it and act up to it, we are not going to suceed or, if I may put it positively, that if we understand it and act up to it, we are bound to succeed. So I wish to stress this moral aspect in its world context and in the more immediate context of India. After all we have to function in this field. India is a big enough field.

There is a great deal of talk of India's leadership, here and there. I discourage this talk. It is just pompous nonsense, this conscious talking about leadership. Let us look after ourselves, and if we look after ourselves properly, we shall have opportunities of serving other countries, not in terms of leadership and imposing ourselves on them, but because they themselves will come and seek our service. But, before we seek to serve others, or guide others, we must be in a position to do so.

India has attained a great name in the world today for various reasons. But the most important of these reasons is Mahatma Gandhi. It is he who has given this great stature to India, and that stature was not given because of India's army or navy or wealth, but because this giant among men showed up the pettiness of the world in the moral sphere, of the politicians of the world. So India gained this place because people thought of India in certain moral terms. And they were right in the sense that India had produced Gandhi, though most of us were petty people, unworthy even of following him. So let us think of this problem in this context of morality. And again, I come back to this, that we may differ as we do—and I do not mind our differing—but whether we differ or not, we must be clear in our minds about this, that we should not stoop to any low means, we should not stoop to any violent means, we should not stoop to any vulgar means. We are not going to make our country great by exhibitions of vulgarity and lowness of action and sporadic violence. Violence is bad enough when nations indulge in it against one another in war. But violence becomes infinitely worse and degrading in the narrow domestic sphere of street violence and the like. Therefore, I would beg of you to consider all this and to realize that if we are living in a time of great moment for our country and the world, a very great responsibility is cast upon us to understand this problem, to understand this question, in order to think of how to solve it and to act aright in this context.

ON INDUSTRY

PRODUCTION, THE FIRST ESSENTIAL

DR. MOOKERJEE, friends and comrades, I venture to address you in this way, more especially on this occasion, because probably no other major problem that we have to tackle requires so much the spirit of friendly co-operation than Industry, Labour and the general economic set-up of the country. It is rather presumptuous for me to come here at this almost last stage of this Conference and the Committees that you have had during the last few days, not having taken part in them, and now presumably in order to offer you good advice. Many of you are experts in your fields, whether it is Labour or Industry and though I am very greatly interested in all these matters, and perhaps sometimes have an advantage over the experts in the sense that a layman can see the whole picture in proper perspective more than a specialist in his special field of activity, nevertheless, I would have liked to have had the chance and opportunity of taking part in your discussions during the last few days, and knowing more how the mind of this gathering, of those who are participating in these discussions, was working.

It is obvious that in these very vital matters there are differences of opinion—vital difference of opinion and approach. There are what are called ideologies, there is what is called the practical approach which, I have often found, is far removed from anything that might really be called practical or that can be practical. A practical approach need not necessarily be just looking one yard ahead of you, it requires looking further ahead also. Well, there are these differences and it would be a little absurd to think that you can charm away those differences and find complete unanimity by just pure good-will and good advice. Nevertheless, I think, without doing away with those differences of approach, if we do appreciate that in a certain context of events it is necessary and highly desirable to function together, well, we create an atmosphere which helps in coming to some—if you like, not permanent, at any rate semi-permanent or temporary conclusions.

Now, why are these approaches different? I suppose, partly

A speech delivered at the Industries Conference, New Delhi, December 18, 1947.

because of some difference in one's outlook on life itself, on the objectives of life, on the social set-up, and the rest, but to put it very crudely, leaving out these wider objectives, the differences arise because various groups aim at getting some prize or other, some benefit or other. Capital may want a certain prize, Labour may want a certain prize ; the consumer, the producer, everybody naturally wants to benefit himself or his group.

But a time comes when it may well happen that while the conflicting groups are fighting against each other, the prize vanishes and there is no prize left for anybody. So it becomes important at that time to moderate one's own ardour or one's own particular desire to win the prize, and save the prize itself. It is not necessary to give up the hope of getting the prize, but rather to put first things first, that is, to preserve the prize and then either in a friendly way come to future decisions or, if you like, have a conflict ; but when the conflict endangers the prize itself, then obviously this is an exceedingly unfortunate and foolish way of approaching a thing.

You all know that India for the last few months has passed through all manner of tremendous crises and we have had to face colossal problems ; we have survived all manner of surgical operations of a major kind, and we are not likely to have another operation of that type, but the consequences of that operation have been so tremendous that few of us realized previously that they would be so bad. We knew they would be bad ; therefore, we resisted the operation and resisted what might be called quack remedies. But unfortunately sometimes quacks succeed, even in the best regulated households. And the result is that we have had operations and you have seen what a tremendously upsetting consequence followed them. We have not yet overcome that consequence and we have to face problems of colossal magnitude still.

While we have had to face this, on the other hand, we see and we have seen a progressively deteriorating economic situation. We talk, and rightly so, of the problems of distribution. In fact, most of our troubles and conflicts and vital ideologies are concerned with distribution. But important as that is, there must obviously be something substantial to distribute before we can start the process of distribution. Therefore, we come to the problem of production. Production becomes the first essential, but with it is intimately associated distribution. You cannot really separate the two. Production depends on many factors and one of the most important of those factors is the psychology for production, apart from the technical apparatus that we may have, one should have efficiency and there must be the capacity and the psychology to produce. If that psychology is lacking, then inevitably production goes down as it has gone down.

Now, you can analyze the past few months or few years as you like ; there are so many factors. There are the consequences of the war—a certain feeling of tiredness after hard work. There are the consequences of political upsets, of the partition, of communal troubles and the like. But I should say, perhaps, one of the major things we have to face in industrial relations is this psychological background, which makes Labour feel that it does not get a square deal, that somehow it is overreached all the time, which makes the employer class feel that they are threatened with all manner of dangers, and that Labour is not pulling its weight and is only threatening strikes and slowing up work and so on and so forth. So they approach each other not only with a complete lack of confidence but in a spirit of extreme hostility.

How are we to get over this? On the one hand, I think it is perfectly true to say that there has been a tendency on the part of Labour or certain Labour groups to take advantage of certain difficulties which the nation has had to face, to organize strikes and stoppages of work and slowing down of work at a time when it meant hitting rather hard the nation. If that kind of thing continues with Labour—which undoubtedly has the sympathy of vast numbers of people in this country—a certain barrier begins to grow up between the large labour element and the rest of the country. And it is not good to have that kind of barrier grow up.

That is so far as Labour is concerned. As far as the employers' side is concerned, I hope no one will challenge me when I say that during this last war a certain section of the employer class did not behave well ; in fact, they behaved exceedingly badly, exceedingly egotistically and far from giving a square deal to anybody, they thought mostly of themselves and of little else. I have yet to understand how, in spite of the tremendous and heavy taxation in India, these vast fortunes were made by certain individuals or groups, I just cannot understand it ; and we have to find some means and machinery to prevent this kind of shameful traffic in human beings and profiting at the expense of the nation.

So it is easy to find fault with certain sections of Labour or certain sections of the employing class. But what we have to do is not merely to find fault but to seek a remedy. You cannot turn everybody into angels ; there would be no problem if people were advanced enough to think and act in that way. One remedy is to create conditions in which—if I may say so—those who are not angelic do not find it easy to flourish and find difficulties in their way. That is, you have to provide inducements to fair dealing and honesty and certain disadvantages should be attached to any other course of action.

Leaving out the people who may not be up to the right standard in fair dealing and honesty, the real difficulty comes when honest people are in conflict. If they are completely honest, they hold different views and they come into conflict. Normally, people who are not honest sometimes make up their differences sooner, because they have nothing strong to hold on to. They are not used to any anchorage, they just float about, and so, under pressure of events, they come to terms. But honest people who hold opinions very stoutly do not come to terms, because they think that any other way is the wrong way. Now, I take it that most of us who are here are honest people and people who have thought about these matters and hold strong opinion about these matters and, therefore, find it a little difficult to accept the other person's view.

Nevertheless, the major fact confronts us : that all manner of perils face us in India today. And although some for the moment are at the forefront, the ultimate peril is the slow drying-up of the capacity of the nation to produce. That affects us politically, economically and in every other way, and gradually our strength goes down to resist these very perils that face us. Therefore, you have to stop this drying-up of our productive capacity.

I believe you have been thinking about this and you have also passed a number of Resolutions on the subject. We must increase our production ; we must increase our national wealth and the national dividend and only then can we really raise the standard of living of our people.

We may here and there make some adjustment by a more equitable distribution of the existing wealth. That must be done really not so much because it makes too much of a difference in raising the standard of life—it does, but not very much—but it must be done because it creates conditions for advance ; because, if that is not done, there is continually that feeling of not having a square deal and people do not put their heart and soul into the work they do, thinking that they are not being properly treated, and so on. Therefore, it becomes essential first of all to see that where there are gross inequalities present, we work for a rapid reduction of those inequalities. But ultimately more wealth can only come from more production of all types and kinds of goods.

Presumably, many of you here represent big industry and I have no doubt that production through big industry is essential. But in the present context of events today—I should like to say that when we talk of increased production, whether of food or of any other commodity—it is necessary for us to encourage small-scale production in a large way also. This question is often considered as if there were an inherent conflict between large-scale production and small-scale production. Perhaps, it might indicate a different approach. But, leaving that idea of conflict aside, it seems to me obvious that, at the present moment more especially, and possibly later, the two have to go on at the same time. And especially as a short-term plan, there must be large-scale small production today of all manner of things that can be produced in a small way, because all kinds of commodities are lacking. But we are really concerned at the present moment with bringing about a psychological atmosphere and bringing about some kind of machinery wherewith to tackle any conflict that may arise.

Now, if we are facing some perils along with the rest of the world, with some special troubles of our own, how are we to proceed? The very first thought that comes to one's mind is that in this dissolving world which is heading again for a big-scale conflict, the sooner we put India on its feet the more chance there is of our pulling our weight and surviving and having some influence in the near future. None, not even the very biggest expert, can say how long this very precarious peace in the world will last. We hope it will last many years, but it may break at any time. And if that happens, you will realize that all manner of unforeseen things will take place. It will shake us up more than anything else has yet done.

And how should we face that emergency? By building up, before anything happens, an economically strong and well-balanced India with a strong enough defence apparatus. And remember what the defence apparatus means today. People talk of the army and navy and air force ; obviously, defence means these. But far more than the army and navy and air force, defence means industry and production, not all the soldiers in the world will be of any good to India otherwise. People talk about compulsory military service. From one point of view, I am not in favour, generally speaking, of compulsory military service. But I am in favour of it in this sense, that it will make our people a little more disciplined, and also from the point of view of physical culture.

But this business of compulsory military service means nothing important from the point of view of defence, because the real problem is not to make people war-minded but to give them the means of fighting. If you have millions and millions of men walking about with antique weapons and lathis, it is not much good. You have to have the production of all the essentials of warfare. In fact, in war weapons and all manner of things are necessary. If you are industrially strong, you can build up your army and navy and air force at short notice. If you depend on buying your warships and everything else in a foreign country and that source dries up, it is quite useless to have only a few thousand men shouting about war. So that, in the ultimate analysis, even this war business brings you back to production and the growth of industries, small and big.

Many things contributed to the winning of the last war, but I think the final reasons were two, the amazing capacity of American industry and scientific research. It is these which won the war, not so much the soldiers and others. Therefore, we must, from every point of view—external and internal—stop this slowing down of production and increase it rapidly by building up new industries; and also tackle problems of unemployment and of raising the standard of living. These can only be done if there is peace in industry ; without peace there, it simply cannot be done. And I take it that the object of this Conference is to have peace in industry for a certain period at least, which will give us a breathing space.

In a draft Resolution that I have been reading, a period of three years is mentioned. I am not interested in any particular period, and for some time past my mind has hardly functioned in terms of long-distance objectives except in an idealistic kind of way. I can make no plan for myself, a few days or a few weeks ahead, I do not know where I shall be. So I am not very much interested whether it is two years or three years.

The point is that it would be a tremendous thing for India, if all of you and all those whom you represent came to the conclusion that you should give a chance to this and have a period of truce during which there would be no strikes and no lock-outs. And how can you do that? Of course, it is too much to expect this to be done unless there is some machinery and apparatus to settle disputes to the satisfaction of the people concerned, or more or less to their satisfaction, because there cannot obviously be hundred per cent satisfaction when two parties are in dispute. I suppose it is not beyond the wit of man or even beyond the wit of this Government to produce some such machinery or scheme. Whenever there are such schemes, it is curious that objection is taken to them on both sides.

The other day I was in Calcutta and the President of the Associated Chambers of Commerce there went on repeating and telling the audience that the Government should not interfere or intervene in any way. He thought that if the Government stood aloof, industry would flourish. It was very interesting for me to hear that, because I had thought that that particular viewpoint had almost vanished from the earth. But still it exists in Calcutta. At any rate, the labour people want governmental interference right enough. But when you talk of arbitration and adjudication, their idea of arbitration and adjudication often is that they should go in for them ; if they succeed, well and good, otherwise they are free to do what they like. That I can understand psychologically. It is a relic of old times, but practically speaking, it becomes impossible to have arbitration and adjudication if you approach it in that spirit. So, if we can, as I think we can, have a proper impartial machinery—which machinery in the modern world is bound to incline towards Labour rather than towards the others—we can resolve these difficulties or such difficulties as may arise from time to time.

I am not for the moment talking about the final resolution, as to the future economic policy and the merits or otherwise of nationalization, although inevitably they arise. For the present, I think the first step should be a kind of adjustment of minor differences while we are considering major objectives of policy. With regard to the major objectives of policy, I have just said something in Calcutta and elsewhere and I will not repeat it here.

Speaking as a person who is a believer in the socialization of industry, I should like to say this, that far too much attention is often paid to acquiring existing industries than to the building of new industries by the State or under State control. In many cases, existing industries of the basic type may have to be acquired by the State and run by the State. But it seems to me a far better approach to the problem for the State to concentrate more and more on new industries of the latest type and to control them in a large measure, because then the resources of the State go towards further progress and controlled progress instead of merely trying to get hold of something which exists. Of course, one sometimes has to do that too.

I say this because I am to some extent—if I may venture to say so—of a scientific bent of mind and I try to think more in dynamic terms than in static terms. The existing industry today that most people think of—capitalists, socialists or communists—is something of which they think in static terms, as if the thing must go on and on, while as a matter of fact the thing is completely out of date and most of it should be scrapped.

If you think in a somewhat dynamic way, you can see that we are at one of the major ages of transition when completely new sources of power are being tapped, something of the nature of the industrial revolution or electrical revolution, but something even more far-reaching. If somebody at the time of the industrial revolution was thinking in terms of the pre-industrial age and talking about acquiring this or that, he would have been completely out of the picture sometime later when the new age came and there were new sources of power. In the same way, we are on the verge of a new industrial age and whether it takes ten, fifteen or twenty years—I doubt if it will take more than that—many of our methods of production will become completely out of date, and what you are thinking of acquiring today may have no value at all. That is a warning. I hope it does not frighten people and make them think that they should not invest money in any industry. But one has to be very wide awake today about these changes and one must think in terms of the future rather than the past, because the past is dead and gone, we cannot go back to it, and even the present is a rapidly changing present. If you approach it in terms of the future, then many of the present conflicts seem out of place: or, at any rate, they assume a new aspect and you get out of the rut of your old mode of thinking.

These are some considerations for us to ponder over. But for the present I do hope that you, who represent great forces in the country—industrial, labour and governmental—will come to an agreement on the period of peace and reconstruction and building up, and meanwhile we shall think of the larger policies for industrial and economic development and give effect to them fairly rapidly. For my part, I attach probably more importance to the development of our big schemes—river valley schemes—than to anything else. I think it is out of those that new wealth is going to flow into this country. When I see a map of India and I look at the Himalayan range—I like the Himalayas myself ; I like mountains and all that—I think of the vast power concentrated there which is not being used, and which could be used, and which really could transform the whole of India with exceeding rapidity if it were properly utilized. It is an amazing source of power, probably the biggest source anywhere in the world—this Himalayan range, with its rivers, minerals and other resources. Therefore, I attach more importance to the development of these big river valley schemes, dams, reservoirs, hydro-electric and thermal power and so forth, which, once released, will simply drive you forward. But before we release power, we have to know how to control it and use it in the proper way.

We have been in some way or other connected with this Government for the last sixteen months or so. One of the first things that I did when we came to this Government was to think of these economic plans and these various schemes, and we appointed an Advisory Planning Board for a rapid survey—not a detailed survey—of these schemes so that we might consider some basic policies. The Planning Board reported fairly soon. It worked necessarily with some superficiality, but nevertheless it did well, and then immediately we got caught up in the business of the approaching partition. After partition again, we got caught up with the business of the after-effects of partition. So all these vital problems could not be solved. There they remained.

But part of the difficulty has also been the wrong psychology in the industrial field. So if we start at this end, governmentally, I hope, we shall approach this problem fairly soon, and I hope also that this procedure which my colleague, Dr. Mookerjee, has initiated—that is, to confer with the representatives of all shades of opinion—will be adopted whenever necessary in the future policy. But in order to approach that properly, one has to have a breathing space. One cannot have it in this world with trouble all over the place. But let us have it in industry.

I do not ask you to give up any of your particular ideologies and beliefs. Stick to them. But just realize that even your particular ideology may have a greater chance of advancement if we have peace and build up something now for the next year or two, and meanwhile we develop those other policies ; and if you want a fight, let us have a fight afterwards, but at any rate let us have something worth fighting for, otherwise the thing we fight for vanishes and that is not good enough or wise enough.

I heard last night—I have not myself seen it in a newspaper —that in Bombay an announcement has been made that there will be what is called a token one-day strike against the adjudication machinery and decontrol. I will not go into these two matters here. But it seems to me quite astoundingly irresponsible for any organization, whatever its views and ideologies, to indulge in strikes at this moment and in this way, even though they may be token one-day strikes. It shows a complete lack of understanding of the political situation, of the international situation, of the national situation, of the economic situation, of the human situation, or for that matter of any situation. I should not like to criticize any people without discussing the matter with them, but I confess that it passes my understanding how any responsible person can indulge in this kind of token strike at a moment when there is always the possibility of its giving rise to even bigger problems and bigger conflicts, when all of us here and all over the country are thinking in terms of finding some way out of this impasse, even though it may be a temporary way out. So just at this moment to indulge in this kind of token strike seems to me to be very unfair and very unfortunate.

Now, the strike, as I have just learnt, is against compulsory adjudication and decontrol. Opinions may differ about these matters, but so far as decontrol is concerned, we have announced a policy which is very cautious. The subject of control is of exceeding complexity and difficulty and opinions differ. The decision that the Government has arrived at has been taken after the most careful thought. And even so we have taken care to see that if anything tends to go wrong, we go back, or we reconsider our position. The whole machinery of control is being kept even where control is being withdrawn. Now, whether we are right or wrong is another matter. We may be wrong, but the only way to proceed in such matters is to be always ready to correct an error as soon as one is convinced that it is an error. We are ready for it, but the point I wish to put before you is this. This Government is supposed to be a popular government and to represent the wishes of a large majority of the people. If that is so and if that Government takes any measure like this, how do those who oppose that measure proceed? Either they are in a majority or in a minority. If they are in the majority, it is very easy for them to put an end to that Government. If they are in a minority, any action that they may want to take means that a minority is trying to coerce the majority and that inevitably leads—it may of course lead to a temporary success for the minority—to the majority getting angry and setting on the minority.

After all, if you start a conflict, two can play at the same game of trying to coerce the other part of the community. Or even from the narrowest point of view of a group, this business is unwise and does not pay ; but it does a lot of harm to the community. I hope, therefore, that this type of token strikes—though the strikers may be justified in expressing their wishes in any way they like, such as meetings and peaceful demonstrations, and show that they disapprove of decontrol and adjudication—is not followed because not only does it mean the loss of production for that day, but it may mean petty conflicts. If someone does not go on strike then you pull him out and then there is trouble. Then some one is arrested by the police and immediately a vicious circle starts.

I would beg those who think in this way to reconsider their decisions and try to think in a larger way, or if I may say so, in a more rational way and consider the consequences of their actions. It may be that many of these things that occur happen because of some cause which does not appear on the surface. For instance, some kind of election may be pending and people think that if they behave in a particular way they may have a pull at the elections—municipal, corporation or provincial.

Ultimately, it becomes a question for all of us to consider whether we are to think in terms of some petty election or some permanent and larger interest. Of course, if we are interested in the former, in the small things, then it is not much good talking about bigger things ; they will escape us. I am sure there is quite enough determination and sense in this country to get over these petty difficulties and to face the larger issues. Therefore, to come back, I hope that this Conference will yield this very substantial result, namely, that we shall start in a friendly way, we shall decide on some kind of truce in industry for a period, and we shall devise means to see that everybody gets a square deal as far as possible, and meanwhile, we shall sit down and think about our larger policies.

PRODUCE OR PERISH

FRIENDS and comrades, I am supposed to speak to you about the production crisis. But my mind is full of other matters and other crises. We talk of the production of many things, but perhaps the most important thing for a nation is to produce men and women, good and true. One such person is in India who through his goodness, truth and power of spirit brightens this ancient land and casts his radiance on us, weak and erring mortals, and stops us when we go astray. We have strayed enough from the right path and wasted our inheritance, and our good repute. We have had enough of this now. We must go ahead on the path of creation and construction and co-operation and goodwill to our brother man.

Production means wealth. If we do not produce we have not enough wealth. Distribution is equally important, so that wealth cannot accumulate in the hands of a few, nevertheless, before we think of distribution, there must be production.

You know we have many problems to face today—economic problems and others. There are questions of control and inflation and so many other things. There is, again, the scarcity of goods. The change over from wartime to peace-time economy has been very slow. And, indeed, instead of progress there has often been going back. Now, this is the most urgent and serious matter for us to consider, because as this kind of thing goes on, there is a kind of creeping paralysis in our economy and the whole of India, the whole nation suffers. Today, in addition, we have to face tremendous problems of vast migration and colossal numbers of refugees. The refugees are not producing. East Punjab is not producing much and all these people become unfortunately a burden on the country. Not that they want to be a burden, not that they are not capable of producing, but circumstances have forced them into this unhappy position. So we have to think of production as an urgent problem even more than what we have otherwise done.

We want a stream of wealth pouring out from our fields, factories and workshops and reaching our country's millions, so

A talk broadcast from New Delhi, January 18, 1948.

that ultimately we may be able to see our dreams for India fulfilled.

We talk of freedom, but today political freedom does not take us far unless there is economic freedom. Indeed, there is no such thing as freedom for a man who is starving or for a country which is poor. The poor whether they are nations or individuals have little place in this world. Therefore, we have to produce in order to have sufficient wealth, distributed by proper economic planning so that it may go to the millions, more especially to the common man. Then not only the millions prosper, but the whole country becomes rich and prosperous and strong. Many people have faith in all manner of dangers and people talk loosely of conflict with other countries. I hope there will be no such conflict.

Nevertheless, a new country—a new State which has recently achieved its independence—must take great care to guard that independence and that freedom. It has been rightly said that eternal vigilance is the price of liberty. How are we to effect this? How are we to put into effect the schemes of reform, or constructive schemes or development schemes unless we have the wealth to put into them? We cannot live on borrowed money for long, and even if we borrow money, we must have the credit for it. We must be strong enough to invest it along proper channels. All these require production—production in the immediate present to fulfil our immediate needs, so that we may have something to lay by for these productive schemes of development. Therefore, we come back to the basic need of production at this moment. Now, production means hard work, unremitting labour ; production means no stoppage of work, no strike, no lock-out.

Now, I am the last man to say that Labour should be denied the right to strike, for the weapon of strike has been a much valued weapon by means of which Labour has gradually gained a position of strength and eminence in most countries. Nevertheless, there are times when strikes are dangerous, when strikes not only injure the cause of the nation, but also ultimately the cause of the worker himself. This is one of those times, and it was for this reason that a short while ago, at a Conference held in Delhi, the representatives of the Government, Labour and Industry decided almost unanimously that we should have a three-year truce, during which there should be no strikes or lock-outs. Obviously, if we have decided on such a course, we must have machinery to see that it is followed. Otherwise some will take advantage of this decision. Therefore, in that Conference it was further decided to have this machinery, so that the worker, labourer or peasant would have his due, would have a fair deal and would even take some part in the management, more especially in regard to his own needs. If we have fair and impartial machinery of this kind, then strikes and lock-outs would have no meaning.

Of course, strikes and lock-outs should have no meaning in a properly constituted State, where everyone has his due. Strikes and lock-outs are the symbols of something radically wrong in the economic system. Well, a great deal is wrong in our economic system today, not only in India, but in the other parts of the world as well. We have to change all this, but in changing we have to take care that we do not smash what we already have. There is the danger that in doing something rashly, we may go further away from the objectives that we aim at. Therefore, at present with all these crises facing us, it is most important for us to have a period of industrial calm and peace so that we may all co-operate together in increasing production in the country and in building up the country by putting through the vast schemes of development.

You know that we have had these schemes for a long time. Unfortunately, many of them still remain paper schemes. It is time that we gave effect to them. There are among them, great river valley schemes which would not only irrigate the land, prevent floods, produce hydro-electric power and prevent malaria and other diseases, but generally produce conditions for the rapid development of industries and the modernization of our agriculture. Do you realize that India is heavily populated, but still has vast tracts of land where no man lives, because these tracts have no water or the soil requires treatment?

Our present population can easily be fully employed, thereby removing unemployment and adding to the wealth of the country. No country can be overpopulated, if there is work for everyone. We propose to have this work, and if we succeed in our endeavour we shall have to give up the idea of unceasing conflict in the economic and labour fields. But that again, as I said, can be solved only if the worker gets his due and if he is not exploited.

We must devise something soon for this purpose. To some extent, this has been done but a great deal has yet to be done.

Meanwhile, we must decide to give full effect to this three-year truce which we have decided upon.

So let us get on with work, hard work. Let us produce, but what we are producing is not for individual pockets but for the nation, to raise the standard of the people and the common man. If we do that we shall see India progressing rapidly and many of the problems that face us today will be solved. It is not an easy task for us to rebuild India. It is a very big problem, though we are a numerous people, and there is no lack of resources in India, there is no lack of human beings, capable, intelligent and hard working. We have to use these resources, this man power in India.

It also depends on peace, international peace, national peace, economic peace and peace in the labour world and in the industrial world. Let us have this peace. At the present moment, I am talking to you particularly for industrial peace and let all of us join together in this campaign of production and remember that this production is not just for enriching individuals, but it is to enrich the nation. For if India lives, we also live. JAI HIND.

OUR ECONOMIC POLICY

SIR, I should like to say a few words right at the beginning of this discussion in order to indicate the general policy of the Government in this behalf. The Honourable Mover has referred to various statements previously made by the National Congress, by me personally and by others ; and then he has drawn attention to other statements made by members of the Government and pointed out certain discrepancies between them. There may be different viewpoints and certain discrepancies if the various statements are compared ; but I think the real fact of the matter is—and I plead guilty to that—that the Government as such have not put forward, before this House or before the country, a fully worked-out policy in regard to these matters. Not that the Government do not attach a good deal of importance to them, but for the simple reason that events of various kinds rather overwhelmed us, and these could not be dealt with—if I may say so with all respect—in the manner that the Honourable Member suggests, by a kind of Resolution vaguely talking about nationalization and putting everything into effect immediately. It is a much more intricate matter. We may call ourselves by any name we like,—socialists or any other name—but if we have to tackle these problems, we cannot tackle them in vague terms. We must tackle them with precision. And it is the Government's business certainly to deal with long-term policies, but even more so with the immediate present. And so, as we have had these other difficulties to face, many matters, which we would probably already have considered by now, have had to be postponed.

For instance, it was our desire to consider the appointment of a Planning Commission which could be given general terms of reference, and which could then precisely lay down priorities, how to plan and co-ordinate various sectors of our economic life.

A speech delivered at the Constituent Assembly (Legislative), New Delhi, February 17, 1948.

The Resolution on which the Prime Minister made this speech was moved by Kazi Syed Karimuddin and it read as follows:

" This Assembly is of opinion that the economic pattern of this country shall be socialist economy based on the principle of nationalization of key industries and co-operative and collective farming and socialization of the material resources of the country and that the Government of India shall adopt the said principle immediately."

We have been unable to do that, I am sorry to say. I hope that before very long, we shall be able to take steps in that direction. Meanwhile, as the House is aware, in a very small way we have appointed a Rehabilitation and Development Board which, though it primarily concerns itself with the rehabilitation of the refugees, is also intimately concerned with development, and it will have to consider the various development schemes and try to plan them with the object of rehabilitating the refugees.

In the past few years, I have had occasion to express my general views on this subject many times, and for some years I was Chairman of the National Planning Committee where all such matters came up for discussion. We did a lot of good work in that Committee. Unfortunately, this work did not bear fruit in the shape of a final report, but the reports issued by a large number of sub-committees and a considerable number of our own resolutions bear witness to the work that has already been done.

I am glad to say that many of these reports of the sub-committees are now available for such persons as are interested in them. If they read these reports as well as the other material which we have, they will find that these questions are extraordinarily intricate, overlapping, and they cannot be solved by a mere formula.

The formula gives the mental outlook of the person who uses it. That is true, but a Government cannot speak in vague formulas. The Government has to consider every aspect of a question and more especially what it can do for the immediate present.

Now, it is wellknown, and we have often stressed this, that production is perhaps one of the most important things before us today: that is, adding to the wealth of the country. We cannot overlook other things. Nevertheless, production comes first, and I am prepared to say that everything that we do should be judged from the point of view of production first of all. If nationalization adds to production, we shall have nationalization at every step. If it does not, let us see how to bring it about in order not to impede production. That is the essential thing.

It is not so easy as the Honourable Member seems to think that we can legislate, and then by some kind of jugglery, we can produce results. To take such a step may possibly lead to some kind of a disaster: actually a graver crisis may follow. So it is not merely a question of adopting a certain economic outlook, but also of timing, of priorities, of how to do it, in what manner and when to do it—that is the most important factor. It is not enough to put aside or break up a certain system, you have to put another system in its place. All these factors have to be borne in mind.

The Resolution that the Honourable Member has put forward, suffers from all manner of defects, including the kind of defect that he was blaming us for. It is vague. It has little meaning except to show the goodness of his heart. He talks about doing things immediately, all over the place in agriculture and industry. I just cannot conceive how any Government, whatever its views may be as regards economic problems, can accept such a resolution. Most of us—and, so far as I am concerned, I, too,—believe that the time has come for a rapid change in the economic system, not only of India but of other parts of the world. I think far too many of our friends and our countrymen here and those in other countries continue to think in terms which were applicable to an age which has more or less passed. They continue to adhere to what might be called the 19th century economic ideology, which may have been very good in its time, but which is largely inapplicable today, and I think many of the ills in the world today are due to the fact that that particular economic system, which grew in the 19th century, does not fit the circumstances of the middle of the 20th century.

We find, therefore, all over the world an economic malaise, and it may be that many of our political ills are due to the fact that we are not settling down in a more sensible manner befitting the times. However that may be, the point we have to consider is not just destructive criticism, but what we can do constructively to meet it. What we can do to meet it depends a great deal, of course, on circumstances in our own country: partly, also, on circumstances in the world outside, because these events act and react on one another.

In judging of the circumstances in our own country, we have to consider all manner of factors and we have to plan accordingly and go ahead, step by step, so as not to break up something we have without replacing it immediately with something better. It is fairly easy to break things up. It is not so easy to construct. It is quite possible that, in an attempt to change the economic system, you may have a period of semi-disaster. You may even stop production which we aim at. Ultimately, perhaps very gradually, you may build up a new kind of apparatus. But for the moment you will break up the existing apparatus. That is undesirable when all our energies have to be concentrated on production.

The Honourable Member referred to a certain report which was issued by a sub-committee of the All-India Congress Committee, of which I had the honour to be Chairman. I would recommend him and other members to read that report carefully, because that report was a carefully drafted document. It was not by any means a final report. It was a report to be considered firstly by the Working Committee of the Congress, and secondly by the All-India Congress Committee. The report itself states that it is only a rough blue-print and that these matters will have to be considered by the Planning Commission which is recommended.

Certain other factors were laid down in it in regard to the nationalization of defence industries and key industries. Now, it is perfectly true that in so far as the National Congress is concerned, it accepted this principle about 17 years ago—the nationalization, ownership or control of defence and key industries and public utilities, and I do believe that such industries will have to be nationalized at some time or other. Then, again, the Congress in its various resolutions has also indicated that this process of nationalization should go a little further in other directions. But when you come down to giving effect to this, you have to think of which to choose first and how to do it without upsetting the present structure and without actually interfering with production.

Now, this document which I have referred to, issued by the Economic Programme Sub-committee of the Congress, has given rise to a great deal of criticism, or, in any event, to some criticism, on either side. Some people think it does not go far enough, and others think it is a revolutionary departure which will upset our economy, and that it is, in fact, a sudden jump to socialism. Of course, it is nothing of the kind either way. It is very far from socialism. It is the continuation of a process which is going on all over the world, including the capitalistic countries of the world, excepting perhaps the biggest of them all, the United States of America. In other countries, you will see this process going on in some places, and in some, faster than in other countries. This report merely indicates a strong tendency towards socialism, with certain industries earmarked for earlier socialization than others, and even in this report, it is stated definitely that every step should be taken so as not to interfere with production.

I should just like to read to the House one or two passages from it. First, "It is emphasized that the report is not a blue-print, but an outline programme, the details of which will have to be filled in by the Permanent Planning Commission which has been recommended." Then, it referred to definite and key industries, and here again, may I say, the use of the word 'key' industry is very vague. Opinions may differ as to what is a key industry, whether we are referring to a few or many. Deliberately it has been left vague, because the stage of defining these industries will come later, when the matter is considered by the Standing Committee. Quite apart from defining them, the question of nationalizing them, and the timing of it, would also depend on the Commission or whatever authority that might have to consider the problem.

There is another matter which has been referred to in this report. We have specifically stated that, apart from certain obvious industries of vital importance, we consider that the State should nationalize or start nationalizing new industries of a particular type, that is to say, we should not waste our resources at the present moment in trying to nationalize existing industries, except where it is absolutely necessary, but rather conserve our resources and start new industries.

I thought that a very sound principle, because, after all, whatever we may do will have to be limited by our own resources. We have to choose which to take up first. If we squander our resources in merely acquiring for the State existing industries (that we have acquired them may be for the nation's good), for the moment we may have no other resources left, and we would have spoiled the field for private enterprise too. So it is far better for the State to concentrate on certain specific vital new industries than to go about nationalizing many of the old ones, though, as I said, in the case of some specific vital industry of national importance, that might be done.

This has many advantages, one advantage being, as I said, that the State's resources are applied to new industries, according to the requirements of production, without interfering with the existing apparatus except where it is absolutely necessary. All the work that the State would do would be to add constructively to production rather than merely effect a change over. After a period (which is hinted at in this report), after five years or so, the State may reconsider the problem and see what else it can do, how far it can go.

Now, what is the point in putting in this five year period? As a matter of fact, whatever period might be put in has little significance in the present changing dynamic world. One does not know, and I doubt if any member of this House can say, what will happen in India two years hence or three years hence, either in the political or economic domain, so that putting down any time table or programme does not help much, except that it gives us something to aim at.

Why five years was the time put down was really to give a kind of assurance to those who might be somewhat put out by the prospect of these changes, that is to say, that we are not going to upset existing things, we are leaving them as they are more or less, but that we are enlarging the domain in other fields, more or less specified fields, so that there may be no grievance that something is done which upsets the existing structure.

I have been surprised to read criticisms of this rough outline report, criticisms from industrial magnates and others, because I thought that this report had carefully considered many of the problems that face the country, even from the point of view of industrialists and others. We had provided for many of those things, maybe some things had to be overlooked which can be considered later, but generally speaking, we had carefully provided that there should be no sudden change which might upset the present structure without its being replaced.

After this report was drawn up, this House decided on the nationalization of the Reserve Bank and the Imperial Bank of India. Changes go on taking place in that way. It may be that if we merely talk in terms of big changes all over the place, the result would be no change at all, because that would be merely a paper decision, which could not easily be given effect to. Therefore, I submit that the proper way of dealing with this matter is not to pass a Resolution of this kind, but to consider it carefully in the context of what can be done, the general policy being laid down, the general outlook, or if you like, the general objective. The ultimate objective may not have to be reconsidered, but many of the things leading up to it may have to be reconsidered from time to time, because, meanwhile, all manner of changes are taking place.

For instance, if I may put one aspect of the case before the House, I think that the progress of technology and of science is so enormous and so rapid, that within a fairly short space of time, let us say, 15 years, the whole conception of modern industry will have changed completely. New sources of power will be discovered and those sources of power will upset the methods of production that exist today, much more so than the Industrial Revolution did 150 years ago in England and in the rest of Europe.

All these enormous changes are going to take place and I find that many of us, whether we call ourselves socialists, communists or capitalists or by any other name, are singularly unaware of the big changes that are taking place. They are so unaware of this that they think merely in terms, not of the greater wealth coming into existence by fresh methods, but rather only of changing the ownership of industry, which, of course, may be important from the point of view of advancing towards equality.

Distribution is most important, but what is far more important is the dynamic future. In the changed situation all over the world, new sources of power might completely revolutionize our agriculture as well as our industry. Therefore, what I think is most important for the State is that whatever may happen to the existing sources of production, these new and novel sources of production should always remain in the hands of the State. We should not allow them to go into private hands and thus become private monopolies. And in regard to the existing sources, we should proceed step by step, and avoid any drop in production or disturbance of the economic structure, as far as possible.

The House knows that we have a large number of big schemes or projects dealing with the river valleys. These schemes deal with the construction of big reservoirs, hydro-electric works, irrigation canals, prevention of erosion and prevention of malaria and so on and so forth. These schemes are going to require a vast deal of money and by far the most important thing is that they will be the basis of all future growth. They will go a long way to solve our food problem, to provide that power which is essential for industrial growth. Once you have that power you can go ahead pretty fast. So the Government decided to concentrate on the rapid development of these river valley schemes and not to fritter away their energy on temporary expedients here and there. If we are going to concentrate on these big schemes, are we going to divert our energy from them by acquiring this or that little industry which may make only some or no difference at all, which will create upsets here and there and not lead to that basic foundation on which all industry should rest in the future?

Therefore, even from the point of view of socialization, we should proceed with the foundations first, lay them down, have a system of priorities and timing, take over a sector of the national economy and socialize it only when the time is ripe for it. When the time will be ripe, I cannot say. We require not only money, but, what is far more important, trained human material.

In fact, in the ultimate analysis, that is the only essential thing whether it concerns industrial or any other department of life. Let us admit, we do not possess a sufficient quantity of that trained human material in any field of life in India today. We have produced very high class persons in every department of life—in science, in industry. We have some of the finest scientists in the world. Nevertheless, they are few. They are not enough. The House may remember that the Government appointed a Scientific Manpower Committee a little time ago, because we attach the greatest importance to using the scientific manpower we have, to increasing it and rapidly augmenting it. That Committee reported and its report was considered by the Government. Many of its recommendations were adopted. We are trying our best to increase our technical and other personnel by sending people abroad, and getting people from abroad to come here to teach our students here. All this is the real basis, the foundation, that is being laid down for future progress, and the other, if I may use the word, theoretical and doctrinaire approach, stating that we are going to make these big changes, does not help us much. On the other hand, it gives a completely wrong picture to the people, who do not realize what is to be done, what preparations have to be made, before the various steps can be taken. Therefore, I submit that a Resolution of this kind will not be helpful at all. I hope that some time during this session, if it is possible, we may come up before this House with certain specific proposal or statements of policy in regard to the industrial programme. Naturally, whatever programme we may adopt would have to have the sanction of this House.

To refer back to the Congress sub-committee's report, naturally, if any programme, economic or other, receives the final sanction of the All-India Congress Committee, and that Committee calls for that programme to be adopted, most of us in this House are bound by that mandate. The final authority, no doubt, is this House for any programme that has to be adopted, but most of us are bound by any programme definitely and precisely put forward by the All-India Congress Committee, and we shall have to place it before this House for adoption. But the All-India Congress Committee, after all, is not an executive body: at the most it is a policy-laying body. It will lay down the general policy, again, naturally, leaving it to this House or to the Government to time it as it thinks expedient, to give certain priorities and to go ahead with it at a pace which may be considered right and proper.

The House knows that in regard to the land system, our general policy has been to put an end to what is called the zamindari system. The pace has been slow, not due to any lack of effort, but because all manner of difficulties have cropped up. Still, I hope that the matter will be gone through fairly soon. That again is one of the foundations on which we can build every thing else. There has been talk about collective and co-operative farming. I should like to have collective and co-operative farming in this country. I hope that, in any event, if not on a large scale, at least on a small scale, we shall begin soon with co-operatives, and, maybe with collectives. But it is obvious that before you can think of them, you have to put an end to the present land system which prevails in the greater part of India—first of all the big zamindari system, then maybe other aspects of it—and that is not such an easy matter.

It is not a matter of a few, whom you might call capitalists, disliking it, but possibly a very large number of peasant proprietors disliking it. Obviously, whatever decision we may make must have the consent of a large number of people. We cannot force it down the throats of the vast majority of our peasants. We have to convert them. The best way to do that is to give them a living example in co-operatives, and show them how they will function: and then only can they be converted. India is a huge country. We may have various types of agricultural economy side by side, and gradually the one that is best suited to the land will prevail. Even in co-operatives, there are so many types. I cannot say immediately which is the most suitable : maybe that one type will be suitable in one part of the country and another in another part.

Finally, therefore, I would assure the House that as far as we are concerned, we are very anxious to draw up a particular statement of policy in regard to our industrial programme. I do not think at this stage that that statement will go very far into the future. It is risky to go far into the future. It is for non-official organizations to look far ahead into the future, but for a Government to commit itself to the long distance is not safe. I should like to assure others who may not be in the House that whatever we may do, we want to put production first. We think it most essential. Production obviously depends on a very great deal of co-operation between those people who are most concerned in production. Obviously, we want the goodwill of the industrialists of the country. The question is often asked, " Have you the personnel to nationalize industries? " Well, as I said just now, we have not enough. But the question rather surprises me, because it is the same personnel that has to be used whether industry is nationalized or not. The personnel which function in private industry will not leave the country when it is nationalized. It is the same personnel, including the captains of industry who will also be utilized because of their very special ability—managerial, executive, etc. Now, the point is that in any programme that we put forward, we must have the largest measure of goodwill. We must not allow it to affect production. At the same time, we must lay the foundations of future progress in the direction we aim at. That was the outlook with which we framed the sub-committee's report. That is a document for you and the country to consider. We paid very special attention to this so that we might not have a break, nor any big upsetting factor, but gradually, though nevertheless fairly quickly, a change over might be made in those sectors of economy which are most capable of bearing it to the national advantage, and then making other changes. I would therefore beg the Honourable Member not to press a Resolution which on the face of it cannot be given effect to.

THE ONLY RIGHT APPROACH

SIR, I must apologize to the House for not having been present here throughout this debate, but sometimes the claims of other work are heavy. I would have liked to be here throughout, because I am vastly interested in this subject, and I should have liked to hear what members had to say. I understand that many of the members have commended this Resolution and spoken in praise of it or in favour of it at least. Some have not liked it and some have disliked it intensely. I am glad of that difference of opinion, and I am sorry if any one of the Honourable Members should feel that he should suppress his own opinion on such a vital matter because of some Whip or some other direction of the Party executive.

I have myself been concerned with the theoretical aspects of planning for a considerable time. I realize that there is a great deal of difference between its theory and practice; as in almost everything in life, the theory is full of poetry as, if I may say so, was the speech of my honourable colleague, the Mover of the Resolution, but when we come down to applying that poetry, all kinds of difficulties crop up. Normally, there would be those difficulties, but as we are situated today in India, after all that has happened in the course of the last seven or eight months, one has to be very careful of the steps one takes so as not to injure the existing structure too much. There has been destruction and injury enough, and certainly I confess to this House that I am not brave and gallant enough to go about destroying any more. I think there is room still for the destruction in India of many things—they will no doubt have to be removed; nevertheless, it is a matter of approach. Are we going to adopt the course of having a clean slate or sweeping away everything so that we may have the pleasure of writing anew, without anything else being written on that slate? That seems to be an easy way of doing things, though perhaps there never has been a clean slate even when

A speech delivered at the Constituent Assembly (Legislative), New Delhi, during the debate on the Industrial Policy Resolution moved by the Hon'ble Dr. Syama Prasad Mookerjee, Minister for Industry and Supply, April 7, 1948.

people imagined that there was going to be a clean slate.

I will not say that one should never try to start with a clean slate. But one has to think of a country and its condition at the time, and see which is the preferable course, which involves less danger. It seems to me that in the state of affairs in the world today and in India, any attempt to start with what might be called a clean slate, that is to say, a sweeping away of all that we have, would certainly not bring progress nearer, but might delay it tremendously. Far from bringing economic progress, it might put us so far back politically that the economic aspect itself might be lost sight of. We cannot separate these two things. We have gone through big political upheavals and cataclysms, and if in our attempt to get something that we liked, to go forward a step in one direction, we lose a few steps in another, then on balance we have lost, not gained. Therefore, the alternative to having a clean slate is to try to rub out here and there in order to write on it again, gradually to replace the writing on the whole slate—not too gradually, I hope, yet not with a great measure of destruction and strain. Maybe I have been affected by recent events, but more and more I have felt that it is wrong to destroy something that is productive or capable of doing good. It takes a long time to build and it does not take very long to destroy, so that if this House and this country think that we should go ahead in a much more constructive spirit than in a destructive spirit, then that approach has necessarily to be different. What your ideals may be is another matter, but even in the realization of those ideals, do you think that the easiest way of approach will be a clean sweep and then starting anew, or to replace as rapidly as possible and as fast as you can, with your available resources and material, the existing structure with a new one? I have no doubt that we have to change the existing structure, and as rapidly as possible.

I was listening to the Honourable Member who spoke before me ; I was listening to his laments on the burdens that are put on industry, on taxation and on this and that. The fact of the matter is that that lament is based on a certain view of the world which, I fear, cannot possibly return. I am not thinking in idealistic terms but just practical terms ; you cannot have it back. There are going to be greater burdens on industry, because the State itself is burdened so much with its social problems ; it has to solve them or cease to be a socialist State, and might well become a police State, or some other State might take its place. It has to face its problems, and if it is to do that, it must necessarily obtain the wherewithal to face these problems, and the burden on industry becomes greater and greater. In fact, not because you think or I think or anybody thinks so, inevitably the trend of events is to make the State more and more the organizer of constructive industry, and not the private capitalist or any one else. This is quite inevitable as far as I can see objectively. I do not rule out entirely the profit motive ; I do not know how long it will last in a limited sense, but in the larger sense of the term it will come more and more into conflict with the new idea of the socialist State. That conflict will go on, and one must survive, and it is clear that the State will survive, not that group which represents the profit motive in industry in its pure essence. That is an inevitable development. How are you to face that development? Are you then to try again to accelerate it as many of us would like to do, because quite apart from the economic aspect, the expert aspect, we have arrived at a stage which, I trust, every sensitive man feels. Sensitive people today cannot easily put up with the vast gap between human beings, the distance between them, the difference between them, the lack of opportunities on the one side and the waste on the other. It seems so vulgar, and vulgarity is the worst thing for a country or individual to support. It was not, if I may say so, so vulgar 50 or 100 years ago. Although the profit motive was at work very strongly and although there was probably greater suffering then, nevertheless, the approach was different. Perhaps, the sense of social values was different. But, in the context of the world today, such a motive is becoming increasingly not only wrong from the economic point of view, but a vulgar thing from any sensitive point of view. So changes are bound to come.

How then are you going to bring about these changes? As I said, I would much rather bring them about without deliberate destruction and obstruction, because destruction and obstruction, whatever the future may bring after them, must undoubtedly lead to a stoppage of growth at present. They stop production. They stop the production of wealth. One has the satisfaction of being able to do something afterwards more rapidly, no doubt, but it is not certain that afterwards you will be able to do it so rapidly. One has, therefore, to compromise. Although I hate the word compromise in this context or in any context, one cannot avoid it.

That brings us to a transitional stage of economy. Call it what you like—mixed economy or some thing else. It brings us to doing things in such a way as continually to add to the wealth of the country, as well as to lead to a more equitable distribution of that wealth in the country. Gradually we arrive at a stage when the centre of gravity of the whole economy has shifted. Now, I rather doubt myself whether it is possible without a conflict or without repeated conflicts to bring about these changes, because people who are used to possessing certain interests or certain ideas do not easily accept new ideas, and nobody likes to give up what he has; at least no groups like it; individuals sometimes do. These conflicts are continually arising, but the point is that even those conflicts are rather foolish conflicts, if I may say so, because they cannot reverse the trend of events. They may delay the process, and in delaying the result probably is that those who hold on to the vested interests get a worse bargain at the end.

Now, there is another aspect which I should like the House to consider. It is an odd thing that many of our most ardent revolutionaries, who think in terms of an idealistic world, are quite extraordinarily conservative in their scientific approach to the world's problems. If I may explain myself, I have used the word 'scientific' in its narrow sense. Most of our friends— socialists or communists—continually think in terms of the technique of production remaining as it is. Of course, they will not admit it. They will say, "No, it is changing." But, in fact, they base their programmes more or less on a static world and not on a continually changing world with new methods of production, new techniques of production. They think in terms, for instance, of changing the land system. Quite right, because the fundamental thing is that the feudal land system must go before you can build another society. So far, so good. Change the land system. They think in terms of acquiring the industries, because a socialist economy means that big industries should be owned by the State. Well, quite good. But they do not think so much in terms of the vast changes in productive methods that are taking place which may render the present industrial apparatus, or the methods adopted in the cultivation of the land, completely obsolete. They say, "Why don't you acquire this

or that?" Spend vast sums of money over acquiring things which
are 90% obsolete? In fact, from the point of view of technological
advance, it may well be a complete waste of money to acquire
such obsolete machinery, factories and other installations. It is
true that they are useful so long as new factories and new technological methods are not introduced, and if you have a vast quantity
of money and resources, certainly acquire them and go ahead
with other things. But if you have limited resources, then the
main thing to do is not to think in terms of static technology,
but to think in terms of changing technology, of the State acquiring the new processes, the new changes, and not the old, except
when the old obstructs, when the old hampers your planning
and progress.

Now, obviously, situated as we are in India, our resources are
not unlimited. We have to think hard where to get the money,
how to get the money, how to get the other resources—technical
and other. If this is so, there has to be a certain system of
priorities about the work we are to do. Even if you start acquiring things—suppose we decide to acquire a large number of industries—and you pass this Resolution, I am quite sure when we
actually work it out in practice, it will take a good deal of time to
acquire them one by one. However rapidly you may do so, it will
take a little time, unless, of course, it is by the process of the
" clean slate ", where you sweep the old thing away and build a
new one on it. Therefore, you have to think in terms of priorities:
which industry must come first and which service ; after that
you must provide the money ; provide the organization ; provide
the technical personnel, etc., etc. So it takes time. Much more
so when you have to think in terms of additional industry and
new industry, new schemes plus old schemes. I have no doubt
in my mind that the priority for the State enterprises must be
in terms of new things as far as possible unless the old things
come in the way.

I attach the greatest importance today to, let us say, the great
river valley projects and schemes that have been framed, the first
one of which, the Damodar Valley scheme, has passed through
this Legislature, and others are coming soon. I think they are far
more important than almost all your existing industries. Here is
something new that you are building out of nothing ; new land
brought into cultivation, many new things which you are creating out of the enormous power of the river valley project. Now,

I want that to be completely State-controlled, but run, as is stated in this Resolution, on the model of public corporation. I do hope that this public corporation is not going to be a departmentally-run organization, but a wholly or partly independent organization. I do hope that it is not going to be run by people who have worked in the ruts of the Departments, but by persons of vision, push and drive ; not by people who write on the files but who do the work. Now, regarding these vast river valley schemes, all the resources of India are not enough to push them through quickly. Am I going to allow these to remain undone and delay them and think in terms of acquiring a tramway system or something else here and there? Let the tramway system be acquired, if you like, but I do not want to give first priority to the tramway system or some such thing.

Now, in this Resolution which has been placed before you, various lists are given—list no. 1, no. 2, etc.—explaining what the Government has done and what it proposes to do. The river valley projects are mentioned rather casually. But remember what that casual mention means. It means that the State is undertaking vast enterprises all over the country which will govern the industry of this country, and all you have acquired will be secondary and minor. These river valley systems are controlled by the State and they will control the economy and industry of the country completely. If you get a grip of all these things, then the process will be swifter, but if we simply lay down fancy schemes, then we shall never come to grips with any particular part of them, then, in fact, we are not advancing at all except on paper and in theory. Therefore, from the poetry of rather vague planning in the air, we have to come down to the prose of the statement. Because it is a prosaic statement, there is very little poetry in it except the poetry of my honourable friend who made the speech at the beginning. It is definitely a prosaic statement ; it is meant to be a prosaic statement ; the House knows it is not difficult to put in fine flourishes of language in a Resolution of this kind, which would have sounded so nice for the public and which would, without any commitment, have pleased the ear and the eye and produced a general impression of how fine we are. Well, we have very deliberately not done so, because we wanted to make it a prosaic statement of what we think we ought to do, and what we can do in the relatively near future. How much we do depends upon this House and a multitude of factors, but, at any rate, this is a thing which is meant to be done, not a thing which is meant to be flourished as a kind of organized programme before the public.

The tempo will depend on so many factors. I mentioned these river valley schemes, because I attach the greatest importance to them. Now, suppose the Damodar Valley scheme is a thundering success and we are responsible for it, then it is a bigger thing from the State's point of view or the industrialization point of view than the fact that this House has passed half a dozen other schemes which are not carried out. So, it is the first step that counts. If we start an industry under State auspices, let us make it a thorough success instead of trying to acquire this and that and making a mess of many things. Of course, once you have laid a good foundation, it will be easy for you to go ahead. Now, it is obvious that this Government or this House may pass this Resolution, may lay down the periods of time for what is to happen five or ten or fifteen years hence, but the fact of the matter is that we are living in an age of very swift change and transition, and nobody can guarantee what will happen and when it will happen ; nobody can guarantee whether there will be war or peace and nobody can guarantee what will happen even if there is peace because things change rapidly in India. We have lived during the last eight months in a state of rapid change, and very undesirable and unhealthy a change it has been in many respects. Nevertheless, when we say ten years, we mean it, that is how we see things at present,—and we say ten years because as far as we can see, the State's hands will be completely full. It is not merely to give an assurance, although we wish to give an assurance to all working industries so that they may be able to function properly, but fundamentally we have enough to do and we want to do it thoroughly ; but whether I give an assurance or the House gives it, ultimately events will determine the pace. Events may go faster or slower ; events may break up our economy or something may happen, not only that, but a hundred and one things may happen.

When we are told—and I suppose it is a fact—that capital is shy and it does not come in readily ; that we cannot find capital for private industry or public loans, etc., it is a fact. Well, that too I imagine is due more to these changing conditions than to anything that we might do or might not do. It is obvious that the country cannot stand aside. Either we give a fair field and a fair chance to the industrialist to go ahead, or if he does not, we go ahead without him. We cannot see things mismanaged or just not managed because he is afraid that he will not have enough profit or something might happen. People cannot wait. We give a fair chance, a fair field and a fair profit and if he does not do his utmost, somebody else has to do it ; there cannot be a vacuum. Also if industries are mismanaged, or not managed, or slowed down or stopped, again we have to consider what to do with them, because the day has passed when industry simply stopped or did not function, because somebody misbehaved, either an employer or Labour—and the whole community suffered. The community cannot afford to suffer, the community must see that it gives a fair deal to Labour, which is a different matter. Therefore, in this Resolution a great deal has been said about it and that is perhaps one of the most important parts of the Resolution, namely, regarding councils and committees, because unless you give a completely fair deal to Labour you cannot come down with a heavy hand in case of misbehaviour. After that you may have people still misbehaving, so that I should like this House to consider this Resolution in this context. I have not touched on the various subjects which might be added. I have no doubt that if the House sat down, it could make some changes in it, but I do submit that the fundamental approach of this statement is the only right approach and the only practical approach at the present time and I hope the House will adopt it.

WE SHOULD PULL TOGETHER

MR. PRESIDENT, and members of the Federation, yesterday in your presidential address you touched upon a variety of problems ; you referred to events in foreign countries and to domestic problems, more especially those affecting the trade, commerce, and industry of this country. I am sorry I was not present to hear that address, but I read it and tried to profit by the reading. You will not expect me to say something on everything that you said, because that would be a complicated story, but I would with your permission, like to say something about certain broad approaches to those problems of ours.

May I just repeat, first of all, a little of what I just said in Hindustani? It is this that while it is very comforting to me to be addressed as you addressed me a little while ago in terms of praise and affection and confidence, nevertheless, I have a feeling, when I come to such gatherings as this, that I am treated, and my Government is treated, as if we were prisoners in the dock. All our faults and errors, failings and deficiences are placed before us pointedly, not merely placed before us, but sometimes even a hint is given that although we are past redemption, nevertheless, the duty has to be performed. That does not happen merely in such gatherings as this, but even in the Assembly Chamber—even colleagues of ours do this, not opponents. Well, I welcome criticism and I welcome your pointing out all our failings—particularly my failings ; in fact, sometimes I recount them myself. I think it is good for an individual and for a nation always to try to find where it is going wrong and to correct itself. Never be afraid of criticism. I welcome criticism. I do not welcome it quite so much if behind that criticism there is an imputation of *mala fides* on our part. Naturally, nobody likes that. But I find this kind of criticism in whatever type of gathering I attend except one of which I shall tell you later; we are criticized by the captains of industry—industrialists—and commercial magnates and the like. We are criticized by the leaders of labour for suppressing them. We are criticized by the refugees

A speech delivered at the meeting of the Federation of Indian Chambers of Commerce and Industry (22nd Annual Session), New Delhi, March 4, 1949.

or displaced persons for not doing enough for them. We are criticized by Provincial Governments for not helping them. We are criticized for not doing this, for not doing that. We are criticized for not being economical enough, for not reducing the bloated staff in the Secretariat. We are criticized for retrenchment and we are criticized in a variety of other ways. Our foreign policy is criticized ; our domestic policy is criticized. If controls are established, we are criticized ; if decontrol is established, we are criticized. Now, that, I take it, is in some measure a healthy sign. I said that I was not criticized in one type of gathering, that is gatherings of the common people of this country. They do not criticize me and I would like you to spend a moment of thought on this. We, as a Government, are existing today because those people have faith in us. I would not be there, for instance, if I had the suspicion that the people of India—the common men of India—did not have faith in us. And it is because of their affection that we are shouldering the burden and you know very well that that burden is not a light burden ; no pleasant burden. Nevertheless, we are shouldering it partly because we think it is our duty to carry on this work till such time as we have completed another stage of it ; till such time as we can hand it over to others stronger and more worthy to shoulder the burden; but in the main because we have the sense of the confidence of the vast majority of the Indian people. Now, criticism, as I said, is welcome. But when we are criticized by friends or by opponents, what exactly should our approach be to this or that problem of India? It seems to me that we have not yet adjusted ourselves to changing conditions sufficiently. When I say " we ", I include all kinds and groups of people in this country, both industrialists and workers, merchants and politicians like me, Congressmen and others. We have not brought our minds into line, in tune with the world as it is. It is a frightfully difficult task to do so, because swift as thought is, the mind lags behind events and in a period of transition such as the one through which we have been passing and through which we are still passing, minds and men's thoughts lag behind events. Most of us have fashioned our thinking—whether it is political thinking or economic thinking—in terms of the India that existed some years ago, certainly before this change over took place in India. We have fashioned our approach to political action also in terms of a past which is not so very distant. We do not realize that things have changed in the world on account of many things, but chiefly on account of the last great war. Tremendous changes have taken place. Tremendous changes—as you all know and as you yourself referred to in your address yesterday—are taking place in various parts of Asia, China, Burma, Indonesia and other places. Now, if the world has changed so much, surely, it should affect our thinking and we should try to understand and adapt ourselves to those changes. Now, our approach to problems here used to be the undiluted criticism of the Government. That was the British Government at the time. It was—and rightly so—an agitational approach, because our first duty then was to upset, to remove and drive that Government away and to have our own Government here. So we fought and struggled and ultimately succeeded. Now, obviously that approach is not in keeping with the present situation in India. Nevertheless, most of us are still under the influence of that approach. We cannot get rid of it. I find most of my colleagues in the Assembly can only function in that way. They cannot function in any other way They are very dear colleagues and all that, but it is rather distressing to find in them a lack of appreciation of changing conditions. If a country or a people do not understand things as they are, then those things run away without them, or in spite of them. You cannot conquer events or control events or affect the course of events unless you understand them thoroughly.

Now, you—many of you are experts in your own field of activity and, no doubt, you analyze events fairly carefully, probably more than many other people do, and bring all your experience to bear upon an understanding of those events. Nevertheless, it is quite possible that the premises with which you start are not always quite correct, although the logic and the reasoning may be correct. It may be that the basis of your thought may be something that is no longer relevant. Maybe, you are thinking in static terms and not in terms of the dynamic world of today. So, because of this fact, there is, I feel, a tremendous unreality in the mental atmosphere of India today whether I talk to you or to Labour or to anybody else. As I am sitting here, a member of your Federation who was moving or supporting a Resolution finished up by saying something about the practical approach to things, because, of course, industrialists and businessmen take pride in being practical ; politicians also talk of being practical. What amazes me, however, is that these men whose God is ' being practical ' are sometimes most amazingly ignorant of men, of what is happening around. Their idea of being practical is to imagine that the world never changes and follow something that they and their forefathers have done in the past ; that is being practical, just as, if I may refer to the class to whom I might be said to belong, the politicians are very hard-headed and practical men too. Being hard-headed and practical, people force them to bring about a huge war in the world ; and dealing with terrific problems they work hard and earnestly, fail to solve them and then have another war and create more problems and so on. So the cycle goes on and we are all trying to be practical. Now, surely, there is something wrong about this approach to things. So I have become a little weary of people who call themselves practical and hard-headed. That hard-headedness often represents a complete lack of resilience. Take another thing. In looking at either the foreign or domestic spheres today, the thing that every person knows is that things are inter-related. You cannot isolate them today ; you cannot consider the problem of India as if it were unrelated to the problems of the world either politically or economically. This involves our understanding of what is happening in other parts of the world. It is not an easy matter, because in other parts of the world there is also the same worship of what is considered practical, with the result that people continue to follow paths which have demonstrably led to disaster in the past. I should have said that while it may be difficult to be wise at the right time, surely it does not require too much wisdom to avoid doing something which has led to disaster in the past. Oddly enough, we have not done that. The point is that we continue to pursue a path knowing full well that it will lead to disaster. Now, if it is true that we have completely lost all sense of wisdom and are in the grip of something in the nature of a great tragedy, an inevitable catastrophe, then what we must do is to face the disaster and catastrophe with a certain dignity. Or else there is some way out and we should look for it and seek that way, though it may not bring the best results. Now, looking at India, the complexity of the problems we have here—and we have had a multitude of them, each one of them a major problem—and looking at the past year and a half or more during which this Government has been functioning, I am conscious of so many things that we have done badly, so many things that we wanted to do and yet have not done ; we put before ourselves rather high ideals and we have failed to achieve them in the measure we had expected. That is perfectly true. Nevertheless, speaking quite deliberately as Prime Minister of this great country and as representative of my Government, I say to you that I have not come here with a note of apology from the Government to you, I am proud of what my Government has done, and I think we have faced our problems with courage, without excitement, problems which might have baffled many a Government and many a people. It is true that we have committed errors and mistakes. But if you take an overall view of the country, whether in foreign relations or in the domestic sphere, and for the moment if you turn your eyes away from the numerous eddies, whirlpools and stagnant waters, you will see the main tide advancing and advancing pretty rapidly. I have not a shadow of doubt that this country is advancing and will advance rapidly in the future. There are many people in this country whose chief business, it seems to me, is to run down their country, to run down their people, to run down the Government, to run down almost everything. I said, I do not mind criticism, however strong, however persistent. We want criticism; we want opposition if you like, I do not mind that. But I do mind this spirit of excessive pessimism, and, if I may use the word, this croaking about India's future. It is folly to be merely optimistic and not to see facts as they are. But it is at least as great a folly to be pessimistic and imagine all kinds of evil happenings over-taking us. So, in spite of the burdens that we have had to face and in spite, if I may say so, of the criticism that overwhelms us, I am in good heart when I think of India and of its future. This does not mean that we should take a complacent attitude. Nothing could be more foolish. We have big problems before us and we have to work very hard to solve them, but if we have to solve these big problems in a democratic way, it requires a very large measure of co-operation between the Government and the people; between the Central and the Provincial Governments; between all classes and groups of people in India. It requires faith in ourselves and in the work ahead of us and in our country. It requires, as I said, criticism certainly, but not the type of criticism which is meant to hinder, but the type of criticism which is meant to help and construct. We must change our old approach, and bring a new and more vital approach to the understanding of our problems.

Now, I just want to ask you another and a very difficult question that always faces me and my Government. We were born and bred, if I may say so, politically in the Gandhian doctrine. We did not adopt Gandhiji's views wholly either in regard to non-violence or in regard to economics. Nevertheless, we accepted many of them as suited to our country—and maybe suited to the world in some ways, if not a hundred per cent, but in a large measure. Now, imagine a people who had carried through their struggle for freedom, trying always to adhere to peaceful methods, having to face an extremity of violence and having to face the armed might of the State. Now, it was no pleasure to us to do so and it brought great problems and conflicts in our minds. We were responsible, as a Government, for peace and order in the country and if we did not maintain peace and order there was danger of the whole country going to pieces. We dared not give up that responsibility or act otherwise. In our minds, however, there was always this conflict and feeling that we were hypocritical in talking about those great doctrines that Gandhiji had taught us. We talked of Gandhiji and then proved false to him at every step. It was a painful thought. The facts as they were in the country compelled us to act in a particular way. I do not know whether it would have been better if we had acted differently. We acted according to our wisdom, not at any time denying the validity or truth of the message that Gandhiji gave us, at the same time doing something which we thought was imperative. Now, that problem comes up again and again in its varying phases. Here we are committed to civil liberty in its broadest form. There can be no freedom in a country without a wide extension of civil liberties. We are also interning people without trial in large numbers and some of our Provincial Governments are passing legislation of a kind to which we took the greatest objection in the old days. It is an irony of fate that we have to do this. Yet, we have done it and done it after full thought, not casually, because the matter was of the most serious concern to us. Now, what are we to do about it? People come to us complaining about civil liberty and they find a certain answering echo in our minds. The fact is that if we do not act, something infinitely worse takes place in the country

—chaos and disorder. Not chaos and disorder only, for you know that brutal murders have taken place in some parts of the country, and if there is one thing that this Government cannot possibly permit as long as it calls itself a government or has a semblance of authority, it is deliberate murder and sabotage that any group may indulge in. I do not mind the preaching of any doctrine, provided there is no violence in it. I do not think any interpretation of civil liberty includes the preaching of violence or acts of violence. And in the past year and a half in this country we have had to deal with various phases of intensive violence whether it came in the early days of August, September and October in the Punjab or Delhi, or whether it came subsequently from communal organizations or from certain labour bodies and a good deal from certain sections of the Communist Party of India, at first chiefly in and around Hyderabad—on both sides of the Hyderabad border—in West Bengal and elsewhere. Now, I want to make it perfectly clear that it still remains our conception of civil liberty that we should allow the fullest freedom to people of all groups to preach their doctrines, provided there are no incitements to violence. It just does not matter whether we agree with that doctrine or not ; if it does not lead to violence, we shall allow it to be preached. But if it does, if it is meant to lead to violence or sabotage, then it will not be allowed and if it is necessary to limit civil liberty for that purpose, civil liberty will be limited. There is no other way. You know of the horror that took place in Calcutta only a few days ago. It is not a question so much of a few persons killed—bad enough though it is ; we have become accustomed to death on a vast scale—but it was the manner that has upset me. What upset me was the feeling that people should deliberately indulge in that kind of thing. What is the background out of which this horror emerges? Why do our people, who normally speaking are gentle and kind to one another, develop this mentality and commit these horrible deeds?

Well, we must face all and must stop this kind of thing happening again however much it may involve putting into prison people with or without trial, because if this continues, then normal life of every kind stops. Only a number of gangsters survive and dominate and terrorize the community. We are not going to allow gangsterism to flourish in this country. Now, it is a great pity that this kind of thing should be associated in people's minds with Labour or the workers as such, because I am covinced that the workers of India, the labour force of India, is a fine labour force, a fine lot of people. Occasionally, they may get excited or be misled but properly approached they are fine material and after all it is out of this material that you are going to build India. You have to deal with that material and you have to deal with it fairly and justly. And what has pained me most is the association in people's minds that some of these horrible deeds are the outcome of what might be called labour work or trade union work. That will be fatal. Our Government has tried to encourage the organization of labour, trade unions and the like, because it is well known that from every point of view, it is better that Labour be properly organized, that it should have freedom to organize, freedom to deal with its own interests than that it should remain unorganized, unable to protect itself or to deliver the goods. So we have encouraged it. As you know, we have also passed legislation for the settlement of disputes, conciliation, etc., so that, as far as possible, strikes may be avoided. Many of you, perhaps, have objected to some of the legislation that we have passed. Yet, there is no alternative ; either you have strikes and major strikes or you have some machinery for the settlement of disputes. Obviously, the latter course is better, provided the machinery is a good machinery, is not meant to harass any party and is meant to see that justice and fairplay is effected. We are proceeding on those lines and we intend proceeding on those lines in spite of the misguided efforts of some workers and some employers. It is not good government to get excited over this and give up the cause when some people misbehave and punish vast numbers of others. That would be a very wrong thing to do. Nevertheless, we have to face the situation today which might lead certain people, certain unions and others affiliated to the Communist party, to indulge not only in strikes of the normal type, but something far worse —sabotage, destruction and disruption. Some days ago, I made a statement in the Assembly which you may have seen. Now, we are going to meet the situation and are going to put an end to this kind of business. Let there be no mistake about it. What troubles me is not our lack of ability to meet it, because we will meet it, we are strong enough to meet it, but that this kind of conflict leaves a trail of evil behind it, and ill-will ; a kind of impression spreads among other sections of the community that

the industrial workers or the railway workers of India are
to blame. But, as a matter of fact, the great majority of them
are decent folk who do not want to do anything of this kind.
But as far as this particular challenge is concerned, it has got to
be met and it will be met.

Now, if I may address you particularly, that is, the industrialists and those concerned with India's commerce, a great deal
of stress has been laid in the past year or two on the sensitiveness
of the investor, of the businessman, of the industrialist. He is
a frightfully delicate person, and if any wrong word is said or
some speech is delivered, his temperature goes up. The sensitiveness of the body or of the mind or of the spirit is as nothing
compared to the sensitiveness of the pocket. I should like you
just to think about it, of the talk that has taken place in the
last year or so, of how the groups which you represent so
well have been frightened by the budget or by something
else that has happened or by certain other measures taken or
not taken. All this has repeatedly been said and there is, no doubt,
some truth in it. I do believe you have been frightened. But do
you think it has redounded to your credit in the country to recount to all and sundry repeatedly that you are frightened by
what happens? May I tell you that instead of adding to your
credit, it has made people think that you are rather timid folk,
and no longer in your prime. When I say not in your prime,
I am not referring to your individual ages but rather to the fact
that—and this is a fundamental fact—the capitalists, industrialists, etc., in India are not big enough to face the problems of
the day or not quite big enough, and generally the idea is
spreading that their stature is rather small and that they get
frightened at the slightest upset and start complaining and
retiring into their shells and asking others to help them.
Now, you are entitled to seek help from the Government,
ask for it, but it is bad for you or for any group to give
the impression of this frailty and feebleness. After all, in the
world today, it is said that various ideologies, economic ideologies,
are in conflict. In the main, there are two—on the one side the
so-called capitalist ideology and on the other the so-called
communist or Soviet ideology. I think this is an extraordinarily
crude way of putting the question. It is a fact that they are
different economic approaches to the problem and each party is
convinced of the correctness of its own approach. But it does not

necessarily follow that you must have either this or that. There may be many intermediate ways. Now, you all know that capitalism or industrial capitalism that came into the world about 150 years or so ago had a big problem before it—the problem of production. It has solved that problem in theory, and largely in practice in many parts of the world. Therefore, industrial capitalism has been, in spite of everything, a tremendous success. It has solved the problem of production. Now, the other question arises: how far has it solved the other problems of the day? It is on its trial today—whether it can also solve the problem of distribution with equal success as it has solved the problem of production. If it cannot solve that problem, then some other way will have to be found. It is not a question of theory; of communism or socialism or capitalism. It is a question of hard fact. In India, if we do not ultimately solve the basic problems of our country—the problems of food, clothing, housing, etc., etc.—it does not matter whether we call ourselves capitalists, socialists, communists or anything else, if we fail to solve these problems, we will be swept away and somebody else will come in and try to solve them. So ultimately these major problems of the day are not going to be solved by argument or by war but by the method that succeeds in delivering the goods. Whatever the method may be, the method which delivers the goods and brings about the necessary change and gives satisfaction to the masses will justify itself and give hope. That method need not necessarily be an extreme method belonging to either of these two rival ideologies. It may be something in between. In fact, you find in the world today, in most countries there is an attempt to find other ways which certainly are completely divorced from the old style capitalism and which go towards what is normally called socialism. They are fast approaching it. It may be that in India also, we may be able to find some way more suited to the conditions of our people, some middle way. Therefore, I am not enamoured of these ' isms ' and my approach is, and I should like to say the country's approach should be, rather a phlegmatic approach in considering the problem and I want to forget the ' ism ' attached to it. Our problem today is to raise the standard of the masses, supply them with their needs, give them the where-withal to lead a decent life, to help them to progress and advance in life not only in regard to material things but in regard to cultural and spiritual things also. What will happen in the distant

future, I do not know, but I should like to set them on the right
road and I do not care what 'ism' it is that helps me to
set them on that road, provided I do it. And if one thing
fails, we will try another. We need not be dogmatic about this
or that approach. Anything that comes in the way has simply
to be ignored, or will be swept away. With all respect, I should
like to inform you that if your demands come in the way of the
good of the masses, your demands will be completely ignored.
Of course, they need not and should not, because your
interests are really tied up with their interests, but I do
object to your going about the country—and I say so in
your own interest—and talking about your demands and how
much your pocket has suffered. Forget your pocket and if
you cannot forget it, do not mention it. It goes against you.
So the only test should be whether it is good for the masses, and
no other.

Now, take another thing which seems to be almost like a red
rag to the proverbial bull—nationalization. What exactly does
that mean in the context of India? Sometime last year, I think,
I spoke on that subject. I forget if I addressed you also on the
subject, but I spoke in the Assembly. Other people have spoken
about it. The Deputy Prime Minister, the other day, said
something about it. People seem to imagine that the Government
is shifting from one policy to another and cannot make up its
mind. Well, as a matter of fact, there has been no doubt in the
Government's mind about the matter. There has not been even
the necessity for us to reconsider anything, because our mind was
quite clear about it. Our mind was clear, not because of certain
theories, though, of course, there is theory behind everything, but
essentially because of certain practical considerations. We think
that in India, as it is today—I will not talk about the world,
because each country has its own problems and has its own way
of approach—certain basic industries—the key industries—should
be under State control. Partly because it is dangerous for those
key and basic industries to be controlled by private interests and
for other reasons also, which I need not go into. As for the other
industries, they can be under private control, but remember again
that when a State plans its industrial or other development, planning itself involves a certain measure of control or direction from
the State. Otherwise there can be no planning. The Indian
National Congress, 17 years ago, laid down the policy of State

control of basic key industries or mother industries and certain other essential industries and services. Now, that is the initial approach to it. Secondly, what should be tackled immediately and what should be tackled later? In a statement on Industrial Policy, we mentioned certain things which we thought must be immediately undertaken by the State or nationalized—if you like to use the word—and for the rest we said, even in regard to certain basic and key industries, that we would not touch them for at least ten years, maybe more. It did not mean that we would necessarily touch them immediately after the 10-year period. Why did we say that? Not, to be perfectly frank with you, because of love for those who control those industries, but because our resources were limited. Because we were anxious to help in industrializing the country, we felt that the resources that we had would be far better used in starting new basic industries or new big schemes we have in view rather than in merely transferring the ownership of some industries from private hands to State control. So, on balance, we thought we would maintain those private industries and give them encouragement in every way. We do not know when we shall nationalize them, but in the meanwhile we want to build up a nationalized structure of new industries, apart from certain essential industries like defence, which must be nationalized anyhow. So it is a question of utilizing our resources to the best advantage and going ahead, in consultation with the people concerned, including representatives of commerce and industry and other interests, so that we may get the best value for our money and at the same time not upset things that are going on.

The Deputy Prime Minister said the other day in Madras or Hyderabad something to the effect that looking at our present resources, we were not just going to nationalize some of the things we had left out, because if we did we would stop development in the other sectors of our national economy. So, entirely from the practical point of view, as well as from the point of view of not upsetting anything which is working today and which we want to continue to work, we have arrived at this decision. Now, you and we and all of us, in fact, have to understand one another, and if you think that we are out to injure your interests, then, of course, co-operation is difficult. Or, if we think that you are out to play a lone hand and to injure our interests, our economy, not as individuals but the State, then there can be no co-operation, because there is lack of faith. Maybe we do not always agree but the fact is that, whether we agree or we do not agree, common sense should dictate that we should pull together. Otherwise, it is good for neither, and I want you to think about this, because you know very well that whatever the rights and wrongs of things may be, the industrialists and the commercial classes in India have become unpopular with the general mass of the people. They have become unpopular, because some people amongst them have not behaved rightly, have taken advantage of situations to obtain profit for themselves at an inordinate rate to the disadvantage of the community at large. That kind of behaviour on the part of perhaps a relatively small number has affected the whole of the commercial community. It has given it a bad name and I do not quite know how you can get rid of that bad name. But I say to you, make every effort to improve your reputation, because ultimately it is not through legislation or through Government protection that we can go very far in the production of goods but through the goodwill of the various parties concerned in that undertaking. If there is a certain feeling that the commercial community has not acted rightly towards the general public, something has got to be done in the nature of, if I may say so, *prayaschith**, and I am quite serious about it. It is a very serious matter that labour has misbehaved, in many places terribly, and the recent example in Calcutta is pretty bad. Now, we can criticize it, but it is one thing for labour to misbehave—after all they are not trained to high behaviour—it is quite another thing for persons who have to set a standard to others to misbehave. That is bad and that, again, gives an opportunity to labour to misbehave, because they see what others do and so the vicious circle continues. So I would like you to think of this and to see to it that the case you put to the public is one in which they do not see much self-interest, but see that you are acting for the community as you ask others to do, because after all we have to sink or swim together in India whether it is the labour force or the industrialists. It amazes me to see in India today people or groups who are out to create trouble and disaster and chaos that has nothing to do with any ' isms '. As far as I am concerned, I cannot imagine, that any communist, if he is honest and if he thinks in

---

* *i.e.*, expiation.

terms of India's future, can indulge in the activities that the Indian Community Party is indulging in today. It is immaterial, whether I agree or disagree with communism, but I say the activities of some groups in India today, regardless of the merits of the social theory they hold, have nothing to do with the future good of India. They are based on entirely extraneous considerations. They are based, I believe, on the deliberate object of creating chaos in India, out of which perhaps ultimately they hope something new may emerge. Now, this is a very curious approach, to ruin the running machine of India and, perhaps, waiting for a generation or two for something else to emerge. That is a thing which I am quite sure the people of India will never tolerate. We are up against certain groups who want chaos and disorder in India as they have created chaos and disorder in Burma and elsewhere. That has to be combated by all and that can only be combated, not if each group pulls in different ways and talks in terms of its own interest but in terms of the State or the general good.

Now, one thing about food. Food has become almost the basic problem for us today. Food is one of the things about which I think it can rightly be said that we have failed to deal with the situation. I think the very ease with which we have been able to get foodstuffs from abroad has rather prevented us from facing the problem properly. I think we should think in terms of not getting any food at all from abroad after a certain period —let us put it at two years, I should not add a day more, and just make up our mind that we shall live on the food that we produce after two years or die in the attempt. Now, I am quite convinced in my own mind that essentially, basically, the food problem of India is not a difficult problem. Somehow or other, we have made it difficult. After all, the deficit in food, I believe, now is about 6% or 7%. Now it may be 10%, because of bad seasons. Now, surely it should easily be possible, quite apart from the long-distance schemes, the schemes which will bear fruit after about five, six or ten years, it should be easily possible in the course of the next two years or so to make adjustments by increasing intensively our growth of food, by bringing fresh areas under cultivation or by a change of food habits, to fill this deficit of 7 to 8%, and that is how I should like both the Central Government and the Provincial Governments and the other agencies to act. It is no good our carrying on as at present, depending on vast quantities of food from outside and getting into greater difficulties.

I have taken a lot of your time and I have not perhaps referred to many of the points that the President referred to in his address. As you know, we are now discussing our Budget in Parliament. And that Budget, like many things that we do, is being fiercely attacked by all kinds of people. That Budget is essentially a cautious budget, a non-adventurous budget and a budget which has come out of our very able Finance Minister's mind after a great deal of thought. It is easy to criticize it, but I want to tell you that we have looked upon this problem deliberately with a view not to results today, but rather to results next year. It was easy enough for us to say or do things now which might have made this Government a little more popular. It was quite easy, but we had the courage not to seek popularity in that way. Instead we tried to lay the foundations for a big advance in the future. Whether that way of working is welcome to the public or not, I do not know, because people often prefer something good immediately to a future promise. But after all we, as a Government, have to think not of today but of tomorrow and the day after. We have to think of building up this great structure of India on firm foundations. We have tried to lay those firm foundations during the last year or two. But before we can even start laying those foundations, we met dragons on the way and we had to fight those dragons, and if not kill them, at least disable them. We have plenty of other wild animals to face. Nevertheless, the foundations of the India of the future are being laid today and we would be false to our own faith in that future if we imperilled it by doing something now which might be pleasing, but might not bear results tomorrow—the results that we seek. We are after all a kind of Caretaker Government waiting for the Indian Republic to come into existence in order to hand over the charge of India and we should like to hand over an India which has already achieved a measure of greatness and is rapidly advancing to higher fields and to a far greater status in every way, both domestically and internationally. JAI HIND.

ON INDIA'S FOREIGN POLICY

INDIA'S FOREIGN POLICY

SIR, I welcome this occasion. Although we are discussing this subject of foreign affairs not directly but by way of a cut motion, nevertheless, it is a novel occasion for this House and I think it is good that we realize what it conveys.

It means ultimately that we are entering into the international field, not only by going into conferences and the like, but by really putting international questions before the country, before this House for its decision. There is no immediate question before this House today. But undoubtedly as time goes on, the major international questions will have to be decided by this House.

Listening to the debate, to the speeches made by Honourable Members, I find, as was perhaps natural, that there was no immediate issue, no particular question for discussion, but rather pious hopes, vague ideals and sometimes a measure of, let us say, denunciation of things that had happened in the world. It has been a vague debate, with nothing pointed about it to which one could attach oneself. Many of the Honourable Members have been good enough to speak gently and generously of what has been done in the realm of foreign affairs on behalf of the Government of India during the past year. I am grateful to them, but may I say in reply that I am in complete disagreement with them?

I think the Government of India during the past year has not done what it should have done. That, perhaps, has not been so much the fault of the Government of India as such, but rather of circumstances. Anyway, what we had envisaged that we ought to do, we have not been able to do, largely because other circumstances arose in this country which have prevented its being done. We are not yet out of those difficulties, internal and other. We have not had a free hand in our external relations, and, therefore, I would beg the House to judge of this period in the context of what has been happening in this country, not only during the past unhappy three or four months, but in the

A speech delivered at the Constituent Assembly (Legislative), New Delhi, December 4, 1947.

This speech was made in reply to Prof. N. G. Ranga's cut motion for the reduction of the demand under the head "Ministry of External Affairs and Commonwealth Relations."

course of the past year when we lived in the middle of internal conflict and confusion which drained away our energy and did not leave us time to attend to other matters.

That has been the dominant feature of our politics during the past year and undoubtedly that has affected our foreign policy in the sense of our not giving enough time and energy to it. Nevertheless, I think we have advanced in that field. Again, it is difficult to say how you measure advance in such a field. My Honourable friend, Dr. Khare, was critical of various things, as he has every right to be, and his criticism took the shape of a written speech to which your attention, Sir, was not drawn! I was glad of the Honourable Dr. Khare's intrusion in this debate, because the debate was getting rather heavy and he brought a touch of comedy and humour into it as well as unreality. When the Honourable Member represented the Government in this House, it was a little difficult to attach much importance to what he said. I suppose now it is less difficult to do so, or a little more difficult to do so! So I will not venture to say anything or to reply to what he said because it seems to me totally inconsequential and without any meaning.

But coming to other subjects, the main subject in foreign policy today is vaguely talked of in terms of " Do you belong to this group or that group? " That is an utter simplification of issues and it is all very well for the Honourable Maulana to hold forth that India will go to war under this banner or that banner. But that surely is not the way that a responsible House or a responsible country views the situation.

We have proclaimed during this past year that we will not attach ourselves to any particular group. That has nothing to do with neutrality or passivity or anything else. If there is a big war, there is no particular reason why we should jump into it. Nevertheless, it is a little difficult nowadays in world wars to be neutral. Any person with any knowledge of international affairs knows that. The point is not what will happen when there is a war. Are we going to proclaim to the world, taking the advice of Maulana Hasrat Mohani, that when war comes, we stand by Russia? Is that his idea of foreign policy or any policy? That shows to me an amazing ignorance of how foreign affairs can be conducted. We are not going to join a war if we can help it: and we are going to join the side which is to our interest when the time comes to make the choice. There the matter ends.

But talking about foreign policies, the House must remember that these are not just empty struggles on a chess board. Behind them lie all manner of things. Ultimately, foreign policy is the outcome of economic policy, and until India has properly evolved her economic policy, her foreign policy will be rather vague, rather inchoate, and will be groping. It is well for us to say that we stand for peace and freedom and yet that does not convey much to anybody, except a pious hope. We do stand for peace and freedom. I think there is something to be said for it. There is some meaning when we say that we stand for the freedom of Asian countries and for the elimination of imperialistic control over them. There is some meaning in that.

Undoubtedly it has some substance, but a vague statement that we stand for peace and freedom by itself has no particular meaning, because every country is prepared to say the same thing, whether it means it or not. What then do we stand for? Well, you have to develop this argument in the economic field. As it happens today, in spite of the fact that we have been for sometime in authority as a Government, I regret that we have not produced any constructive economic scheme or economic policy so far. Again my excuse is that we have been going through such amazing times which have taken up all our energy and attention that it was difficult to do so. Nevertheless, we shall have to do so and when we do so, that will govern our foreign policy, more than all the speeches in this House.

We have sought to avoid foreign entanglements by not joining one bloc or the other. The natural result has been that neither of these big blocs looks on us with favour. They think that we are undependable, because we cannot be made to vote this way or that way.

Last year when our delegation went to the United Nations, it was the first time that a more or less independent delegation went from India. It was looked at a little askance. They did not know what it was going to do. When they found that we acted according to our own will, they did not like it. We were unpopular last year at the United Nations. I do not mean individually, but in regard to our policy. They could not quite make out what we were or what we were aiming at. There was a suspicion in the minds of the first group that we were really allied to the other group in secret, though we were trying to hide the fact, and the other group thought that we were allied to the first group in secret though we were trying to hide the fact.

This year there was a slight change in this attitude. We did many things which both the groups disliked, but the comprehension came to them that we were not really allied to either group, that we were trying to act according to our own lights and according to the merits of the dispute as they seemed to us. They did not like that, of course, because the position today is that there is so much passion and so much fear and suspicion of each other between these great rival Powers and groups that anybody who is not with them is considered against them. So they did not like what we did in many instances: nevertheless, they respected us much more, because they realized that we had an independent policy, that we were not going to be dragooned this way or that, that we might make a mistake just like anyone else, nevertheless, we were going to stick to our own policy and programme, so that while possibly we irritated some of our friends even a little more than last year, we got on much better with everybody, because they understood that we did stand for something.

To give the House an instance of how we acted, take the Palestine affair which has given rise and will give rise to a great deal of trouble. We took up a certain attitude in regard to it which was roughly a Federal State with autonomous parts. It was opposed to both the other attitudes which were before the United Nations. One was partition which has now been adopted: the other was a unitary state. We suggested a Federal State with, naturally, an Arab majority in charge of the Federal State but with autonomy for the other regions—Jewish regions.

After a great deal of thought we decided that this was not only a fair and equitable solution of the problem, but the only real solution of the problem. Any other solution would have meant fighting and conflict. Nevertheless, our solution—which as the House will remember was the solution given in the minority report of the Palestine Committee—did not find favour with most people in the United Nations. Some of the major Powers were out for partition; they, therefore, pressed for it and ultimately got it. Others were so keen on the unitary State idea and were so sure of preventing partition at any rate or preventing a two-thirds majority in favour of partition that they did not accept our suggestion.

When during the last few days somehow partition suddenly became inevitable and votes veered round to it, owing to the pressure of some of the great Powers, it was realized that the Indian solution was probably the best and an attempt was made in the last 48 hours to bring forward the Indian solution, not by us but by those who had wanted a unitary State.

It was then too late. There were procedural difficulties and many of the persons who might have accepted this solution had already pledged themselves to partition. And so ultimately partition was decided upon by a two-thirds majority, with a large number abstaining from voting, with the result again of trouble now and a great deal of trouble in the future in the Middle East.

I point this out to the House as an instance, that in spite of considerable difficulty and being told by many of our friends on either side that we must line up this way or that, we refused to do so and I have no doubt that the position we had taken was the right one and I still have no doubt that ours would have brought about the best solution.

This applies to many other things. But inevitably it means that to some extent we have to plough a lonely furrow in the United Nations and at international conferences of this type. Nonetheless, that is the only honourable and right position for us to take and I am quite sure that by adopting that position, we shall ultimately gain in national and international prestige, that is to say, when we take a long view of the situation, not a short view of getting immediately a vote here or there.

I have no doubt that fairly soon, in the course of two or three years, the world will find this attitude justified and that India will not only be respected by the major protagonists in the struggle for power, but a large number of the smaller nations which today are rather helpless will probably look to India more than to other countries for a lead in such matters.

May I in this connection say that during this last session of the United Nations General Assembly, many very difficult and very controversial issues were raised, and our delegation had to face extraordinarily intricate situations? I should like to pay a tribute to our delegation, especially to the leader of the delegation. The Honourable Members often put questions about the appointment of Ambassadors, members of delegations and the like and rightly so, because the House should be interested in such important appointments. May I say to the House that nothing is more difficult than to make these appointments, because they are not just appointments of able persons, but appointments of parti- cular persons to particular places where they must fit in, which is an extraordinarily difficult thing?

In the key places of the world the ideal Ambassador must be some kind of a superman. It is so difficult now not only to under- stand the intricacies,—that is not difficult,—but to remain friends with everybody and yet to advance your cause. After all we have in the past discussed foreign affairs from the outside, in other assemblies, or here perhaps, rather in an academic way, rather as in a college debating society. That is, we talked of high policies, but we did not come to grips with them when we had to say ' yes ' or ' no ' to a question and face the consequences.

If the House will forgive my saying so, even in today's debate many of the speeches were of an academic kind which did not take into account the vital questions which concern the world today, which may mean peace or war. But when the House does have to face the question and take a decision which may lead to war or peace, when one comes face to face with realities, then one cannot rely merely on idealistic principles.

Foreign affairs are utterly realistic today. A false step, a false phrase, makes all the difference. The first thing that an Ambassa- dor of ours has to learn is to shut his mouth and give up public or even private speaking. It is not a habit which we have develop- ed in our past careers—that of being completely silent. Yet this habit has to be developed, and in private one has to be silent lest what one says injures the cause of the nation, creates international ill-will.

It is in this background that I should like the House to consider international affairs—this realistic background, this notion that it is not merely some naughty men playing about and quarrel- ling with one another, some statesmen in America and the U.S. S.R. or British imperialism lurking behind the curtain in the dis- tance. We have talked so much about British imperialism that we cannot get rid of the habit.

To come to grips with the subject, in its economic, political and various other aspects, to try to understand it, is what ulti- mately matters. Whatever policy you may lay down, the art of conducting the foreign affairs of a country lies in finding out what

is most advantageous to the country. We may talk about international goodwill and mean what we say. We may talk about
peace and freedom and earnestly mean what we say. But in the
ultimate analysis, a government functions for the good of the
country it governs and no government dare do anything which
in the short or long run is manifestly to the disadvantage of that
country.

Therefore, whether a country is imperialistic or socialist or
communist, its Foreign Minister thinks primarily of the interests
of that country. But there is a difference, of course. Some people
may think of the interests of their country regardless of other
consequences, or take a short distance view. Others may think
that in the long-term policy the interest of another country is as
important to them as that of their own country. The interest of
peace is more important, because if war comes everyone suffers,
so that in the long distance view, self-interest may itself demand
a policy of co-operation with other nations, goodwill for other
nations, as indeed it does demand.

Every intelligent person can see that if you have a narrow
national policy it may enthuse the multitude for the moment,
just as the communal cry has done, but it is bad for the nation
and it is bad internationally, because you lose sight of the ultimate good and thereby endanger your own good. Therefore, we
propose to look after India's interests in the context of world
co-operation and world peace, in so far as world peace can be
preserved.

We propose to keep on the closest terms of friendship with
other countries unless they themselves create difficulties. We shall
be friends with America. We intend co-operating with the United
States of America and we intend co-operating fully with the
Soviet Union. We have had, as the House knows, a distinguished
Representative of the United States here for some time past
Within a week or two we shall have a distinguished Representative of the Soviet Union here, in the Soviet Embassy which is
being opened in New Delhi.

I do not want to say much more at this stage about foreign
affairs partly for lack of time, partly because it is a little difficult
to discuss these matters. Some of the Honourable Members might,
perhaps, want to talk about what should be done in China,
Japan, Siam and Peru, but I fear it would be a little irresponsible
of me to talk about these various matters. Naturally India is in-

terested in Asian countries even more than the rest of the world. We have had an Asian Conference, and at this moment we have a distinguished visitor here, the Prime Minister of Burma.

May I say in this connection that some people are under a misapprehension? They think that we are conducting special negotiations with the Burmese delegation here. That is not quite true. It is primarily a visit of courtesy. At the same time, of course, we have broadly explored various questions, discussed various matters of common concern, not with the idea of suddenly coming to decisions in regard to these intricate matters now, but rather with a view to laying the foundations for future talks. May I also say that the Prime Minister of Burma is interested, as many of us have been, in closer association, not only between Burma and India, but between various other countries of Asia also? We have discussed that also, again not with a view to coming suddenly to decisions, because these things take a little time to grow. It all indicates the new spirit of Asia which wants Asian countries to draw closer together in their own defence and to promote world peace.

Coming to another part of this cut motion in regard to Indians in the British Commonwealth, this is an old subject and a painful subject. I entirely agree with any criticism that may be made that we have not been able to do anything substantial in this direction. Something has been done in Canada and elsewhere, but nothing substantial has yet been done. Now, the odd thing is that this subject becomes more and more difficult to deal with and not easier. Indians have gone to the British Colonies and Dominions in the past in various capacities, as merchants, traders, workers, indentured labourers and the rest.

The history of Indian emigration abroad, including that of the humblest of those who went from India, reads almost like a romance. How these Indians went abroad! Not even citizens of a free country, working under all possible disadvantages, yet they made good wherever they went. They worked hard for themselves, and for the country of their adoption. They made good themselves and profited the country they had gone to.

It is a romance and it is something which India can be proud of, and may I say most of all of those poor indentured labourers who went out under unhappy conditions, through their labour, gradually worked their way up? It is aso true that India is a country, which in spite of everything, has abounding vitality and spreads abroad. It rather frightens our neighbour countries, just as China which is also a country with abounding vitality and an abounding population. We spread. We tend to overwhelm others both by virtue of our numbers, and sometimes by virtue of the economic position we might develop there.

That naturally frightens others who may not have that vitality in them, and they want to protect themselves against it. Questions then arise of vested interests which India has developed or Indians have developed there. Such questions have arisen, and while on the one hand we are obviously intent on protecting the interests of Indians abroad, on the other hand we cannot protect any vested interests which injure the cause of the country they are in. There is that difficulty. Nevertheless, undoubtedly we shall try to do our best to protect all legitimate interests.

Now, one word more. I will not take more of the time of the House. An Honourable Member, Mr. Kamath I think, referred to the expenditure incurred by the Embassies. Now, first of all, one of the minor headaches I have had to suffer from is a relatively new tendency in old and new newspapers alike to publish without check or hindrance the most amazing lies. It is impossible to keep pace with it. It is undesirable always to go about contradicting every little thing they say. It just cannot be done, and new types of papers and journals which have been inflicted by some I have come across, which do not raise either the stature of Indian journalism or anything else. So many of these stories are untrue. I think I read somewhere in a Delhi paper about the U. P. Government presenting Rs. 20,000 and 200 *saris* to Mrs. Vijayalakshmi Pandit on her departure to Moscow. I read all manner of the most malicious and unfounded and false statements in these papers about Mr. Asaf Ali.

Now, coming to the question of cost, the figure Mr. Kamath mentioned, 5 lakhs, has of course no relation to fact. I do not know what the figure is.

I suggest that if Mr. Kamath makes any statements, he might investigate the facts before he makes them.

What I should like this House to remember is that these ambassadorial appointments have to keep up a certain dignity and a certain status. It is no good our sending an Ambassador and not giving him a house to live in, not giving him furniture in the house, not providing him with the minimum wherewith he can meet and entertain other diplomats properly and decently. I doubt if any country, big or small, is conducting its ambassadorial establishments so cheaply as we are doing.

A great deal of criticism has been made about our Ambassador in Moscow getting furniture from Stockholm. Well, how a house has to be furnished in Moscow, of course, Honourable Members do not realize. It just is not possible to furnish easily in Moscow. You get an empty house. We thought of sending things from India, but it was almost a physical impossibility unless you spent vast sums on aeroplanes to carry chairs and tables from here. Of course, it could have been furnished alternatively with Russian furniture. The Russian people, and all credit to them for this, ever since the war, are so intent on doing what they consider to be the fundamental things, that they refuse to waste their time on the accessories of life. They have to rebuild their country after the most horrible suffering and damage suffered in the war and they are concentrating on major undertakings. They go about in patched-up clothes and broken down shoes. It does not matter, but they are building dams, reservoirs and factories and the rest which they consider more important. So it is not easy to get any of these small accessories of life for the moment.

The only things you can get in Russia are antique pieces of Czarist days which are frightfully expensive. The result is that our Embassy in Moscow had to go to Stockholm for its chairs and tables, and as these were urgently required—office equipment, etc.—our Ambassador had to go there. But, of course, the visit to Stockholm was not merely, members of the House should realize, to buy furniture. When an Ambassador goes somewhere, that Ambassador does other work too, and any kind of shopping that might be done is incidental.

I am grateful to the House for their kind sentiments and their expressions of goodwill for our attempt to follow a certain rather vague policy in regard to foreign affairs. I wish it were a more definite policy. I think it is growing more definite, and in this connection may I say that at the present moment no country, including the Big Powers with their long traditions in foreign affairs, has anything which could be called a precise and definite foreign policy, because the world itself is in a fluid condition. Of course, if you call this a definite policy, that of one great country looking with bitter dislike upon another and suspecting it,—

that may be the foundation of a policy, but that is not a policy, it is mere passion and prejudice. Otherwise, there is hardly any very definite policy in any country and each country is trying to fit in its policy from day to day to changing circumstances.

INDIA KEEPS OUT OF POWER BLOCS

Sir, I have taken interest in the various suggestions and criticisms made. I think possibly, if I had been speaking not from my place here, but from somewhere else I might have produced a longer list of criticisms. So I am grateful for the gentle way in which the Honourable Members have treated the External Affairs Department.

In criticizing the foreign policy of the Government of India during the last year, I should like this House for an instant to turn its mind to any country today and think of its foreign policy —whether it is the U.S.A., the United Kingdom, the U.S.S.R., China or France. These are supposed to be the great Powers. Just think of their foreign policy and tell me if you would say that the foreign policy of any one of those countries has succeeded from any point of view, from the point of view of moving towards world peace or preventing world war, succeeded even from the mere opportunist and individual point of view of that country.

I think if you will look at this question from this point of view, you will find that there has been a miserable failure in the foreign policy of every great Power and country. It is in that context that we shall have to view these matters. It is not really the failure of the foreign policy of any particular Power, though perhaps two or three major Powers do influence foreign policy greatly.

Now, surely the responsibility for the deterioration of the international situation might lie with some Powers. In India, our responsibility is very little. We may have acted well or badly on the international stage, but we are not, frankly speaking, influential enough to affect international events very much. Therefore, if a great deterioration has taken place in the international sphere it is not due to our policy. We suffer from it just as every other

A speech delivered at the Constituent Assembly (Legislative), New Delhi, March 8, 1948.

Speaking on two cut motions moved by Prof. Ranga and Seth Govinddas to discuss India's foreign policy, some members criticized certain aspects of that policy and advocated alliance with one of the power blocs at the U.N.O. The Prime Minister made this speech in reply to the debate.

nation suffers from it and I think it is this vague feeling that we have suffered that induces the members of the House to search for reasons why we have suffered.

I think that is a very right approach, because we must find the reasons for our having erred, how we might have bettered our lot and so on and so forth. Nevertheless, I think the real reason is that the causes lie entirely outside any policy that we have pursued. There are bigger and deeper causes affecting the world and we, like the strongest of nations, are pulled hither and thither by these forces. That is one fact that I should like the House to bear in mind.

Another factor—and that is more applicable to us—is that owing to the unfortunate events that have happened in India since the 15th August, 1947, anything we did in the world outside suddenly lost weight or lost weight for a time. We counted for something, not very greatly, of course, more potentially than in actuality, indeed, potentially we counted for a great deal, though actually we need not have counted for much. But the events that occurred after 15th August in India and Pakistan,—Pakistan I might say naturally did not count for much because it had no background ; it was a newcomer ; it was we who counted—those events suddenly brought down our credit in the international domain tremendously.

It affected the United Nations when they met last October to consider the South Africa issue. Undoubtedly the events in India affected the decision of the United Nations General Assembly in regard to the South Africa issue ; so also in regard to other matters. All these facts have nothing to do with foreign policy.

The point I wish to make before the House is this, that it may be desirable for us to adopt this or that foreign policy one of which is called a policy of neutrality or, as Pandit Kunzru said, a more positive one.

But all this has no relationship, it has nothing to do, with what has happened. Other factors govern it. If you like, it was a fault, but we have been rather passive about all these matters, and where we have been somewhat active are the very things in which some of the Honourable Members desire us to be more active. We are asked to collect the smaller nations of the world round us. . . . . . But the point is the very activity—call it idealistic ; I do not think it is purely idealistic ; I think it is, if you like, opportunist in the long run—this policy that we have so far pursued before we became a Government, and to some extent after we became a Government, that is, standing up, in so far as we could, for the weak and the oppressed in various continents, is not a policy which is to the liking of the great Powers who directly or indirectly share in their exploitation. It is this that puts us in the wrong with them.

There has been a lot said about other matters. Here is Indonesia. It is a clear issue before this House. We have done precious little in the way of actual active help ; we are not in a position to do so. But we have sympathy for the Indonesians and we have expressed it as publicly as possible. Because we give our sympathy and some degree of help to Indonesia and because this offends and irritates some of the major Powers of the world, are we to withdraw that help? Are we to submit tamely and say, " No, this might irritate this Power or that ", because it does irritate this or that Power and there is no doubt about it?

Naturally, we cannot as a Government go as far as we might have done as a non-official organization in which we can express our opinions as frankly and as aggressively as possible. Speaking as a Government we have to moderate our language. We have sometimes to stop doing things which we might otherwise do. Nevertheless, the fundamental thing is, do we sympathize and openly sympathize with a country like Indonesia in her struggle for freedom, or do we not? That applies not to Indonesia only, but to several other countries. In each case, we have to face the passive hostility of various interests, not only the direct interests involved, but also the indirect interests involved, because the direct and the indirect interests hang together in such matters.

It has been an astonishing thing to see how for many months, the Good Offices Committee functioned in Indonesia—all good people—and as it happens the Secretary of the Committee was an Indian. The way it has functioned and the results it has produced are not at all satisfactory. If this House is dissatisfied with what the Security Council has done this year or considered in regard to Kashmir, they would be still more dissatisfied, I think, if they considered the Indonesian Good Offices Committee's work. Unfortunately, their approach to such problems is an approach with which this House cannot agree, on account of our past traditions, on account of our ideals.

Now, I am not talking in terms of this bloc or that bloc ; I am talking independently of the blocs as they have appeared on the world stage. We have either to pursue our policy generally within limitations—because we cannot pursue it wholeheartedly, nevertheless openly—or give it up. I do not think that anything could be more injurious to us from any point of view—certainly from an idealistic and high moral point of view, but equally so from the point of view of opportunism and national interest in the narrowest sense of the word—than for us to give up the policies that we have pursued, namely, those of standing up for certain ideals in regard to the oppressed nations, and trying to align ourselves with this great Power or that and becoming its camp followers in the hope that some crumbs might fall from their table.

I think that would undoubtedly, be even from the narrowest point of view of national interest, a bad and harmful policy.

I can understand some of the smaller countries of Europe or some of the smaller countries of Asia being forced by circumstances to bow down before some of the greater Powers and becoming practically satellites of those Powers, because they cannot help it. The power opposed to them is so great and they have nowhere to turn. But I do not think that consideration applies to India.

We are not citizens of a weak or mean country and I think it is foolish for us to get frightened, even from a military point of view, of the greatest of the Powers today. Not that I delude myself about what can happen to us if a great Power in a military sense goes against us ; I have no doubt it can injure us. But after all in the past, as a national movement, we opposed one of the greatest of World Powers. We opposed it in a particular way and in a large measure succeeded in that way, and I have no doubt that if the worst comes to the worst—and in a military sense we cannot meet these great Powers—it is far better for us to fight in our own way than submit to them and lose all the ideals we have.

Therefore, let us not be frightened too much of the military might of this or that group. I am not frightened and I want to tell the world on behalf of this country that we are not frightened of the military might of this Power or that. Our policy is not a passive policy or a negative policy.

Two or three instances that were given perhaps gave an indication of what was working in the minds of some of the Honourable Members, although they have not had the time or the desire to say it clearly. I shall give one instance. It was stated . . that we supported the veto in the United Nations presumably because we did not wish to offend the Soviet group.

Now, I want to place the facts before the House as far as I remember them. The veto was put there, as the House will remember, by the common consent of all the great Powers belonging to every group. It was put there because they felt—and may I say that the Soviets felt that way, the United States also felt that way,—because these huge and great Powers did not like the idea of half a dozen little countries just telling them to do this or that.

Both felt that way and neither of these was prepared to submit to a kind of majority voting of the little nations put together, so that it was put there in the Charter right at the beginning. Whether the veto was used or misused, I am not going into that question, but now the question arose that the veto should be removed. This was not liked by several great Powers. It was not a question of supporting this bloc or that bloc. Neither bloc liked the removal of that veto.

Now, the problem before us was that if that veto was removed by a vote or decision of the United Nations, there was little doubt that the United Nations would cease to be that very instant. That was the choice. It was not a question of liking the veto. On behalf of India, as on behalf of many countries, it was stated openly that we disliked the veto and that it should go. It was pointed out, however, that this could only come about by some kind of general agreement.

Now, we agree with what Mr. Santhanam said that the United Nations, in spite of its failings and weaknesses, is something that is good. It should be encouraged and supported in every way, and should be allowed to develop into some kind of world government or world order. Therefore, we instructed our delegates not to press the question of the veto to the breaking point and to say that, although we did not like it, it should remain there so long as it could not be removed by some kind of agreement among the major groups involved.

In that way various questions come up and each question has to be considered on its merits. I do not know if any Honourable Member has analyzed our voting at these international conferences. It would help them perhaps to appreciate the scene better if they took up any one of the major issues during the last year at the United Nations or its various Committees and Councils and found out what India had done.

It is certainly true that our instructions to our delegates have always been firstly, to consider each question in terms of India's interest, secondly, on its merits—I mean to say if it did not affect India, naturally, on its merits and not merely to do something or give a vote just to please this Power or that Power, though, of course, it is perfectly natural that in our desire to have friendship with other Powers, we avoid doing anything which might irritate them.

As a matter of fact, we go as far as possible to try and win them over. It is not our purpose to enter into other people's quarrels. Our general policy has been to avoid entering into anybody's quarrels. If I may say so, I have come more and more to the conclusion that the less we interfere in international conflicts the better, unless, of course, our own interest is involved, for the simple reason that it is not in consonance with our dignity just to interfere without producing any effect. We should either be strong enough to produce some effect or we should not interfere at all. I am not anxious to put my finger into every international pie. Unfortunately, sometimes one cannot help it. One is dragged into it. For instance, there is the Korea Committee. Well, not only are we in that Committee, but ultimately our representative becomes the Chairman of that Committee.

Now, this leads to another matter, to which reference has been made by an Honourable Member. It is an odd contrast today that while in the official councils of the United Nations we may not perhaps pull the weight we ought to, nevertheless, in the unofficial councils outside, our weight has considerably increased. Why is this so? Because progressively, people see that within the United Nations things are done far from idealistically or morally, or in terms of the underdog, the smaller nations, or the Asian nations, and so more and more of these people try to find someone else and in their search for someone else who might perhaps give a lead in these matters, almost automatically their eyes turn towards India.

Now, I do not wish to enter into any comparisons with other countries, and certainly we have done nothing in India to merit leadership of anybody. It is for us to lead ourselves, then only can we lead others properly and I do not wish to place the case of India at any higher level. We have to look after ourselves.

That is why I am, if I may say so, in spite of being Minister in charge of External Affairs, not interested in external affairs so much as internal affairs at the present moment. External affairs will follow internal affairs. Indeed, there is no basis for external affairs if internal affairs go wrong. Therefore, I am not anxious to widen the scope of our representation all over the world. It is fairly wide already. That too we have been almost compelled by circumstances to do, because as an independent nation we simply cannot do without that representation, but I am not anxious to extend it any further unless some very special reason arises.

That being so, the fact remains that we stand for certain things. Now, when we come into contact with the external world, do we stand for them or do we not? We have to choose. I have no doubt at all, as I said right at the beginning of my remarks, that in the long run, it is to the great advantage of India to try to attract to itself the sympathy and the hope of millions of people in the world without offending others. It is not our purpose to offend others or to come into conflict with others. The world, however, is in a pretty bad way and it is easy enough for people to tell me, " Oh, you talk idealistically, you should be practical."

May I remind the House that we have seen, these many years, the results of persons and things being very practical? I have had about enough of this practicalness, which leads to incessant conflict and which leads to all the misery and suffering that we have seen. If that is the meaning of being practical, the sooner we are not practical, the better.

But that is not being practical. That is being grossly impractical. To march without looking to the left or to the right, each group just contracting into an ever smaller circle, full of danger for the other group, trying to win over other small or big nations by offering some immediate advantage. I do not say that this is good enough for this country and we really are not even compelled by circumstances to submit to it. We might have been compelled by circumstances, but we are not compelled by circumstances to give up, because it does amount to giving up our independence in order to gain the goodwill of this country or that country.

I think that not only in the long run, but also in the short run, independence of opinion and independence of action will count. This again does not mean that we should not associate closely with particular countries in certain activities." Pandit Kunzru referred to the necessity for our developing economically, militarily and otherwise. Surely this House realizes that nothing is more important in the opinion of this Government than to make India economically strong and militarily—not strong in the Big Power sense, because that is beyond our capacity,—but as strong as we can to defend ourselves if anybody attacks us.

We want to do that. We want the help of other countries ; we are going to have it and we are going to get it too in a large measure—I am not aware of this having been denied to us to any large extent. Even in accepting economic help, or in getting political help, it is not a wise policy to put all your eggs in one basket. Nor should one get help at the cost of one's self-respect. Then you are not respected by any party ; you may get some petty benefits, but ultimately even these may be denied you.

Therefore, purely from the point of view of opportunism, if you like, a straightforward honest policy, an independent policy is the best. What that policy should be at a particular moment, it is very difficult for me or for this House to say, because things change rapidly from day to day. It may be that we have to choose what might be a lesser evil in certain circumstances—we must always choose the lesser evil.

We stand in this country for democracy, we stand for an independent Sovereign India. Now obviously, anything that is opposed to the democratic concept—the real, essentially democratic concept, which includes not only political but economic democracy—we ought to oppose. We will resist the imposition of any other concept here or any other practice.

But there was a curious confusion in the speeches of some Honourable Members when on the one hand, they talk about our standing up for the weak and the oppressed against imperialism, and on the other hand, they ask us more or less to side with a Power here or there which may stand for imperialism. It may be that sometimes we have to side with this Power or that Power. I can quite conceive of our siding even with an imperialist Power —I do not mind saying that; in a certain set of circumstances that may be the lesser of the two evils. Nevertheless, as a general policy it is not a worthy policy or a worthwhile policy.

May I state another fundamental difficulty before us? Because of our past record in India, that is the anti-imperialist record, we have not been *persona grata* with many groups and peoples outside. We have not yet overcome their antipathy. With the best will in the world, those people do not like us. Those people govern opinion elsewhere, they govern the Press. It is amazing how a certain section of the Press, say in the United Kingdom, deliberately and offensively misrepresents us. Now, as I was sitting here, a telegram came to me, a telegram from a foreign correspondent in this country, sending a long message to his paper in London, which is the most offensively false thing that I have seen. It amazes me that any person who has been here for some months should have the temerity to send such false messages, and it is about time that the Government of India dealt with this matter more firmly.

We have been extraordinarily lenient towards the Press, Indian and foreign. We have gone out of our way to tell them that we will not do anything even if they send messages which are extremely disagreeable to us. But there is a limit to falsehood and that limit has been reached, I think, in regard to some messages.

Well, it is in this context that I should like Honourable Members to see the picture. Mr. Kamath said in a kind of peroration that we must join this bloc or that. He said, " I do not know which, but join this bloc or that." I remember later he inclined towards one bloc, but that was his first statement—evidently in the course of his speech he changed his mind.

What does joining a bloc mean? After all it can only mean one thing: give up your view about a particular question, adopt the other party's view on that question in order to please it and gain its favour. It means that—it means nothing else as far as I can see, because if our view is the view of that party, then there is no giving up and we do go with that bloc or country. The question only arises when we are opposed to it on that point ; therefore we give up our view-point and adopt the other one in order to gain a favour.

Now, I am prepared to agree that on many occasions, not only in international conferences, but in this House, one gives up one's point to gain a compromise, and I am not prepared to rule out the possibility of our subordinating our viewpoint in international conferences in order to gain something worthwhile. That is perfectly legitimate, and it is often done. But this general approach is the worst possible approach to get anything from another country. I should like this House to realize that even if we wanted to adopt that policy, this approach is the worst approach to get a thing done.

The fact of the matter is that in spite of our weakness in a military sense—because obviously we are not a great military Power, we are not an industrially advanced Power—India even today counts in world affairs, and the trouble that you see in the United Nations or the Security Council is because she does count, not because she does not count. That is a fact you should remember. If we had been some odd little nation somewhere in Asia or Europe, it would not have mattered much. But because we count, and because we are going to count more and more in the future, everything we do becomes a matter for comment, and many people do not like our counting so much. It is not a question of our viewpoint or of attaching ourselves to this or that bloc ; it is merely the fact that we are potentially a great nation and a big Power, and possibly it is not liked by some people that anything should happen to strengthen us.

There are these various things to be considered. It is not such a simple matter for us to affiliate ourselves to this organization or that organization just by a Resolution and get all the privileges of membership of that organization. That kind of thing is not going to happen. And, therefore, Sir, I do submit to this House that while undoubtedly much has happened in the past year which is very undesirable, so far as the External Affairs Department is concerned it has not functioned at all well, if I may frankly admit to this House. Also, as far as our Information Services are concerned, they have not functioned at all well. That is all perfectly true. But so far as our fundamental approach to the problem of foreign policy is concerned, I just do not see how we can vary it. As occasion arises we adapt ourselves to circumstance—that I can understand—but the fundamental approach, I do think, has to remain the same, because the more you think about it, the more you analyze it, there is no other way. It is not a question of your adopting a certain policy, because idealistically you think it a good one, but I do submit that if you give it up, there is no other policy for this country to adopt with the slightest advantage.

Now, I just mentioned our Information Services and the rest. Mr. Shiva Rao has made one or two suggestions, which I welcome. One was in regard to the various delegations, deputations, etc., etc., that go abroad. Each Ministry chooses its delegations, gives it a brief and that delegation goes to a particular Conference. Often enough, the briefs of two delegations do not fit in with each other and there is a slight conflict, so much so that the two delegations speak with two different voices. Frequently also, the choice made of people who are sent abroad is not good enough. So there is this conflict and lack of co-ordination. That is why we are trying to set up, in accordance with Mr. Shiva Rao's suggestion, some kind of an agency in External Affairs. In fact, it is there already in embryo stage. It is called the Conference Section. Every delegation will be chosen by the Ministry concerned—the External Affairs Ministry will not choose every delegation—but the proposal will in essence be vetted by the Conference Section of the External Affairs Ministry in order to prevent overlapping and possible conflict.

Then in regard to publicity, there is at the present moment, may I whisper to the House, a small discussion going on between the External Affairs Ministry and the Ministry of Information and Broadcasting. So far external publicity has been handled by the Information and Broadcasting Ministry. Now, external publicity as such should obviously be organized and looked after by the External Affairs Ministry. That is so, in fact, in every country. In England, external publicity is under the Foreign Office, not under the Home Publicity Service. The two are different, because external publicity has continually to keep in touch with external affairs. Of course, we will come to an agreement and make proper arrangements about it. But there has unfortunately been a great lack in our approach to foreign publicity in the last few months. At the same time, I do not want this House to imagine that by improving our publicity, some wonderful change will come about, because the reasons for the people thinking as they do in other countries and in the Government Departments are far deeper than just lack of publicity. Mr. Shiva Rao pointed out that our publicity in America, however efficient, consists after all in a small organization. That is all that we can afford. At the present moment, Pakistan's publicity has been undertaken at their request by the British Information Service in New York which is a tremendous organization. Now, it is not for me to judge or appreciate the propriety of this step. It is for the United Kingdom to do so. Today, publicity in America is organized on such a big scale that it is absurd for us to think of competing with them.

I understand that the British Information Service has 600 men working in New York. We are certainly not going to send 600 men. We shall try and send probably 6 men, i.e., a hundred times less. And all this publicity organization has unfortunately been built up on an anti-Indian basis during the past few years. The British publicity organization in America, the House will remember, was functioning some years ago with anti-Indian propaganda as one of its main objectives. The same people are still working there today, so that whatever propaganda they do, they do with an anti-Indian bias, whether they want it or not. We cannot get out of that rut. In fact, I regret to say that some Indians who used to do anti-Indian propaganda are still employed by the British Information Service in America.

Now, may I apologize to the House for not dealing with so many matters that have been mentioned, especially by my honourable friend, Seth Govinddas, about Indians overseas? I should like the House to consider this question again in this background that it is not a question of the External Affairs Department or this House turning a switch this way or that way and everything will be all right. It is far more complicated than that, and when the time comes, if necessary, we are prepared to switch over to this or that policy, provided we are firmly convinced that it is for the good of the country.

As for the Indians overseas, I will just say one or two words. Many of these difficulties continue and they are likely to continue. I am sorry to say that we do not get much help from the British Colonial Office. Not only do we not get much help, but it astonishes me, used as I am to the delays of the Government of India—and they are pretty remarkable—but the delays of the British Colonial Office are, indeed, a revelation.

I remember that we sent it some urgent letters and also reminders by cable. It took us exactly ten months to get a reply. The matter was about sending a deputation to some of the British colonies just to see the Indians there. It was a very simple matter, with no great principle involved, but still it took them ten months to reply, and during that period, events happened and nothing could be done. So we come up against this bureaucratic red tape in all these offices, here as well as there.

But the real difficulty is the question of citizenship. Now, these Indians abroad, what are they? Are they Indian citizens? Are they going to be citizens of India or not? If they are not, then our interest in them becomes cultural and humanitarian, not political. That interest of course remains. For instance, take the Indians in Fiji or Mauritius. Are they going to retain their nationality or will they become Fiji nationals or Mauritians? The same question arises in regard to Burma and Ceylon. It is a difficult question. This House wants to treat them as Indians and in the same breath, wants complete franchise for them in the countries where they are living. Of course, the two things do not go together. Either they get franchise as nationals of the other country, or you treat them as Indians minus the franchise and ask for them the most favoured treatment given to an alien.

Finally, right at the beginning, Prof. Ranga asked a question about India being in the British Commonwealth. Apparently, he has been misled by some newspaper reports that have been appearing recently that a delegation has gone from here to London to discuss this matter. It surprises me how people give rein to their imagination. I suppose, the delegation referred to is the Defence Ministry delegation led by Mr. H. M. Patel. It had nothing to do with this matter ; it was concerned entirely with defence matters and certain materials that we wanted to purchase in England and elsewhere. No such question has been discussed.

As to our general position, however, that was defined in this Constituent Assembly in the early stages and it will finally be decided by the Constituent Assembly itself. There is no question of any committee or any individual discussing it or even coming to preliminary conclusion about it. Whatever the final decision may be, it is quite certain, I believe, that India will be a completely independent and sovereign Republic or Commonwealth or State or whatever you may like to call it.

Now, that does not do away with the consideration of the problem of what our relations should be with England or the British Commonwealth or any other group. That is not merely a theoretical question, but a very practical one. Again in regard to citizenship, it affects all Indians abroad in the various British colonies. Exactly what type of relationship should we have, what type of citizenship, so that they may not become aliens? All these questions must be considered, but apart from that politically and otherwise, India must be a completely independent country.

THE PROBLEM OF EXTERNAL PUBLICITY

SIR, with your permission, before I deal with the subject matter of the debate, I should like to make a reference to the tragedy that occurred in Europe a few days ago. I refer to the death of M. Jan Masaryk, the Foreign Minister of the Czechoslovakian Republic. Not only is this in itself a very tragic event (as far as I am personally concerned I was acquainted with him and it is a personal loss to me), but in the circumstances in which it has occurred, it may have grievous consequences. I took the liberty of sending to the Ambassador of the Republic of Czechoslovakia here the sympathy and condolences of the Government and the people of this country and I am sure the members of this House will also like to add their own sympathy to that message.

Now, Sir, on the occasion of a cut motion in regard to the policy of the External Affairs Ministry, rather incidentally and casually, I made a reference to the British Information Services in America—in fact my colleague Mr. Shiva Rao had mentioned it and I also referred to the fact that he had mentioned it— and I stated that they had been asked and they had been carrying on publicity at the request of the Pakistan Government. Further, I mentioned that they had employed some Indians. Now, the British Information Services in America have contradicted that statement and have clearly stated that they are not carrying on any propaganda, or rather publicity, on behalf of the Pakistan Government and that they have not employed any Indian on their staff. I must accept their statement and I express my regret at having made a statement which was not factually true. I do not wish to enter into this argument. But apart from being factually true or not, it is possible to point out many things which occur, and which occur simply because they have been occurring for a long time past and it is difficult to get out of the old rut. A little while ago, an article by an eminent British journalist dealing with Kashmir was circulated by the British Information Services, not only in America but in various foreign countries. Now this article contained certain statements which were completely

A speech delivered at the Constituent Assembly (Legislative), March 15, 1948.

untrue. For instance, to mention one, it stated that it was after the accession of Kashmir to the Indian Union that the tribal people, irritated by that accession, invaded Kashmir, which was just the reverse of what took place. This is a minor matter. I merely mention this, because people who have been connected in the past with a certain type of work naturally tend to look at a problem from that point of view ; it is difficult to get out of that rut. However, I am sorry if I made a statement on the last occasion which was not correct. I regret it.

Now, in regard to external publicity, I have very little to say except to welcome many of the suggestions that Mr. Shiva Rao has made. External Publicity it is called, and, perhaps, the Honourable Members may think that we should try to flood foreign countries with facts and figures in the nature of propaganda. I do not think that it is desirable for us to do so or that we can, in fact, do so. I do not think our approach should be the pure publicity or the advertisement approach. We cannot do it because the way to do this would be to spend far vaster sums than we can ever afford, to engage far bigger personnel and so on. But my main reason for not desiring to do so is that I do not like that approach at all. That approach tends inevitably to become a tendentious approach, and while it may, perhaps, create an impression now and then, the value of it lessens progressively when people realize that it is excessive propaganda of a particular type. I would much rather place the facts before the public here in India or outside. Naturally, I shall place them, from our point of view, try to give the background of the facts—but facts and nothing more than facts as far as possible—and allow other people to judge. Of course, it makes all the difference in the world how facts are placed before the public. Statistics may be made to tell almost any tale. Anyhow, this business of publicity, whether factual publicity or any other kind of publicity, is an extraordinarily tricky business anywhere, and more especially in foreign countries. It is easy to criticize it, and I think many of the criticisms advanced are justified. It is also easy, perhaps, to draw up schemes which appear good on paper, but which may not succeed so well in practice. As I told the House on the last occasion when we discussed this problem, the problem of external publicity, because external publicity is so intimately aligned to external policy that normally every country has its external publicity organized by its Foreign Office and not by

its internal publicity machine. Here, owing to various developments, war-time developments—because this was only thought
of in war time—external publicity became a part of our Information Department. The more I have given thought to it,
the more I have realized that this is not a very satisfactory
arrangement. Obviously, there must be the closest co-operation
between the internal publicity machine and external publicity.
But it is far better, I think, that the External Affairs Ministry
should have a greater part in the organization of external
publicity than it has had so far.

I agree with Mr. Shiva Rao when he refers to the Public
Relations officers rather than the publicity agents abroad. That
conveys far better the idea of the work they ought to do. At the
present moment, the various hand-outs and other material that
are issued, no doubt serve some useful purpose, but I do not think
they are worth the money we spend upon them. My own impression, not now I mean, but previously, and my own, because I have
myself tried to do—not as a member of the Government but as
a private individual or as a member of the Congress organization—some kind of external publicity, is that all these hand-outs
and pamphlets and leaflets find their way to the waste-paper
basket. They influence very few persons except those who are
already converted and who use them and keep them for their own
benefit. The whole thing has to be looked upon from an entirely
different point of view, from a psychological point of view, from
the point of view of the requirements of each country concerned.
For instance, the approach in the United States of America is
likely to be different—I think completely different—from the
approach in France and even more different from the approach in
the Soviet Republic. The kind of paper that one may produce in
America ought to have some bearing on the kind of information
that America requires. In France, it will not be the same. I can
say that with assurance. They have a different outlook and attach
different values. The kind of information that we send to the
Soviet Republic will be entirely different or almost entirely
different again. The kind of information that the Soviet Republic
asks us, our Ambassador tells us, is almost entirely economic information concerning, for instance, what is being done in our various
projects, various schemes, dams, reservoirs, river valley schemes,
irrigation and education. They ask us for these; they are interested
in them. No particular enquiry about politics as such has come

from them. Now, it may be that they deliberately put forward that kind of enquiry, because they are mostly put forward by governmental agencies there. But my point is that the approach has to be different in every country. What is required and how it can be done properly can only be fully appreciated by competent Public Relations Officers as well as our Embassies and Legations abroad. And then it has to be co-ordinated with our publicity arrangements here. So I do think that all this matter has to be considered fully, and in fact the External Affairs Ministry and the Home Ministry are considering it. We hope to evolve a more feasible and better method. Inevitably we shall have to approach this question by the method of trial and error. There is no way of finding the perfect method of doing things except by experience. Then, again, the other countries that engage in this kind of publicity have done so for many years and have a great deal of experience. They spend vast sums of money, employ very large numbers of people, and have already developed very intimate contacts with the publicity organizations in the countries in which they function. It is easy for them. We may send the brightest of our young men from here. It takes time for him to develop those contacts, and not only physical contacts, but psychological and other contacts, so that if results are not brilliant, the House should realize that it is not a mechanical matter of sending shoals of pamphlets, leaflets or lecturers and others, but developing something which is much more intricate and difficult. Undoubtedly, the present arrangements are not very happy, and they have to be changed, I think, more or less on the lines of some of the suggestions made in this House.

Now, coming to Information and Broadcasting, may I say that both in regard to information and broadcasting, and publicity, etc., the Ministry has very kindly given me full notes containing a large number of particulars. I do not propose to read them to the House, because that will take too long a time and the House might get lost in a large number of figures ; but the House should know those particulars, of course, and I shall suggest to the Ministry that they should be placed before the House or before the public in the proper form so that they may know exactly what is being done. Now, my own view of the set-up for broadcasting is that we should approximate as far as possible to the British model, the B.B.C.: that is to say, it would be better if we had a semi-autonomous corporation under the Government, of course, with the policy controlled by the Government, otherwise being not conducted as a Government department but as a semi-autonomous corporation. Now, I do not think that is immediately feasible. I have merely mentioned this to the House. I think we should aim at that, even though we may have many difficulties. In fact, in most matters we should aim at these semi-autonomous corporations, the policy and other things being distantly controlled by the Government, but the Government or Government departments not interfering in their day-to-day activities. But that is not an immediate issue. Obviously, these debates about the policy to be pursued, about our various services—news services, the language question and the rest—have given an indication of the mind of the House. That helps. But if they are to bear real fruit, there should be far more discussions more or less on the—shall I say—not academic level, but certainly on the scholarly level, carefully by committees, etc. It is impossible really to consider these matters in vague speeches connected with cut motions. I am sorry to learn from an Honourable Member that these Advisory Committees have not been functioning in some of the provinces. I should have thought that in regard to broadcasting, it was necessary for such committees to function very frequently, for advice to be taken, for them to be told what was happening, and generally for co-ordination between the non-official element and the official element. I should have liked the Standing Committee attached to this Department also to consider all the matters that are raised in this House and discuss them with the officials in the Department. That is the proper way of dealing with them. It is not very satisfactory for the Honourable Members to make speeches here and for me or some one else to make a reply, and to let the matter end there for the year. I hope, therefore, that this kind of intimate contact and intimate discussion over these matters will take place much more frequently in future than in the past. Now, take a question like the language question. It is obviously a matter for high scholastic consideration, not a matter which can be disposed of properly in the heat of a political debate. More especially, a broadcasting organization should consider it from that point of view, should have indeed high class advisers who know something about languages and the rest and who can advise them. In England, there is no such language issue, of course, as to what language should be employed, but the best literary figures in England are employed to advise the B.B.C.—men like Bernard Shaw and others. They have them on the permanent Advisory Committee as to the use of language. I am not quite sure, if the biggest literary figures were asked to advise us, whether the results would be very happy, because their advice would propably apply to other literary figures, and persons like myself would not understand at all what was happening. That is a conceivable possibility. Nevertheless, my point is that persons capable of understanding this problem, in its educational as well as public aspect, should consider it dispassionately, should be attached to the Broadcasting Ministry, and should advise it, and should make lists of words, vocabularies, etc., to be used. That is done in every country, even though there is no such type of controversy as exists here. That applies also to the kind of news that is to be given.

Now, there can be no two opinions in this House as to the importance of the development of broadcasting in the rural areas. I did not quite understand what, I think, Shrimati Kamala Chaudhri said, something about much more time being given to the rural areas. It is not a question of time at all, I think. Suppose you give, instead of one hour a day, five hours a day. They can only listen at certain times and there is such a thing as overdoing it. Nor do I think that it would be at all right for us to proceed in our broadcasting programmes with the fixed desire to benefit the other person concerned. I do not know how Honourable Members react to attempts made to improve them, but I react strongly against them. If anybody is going to sermonize me, well, I am not going to listen to that sermon. I think that is the general public's psychological reaction: too much sermonizing, too much attempt to give you advice for your benefit, being told to be good too often, does not bring in good results. One must approach the problem differently. If you want to educate, you must do it in an amusing way, entertaining way, in a light way, sometimes in a heavy way, too, if you like, just as you cannot train a child by simply dosing him with heavy stuff all the time. You just ruin his life if you do that. So you must treat him better. I suggest these are matters for experts to consider. So I think it would be desirable for the members of separate committees to consider them and co-ordinate their activities and advise the Ministry, and thus gradually we might improve.

I am sorry I have not dealt with many of the matters raised, but I have suggested the way that should be followed in order to deal with them.

EMERGENCE OF INDIA IN WORLD AFFAIRS

THIS House is no doubt interested in the many aspects of our foreign policy and foreign affairs and how they affect India. Probably, in the course of the debate today, attention will be drawn to many of these factors, but with your permission, Sir, and the indulgence of the House, I should like to deal with the general aspects of foreign affairs and foreign policy as they affect India and as we look at them rather than say much about the smaller aspects of the main problem.

Even before that, I should like to make something in the nature of a general survey not only of foreign affairs, but of India itself. We have had in the course of the last few days a great deal of criticism of the Budget proposals and many of the failings of the Government have been pointed out with more or less force. As far as I am concerned, I welcome every type of criticism and I do believe that it would be unfortunate if this House became just, shall I say, a static House, a subservient House, a House which just says "Yes" to anything that the Government might put forward. Eternal vigilance is the price of liberty and every member of this House has to be vigilant and the Government, of course, must be vigilant. But there is always a possible tendency for those in authority to become a little complacent. Therefore, I repeat, that for my part I welcome the vigilance of the Honourable Members of this House in drawing our attention to our failings or any error or delinquency on the part of the administration. I hope that the criticism is offered in good spirit, in a friendly way, and that it does not challenge the *bona fides* of the Government. Of course, if the *bona fides of* the Government are sought to be challenged, I do not mind, provided it is clear that that is the issue.

I have felt while listening to these criticisms during these days or reading about them that perhaps we were concentrating too much on the trees and not looking at the wood. We are not looking at the whole picture of India today and what has

A speech delivered at the Constituent Assembly (Legislative), New Delhi, March 8, 1949.

happened in the course of the last eighteen months or so. Look at it, as far as you can, objectively—as if you were at a distance and saw this changing scene. I think if you could transport yourself to the period a year and a half ago and to all that was happening then and to all that has happened since then, you would find that there has been not only a great change in India, but that India has gone ahead in many ways in spite of all her difficulties and all the travails that she too has passed through. Our Government, particularly myself to some extent, have had to carry very heavy burdens and we have to carry them still and there are great difficulties ahead of us. Nevertheless, in all honesty, I have a feeling of achievement, not failure, and look upon the future, I do not mean the distant future but the near future, with full confidence and feel a certain secret emotion at being privileged to participate in the service of India at this tremendous stage of her history.

May I say, as you have referred to the budget proposals, that this budget itself contains provisions, many of which may not perhaps be pleasing to some members, maybe we might have done better here and there, but the budget itself, I think, is a sign of our strength and the strength of the nation. I think that the House and the country will see that the care and foresight given to this budget by our Finance Minister will be paid in full measure in the months and years to come. We have proceeded cautiously, because, frankly speaking, we dare not take risks with the great trust that has been placed in our hands. Many a thing that we would have liked to do we have refrained from doing, because we cannot gamble with India's future or India's present. It is too serious a matter for us to go ahead even with our own theories or ideas on the subject, if there is any risk or danger involved in them. So we have proceeded cautiously. It may be that somewhat quicker results might have come to us if we had been a little more dashing in this matter, but I personally entirely agree with the cautious approach at this present critical time. Apart from any small matters here and there, I should like to pay my tribute to my colleague, the Finance Minister, for the courage and vision and high ability with which he has tackled our problem.

The Indian Union is an infant State, infant free State, a year and a half old, but remember that India is not an infant country. India is a very ancient country with millenia of history behind her—history in which she has played a vital part not only within her own vast boundaries, but in the world and in Asia in particular. India now, in this last year or more, emerges again into the main trend of human affairs.

Now, that is something of great historical significance. I could have said that Asia emerges in this main trend of history. Asia, in the long millenia of her history, has played a very important part. So has India, of course ; but during the last two hundred years or so, certain developments of science and technology in Europe, and in America a little later, led to the domination of Asia by Europe and to a restriction of her activities in the world at large. She became confined and restricted. Various changes took place internally in India and in Asia during this period. But generally speaking, India and the other countries of Asia withstood the political and economic domination of Europe. Now, that period and epoch has ended, and India now comes, I think, into the forefront in national events and world affairs.

One of the major questions of the day is the readjustment of the relations between Asia and Europe. When we talk of Asia, remember that India, not because of any ambition of hers, but because of the force of circumstances, because of geography, because of history and because of so many other things, inevitably has to play a very important part in Asia. And not only that ; India becomes a kind of meeting ground for various trends and forces and a meeting ground between what might roughly be called the East and the West.

Look at the map. If you have to consider any question affecting the Middle East, India inevitably comes into the picture. If you have to consider any question concerning South-East Asia, you cannot do so without India. So also with the Far East. While the Middle East may not be directly connected with South-East Asia, both are connected with India. Even if you think in terms of regional organizations in Asia, you have to keep in touch with the other regions. And whatever regions you may have in mind, the importance of India cannot be ignored.

One of the major questions of the day is the readjustment of the relations between Asia and Europe. In the past, especially by virtue of her economic and political domination, the West ignored Asia, or at any rate did not give her the weight that was due to her. Asia was really given a back seat and one unfortunate result of it was that even the statesmen did not recognize the changes that were taking place. There is, I believe, a considerable recognition of these changes now, but it is not enough yet. Even in the Councils of the United Nations, the problems of Asia, the outlook of Asia, the approach of Asia have failed to evoke the enthusiasm that they should. There are many ways of distinguishing between what may be called the approach of Asia and the approach of Europe. Asia today is primarily concerned with what may be called the immediate human problems. In each country of Asia—under-developed countries more or less—the main problem is the problem of food, of clothing, of education, of health. We are concerned with these problems. We are not directly concerned with problems of power politics. Some of us, in our minds, may perhaps think of that.

Europe, on the other hand, is also concerned with these problems, no doubt, in the devastated regions. Europe has a legacy of conflicts of power, and of problems which come from the possession of power. They have the fear of losing that power and the fear of some one else getting greater power and attacking one country or the other. So that the European approach is a legacy of the past conflicts of Europe.

I do not mean to say that we in Asia are in any way superior, ethically or morally, to the people of Europe. In some ways I imagine we are worse. There is, however, a legacy of conflict in Europe. In Asia, at the present moment at least, there is no such legacy. The countries of Asia may have their quarrels with their neighbours here and there, but there is no basic legacy of conflict such as the countries of Europe possess. That is a very great advantage for Asia and it would be folly in the extreme for the countries of Asia, for India to be dragged in the wake of the conflicts in Europe. We might note that the world progressively tends to become one—one in peace and it is likely to be one, in a sense of war. No man can say that any country can remain apart when there is a major conflagration. But still one can direct one's policy towards avoiding this conflict and being entangled in it.

So the point I wish the House to remember is this: first of all, the emergence of India in world affairs is something of major consequence in world history. We who happen to be in the Government of India or in this House, are men of relatively small stature. But it has been given to us to work at a time when India is growing into a great giant again. So, because of that, in spite of our own smallness, we have to work for great causes and perhaps elevate ourselves in the process.

When India became independent a year and a half ago, we chose the time, or if you like, fate and circumstance chose the time for us, which was one of exceeding difficulty. There were the damages and the consequences of the last great war. And immediately we were independent there were volcanic up-heavals in India. It would have been difficult enough for us if there had been complete peace in India to face all the problems that had accumulated during the period of our arrested growth in the past, but added to that came new problems of colossal magnitude. How we faced them the House well knows, and it will be for history to record whether we failed completely or we succeeded or succeeded partially. Anyhow we survived and made good in many ways, apart from mere survival. And gradually we have overcome those problems and gradually we have made of India a single political unit.

And may I point out to this House that the political unit that is India today is, in terms of population, the largest political unit in the world? But population and numbers do not count, it is quality that counts. I would say further that from the point of view of our potential resources and our capacity to use those potential resources, we are also potentially the biggest unit in the world. I say that not in any spirit of vainglory, but let us recog-nize the huge trust we have in our keeping and let us then think of it in terms of the great burden and the great responsibility.

Shall I put another matter to you? It is this. We, the great majority of the members of this House and vast numbers of people in this country, have spent our lives in what might be called revolutionary activity, in conflict with authority. We are bred in the tradition of revolution and now we sit in the seat of authority and have to deal with difficult problems. That adjustment is not an easy adjustment at any time for any-one. Then again, not only were we revolutionaries and agitators and breakers up of many things, but we were bred in a high tradition under Mahatma Gandhi. That tradition is an ethical tradition, a moral tradition and at the same time it is an applica-tion of those ethical and moral doctrines to practical politics. That great man placed before us a technique of action which was unique in the world, which combined political activity and political conflict and a struggle for freedom with certain moral and ethical principles. Now, I dare not say that any of us, not all of us, lived up to those ethical and moral principles and I do dare to say that in the course of the past 30 years or so all of us, in a smaller or greater degree, and the country itself in a smaller or greater measure, was affected by those ethical and moral doctrines of the Great Master and Leader.

And with that idealism and ethical background we now face practical problems and it becomes an exceedingly difficult thing to apply that particular doctrine to the solution of these problems. That is a conflict which individuals and groups and nations have often had to face. It came to us in very peculiar circumstances and it was intensified by those circumstances and so there has been this travail of the spirit in most of us. We have not often thought enough of Gandhiji and his great doctrine, of his great message, and while we praised it often enough, we felt: "Are we hypocrites, talking about it and being unable to live up to it? Are we deluding ourselves and the world?" Because if we are hypocrites, then surely our future is dark. We may be hypocritical about the small things of life, but it is a dangerous thing to be hypocritical about the great things of life. And it would have been the greatest tragedy if we exploited the name and prestige of our Great Leader, took shelter under it and denied in our hearts, in our activities, the message that he had brought to this country and the world. So we have had these conflicts in our minds and these conflicts continue and perhaps there is no final solution of these conflicts except to try continually to bridge the gulf between the idealism and the practice which is forced upon us by circumstances. We cannot and I am quite positive that our great leader would not have had us behave as blind automatons just carrying out what he had said without reference to the changes in events. On the other hand, we have to keep in mind those very ideals to which we have pledged ourselves so often.

There is always a great difference between a prophet and a politician in their approach to a problem. We had the combination of a prophet and a great statesman ; but then we are not prophets nor are we very great in our statesmanship. All we can say is that we should do our utmost to live up as far as we can to that standard, but always judging a problem by the light of our own intelligence, otherwise we will fail. There is the grave danger, on the one hand, of denying the message of the prophet, and on the other, of blindly following it and missing all its vitality. We have, therefore, to steer a middle course through these. Then a politician or a statesman, or call him what you will, has to deal not only with the truth, but with men's receptivity of that truth, because if there is not sufficient response to it from the politician's or statesman's point of view that truth is banished into the wilderness till minds are ripe for it. And certainly a statesman cannot act and much less can he act in a democratic age unless he can make people believe in that truth. So unfortunately, but inevitably, compromises have to take place from time to time. You cannot do without compromises, but a compromise is a bad compromise if it is opportunist in the sense that it is not always aiming at the truth. It may be a good compromise if it is always looking at that truth and trying to take you there. So in the past year and a half we have faced these difficult problems, and the difficulty has been obvious enough to many, but perhaps no one would have thought of this travail of the spirit under which we suffered all the time. All we can do is to pull ourselves up occasionally, look at our activities and examine them from the high standard which was laid down and try to remain as close to it as possible.

It was a curious thing that we who carried on the struggle for freedom in a non-violent and peaceful way should immediately have had to be confronted with violence of the intensest form, civil violence as well as, what may be called, military violence, that we should have had to undertake a kind of war in a part of the country. The whole thing seemed to be a complete reversal of all that we stood for ; and yet circumstances were such that I am quite convinced that we had no other way and that the way we took was the right one.

May I mention to the House that towards the end of October, 1947, when the question of Kashmir suddenly came upon us, when we heard that raiders had come into Kashmir and were destroying and looting, it was a very difficult question for us to decide? It was difficult enough from the military point of view, because we were isolated and far away and the sending of arms or troops by air was no light undertaking from the purely military point of view. But the real difficulty before us arose from within us, it was a difficulty of the spirit. What would this land us in? On the other hand, there was the powerful call of the people of Kashmir, those people who were being attacked and destroyed.

We could not say "No" to them. On the other hand, we did not quite know where it would lead us. And in that difficulty of spirit I went—as I often did—to Mahatma Gandhi, for his advice. It was not natural for him to give advice about military matters. What did he know about them? His struggles were struggles of the spirit. But listening to me, if I may with all respect say so, he did not say "No" to the course of action that I proposed. He saw that a government, as we were, had to follow its duty even to military obligations when certain circumstances arose. And throughout those few months, before he was taken from us, I conferred with him on many occasions about Kashmir and it was a great happiness to me that I had his blessings in the steps we took!

So looking back on this year and a half, we have built up India as a single organized political unit, and in this, as the House knows, my respected colleague, the Deputy Prime Minister, has played a supremely vital part. We have a little further to go in this matter. But I hope these further problems also will be settled very soon. There is the problem of Kashmir. There are the problems of what are called foreign possessions in India, Pondicherry, Chandernagore, Goa and the rest. And all along we have stated that we wanted a peaceful solution in regard to these foreign possessions. But it is quite clear that there is only one future for these possessions and that is complete integration with India. We are prepared to wait a little for it, to avoid conflict. We want peaceful solutions of these and other problems. But it is an inconceivable thing that in this new, resurgent India, bits of territory should belong to Powers far away.

May I point out another thing? The House, very rightly, is vigilant about the avoidance of waste, about the growth of our administrative services. There is an Economy Committee sitting, and there are other committees considering this problem. Please remember that the Government of India which has been functioning since the 15th August, 1947, has had to face many more problems than any other Government of India has had to face previously. First of all, the previous Governments, although they were endowed with certain social objectives, did not think of them as primary functions or of the same importance as we necessarily must. Secondly, take this field of foreign affairs about which I am speaking. There were no foreign affairs then. It has been an entirely new adventure for us, building up our foreign

and international position. This has meant necessarily additions
to our staff here and in foreign countries ; large additions and
large expenditure of money. It may be that some economy is
possible ; that should be considered and looked into. But you
cannot be an independent nation and not have those foreign
relations. Indians are spread all over the world. We have
to look after their interests. Apart from Indians living in other
countries, we have various interests, trade interests and other
interests. We have to buy things. We have to sell things. It is
quite impossible for any independent country, more especially
a great and big country like India, to carry on its normal existence
without these foreign relations, with foreign establishments,
foreign embassies, legations, trade missions and the like.

I mention this because often enough there is criticism of our
spreading out all over the world with our foreign embassies.
It is perhaps thought that this is just a gesture to satisfy our
own vanity. And I am told, sometimes, that I have some
kind of a bee in my bonnet ; that I forget the trouble in India
and I do not consider them, our domestic problems, and that I
think only of sending ambassadors from Timbuktu to Peru. Well,
I should like the House to consider this matter and be quite clear
about it, because to refer to Timbuktu and Peru in this connection
does not appear to me to be the height of wisdom. It shows quite
an extraordinary lack of appreciation of what India is and what
internally and domestically India requires. If we do not go out
and have our foreign establishments, somebody will have to look
after our interests. Who is that somebody? Are we going to ask
England to look after our foreign interests in other countries as
Pakistan has done in many countries? Is that the type of
independence that we imagine? What does independence consist
of? It consists fundamentally and basically of foreign relations.
That is the test of independence. All else is local autonomy. Once
foreign relations go out of your hand, into the charge of somebody else, to that extent and in that measure you are not
independent. If we are an independent nation, we must have
foreign relations. In fact, we cannot carry on without them. If
we have foreign relations, we have to have the establishment
necessary to carry on these foreign relations. And foreign relations though they involve trade, business, etc., are not like opening
a branch of a business or firm, as sometimes some of our business
magnates seem to imagine. It is a very intricate and very

difficult business dealing with the psychology of human beings, the psychology of nations, involving considerations of their background and culture, language and so on.

Beginning from scratch, we have developed our Foreign Service rather rapidly. It has been a difficult business and it would be absurd for me to say that everything we have done in the development of our Foreign Service has been entirely to my satisfaction. But I would like to say from the experience I have gathered during the last eighteen months or so that we have on the whole done remarkably well and that the test—the one test of that of course—is the status of India in the eyes of the world. Individuals may have erred here and there, but the final test is: Does our foreign policy yield results or not? Does it deliver the goods or not? I think it has delivered the goods to some extent, to a considerable extent, indeed, to a surprising extent. I should like to express my high appreciation here in this House of the work of many of our Ambassadors and Ministers abroad and of the work of our delegations to the United Nations. And allow me to inform the House that the reputation of India in the United Nations Assemblies is very high.

Our three chief foreign missions are, as the House knows, in London, Washington and Moscow. There have been criticisms about relatively small matters. It may be about appointments and the like. I will not go into them. But I should like to tell the House, speaking always as Foreign Minister, that I would welcome any query which is brought to me and I shall either enquire into it or give the information that I have in my possession to any member of the House. There are bound to be many such things deserving enquiry, arising out of a vast establishment. I think these principal missions of ours in London, Washington and Moscow have done remarkably well. In China we have had to face very difficult situations and our Embassy there has faced them with great credit. In Paris, we have had a succession of misfortunes for many reasons, but chiefly because we have hardly had any place to stay in for a year. There is no proper place and our representatives have lived in very undesirable quarters. On the whole, we have succeeded in building up our Foreign Service in a very short time with considerable success. Naturally, we shall go on trying to improve it.

Then the main question that troubles this House often enough is the position of Indians abroad. Now, that question has to be viewed in a different light from the one it was viewed in the past. In the past our main effort was to persuade the British Colonial Office to interest itself in bettering the conditions of Indians abroad. We as an independent nation have to deal with other independent nations. Naturally, we try to do our best. I believe the conditions of Indians abroad are being bettered, but the main thing that has happened is that the status of Indians abroad has gone up tremendously in the eyes of the world.

The problems we have to face in world affairs at the present moment bear a great deal of relation to the conflicts that are going on. We have stated repeatedly that our foreign policy is one of keeping aloof from the big blocs of nations—rival blocs—and being friendly to all countries and not becoming entangled in any alliances, military or other that might drag us into any possible conflict. Some people have criticized and suggested to us that that is not a good enough policy ; and that we are losing what we might get by a closer association or alliance. Others, on the other hand, have criticized us by saying that while we say one thing, we act secretly or otherwise in another way. It is a little difficult, of course, to give an answer to an imputation of motives, but as a matter of fact we have very strictly followed the policy of not getting entangled in any kind of commitment, certainly not military commitment with any other Power or group of Powers, and we propose to adhere to that policy, because we are quite convinced that that is the only possible policy for us at present and in the future. That does not, on the other hand, involve any lack of close relationships with other countries.

The House will remember that sometime back I mentioned the question of India's possible relationships with the Commonwealth and I informed the House of the broad lines of our approach to this problem and I gathered that the House agreed with it. Subsequently, the question was considered by the National Congress at its Jaipur Session and in broad lines they also laid down the policy to be pursued. As far as we are concerned, we propose strictly to adhere to those directions. Of course, changing circumstances have to be understood and interpreted in different ways, but the broad lines of policy have been laid down and the broad lines of policy are these:

(*a*) that India will naturally and inevitably in the course of a few months become an Independent Republic.

(*b*) that in our external, internal or domestic policy, in our political policy, or in our economic policy, we do not propose to accept anything that involves in the slightest degree dependence on any other authority.

Subject to that, we are prepared to associate ourselves with other countries in a friendly way. We are associated today in the United Nations with a great number of countries in the world. Anything else that we might do will naturally have to be something that does not go against our association with the United Nations. It is only in terms of independent nations co-operating together that we can consider the problem of our association with the Commonwealth. There may be, as some people have suggested, alliances with this or that nation. Alliances usually involve military and other commitments and they are more binding. Other forms of association which do not bind in this manner, but which help in bringing together nations for the purpose of consolidation and, where necessary, of co-operation, are, therefore, far more preferable than any form of alliance which does bind. What the outcome may be I do not know. As soon as I know, I shall inform the House, but what I am placing before the House today is this: that our policy in regard to this matter is going to be strictly determined by the Jaipur Congress resolution.

Recently there was a conference on Indonesia held at India's instance in New Delhi and many countries from Asia attended it, besides Egypt, Ethiopia, Australia and New Zealand. That conference forcibly brought several matters before the world's eye and at that conference one of the resolutions passed was that we should explore methods of closer co-operation. We are pursuing that line of enquiry and perhaps in the course of a month or two or perhaps more we may have some more definite results to consider ; possibly we might have another conference to consider the possible lines of co-operation. Again, that co-operation can only be the co-operation of independent nations without the least commitment of one to the other. But it is a fact that there are so many matters in common between us that it is helpful for us to co-operate with one another. We have not yet decided what the region of co-operation might be, because, as I said a little while ago, India is interested in several regions in Asia. Whether all should be grouped together or separately, I do not know. That is for us to consider together and to decide what is more feasible, but in any event two facts have to be borne in mind. One is that whatever structure of co-operation we may build up will be entirely within the scope of the Charter of the United Nations. Secondly, there will be no binding covenant in it, and this will largely be an organization for the consultation and co-operation that naturally flow from common interests.

So our policy will continue to be not only to keep aloof from power alignments, but try to make friendly co-operation possible. Fortunately we enter upon our independence as a country with no hostile background in regard to any country. We are friendly to all countries. Our hostility during the last 200 years was mainly directed towards the dominating power here and because of India's independence that hostility has largely vanished, though it may survive in some people's minds. So we approach the whole world on a friendly basis and there is no reason why we should put ourselves at a disadvantage, if I may say so, by becoming unfriendly to any group. I think that India has a vital role to play in world affairs.

The various ideologies that confront the world today, the various *isms* which threaten conflict repeatedly may have a great deal, I think, to commend themselves, but all of them have been derived, if I may say so, from the background of Europe. Well, the background of Europe is not something apart from the background of the world and there is much in the background of Europe which is present in India or in other countries. Nevertheless, it is true that the background of Europe is not completely the background of India or the world and there is absolutely no reason why we should be asked to choose between this ideology or the other in toto.

India is a country with a tremendous vitality which it has shown through its history. It has often enough imposed its own cultural pattern on other countries not by force of arms, but by the strength of her vitality, culture and civilization. There is no reason why we should give up our way of doing things, our way of considering things, simply because of some particular ideology which emanates from Europe. I have no doubt at all that we have to learn a great deal from Europe and America and I think that we should keep our eyes and ears completely open. We should be flexible in mind and we should be receptive, but I have also no doubt at all that we should not allow ourselves, if I may use the words of Gandhiji, we must not allow any wind from anywhere to sweep us off our feet.

So we should approach these problems, whether domestic or international problems, in our own way. If by any chance we align ourselves definitely with one power group, we may perhaps from one point of view do some good, but I have not the shadow of a doubt that from a larger point of view, not only of India but of world peace, it will do harm. Because then we lose that tremendous vantage ground that we have of using such influence as we possess (and that influence is going to grow from year to year) in the cause of world peace. What are we interested in world affairs for? We seek no domination over any country. We do not wish to interfere in the affairs of any country, domestic or other. Our main stake in world affairs is peace, to see that there is racial equality and that people who are still subjugated should be free. For the rest we do not desire to interfere in world affairs and we do not desire that other people should interfere in our affairs. If, however, there is interference, whether military, political or economic, we shall resist it.

So it is with this friendly approach that we look at the world. It is true that in doing so we are often likely to be misunderstood, because passions have been roused all over the world and sometimes each country thinks that if you are not completely lined up with it you are its enemy or opponent. It is unfortunate if people think so ; we cannot help it. We may sometimes even lose some petty advantage because of this fear and suspicion in other people's minds. But even now other countries are beginning to realize that we are playing an independent role, that we are not tied up to anybody, that we consider problems dispassionately and objectively in so far as we can judge them on their merits and not from that other point of view, which is becoming very common, that is to say from the point of view of a certain manoeuvring for a possible future war. That is the point of view from which problems are dealt with today.

It is not for me to criticize other nations and their policies. But I just do not see why India should act in this way or should become a part of the manoeuvring that is going on in the world. We have to keep aloof from that and at the same time develop the closest relations with all those countries. It so happens that because of history and chance, our relations—economic and trade—are far greater with some countries than with others. Well, we will continue them always seeing that they do not come in the way of our growth, do not hamper us in our progress. Otherwise, we keep them so that we can play a very important part in world affairs.

The supreme question that one has to face today in the world is, how can we avoid a world war? Some people seem to think that it is unavoidable and, therefore, they prepare for it and pre- pare for it not only in a military sense, but in a psychological sense and thereby actually bring the war nearer. Personally, I think that is a very wrong and a very dangerous thing. Of course, no country dare take things for granted and not prepare for possible contingencies. We in India must be prepared for all possible danger to our freedom and our existence. That is so. But to think in terms of the inevitability of world war is dangerous thinking. I should like this House and the country to appreciate what a world war means, what it is likely to mean. It just does not matter who wins in the world war, because it will mean such utter catastrophe that for a generation or more everything that we stand for in the way of progress and advancement of humani- ty will be put an end to. That is a terrible thing to contemplate and everything should be done to avoid this catastrophe.

I feel that India can play a big part, and maybe an effective part, in helping to avoid war. Therefore, it becomes all the more necessary that India should not be lined up with any group of Powers which for various reasons are full of fear of war and preparing for war. That is the main approach of our foreign policy and I am glad to say that I believe that it is more and more appreciated.

We are at the present moment on friendly terms with all countries. With our neighbour, Pakistan, I think the situation is improving from day to day. It is much better than it was a few months ago. I hope it will improve more. With Afghanistan and Nepal we are on the friendliest terms. With other countries in Asia and in Europe our relations are getting closer and closer, our trade is extending.

We should utilize this position, I think, in the United Nations and elsewhere to fulfil the cause of peace, and it is possible that a number of other countries which are not happy at the prospect of war may also support the attitude that India may take up. We have dealt with questions in the United Nations as individual separate questions,—for instance, in regard to Korea, in regard to Palestine, in regard to some other matters too, and we have displeased people, because we have dealt with individual questions and gave our opinion on their merits. Of course, the merits cannot be divorced from various other possible consequences. I think people have realized often enough that the advice that India gave and which was not accepted then was the right advice and that the trouble would have been far less if the advice had been accepted then. There are many aspects of this question which I can speak about, but I have already taken a great deal of the time of the House.

I would beg the House to look upon the matter from the wider point of view that I have placed before it, that is the emergence of India and Asia in the modern trend of human affairs, the inevitability of India playing an important part by virtue of her tremendous potential, by virtue of the fact that she is the biggest political unit in terms of population today and is likely to be in terms of her resources also. She is going to play that part. If we have to play that part we have to look upon this question from this bigger point of view and not from the small difficulties and problems that may face us and that part must essentially be one of promoting peace and freedom in the world, of removing racial inequalities.

And may I in this connection say that it has been a matter of deep grief to us to learn of the racial riots that took place at Durban in South Africa? I do not wish to say much in regard to this except that if racialism is encouraged anywhere it is bound to yield such trouble. But it is a matter of deep grief to us that Indians and Africans should be involved in such rioting. It has been, not today but over years past, our definite instruction to our envoys in Africa and elsewhere that we do not want Indians to have any special interests at the cost of the Africans anywhere. We have impressed upon them the need for co-operation with the Africans in order to gain freedom for these Africans and we have repeated these instructions again. I hope that after the unfortunate experience of Durban, Indians and Africans will come together again. Indeed, there is evidence from East Africa and elsewhere of a great measure of co-operation between Indians and Africans.

I hope that this House and this country will approve of the general lines of policy that I have suggested and indicate that it is India's desire to play this important part in favour of world peace and thereby perhaps help in avoiding that supreme catastrophe, that is, a world war.

OUR FOREIGN POLICY

MR. CHAIRMAN and friends, first of all, may I congratulate you on the conception of having this dinner called the Annual Dinner Meeting? I think it is a good idea for an organization of this kind to meet periodically not only to feast together, but also to have discourses, if you like, on certain subjects for which this organization is formed. There is just one suggestion which, perhaps, I may offer that in future dinners care may be taken to make them a little less hot. I say this, because I feel a sort of victim of the chillies that have been used in the dishes.

I think the first matter which must be in your mind is the fact that two of our most eminent members who built up this organization in the past passed away within the last few months, our President Dr. Tej Bahadur Sapru and Mrs. Sarojini Naidu. Our Chairman referred to the Asian Conference that was held two years ago and connected my name with it. As a matter of fact, all of you know that Mrs. Naidu was not only the President of the Conference, but took enormous pains in spite of her illness and really made it the success that it was. There is a proposal that we should have a memorial for Dr. Sapru here in Delhi and that the memorial should take the form of a building with a hall and some rooms for the Indian Council of World Affairs. I feel it is an excellent proposal—a fitting memorial for Dr. Sapru and also something which is urgently needed here in Delhi. I hope there will be no difficulty whatever in raising sufficient funds for this memorial. All of you who are present here in such large numbers, if you took a little interest, the matter would be concluded very soon.

Now, although I welcome this opportunity of meeting you all at dinner, I am not quite sure if I or other Foreign Ministers who may come after me would always welcome the idea of having to speak on foreign policy. I sometimes think that it would be a good thing for the world if all the Foreign Ministers remained silent for some time. I think more trouble is being caused in foreign affairs by the speeches that the Foreign Minis-

A speech delivered at the Indian Council of World Affairs, Constitution Club, New Delhi, March 22, 1949.

ters or their representatives deliver either in their own respective
Assemblies or in the United Nations. They talk about open
diplomacy and I suppose in theory most of us believe in it.
Certainly, I have believed in it for a long time and I cannot say
that I have lost that belief entirely. Open diplomacy is good
enough, but when that open diplomacy takes the form of very
open conflicts and accusations and strong language hurled at one
another, then the effect, I suppose, is not to promote peace.
It becomes a contest, an open contest in the use of violent language
towards one another. Now, it is all very well to talk about foreign
policy, but you will appreciate that no person charged with a
country's foreign policy can say really very much about it. He
can say something general about it ; he can sometimes say something very specific about it when occasion arises, but there are
many things connected with it which are supposed to lie in
what are called top-secret files. In spite of this, they are not
frightfully secret, but still they are not to be talked about
in public.

Now, foreign policy in the past, I suppose, related chiefly to
the relations of a country with its immediate neighbours—whether they were friendly or otherwise.

As our Chairman reminded you, our neighbours now are all
the countries of the world so that we cannot relate our foreign
policy just to a few countries around us, but have to think of
practically every country in the world and take into consideration
all the possible areas of conflict, trade, economic interest, etc. It has
been recognized now that if there is a conflict on a big scale anywhere in the world, it is apt to spread all over the world, i.e., that
war has become indivisible and, therefore, peace is indivisible.
Therefore, our foreign policy cannot limit itself to the nearby
countries. Nevertheless, the nearby countries always have a
special interest in one another and India must, inevitably, think
in terms of its relations with the countries bordering her by land
and sea. What are these countries? If you start from the left,
Pakistan ; I would also include Afghanistan, although it does not
touch India's borders ; Tibet and China, Nepal, Burma, Malaya,
Indonesia and Ceylon. In regard to Pakistan, the position has been
a very peculiar one owing to the way Pakistan was formed and
India was divided. And there have been not only all the upsets
that you all know, but something much deeper, and that is, a
complete emotional upset of all the people in India and Pakistan

because of this. It is a very difficult thing to deal with, a psychological thing, which cannot be dealt with superficially. A year and a half or more has passed, and there is no doubt at all that our relations have improved and are improving. There is also no doubt at all in my mind that it is inevitable for India and Pakistan to have close relations—very close relations—sometime or other in the future. I cannot state when this will take place, but situated as we are, with all our past, we cannot really be just indifferent neighbours. We can either be rather hostile to each other or very friendly with each other. Ultimately, we can only be really very friendly, whatever period of hostility may intervene in between, because our interests are so closely interlinked. It is an astonishing thing—this partition that has taken place, and although we know a great deal about it, because we have lived through these troubled times, nevertheless, it is interesting to list the things that were upset by it. All our communications were upset and broken. Telegraphs, telephones, postal services, railway services and almost everything as a matter of fact was disrupted. Our Services were broken up. Our army was broken up. Our irrigation systems were broken up and so many other things happened. If we were to go on making a list of all, there would be a large number of them. But above all, what was broken up which was of the highest importance was something very vital and that was the body of India. That produced tremendous consequences, not only those that you saw, but those that you could not imagine, in the minds and souls of millions of human beings. We saw enormous migrations as a result of them, but what was deeper than that was the hurt and injury to the soul of India. We are getting over it, as people get over almost any type of injury, and we are again developing closer relations with Pakistan. There are many problems still to be solved, and I suppose they will gradually be solved.

As far as other countries are concerned, our relations with them are quite friendly. Take for instance, Afghanistan. Our relations with Afghanistan are exceedingly friendly and our relations with Tibet, Nepal and all the neighbouring countries are also very friendly. In fact, I think I am justified in saying that there is no country in this wide world today with which our relations may be said to be inimical or hostile. Naturally we will be attracted more towards some or our trade or economic interests might link us more with some countries and less with others, but there can be no doubt about it that we are friendly with all and I think that is a good thing and some achievement.

If our neighbouring countries have in a sense first place in our minds, then the second place goes to the other countries of Asia with whom we are also fairly intimately connected. Now, India is very curiously placed in Asia and her history has been governed a great deal by the geographical factor plus other factors. Whichever problem in Asia you may take up, somehow or other India comes into the picture. Whether you think in terms of China or the Middle East or South-East Asia, India immediately comes into the picture. It is so situated that because of past history, traditions, etc., in regard to any major problem of a country or a group of countries of Asia, India has to be considered. Whether it is a problem of defence or trade or industry or economic policy, India cannot be ignored. She cannot be ignored, because, as I said, her geographical position is a compelling reason. She cannot be ignored also, because of her actual or potential power and resources. Whatever her actual strength may or may not be, India is potentially a very powerful country and possesses the qualities and factors that go a long way to make a country grow strong, healthy and prosperous. She is rich in those elements and I think she has a population which has the capacity to use those elements. Naturally we have our failings and the difficulties are there, but if you view the problem in a certain perspective, there can be no doubt in anyone's mind that India's potential wealth will become actual and that in not too distant a future.

Therefore, whatever our own views may be, by virtue of her practical position and other reasons that I mentioned, India is bound to play an important part in Asia—in all parts of Asia—whether it is Western Asia or the Far East or South-East Asia. It so happens, of course, that even culturally speaking, our bonds are very great with all these parts of Asia, whether it is Western Asia or the Far East or South-East Asia, and these bonds are very old and very persistent.

A very curious thing happened when, roughly speaking, British power came to India and British dominion was established here. This was the reason why we were cut off from our neighbouring countries of Asia. Our contacts were then with England across the seas and while we to some extent struggled against that domination and resented those contacts, nevertheless, they were there and we saw the world more and more through that window

—through the British window. Very few people went to the Asian countries from India and very few came here from there. And even those few people from Asia we met, we met in Europe and not in Asia. Now in recent years that process has been reversed or is being reversed for a variety of reasons. Originally, I suppose, the one major factor was air travel. Immediately air travel brought us into close contact with our neighbours, because if we went to Europe, we passed through Baghdad and Teheran and other places. Air travel was not the only factor ; also there were political reasons that are now bringing about this change. And more especially since India became a free and independent country, you find several things happening. As you know, the Asian Conference was convened two years ago and various matters of common interest were discussed there. I will tell you what happened about that Conference. When a proposal was made to hold the Asian Conference—it was tentatively put forward—we did not quite know what the reaction to it would be. And invitations were sent to a number of countries and I may tell you we were amazed to find what the reaction was. It was an overwhelming reaction in favour of it and the Conference, as you very well know, was a very great success.

So you see something working in the mind of Asia, not only in India, but all over Asia. You find something germinating and whenever you give it a chance to come out, it comes out. We are convinced that there is a keen desire on the part of Asian countries to work together, to confer together and generally to look to each other. Possibly, this may be due to a certain resentment against the behaviour of Europe in the past. Undoubtedly, it was partly also a feeling that the Asian countries might still be exploited or dominated by Europe or the countries elsewhere. But it was also I think largely due to a certain flowback in memory of our ancient contacts, for our literature is full of them. We earnestly hope that we shall be able to develop our contacts still more for our future growth. That is why whenever any step is taken such as the recent Conference on Indonesia in Delhi, there is immediately a good response. This Conference was held at very short notice. But it attracted all these people. It attracted them, no doubt, because they were interested in Indonesia, but I think even more important was the desire to confer together and co-operate together, and a certain looking in the direction of India on the part of all these countries, the feeling that India might possibly play a fairly important part in bringing Asian countries together.

Some people talk rather loosely, and, if I may say so, rather foolishly, of India becoming the leader of this or the leader of that or the leader of Asia. Now, I do not like that at all. It is a bad approach, this business of leadership. But it is true that, because of the various factors I have mentioned, a certain special responsibility is cast on India. India realizes it, and other countries realize it also. The responsibility is not necessarily for leadership, but for taking the initiative sometimes and helping others to co-operate.

There are many factors that join the countries of Asia together apart from geography. There is the factor that for the last 150 to 200 years Asia has been dominated by Europe, by certain European countries. They came here, exploited this continent, dominated it, and various consequences flowed from this. We are today rather overwhelmed with the recent history of 200 years of European domination. But if we look at the long process of history, going back more than a few hundred years, we get a truer perspective, and in that perspective, of course, whether you look at Asia, or whether you look at India, the period of foreign domination is a very limited one. And now, the foreign domination of most Asian countries has ended, and it will no doubt end soon, there is a certain process of finding oneself, which each of the Asian countries is going through in various stages of advance according to modern standards ; there is this looking into oneself, finding oneself, feeling a certain assurance, self-confidence, fear also it may be in the case of some countries, because of economic and other weaknesses—but on the whole, finding oneself. This is also a certain binding factor.

Then again, the problems of Asia today are essentially problems of supplying what may be called the primary human necessities. They are not problems which may be called problems of power politics. Of course, every country to some extent has something to do with power politics in this world. But whichever countries we may take in Asia, one problem they always have, and that is the problem of preserving their freedom—the fear that somebody might take away their freedom. That problem is always there, quite apart from the fundamental problem, the problem of supplying primary necessities—food, clothing, housing, health, education and the like. These are common problems all over the world undoubtedly, but a great part of the rest of the world has advanced in its standards much further than the countries of Asia. The countries of the rest of the world have room for still further advance no doubt, and they have suffered a great deal from the last war. They have had to make up the tremendous losses caused by the last war. Unfortunately the whole outlook of Europe in the past 100 years has been the outlook of countries possessing great power, and being afraid of losing that power, afraid of one another, or desirous of extending that power. So that today Europe is much more tied up with power politics than Asia is at present. I do not know about the future. There is a fundamental difference of approach between them. And now, since the last war, Europe has been tied up to a number of very grave problems and conflicts. If I may say so, the past *karma* of Europe pursues it. We cannot easily get rid of the curse of our past *karma* ; it pursues our country in various ways. But there is this basic difference, I think, in the European approach to problems and the Asian approach. The whole world wants peace ; I have no doubt about it. And if there are any individuals who really want war, they cannot be many, and they cannot be completely balanced in mind. But what does happen is that in the case of people wanting war, a certain obsession, a certain fear, oppresses them, and, therefore, whether they want to or not, they go towards war. This is a terrible thing, this fear complex that we see all over the world today, or nearly all over the world. Europe is full of it at the present moment. Why Europe? Other parts of the world, too. And, of course, Asia has it too, and, I suppose a good deal of it ; but compared with Europe, I think, there is much less of it.

Let me put it in another way—the countries which have been the 'haves' in the world are very much afraid of losing what they have, while countries not having had so much to lose are not obsessed by that fear so much. Anyhow, there are these different psychological approaches to these various problems.

Now, take the United Nations. The United Nations Organization has most of the nations of the world in it, but it is true that it is dominated more or less by certain great nations of Europe and America, with the result that the main problems discussed there are the problems of Europe and America. Naturally we are interested in those problems, because they affect us too ;

and if there is war, obviously we are affected. But we cannot possibly get as excited about those problems as the people of Europe and America. For instance, the problem of Indonesia is more important to us than many European problems. Geography, perhaps, is responsible if you like. Whatever the reason may be, the real reason ultimately is not merely geography, but a feeling deep down in our minds that if some kind of colonial domination continues in Indonesia, if it is permitted to continue, it will be a danger to the whole of Asia, it will be a danger to us in India as well as to other countries. Further, if it is allowed to continue there, obviously it can only continue with the passive or active acquiescence of some of the great Powers, the result being that those great powers who may acquiesce in it themselves become in the eyes of Asia partners to that guilt. This is an important point to remember, that it is not merely a political game of chess for us in India ; it is, apart from the freedom of Indonesia, a most vital problem affecting the whole of Australia, Asia, and perhaps America. From this point of view, Europe and America are being tested in the eyes of Asia, just as we may be tested in the eyes of Europe and America.

I give you one instance. Now, if I may be quite frank before you, I have no doubt that the countries in Europe and America are themselves very much disturbed and distressed by what is taking place in Indonesia. They want to help Indonesia. I think they realize that Indonesian freedom is not only desirable in itself, but in the larger scheme of things which they have before them it is also desirable, and if by any chance any kind of imperialistic domination succeeds in Indonesia it will affect the larger plans they have for the future. And I realize that the Asian nations as a whole will be very much affected and our action in future may be governed by what happens in Indonesia. Therefore, I have heard that they are very anxious to solve the Indonesian problem satisfactorily and bring about freedom and independence in Indonesia. True, but then there comes the difficulty when you forget or you do not act up to certain definite principles. Any action taken in Indonesia concerns more especially the Indonesian people on the one side and the Netherlands Government on the other. Now, in an entirely different context, some of the Powers of Western Europe and America have, as you well know, arrived at a settlement in which the Netherlands Government is also included—the Atlantic Pact. They were apparently justified in looking after their interests. It is another matter, I am not discussing that. But here a conflict arises in the minds of all these countries. While, on the one hand, they wish to have Indonesian freedom, on the other, they are very anxious to have the Netherlands in their political grouping. Sometimes they do not take up the strict and direct line that they might otherwise take up, because they are pulled in other directions by these very difficulties.

So that while generally we may agree about various matters, the emphasis may be very different. We may look upon something as No. 1 which for them is No. 2, and what is for them No. 1 may be No. 2 for us. Although we may not be against No. 2, it is, nevertheless, for us not No. 1. It does make a lot of difference what priorities you give to things. It makes all the difference in the world whether you give truth the first place or the second place in life and in politics.

The other day I was speaking about the foreign policy of India and naturally I was rather general, because it is very difficult to be precise and particular. When we are students at colleges, we discuss almost all matters and problems and foreign policy and give expression to our opinions freely and frankly, because we deal normally with these questions as if we had isolated them from other questions. It is fairly easy to give an opinion about any question isolated from others. But when you have to deal with the business of life, you find that no question is isolated from another. While you may say 'yes' in answer to a particular question, when you look at it in relation to other problems your 'yes' may well become 'no' or something in between.

Now, foreign policy is normally something which develops gradually. Apart from certain theoretical propositions you may lay down, it is a thing which, if it is real, has some relation to actuality and not merely to pure theory. Therefore, you cannot precisely lay down your general outlook or general approach, but gradually it develops. We are as an independent country a fairly young country at present, although we are a very ancient country, and we have all the advantages and disadvantages of being an ancient country. Nevertheless, in the present context of foreign policy we are a young country and, therefore, our foreign policy is gradually developing and there is no particular reason why we should rush in all over the place and do something that comes in the way of this gradual development. We may and we should express our general view as to where we wish to go and how we wish to go there, but laying down our policy precisely in regard to any particular country would probably lead us into some difficulties. As I said, our general policy has been to try to cultivate friendly relations with all countries, but that is something which any one can say. It is not a very helpful thought. It is almost outside, if I may say so, of politics. It may be just a verbal statement or a moral urge. It is hardly a political urge. Nevertheless, something can be said for it even on the political plane. We cannot perhaps be friendly always with every country. The alternative is to become very friendly with some and hostile to others. That is the normal foreign policy of a country—very friendly with close relations with some, with the consequence that you are hostile to others. You may be very friendly to some countries and you cannot just be equally friendly with all countries. Naturally you are more friendly with those with whom you have closer relations, but that great friendliness, if it is active friendliness is good ; if it merely reflects hostility to some other country, then it is something different. And ultimately your hostility provokes other people's hostility and that is the way of conflict and leads to no solution. Fortunately, India has inherited no past hostility to any country. Why should we then start this train of hostility now with any country? Of course, if circumstances compel us it cannot be helped, but it is far better for us to try our utmost to keep clear of these hostile backgrounds. Naturally, again, we are likely to be more friendly to some countries than to others, because this may be to our mutual advantage. That is a different matter, but even so, our friendship with other countries should not, as far as possible, be such as brings us inevitably into conflict with some other country. Now, some people may think that this is a policy of hedging or just avoiding pitfalls, a middle-of-the-road policy. As I conceive it, it is nothing of the kind. It is not a middle-of-the-road policy. It is a positive, constructive policy deliberately aiming at something and deliberately trying to avoid hostility to other countries, to any country as far as possible.

How can we achieve this? Obviously, there are risks and dangers, and the first duty of every country is to protect itself. Protecting oneself unfortunately means relying on the armed forces and the like and so we build up, where necessity arises, our defence apparatus. We cannot take the risk of not doing so, although Mahatma Gandhi would have taken that risk no doubt and I dare not say that he would have been wrong. Indeed, if a country is strong enough to take that risk it will not only survive, but it will become a great country. But we are small folk and dare not take that risk. But in protecting oneself, we should do so in such a way as not to antagonize others and also so as not to appear to aim at the freedom of others. That is important. Also we should avoid in speech or writing anything which worsens the relationship of nations. Now, the urge to do or say things against countries, against their policies and sometimes against their statesmen is very great, because other people are very offensive at times ; they are very aggressive at times. If they are aggressive we have to protect ourselves against their aggression. If there is fear of future aggression we have to protect ourselves against that. That I can understand, but there is a distinct difference between that and shouting loudly from the house tops all the time attacking this country or that—even though that country may deserve to be criticized or attacked. It does not help—this shouting business ; it only makes matters worse, because this increases tremendously that fear complex to which I referred. And in the shouting that takes place on either side, logic and reason disappear, because people's passions are roused and ultimately they land themselves in war.

If war comes, it comes. It has to be faced. To some extent it has to be provided for and all the consequences of war have to be accepted with it if it comes. But surely we do not want war. As I said some time ago, I take it that the vast majority of people of this world do not want war. Then our policy should primarily aim at avoiding war or preventing war. The prevention of war may include providing for our own defence and you can understand that, but that should not include challenges, counter-challenges, mutual cursings, threats, etc. These certainly will not prevent war, but will only make it come nearer, because they frighten the other Governments and the other Governments issue similar challenges and then you are frightened and so everybody lives in an atmosphere of fear and anything may come out of such an atmosphere of fear.

Now, can any country, can India succeed in preventing this kind of mutual recrimination? Can we succeed, as we want to, in dealing with every question on its merits? Today international questions are looked upon from the point of view of how they will affect some future conflict, with the result that you find groupings on either side forgetful of the actual merits of the case. And a country like India which talks in a different language is looked upon as a nuisance in every way ; unfortunately, not only as a nuisance, but every group suspects it of joining hands with the opposite group. But now, I think, there is a certain amount of realization by other countries that we really mean what we say. It is not some deep game or plot and we mean to consider these questions on their merits, and of course merits include other factors also in relation to which we consider such questions. Take our attitude in regard to two or three recent issues—Korea, Palestine and atomic energy. This atomic energy business came up in the last session of the U. N. General Assembly in Paris and there was a fierce debate on it as to what should be done. India was made a member of the Committee appointed to consider this problem and our distinguished representative on that Committee, who is an ideal person for this kind of thing and who never gets excited—while others get excited he gives calm and dispassionate thought to the problem—was able to change the atmosphere in the Committee. Whether any wonderful result was achieved or not is not the point, but the way to achieve the result was shown by us. Some countries refuse to be thrown off their feet whatever happens. Now, I do not say that we are so wise and steady on our feet that nothing pushes us off our balance. Of course, not. It is anyhow an attempt to stand on our feet, not to hop about or dance about or fall down.

May I say that I do not for an instant claim any superior vantage point for India to advise or criticize the rest of the world? I think we are merely trying not to get excited about these problems and anyhow there is no reason why we should not try. It follows, therefore, that we should not align ourselves with what are called power blocs. We can be of far more service without doing so and I think there is just a possibility—and I shall not put it higher than that—that at a moment of crisis our peaceful and friendly efforts might make a difference and avert that crisis. If so, it is well worth trying. When I say that we should not align ourselves with any power blocs, obviously it does not mean that we should not be closer in our relations with some countries than with others. That depends on entirely different factors, chiefly economic, political, agricultural and many other factors. At the present moment you will see that as a matter of fact we have far closer relations with some countries of the western world than with others. It is partly due to history and partly due to other factors, present-day factors of various kinds. These close relations will no doubt develop and we will encourage them to develop, but we do not wish to place ourselves in a position where, politically speaking, we are just lined up with a particular group or bound up to it in regard to our future foreign activities. India is too big a country herself to be bound down to any country, however big it may be. India is going to be and is bound to be a country that counts in world affairs, not I hope in the military sense, but in many other senses which are more important and effective in the end. Any attempt on our part, i.e., the Government of the day here, to go too far in one direction would create difficulties in our own country. It would be resented and we would produce conflicts in our own country which would not be helpful to us or to any other country. While remaining quite apart from power blocs, we are in a far better position to cast our weight at the right moment in favour of peace, and meanwhile our relations can become as close as possible in the economic or other domain with such countries with whom we can easily develop them. So it is not a question of our remaining isolated or cut off from the rest of the world. We do not wish to be isolated. We wish to have the closest contacts, because we do from the beginning firmly believe in the world coming closer together and ultimately realizing the ideal of what is now being called One World. But India, we are convinced, can help in that process far more by taking an individual stand and acting according to her own wishes whenever any crisis arises than by merging herself with others and getting tied up in hard and fast rules.

That is our general outlook in regard to our policy and we feel that looking at the world today we find that there is a great deal of talk of war. Unless some very unfortunate thing happens, say a grave accident or something like that takes place, I do not think there is going to be any war, at least in the next few years. Nobody can guarantee peace for any great length of time. If there is not going to be any war in the next few years—and if I may say so, there is not going to be any war—primarily it is because the countries are not prepared for war. That is to say while, politically speaking, in the course of the last year we might have been said to be near the war, because passions were aroused and many things happened that usually led the nations to war, but even then war did not take place. That is because in a military sense or otherwise, the countries were not prepared for war. War takes place when two factors are present at the same time. Firstly, the political urge for war and secondly the preparation for war. Now if one of them is absent, then war is not likely to take place. Well, one was actually absent and that was the preparation for war. The result was that the great crisis through which Europe struggled during the last summer and autumn, passed. Now, you cannot live for ever at a high pitch of crisis. It either bursts into war or gradually tones down. If, therefore, a political crisis takes place and if for certain reasons it cannot burst into war, then it is bound to tone down and this has happened in practice. But in any case that does not mean that the danger is not there. All you can say is that you get a few years of peace and you know in this mad world of ours a few years of peace are worthwhile. This short period of peace gives you definitely a chance to work to make that peace more enduring. I feel strongly that there is certainly a good possibility of that chance being utilized by the countries of the world and peace being very firmly established.

But what has happened today? We find that there has developed a fatalistic tendency to think in terms of war. It is rather difficult to say anything with certainty, yet the prospect of war is so bad and the consequences of war are going to be so bad, that, regardless of the result of war, I wish every human being to try his utmost to avoid war as far as possible. We do not want war anywhere. We want at least 10 or 15 years of peace in order to be able to develop our resources. If there is war anywhere in the world, then what happens to the rest of the world? You can imagine starvation for millions following the war.

So if we strive earnestly for peace and try to take advantage of the fact that the very grave crisis of the past autumn has toned down and might tone down still further, I think we can well increase the chances of peace. As far as we are concerned, we ought to try to do that. Now, there are other conflicts—whether it is in Berlin or in other places in Europe. Apart from these, there are two other issues in the world which, unless satisfactorily solved, may well lead to conflict and a conflict on a big scale. One is the issue typified by Indonesia, that is the issue of domination of one country over another. Where there is continued domination, whether it is in Asia or Africa, there will be no peace either there or in the people's minds elsewhere. There will be a continuous conflict going on, continuous suspicion of each other and continuous suspicion of Europe in the minds of Asia and, therefore, the friendly relationship which should exist between Asia and Europe will not come about easily. It is, therefore, important that all these areas of colonial domination should be freed and they should be able to function as free countries.

The second important factor is that of racial equality. That too, in some parts of the world, you know, has come very much to the forefront. For example, take the question of Indians in South Africa. It is a matter which concerns us all. It is not merely a question of Indians or South Africans, but it is a matter of vital significance to the world, because that too symbolises something in the world. If that is to continue in the world, then there is bound to be conflict and conflict on a big scale, because it is a continuous challenge to the self-respect of a vast number of people in the world and they will not put up with it. The matter is thus before the United Nations and I hope the United Nations will help in its solution. But quite apart from the United Nations, there can be not a shadow of doubt that if such a policy is continued, it will breed conflict. And that conflict will not be confined to particular areas in South Africa or elsewhere ; it will affect peoples in vast continents.

I am not touching upon the third matter, the basic matter, that is, economic policies,—it is too big a subject—except that I would like to say this in regard to it, that the only way to proceed in the world today as far as I can see is for each country to realize that it must not interfere with another country's economic policy. Ultimately the policies that deliver the goods will succeed, those that do not will not succeed. This policy of interfering aggressively with other countries' policies inevitably leads to trouble. We must realize that there are different types of economic policy in the world today, in different countries, and they are believed in by their people. Well, the only thing to do is to leave them to work out their destiny. It may be that one of them justifies this policy, another justifies another. It may be that a third follows a middle course. Whatever it may be, the future will show. Whatever that may be, the point is that we must proceed on the basis of leaving every country to shift for itself in regard to its internal affairs. Any effort to change the economic policy, or any other internal policy, forcibly, or to bring pressure to bear upon it, leads to counter-pressure and to continuous conflict.

May I just say one word before I close? We are striving for

One World, and what with the development of communications and everything, we come closer to one another. We know a great deal more about one another than we used to do. Nevertheless, I have a feeling that our knowledge of one another is often extraordinarily superficial, and we, living in out grooves, big or small, seem to imagine, each country seems to imagine, that we are more or less the centre of the world, and the rest is on the fringe, that our way of living is the right way of living and other people's way of living is either a bad way or a mad way, or just some kind of backward way. Now, I suppose it is a common human-failing to imagine that we are right and others are wrong. But, of course, apart from being right or wrong, it may be, both are right, and both are wrong ; anyhow, in so far as the people's manner of living is concerned, there may be differences, not only as between Europe, America, Asia and Africa, but also internally in some of the continents. Now, Europe and America, because they have been dominant countries, with a dominant culture, have tended to think that ways of living other than theirs are necessarily inferior. Whether they are inferior or not I do not know. If they are inferior, probably their own people will change them. But this method of approach of one country to another is a very limited approach and does not indicate much wisdom, because this world is a very varied place. Even in India, our whole culture testifies to our understanding of the variety of humanity—laying stress always on the unity, but also on the variety, the diversity. The world is a very diverse place, and I personally see no reason why we should regiment it along one line. And yet there is this attitude in people's minds to some extent, to regiment it and shape it after one particular pattern. Perhaps it may be due to the whole philosophy of life behind us in India. Whatever we may do in our limited outlook and failings, we have had a type of philosophy which is a live-and-let-live philosophy of life. We have no particular desire to convert other people to any view or thought. We are prepared to talk it out with everybody and convince him, and it is for him to accept it or not, and we are quite happy if he goes his own way. We are not at all happy if he interferes with our way. Other philosophies apparently are to compel a man to think and act according to their own ways, and that leads to conflict, apart from the fact that it is not probably, psychologically speaking, a right approach.

So if we recognize that this world is a diverse place and there

are diverse ways of living and functioning and thinking in it,
then let us try to get rid of the evil in the world and allow the
variety of the world to continue. There are forces strong enough
to unify it today, and probably it will come together, and the
diversity will probably grow less. It would be unfortunate if it
were to disappear one day and we were to become one regimented
whole ; it is a terrible thought. If it so happens, well, those who
live then will face the problems of the day. Most of us will not
be alive then. I suppose if we approach it in this way, there will
be far greater understanding between countries.

It surprises me to see some of our friends from abroad coming
here and doling out good advice to us, which we listen to patiently,
realizing that the advice that is given to us is not necessarily very
wise advice, and that the manner of giving it is also perhaps not
very wise ; nor does it show much profundity of thought, because,
with all our failings, we are a very ancient people, and we have
gone through thousands and thousands of years of human experience ; we have seen much wisdom, and we have seen much
folly, and we bear the traces of both that wisdom and that folly
around us. We have to learn much, and we shall learn much ;
and perhaps we have to unlearn a great deal too. But it is curious
when people, not even trying to understand what we are, seek
to improve us. We do not mind very much, but it does not help.
Now, that applies to us too, because we go about thinking in terms
of improving others. I wish all of us would give up the idea of improving others, and improve ourselves instead. Thank you.

INDIA & THE COMMONWEALTH

A FATEFUL AND HISTORIC DECISION

THREE days ago I returned to Delhi after attending the meeting of the Commonwealth Prime Ministers in London. It is right that I should report to you about this meeting which resulted in a fateful and historic decision. That decision will have to be placed before the Constituent Assembly for their approval. It will also be considered by the All India Congress Committee which has been the torch-bearer of India's freedom these many years. It is for these great and representative organizations to give the final verdict on what was done by me and others in London last month.

You have already read the declaration embodying the conclusions reached by the London meeting. The impression that I have gathered since my return is that the vast majority of our people has welcomed the decision, though there are some who have criticized in strong language what I did and have even called it " a great blunder," and " an outrage on the national sentiments of the Indian people." During a fairly long career in India's service I have often been accused of errors and mistakes, but I have never yet been charged with doing anything which was against the honour and self-respect of India or her people. It is a serious matter, therefore, if even a few persons, whose opinions I value, should consider that I have committed an outrage.

I want to tell you that I have not the least doubt in my mind that I have adhered in letter and spirit to every pledge that I, in common with millions of my countrymen, have taken in regard to the independence of India during the past twenty years and more. I am convinced that far from injuring the honour or interest of India, the action I took in London has kept that honour bright and shining and enhanced her position in the world.

Though the critics are few, I would rather address myself to them than to the much larger number of my people who have already expressed their approval. I can only imagine that these critics are labouring under some misapprehension, or are under the impression that something else has been done in secret

A talk broadcast from New Delhi, May 10, 1949.

which has not seen the light of day. I wish to say that nothing has been done in secret and that no commitments of any kind limiting our sovereignty or our internal or external policy have been made, whether in the political or economic or military spheres. Our foreign policy has often been declared by me to be one of working for peace and friendship with all countries and of avoiding alignments with power blocs. That remains the keystone of our policy still. We stand for the freedom of suppressed nationalities and for the ending of racial discrimination. I am convinced that the Sovereign Indian Republic, freely associating herself with the other countries of the Commonwealth, will be completely free to follow this policy, perhaps in an even greater measure and with greater influence than before.

We took a pledge long ago to achieve Purna Swaraj (complete independence). We have achieved it. Does a nation lose its independence by an alliance with another country? Alliances normally mean mutual commitments. The free association of sovereign Commonwealth nations does not involve such commitments. Its very strength lies in its flexibility and its complete freedom. It is well-known that it is open to any member nation to go out of the Commonwealth if it so chooses.

It must be remembered that the Commonwealth is not a super State in any sense of the term. We have agreed to consider the King as the symbolic head of this free association. But the King has no function attached to that status in the Commonwealth. As far as the Constitution of India is concerned, the King has no place and we shall owe no allegiance to him.

I have naturally looked to the interests of India, for that is my first duty. I have always conceived that duty in terms of the larger good of the world. That is the lesson that our Master taught us and he told us also to pursue the ways of peace and of friendship with others, always maintaining the freedom and dignity of India. The world is full of strife today and disaster looms on the horizon. In men's hearts there is hatred and fear and suspicion which cloud their vision. Every step, therefore, which leads to a lessening of this tension in the world, should be a welcome step. I think it is a good augury for the future that the old conflict between India and England should be resolved in this friendly way which is honourable to both countries. There are too many disruptive forces in the world for us to throw our weight in in favour of further disruption and any opportunity that offers itself to heal old wounds and to further the cause of co-operation should be welcomed.

I know that much is being done in parts of the Commonwealth which is exceedingly distasteful to us and against which we have struggled in the past. That is a matter to be dealt with by us as a sovereign nation. Let us not mix things up which should be kept separate.

It has been India's privilege in the past to be a meeting place for many cultures. It may be her privilege in the present and the future to be a bridge to join warring factions and to help in maintaining that most urgent thing of today and the future— the peace of the world. It is in the belief that India could more effectively pursue this policy of encouraging peace and freedom and of lessening the bitter hatreds and tensions in the world, that I willingly agreed to the London agreement. I associated myself with the decisions taken in London at the Prime Ministers' meeting in the full belief that they were the right decisions for our country and for the world. I trust that the Indian people will also view them in that light and accept them in a manner worthy of the stature and culture of India and with full faith in our future. Let us not waste our energy at this critical moment in the world's history over empty debates, but rather let us concentrate on the urgent tasks of today, so that India may be great and strong and in a position to play a beneficent part in Asia and the world.

THIS NEW TYPE OF ASSOCIATION

I HAVE the honour to move the following motion :—

"Resolved that this Assembly do hereby ratify the declaration, agreed to by the Prime Minister of India, on the continued membership of India in the Commonwealth of Nations, as set out in the official statement issued at the conclusion of the Conference of the Commonwealth Prime Ministers in London on April 27, 1949."

All Honourable Members have been supplied with copies of this declaration and so I shall not read it over again. I shall merely point out very briefly some salient features of this declaration. It is a short and simple document in four paragraphs. The first paragraph, it will be noticed, deals with the present position in law. It refers to the British Commonwealth of Nations and to the fact that the people in this Commonwealth owe a common allegiance to the Crown. That in law is the present position.

The next paragraph of this declaration states that the Government of India have informed the Governments of the other Commonwealth countries that India is soon going to be a sovereign independent Republic ; further that they desire to continue her full membership of the Commonwealth of Nations, accepting the King as a symbol of the free association.

The third paragraph says that the other Commonwealth countries accept this and the fourth paragraph ends by saying that all these countries remain united as free and equal members of the Commonwealth of Nations. You will notice that while in the first paragraph this is referred to as the British Commonwealth of Nations, in the subsequent paragraph it is referred to only as the Commonwealth of Nations. Further you will notice that while in the first paragraph there is the question of allegiance to the Crown which exists at present, later, of course, this question does not arise, because India by becoming a Republic goes outside the Crown area completely. There is a reference, in connection with the Commonwealth, to the King as the symbol of that association. Observe that the reference is to the King and not to the

A speech moving a Resolution for the ratification of the Commonwealth Decision, delivered at the Constituent Assembly, New Delhi, May 16, 1949.

Crown. It is a small matter, but it has a certain significance. But the point is this that in so far as the Republic of India is concerned, her Constitution and her working are concerned, she has nothing to do with any external authority, with any king, and none of her subjects owe any allegiance to the King or any other external authority. The Republic may however agree to associate itself with certain other countries that happen to be monarchies or whatever they choose to be. This declaration, therefore, states that this new Republic of India, completely sovereign and owing no allegiance to the King, as the other Commonwealth countries do owe, will, nevertheless, be a full member of this Commonwealth and it agrees that the King will be recognized as a symbol of this free partnership or rather association.

Now, I am placing this declaration before this Honourable House for their approval. Beyond this approval, there is no question of any law being framed in accordance with it. There is no law behind the Commonwealth. It has not even the formality which normally accompanies treaties. It is an agreement by free will, to be terminated by free will. Therefore, there will be no further legislation or law if this House approves of this. In this particular declaration nothing very much is said about the position of the King, except that he will be a symbol. It has been made perfectly clear—it was made perfectly clear—that the King has no functions at all. He has a certain status. The Commonwealth itself, as such, is not a body, if I may say so ; it has no organization through which to function and the King also can have no functions.

Now, some consequences flow from this. Apart from certain friendly approaches to one another, apart from a desire to co-operate, which will always be conditioned by each party deciding on the measure of co-operation and following its own policy, there is no obligation. There is hardly any obligation in the nature of commitments. But an attempt has been made to produce something which is entirely novel, and I can very well understand lawyers on the one hand feeling somewhat uncomfortable at a thing for which they can find no precedent or parallel. There may also be others who feel that behind this there may be something which they cannot quite understand, something risky, something dangerous, because the thing is so simple on the face of it. That kind of difficulty may arise in people's minds. What I have stated elsewhere I should like to repeat. There is absolutely nothing behind this except what is placed before this House.

One or two matters I might clear up which are not mentioned in this declaration. One of these, as I have said, is that the King has no functions at all. This was cleared up in the course of our proceedings ; it has no doubt been recorded in the minutes of the Conference in London. Another point was that one of the objects of this kind of Commonwealth association is now to create a status which is something between being completely foreign and being of one nationality. Obviously, the Commonwealth countries belong to different nations. They are different nationalities. Normally either you have a common nationality or you are foreign. There is no intermediate stage. Up till now in this Commonwealth or the British Commonwealth of Nations, there was a binding link which was allegiance to the King. With that link, therefore, in a sense there was common nationality in a broad way. That snaps, that ends when we become a Republic, and if we should desire to give a certain preference or a certain privilege to any one of these countries, we would normally be precluded from doing so, because of what is called the " most favoured nation clause" every country would be as much foreign as any other country. Now, we want to take away that foreignness, keeping in our own hands what, if any, privileges or preferences we can give to another country. That is a matter entirely for two countries to decide by treaty or arrangement, so that we create a new state of affairs—or we try to create it— that the other countries, although in a sense foreign, are, nevertheless, not completely foreign. I do not quite know how we shall proceed to deal with this matter at a later stage. That is for the House to decide—that is to say, to take the right, only the right, to deal with Commonwealth countries, should we so choose, in regard to certain preferences or privileges. What they are to be, of course, we shall in each case be the judge ourselves. Apart from these facts, nothing has been decided in secret or otherwise which has not been put before the public.

The House will remember that there was some talk at one stage of a Commonwealth citizenship. Now, it was difficult to understand what the status of Commonwealth citizenship might be except that it meant that its members were not completely foreign to one another. That un-foreignness remains, but I think it is as well that we left off talking about something vague, which could not be surely defined, but the other fact remains, as I have just stated: the fact that we should take the right to ourselves if we so chose to exercise it at any time to enter into treaties or arrangements with Commonwealth countries assuring us of certain mutual privileges and preferences.

I have briefly placed before this House this document. It is a simple document and yet the House is fully aware that it is a highly important document or rather what it contains is of great and historical significance. I went to this Conference some weeks ago as the representative of India. I had consulted my colleagues here, of course, previously, because it was a great responsibility and no man is big enough to shoulder that responsibility by himself when the future of India is at stake. For many months past we had often consulted one another, consulted great and representative organizations, consulted many members of this House. Nevertheless, when I went, I carried this great responsibility and I felt the burden of it. I had able colleagues to advise me, but I was the sole representative of India and in a sense the future of India for the moment was in my keeping. I was alone in that sense and yet not quite alone, because, as I travelled through the air and as I sat there at the Conference table, the ghosts of many yesterdays of my life surrounded me and brought up picture after picture before me, sentinels and guardians keeping watch over me, telling me perhaps not to trip and not to forget them. I remembered, as many Honourable Members might remember, that day 19 years ago when we took a pledge on the bank of the river Ravi, at the midnight hour, and I remembered the 26th January the first time and that oft-repeated pledge year after year in spite of difficulty and obstruction, and finally I remembered that day when standing at this very place, I placed a resolution before this House. That was one of the earliest resolutions placed before this Honourable House, a resolution that is known as the Objectives Resolution. Two years and five months have elapsed since that happened. In that Resolution we defined more or less the type of free Government or Republic that we were going to have. Later in another place and on a famous occasion, this subject also came up, that was at the Jaipur session of the Congress, because not only my mind, but many minds were struggling with this problem, trying to find a way out that was in keeping with the honour and dignity and independence of India, and yet also in keeping with the changing world and with the facts as they were. Something that would advance the cause of India, would help us, something that would advance the cause of peace in the world, and yet something which would be strictly and absolutely true to every single pledge that we had taken. It was clear to me that whatever the advantages might be of any association with the Commonwealth or with any other group, no single advantage, however great, could be purchased by giving up a single iota of our pledges, because no country can make progress by playing fast and loose with the principles which it has declared. So during these months we had thought and we had discussed amongst ourselves and I carried all this advice with me. May I read to you, perhaps, just to refresh your minds, the Resolution passed at the Jaipur session of the Congress? It might be of interest to you and I would beg of you to consider the very wording of this Resolution:

" In view of the attainment of complete independence and the establishment of the Republic of India which will symbolize Independence and give to India the status among the nations of the world that is her rightful due, her present association with the United Kingdom and the Commonwealth of Nations will necessarily have to change. India, however, desires to maintain all such links with other countries as do not come in the way of her freedom of action and independence and the Congress would welcome her free association with the independent nations of the Commonwealth for their commonweal and the promotion of world peace."

You will observe that the last few lines of this Resolution are almost identical with the lines of the declaration of London.

I went there guided and controlled by all our past pledges, ultimately guided and controlled by the Resolution of this Honourable House, by the Objectives Resolution and all that had happened subsequently ; also by the mandate given to me by the All India Congress Committee in that Resolution, and I stand before you to say with all humility that I have fulfilled the mandate to the letter. All of us have during these many years past been through the valley of the shadow ; we have passed our lives in opposition, in struggle and sometimes in failure and sometimes success and most of us are haunted by these dreams and visions of old days and those hopes that filled us and the frustrations that often followed those hopes ; yet we have seen that even from that prickly thorn of frustration and despair, we have been able to pick the rose of fulfilment.

Let us not be led away by considering the situation in terms of events which are no longer here. You will see that the Resolution of the Congress that I have read out says that because India becomes a Republic, the association of India with the Commonwealth must, of course, change. Further it says that free association may continue subject only to our complete freedom being assured. Now, that is exactly what has been tried to be done in this declaration of London. I ask you or any Honourable Member to point out in what way the freedom, the independence of India has been limited in the slightest. I do not think it has been. In fact, the greatest stress has been laid not only on the independence of India, but on the independence of each individual nation in the Commonwealth.

I am often asked, how we can join a Commonwealth in which there is racial discrimination, in which there are other things happening to which we object. That, I think, is a fair question and it is a matter which must necessarily give us some trouble in our thinking. Nevertheless, it is a question which does not really arise. That is to say, when we have entered into an alliance with a nation or a group of nations, it does not mean that we accept their other policies ; it does not mean that we commit ourselves in any way to something that they may do. In fact, this House knows that we are carrying on at the present moment a struggle, or our countrymen are carrying on a struggle in regard to racial discrimination in various parts of the world.

This House knows that in the last few years one of the major questions before the United Nations, at the instance of India, has been the position of Indians in South Africa. May I, if the House will permit me, for a moment refer to an event which took place yesterday, that is, the passing of the Resolution at the General Assembly of the United Nations, and express my appreciation and my Government's appreciation of the way our delegation has functioned in this matter and our appreciation of all those nations of the United Nations, almost all, in fact all barring South Africa, which finally supported the attitude of India? One of the pillars of our foreign policy, repeatedly stated, is to fight against racial discrimination, to fight for the freedom of suppressed nationalities. Are you compromising on that issue by remaining in the Commonwealth? We have been fighting on the South African Indian issue and on other issues even though we have thus far been a Dominion of the Commonwealth. It was a dangerous thing for us to bring that matter within the purview of the Commonwealth. Because then the very thing to which you and I object might have taken place. That is, the Commonwealth might have been considered as some kind of a superior body which sometimes acts as a tribunal, or judges, or in a sense supervises the activities of its member nations. That certainly would have meant a diminution in our independence and sovereignty, if we had once accepted that principle. Therefore, we were not prepared and we are not prepared to treat the Commonwealth as such or even to bring disputes between member nations of the Commonwealth before the Commonwealth body. We may, of course, in a friendly way discuss the matter ; that is a different matter. We are anxious to maintain the position of our countrymen in other countries in the Commonwealth. As far as we are concerned, we could not bring their domestic policies in dispute there ; nor can we say in regard to any country that we are not going to associate ourselves with that country because we disapprove of certain policies of that country.

I am afraid that if we adopted that attitude, then there would hardly be any association for us with any country, because we have disapproved of something or other that that country does. Sometimes, it so happens that the difference is so great that either you cut off relations with that country or there is a conflict. Some years ago, the United Nations General Assembly decided to recommend its member States to withdraw diplomatic representatives from Spain, because Spain was supposed to be a Fascist country. I am not going into the merits of the question. Sometimes, the question comes up in that way. The question has come up again and they have reversed that decision and left it to each member State to do as it likes. If you proceed in this way, take any great country or a small country ; you do not agree with everything that the Soviet Union does ; therefore, why should we have representation there or why should we have a treaty of alliance in regard to commercial or trade matters with it? You may not agree with some policies of the United States of America ; therefore, you cannot have a treaty with them. That is not the way nations carry on their foreign work or any work. The first thing to realize, I think, in this world is that there are different ways of thinking, different ways of living and different approaches to life in different parts of the world. Most of our troubles arise from one country imposing its will and its way of

living on other countries. It is true that no country can live
in isolation, because, the world as constituted today is progressively becoming an organic whole. If one country living in isolation
does something which is dangerous to the other countries, the
other countries have to intervene. To give a rather obvious
example, if one country allowed itself to become the breeding
ground of all kinds of dangerous diseases, the world would have to
come in and clear it up, because it could not afford to allow
disease to spread all over the world. The only safe principle to
follow is that, subject to certain limitations, each country should
be allowed to live its own life in its own way.

There are at present several ideologies in the world and major
conflicts flow from these ideologies. What is right or what is
wrong, we can consider at a later stage, or maybe something else
altogether is right. Either you want a major conflict, a great war
which might result in the victory for this nation or that, or else
you must allow them to live at peace in their respective territories
and to carry on their way of thinking, their way of living, their
structure of State, allowing the facts to prove which is right ultimately. I have no doubt at all that ultimately it will be the system
that delivers the goods—the goods being the advancement and
the betterment of the human race or the people of the individual
countries—that will survive and no amount of theorizing and no
amount of warfare can make the system that does not deliver the
goods survive. I refer to this because of the argument that was
raised that India could not join the Commonwealth, because
it disapproved of certain policies of certain Commonwealth
nations. I think we should keep these two matters completely
separate.

We join the Commonwealth, obviously because we think it is
beneficial to us and to certain causes in the world that we wish
to advance. The other countries of the Commonwealth want us
to remain, because they think it is beneficial to them. It is
mutually understood that it is to the advantage of the nations
in the Commonwealth and therefore they join. At the same time,
it is made perfectly clear that each country is completely free to
go its own way ; it may be that they may go, sometimes go so far
as to break away from the Commonwealth. In the world today
where there are so many disruptive forces at work, where we are
often on the verge of war, I think it is not a safe thing to encourage
the breaking up of any association that one has. Break up the evil

part of it ; break up anything that may come in the way of your growth, because nobody dare agree to anything which comes in the way of a nation's growth. Otherwise, apart from breaking the evil parts of the association, it is better to keep a co-operative association going which may do good in this world rather than break it.

Now, this declaration that is placed before you is not a new move and yet it is a complete reorientation of something that has existed in an entirely different way. Suppose we had been cut off from England completely and we had then desired to join the Commonwealth of Nations, it would have been a new move. Suppose a new group of nations wanted us to join them and we joined them in this way, that would have been a new move from which various consequences would have flowed. In the present instance, what is happening is that a certain association has been in existence for a considerable time past. A very great change came in the way of that association about a year and eight or nine months ago, from August 15, 1947. Now another major change is contemplated. Gradually the conception is changing. Yet that certain link remains in a different form. Now, politically we are completely independent. Economically we are as independent as independent nations can be. Nobody can be 100% independent in the sense of absolute lack of inter-dependence. Nevertheless, India has to depend on the rest of the world for her trade, for her commerce and for many supplies that she needs, today for her food unfortunately, and so many other things. We cannot be absolutely cut off from the world. Now, the House knows that inevitably during the past century and more all kinds of contacts have arisen between England and this country, many of them were bad, very bad, and we have struggled throughout our lives to put an end to them. Many of them were not so bad, many of them may be good and many of them, good or bad, irrespective of what they may be, are there. Here I am the patent example of these contacts, speaking in this Honourable House in the English language. No doubt we are going to change that language for our use, but the fact remains that I am doing so and the fact remains that most other members who will speak will also do so. The fact remains that we are functioning here under certain rules and regulations for which the model has been the British Constitution. Those laws which exist today have been largely forged by them. Gradually, the laws which are good we will keep and those that are bad we will throw away. Any marked change in this without something to follow creates a hiatus which may be harmful. Largely our educational apparatus has been influenced. Largely our military apparatus has been influenced by these considerations and we have grown up naturally as something rather like the British Army. I am placing before the House certain entirely practical considerations. If we break away completely, the result is that without making sufficient provision for carrying on in a different way, we have a period of gap. Of course, if we have to pay a price, we may choose to do so. If we do not want to pay the price, we should not pay it and face the consequences.

But in the present instance, we have to consider not only these minor gains, which I have mentioned to you, to us and to others but, if I may say so, the larger approach to world problems. I felt as I was conferring there in London with the representatives of other Governments that I had necessarily to stick completely and absolutely to the sovereignty and independence of the Indian Republic. I could not possibly compromise on the question of allegiance to any foreign authority. I also felt that in the state of the world today and in the state of India and Asia, it would be a good thing if we approached this question in a friendly spirit which would solve the problems in Asia and elsewhere. I am afraid I am a bad bargainer. I am not used to the ways of the market place. I hope I am a good fighter and I hope I am a good friend. I am not anything in between and so when you have to bargain hard for anything, do not send me. When you want to fight, I hope I shall fight and then when you are decided about a certain thing, then you must hold on to it and hold to it to the death, but about minor things I think it is far better to gain the goodwill of the other party. It is far more precious to come to a decision in friendship and goodwill than to gain a word here and there at the cost of ill will. So I approached this problem and may I say how I felt about others? I would like to pay a tribute to the Prime Minister of the United Kingdom and also to others there, because they also approached the problem in this spirit, not so much to score a debating point or to change a word here and there in this declaration. It was possible that if I had tried my hardest I might have got a word here and there changed in this declaration, but the essence could not have been changed, because there was nothing more for us to get out of that declaration. I preferred not to do so, because I preferred creating an impression and I hope the right impression that the approach of India to these and other problems of the world was not a narrow-minded approach. It was the approach based on faith and confidence in her own strength and in her own future and, therefore, it was not afraid of any country coming in the way of that faith, it was not afraid of any word or phrase in any document, but it was based essentially on this that if you approach another country in a friendly way, with goodwill and generosity, you would be paid back in the same coin and probably the payment would be in an even larger measure. I am quite convinced that in the treatment of nations to one another, as in the case of individuals, only out of goodwill will you get goodwill and no amount of intrigues and cleverness will get you good results out of evil ways. Therefore, I thought that this was an occasion not only to impress England, but others also, in fact to some extent the world, because the matter that was being discussed at 10 Downing Street, in London, was something that drew the attention of the entire world. It drew the attention of the world, partly because India is a very important country, potentially so, and actually so too. And the world was interested to see how this very complicated and difficult problem which appeared insoluble, could be solved. It could not be solved if we had left it to eminent lawyers. Lawyers have their uses in life ; but they should not be spread out everywhere. It could not have been solved by those extreme, narrow-minded nationalists who cannot see to the right or to the left, but live in a narrow sphere of their own, and, therefore, forget that the world is going ahead. It could not be solved by people who live in the past and cannot realize that the present is different from the past and that the future is going to be still more different. It could not be solved by any person who lacked faith in India and in India's destiny.

I wanted the world to see that India did not lack faith in herself, and that India was prepared to co-operate even with those with whom she had been fighting in the past ; provided the basis of co-operation today was honourable, that it was a free basis, a basis which would lead to the good not only of ourselves, but of the world also. That is to say, we would not deny that co-operation, simply because in the past we had fought, and thus carry on the trail of our past *karma* along with us. We have to wash out the past with all its evil. I wanted, if I may say so in all humility, to help in letting the world look at things in a slightly different perspective, or rather try to see how vital questions could be

approached and dealt with. We have seen too often in the arguments that go on in the assemblies of the world, this bitter approach, this cursing of each other, this desire, not in the least
to understand the other, but deliberately to misunderstand
the other, and to make clever points. Now, it may be a satis-
fying performance for some of us, on occasions to make clever
points and be applauded by our people or by some other people.
But in the state of the world today, it is a poor thing for any
responsible person to do, when we live on the verge of catastrophic
wars, when national passions are roused, and when even a casually
spoken word might make all the difference.

Some people have thought that by our joining or continuing
to remain in the Commonwealth of Nations we are drifting away
from our neighbours in Asia, or that it has become more difficult
for us to co-operate with other countries, great countries in the
world. But I think it is easier for us to develop closer relations with
other countries while we are in the Commonwealth than it might
have been otherwise. This is rather a peculiar thing to say.
Nevertheless, I say it, and I have given a great deal of thought to
this matter. The Commonwealth does not come in the way of our
co-operation and friendship with other countries. Ultimately we
shall have to decide, and ultimately the decision will depend on
our own strength. If we dissociate ourselves completely from the
Commonwealth, then for the moment we are completely isolated.
We cannot remain completely isolated, and so inevitably by stress
of circumstances, we have to incline in some direction or other.
But that inclination in some direction or other will necessarily be
a basis of give-and-take. It may be in the nature of alliances, you
give something yourself and get something in return. In other
words, it may involve commitments far more than at present.
There are no commitments today. In that sense, I say we are freer
today to come to friendly understandings with other countries and
to play the part, if you like, of a bridge for the mutual understanding of other countries. I do not wish to place this too high ;
nevertheless, it is no good placing it too low either. I should like
you to look round the world today and look, more especially
during the last two years or so, at the relative position of India
and the rest of the world. I think you will find that during this
period of two years or less, India has gone up in the scale
of nations in its influence and in its prestige. It is a little
difficult for me to tell you exactly what India has done or has not

done. It would be absurd for anyone to expect that India can become the crusader for all causes in the world and bring forth results. Even in cases that have borne fruit, it is not a thing to be proclaimed from the housetops. But something which does not require any proclamation is the fact of India's prestige and influence in world affairs. Considering that she came on the scene as an independent nation only a year and a half or a little more ago, it is astonishing—the part that India has played.

One more thing I should like to say. Obviously a declaration of this type, or the Resolution that I have placed before the House is not capable of amendment. It is either accepted or rejected. I am surprised to see that some Honourable Members have sent in notice of amendments. Any treaty with any foreign power can be accepted or rejected. It is a joint declaration of eight—or is it nine countries?—and it cannot be amended in this House or in any House. It can be accepted or rejected. I would, therefore, beg of you to consider this business in all its aspects. First of all make sure that it is in conformity with our old pledges, that it does violence to none. If it is proved to me that it does violence to any pledge that we have undertaken, that it limits India's freedom in any way, then I certainly shall be no party to it. Secondly, you should see whether it does good to us and to the rest of the world. I think there can be little doubt that it does us good, that this continuing association at the present moment is beneficial for us, and it is beneficial in the larger sense, to certain world causes that we represent. And lastly, if I may put it in a negative way, not to have had this agreement would certainly have been detrimental to those world causes as well as to ourselves.

And finally, about the value I should like this House to attach to this declaration and to the whole business of those talks resulting in this declaration. It is a method, a desirable method, and a method which brings a touch of healing with it. In this world which is today sick and which has not recovered from so many wounds inflicted during the last decade or more, it is necessary that we touch upon the world problems, not with passion and prejudice and with too much repetition of what has ceased to be, but in a friendly way and with a touch of healing, and I think the chief value of this declaration and of what preceded it was that it did bring a touch of healing in our relations with certain countries. We are in no way subordinate to them, and they are in no way subordinate to us. We shall go our way and they will go their way. But our way, unless something happens, will be a friendly way ; at any rate, attempts will be made to understand one another, to be friends with one another and to co-operate with one another. And the fact that we have begun this new type of association with a touch of healing will be good for us, good for them, and I think, good for the world.

WE HAVE NOT BOUND THE
FUTURE DOWN

WE have had a fairly full debate since yesterday and many Honourable Members have spoken in approval of this motion. In fact, if I may say so, some of them have even gone a little further than I might perhaps have gone. They have drawn some consequences and pointed out some implications which for my part I would not have approved or accepted. However, it is open to all of us and to each one of us to see the future in a particular way.

As far as this Resolution of mine and the Declaration of London are concerned, what we have got to see is this: One, that it fulfils, or at any rate it does not go against, any pledges of ours ; that is to say, that it takes India forward, or does not come in the way of India going forward to her natural destination of a Sovereign Independent Republic. Secondly, that it helps India, or does not hinder India from making rapid progress in the other domains in the course of the next few years. We have, in a sense, solved the political problem, but the political problem is intimately connected with the economic condition of the country. We are being faced by many economic difficulties. They are our domestic concern, no doubt, but obviously the world can help or hinder any policy that we may adopt. Now, does this proposal which is contained in this Declaration help our speedy progress economically and otherwise or not? That is another test. I am prepared to admit that even without external help, we will go ahead. But obviously it will be a far more difficult task and it will take a much longer time. It is not an easy matter to do that.

The third test is whether in the world, as it is today, it helps in the promotion of peace and the avoidance of war. Some people talk about encouraging this particular group or that, this bloc or that. We are all, I am afraid, in the habit of considering ourselves or our friends as angels and others the reverse of angels. We are all apt to think that we stand for the forces of progress and democracy and others do not. I must confess that in spite of my own

A speech in reply to the debate on India's decision to remain in the Commonwealth of Nations, delivered at the Constituent Assembly, New Delhi, May 17, 1949.

pride in India and her people, I have grown more humble about talking in terms of our being in the vanguard of progress or democracy.

In the last two or three years we have passed through difficult times, humiliating times. We have lived through them. That has been something in our favour. We have survived them. But I hope we have learned our lesson from them. For my part I am a little chary now of condemning this or that person or this or that nation, because the hands of no individual or nation are clean in such matters. And there is far too much of the habit of condemning other nations as the wrong-doers or the war-mongers, and yet doing exactly the same thing oneself.

If one looks round the world—of course, one favours certain policies—one is against some things and thinks that these are dangerous and might lead to war, but others are not. But the most amazing thing that strikes me is this: if you look back during the last 30 years or more which have comprised two wars and the period between these wars, you will find the same cries, changing slightly with the changed situation, of course, nevertheless, the same cries, the same approaches, the same fears and suspicions and the same arming on all sides and war coming. The same talk of this being the last war, the fight for democracy and all the rest of it is heard on every side. And then the war ends, but the same conflicts continue and again the same preparation for war. Then another war comes. Now, that is a very extraordinary thing, because I am convinced that hardly anybody in this wide world wants war, barring a few persons or groups who make profit by war.

Nobody and no country wants war. As war becomes more and more terrible they want it still less. Yet some past evil or *karma* or some destiny goes on pushing people in a particular direction, towards the abyss and they go through the same arguments and they perform the same gestures like automatons.

Now, are we fated to do that? I do not know, but anyhow I want to fight against that tendency of talking about war and preparation for war. Obviously, no country and no Government of any country dare allow its country to be unprepared for contingencies. We have to prepare ourselves unfortunately, unless we are brave enough to follow the policy that Mahatmaji laid down. If we are brave enough, well and good, we take the chance. I do believe that if we are brave enough that policy will be the right policy. But it is not so much a question of my being brave or your being brave, but of the country being brave enough to follow and understand that policy. I do not think we have been brought up to that level of understanding and behaviour. Indeed, when we talk about that great level, I should say that in the last year and a half we have sunk to the lowest depths of behaviour in this country. So let us not take the name of the Mahatma in vain. Anyhow we cannot ; no Government can say that it stands for peace and do nothing about it. We have to take precautions and prepare ourselves to the best of our ability. We cannot blame any other Government which does that, because that is an inevitable precaution that one has to take. But, apart from that, it seems to me that some Governments or many Governments go much further. They talk all the time of war. They blame the other party all the time. They try to make out that the other party is completely wrong or is a war-monger and so on. In fact they create the very conditions which lead to war. In talking of peace and our love of peace we or they create the conditions that in the past have invariably led to war. The conditions that ultimately lead to war are generally economic conflicts. But I do not think today it is economic conflict or even political conflict that is going to lead to war, but rather the overmastering fear, the fear that the other party will certainly overwhelm one, the fear that the other party is increasing its strength gradually and would become so strong as to be unassailable and so each party goes on arming and arming with the deadliest weapons. I am sorry I have drifted off in this direction.

How are we to meet this major evil of the day? Some people may join up with the group which stands for peace while others may join up with the other group which, according to them, stands for some other kind of peace or progress. But I am quite convinced in my own mind that by joining up in this way, I do not help the cause of peace. That, in fact, only intensifies the atmosphere of fear. Then what am I to do? I do not believe in sitting inactive or practising the policy of escapism. You cannot escape. You have to face the problem and try to beat it and overcome it. Therefore, the people who think that our policy is a kind of passive negation or is an insane policy,—they are mistaken. That has not been ever my idea on this subject. I think it is and it ought to be our policy, a positive policy, a definite policy, to strive to overcome the general trend towards war in people's minds.

I know that in the huge problem before the wor'd, India may not be a strong enough factor. She may be a feeble factor to change it or alter it. That may be so. I cannot claim any necessary results. Nevertheless, I say that the only policy that India should pursue in this matter is a positive, definite policy of avoiding the drift to war on the part of other countries and also of avoiding the atmosphere becoming so charged with fear and suspicion, and of not acclaiming this country or that, even though they may claim to make the world rational, but rather laying stress on the qualities of those countries which are good, which are acceptable and drawing out the best from them and thereby, in so far as it may be possible, to work to lessen the tensions and work for peace. Whether we succeed or not is another thing. But it is in our hands now to work with might and main in the direction we consider right, not because we are afraid or fear has overwhelmed us. We have gone through many frightful things and I do not think anything is going to happen in India or the world that is going to frighten us any more. Nevertheless, we do not want the world to suffer or go through another world disaster from which you and I cannot escape and our country cannot escape. No policy can make us escape from it. Even if war does not spread to this country, even so, if war comes from abroad, it will engulf India as well as the world. We have to face this problem.

This is more a psychological probelm than a practical one, although it has practical applications. I think that in a sense India is partly suited to face it, because in spite of our being feeble and rather unworthy followers of Gandhiji, we have imbibed to some small extent what he taught us. Secondly, in these world conflicts you will see there is a succession of one action following another ; inevitably one leading to another and so the chain of evil spreads ; war comes and the evils that follow wars come and they themselves lead to another war and the chain of events goes on and each country is caught in the cycle of *karma* or evil or whatever you call it. Now, so far these evils have brought about wars in the West, because in a sense these evils were concentrated in the Western powers ; I do not by any means say that the Eastern powers are virtuous. So far the West or Europe has been the centre of political activity, has dominated the politics of the world. Therefore, their disputes and their quarrels and their wars have dominated the world.

Now, fortunately we in India are not inheritors of the hatreds of Europe. We may like a person or dislike something or an idea, but we have not the past inheritance to crush us. Therefore, it may be slightly easier for us in facing these problems, whether in international assemblies or elsewhere, to deal with them not only objectively and dispassionately, but also with the goodwill of others who may not suspect us of any ill will derived from the past. It may be that a country can only function effectively if it has a certain strength behind it. I am not for the moment thinking of material or war strength—that, of course, counts—but the general strength behind it. A feeble country which cannot look after itself, how is it to look after the world and others? All these considerations I should like this House to have before it and then to decide on this relatively minor question which I have placed before the House, because I had all these considerations and I felt first of all that it was my duty to see that Indian freedom and independence was in no way touched.

It was obvious that the Republic that we have decided on will come into existence. I think we have achieved that. We would have achieved that, of course, in any event, but we have achieved that with the goodwill of many others. That, I think, is some additional achievement. To achieve it with the goodwill of those who perhaps are hit by it is some achievement. It shows that the manner of doing things—the manner which does not leave any trace of hatred or ill will behind it but starts a fund of goodwill—is important. Goodwill is always precious from any quarter. Therefore, I had a feeling when I was considering this matter in London and later, in a small measure, perhaps, I had done something that would have met with the approval of Gandhiji. The manner of it I am thinking of, more than the thing itself. I thought that this in itself would raise a fund of goodwill in the world—goodwill which in a smaller sense is to our advantage certainly, and to the advantage of England, but also in a larger sense to the advantage of the world in the psychological conflicts which people try to resolve by blaming one another, by cursing one another and saying that the others are to blame. Maybe somebody is to blame ; maybe some politicians or big men are to blame, but nobody can blame those millions of men who will die in these catastrophic wars. In every country, the vast masses of human beings do not want war. They are frightened of wars. Sometimes this very fright is exploited to revive wars, because it can always be said that the other party is coming to attack you.

Therefore, I want this House to consider not only what we have achieved in any event, nobody would have been able to prevent us from achieving it—but what has a certain relevancy and importance is that we have achieved it in a way that helps us and helps others, in a way which does not leave evil consequences behind it, for otherwise when we think that we have profited at other people's expense, they think of that always and want to take revenge later. So that is the way and if the world acts in that way, problems will be solved far more easily and wars and the consequences of war will perhaps be fewer. They would be no more. It is easy to talk about the faults of the British or of the imperialism and the colonialism of other countries. Perfectly true. You can make out a list of the good qualities and the bad qualities of every nation today, including India. Even if you made that list, the question would still remain how anyone was going to draw the good from the other parties and yourself and lay the foundations for good in the future.

I have come to the conclusion that it does not help us very much either on the government plane or on the national plane to lay stress on the evil in the other party. We must not ignore it ; we have to fight it occasionally. We should be prepared for that, but with all that, I do not think this business of maintaining our own virtues and blaming the other party is going to help us in the understanding of our real problem. It no doubt gives an inner satisfaction that we are virtuous while others are sinners. I am talking in religious phraseology which does not suit me, but the fact is that I do wish to bring this slightly moral aspect of this question before this Honourable House. I would not dare to do any injury to the cause of India and then justify it on some high moral ground. No Government can do that. But if you can do a profitable business and at the same time it is good on moral grounds, then obviously it is worthy of our understanding and appreciation. I do submit that what we have done in no way, negatively speaking, injures us or can injure us. Positively, we have achieved politically what we wanted to achieve and we are likely to progress, to have more opportunities of progress, in this way than we would otherwise have in the next few years.

Finally, in the world context, it is something that encourages and helps peace, to what extent I do not know ; and, of course, it is a thing which in no way binds this country down to any country. It is open to this House or Parliament at any time to break this link, if they so choose. Not that I want that link broken. But I am merely pointing out that we have not bound the future down in the slightest. The future is as free as air and this country can go any way it chooses. If it finds this way is a good way, it will stick to it ; if not, it will go some other way and we have not bound it down. I do submit that this Resolution that I have placed before this House embodying approval of the Declaration, the decision at the Conference in London, is a motion which deserves the support and approval of this House, not merely, if I may say so, a passive approval and support, but the active appreciation of all that lies behind it and all that it may mean for the future of India that is gradually unrolling before our very eyes. Indeed, all of us hitched our wagons to the star of India long ago. Our future, our individual future, depends on the future of India, and we have thought and dreamt of the future for a long time. Now, we have arrived at a stage when we have to mould, by our decisions and activities, this future at every step. It is no longer good enough for us to talk of that future in terms merely of resolutions, merely in terms of denunciations of others and criticism of others ; it is we who have to make it for good or ill ; sometimes some of us are too fond of thinking of that future only in negative terms by denouncing others. Some members of this House who have opposed this motion and some others who are not in this House, who have opposed this motion, I have felt, have been totally unable to come out of the cage of the past in which we all of us lived, even though the door was open for them to come out mentally. They have reminded us, and some of our friends have been good enough to quote my speeches, which I delivered 15 or 20 years ago. Well, if they attach so much value to my speeches, they might listen to my present speeches a little more carefully. The world has changed. Evil still remains evil, and good is good ; I do not mean to say that it is not: and I think imperialism is an evil thing and wherever it remains it has to be rooted out and colonialism is an evil thing, and wherever it remains, it has to be rooted out, and racialism is an evil and has to be fought. All that is true. Nevertheless, the world has changed; England has changed ; Europe has changed ; India has changed : everything has changed and is changing: and look at it now. Look at Europe which for the last three hundred years has had a period of magnificent achievement in the arts and sciences and it has built up a new civilization all over the world. It is really a magnificent period of which Europe or some countries of Europe can be greatly proud, but Europe during those three hundred years or more has also gradually spread out its domination over Asia and Africa, has been an imperialist power and exploited the rest of the world and in a sense dominated the political scene of the world. Well, Europe has still, I believe, a great many fine qualities and those people there who have fine qualities will make good, but Europe can no longer be the centre of the world politically speaking or exercise that influence over other parts of the world, which it had in the past. From that point of view, Europe belongs to the past and the centre of world history, of political and other activities, shifts elsewhere. I do not mean to say that any other continent becomes a dominating force, dominates the rest, not in that way. However, we are looking at it in an entirely changed scene. If you talk of British imperialism and the rest of it, I would say that there is no capacity left for imperialism even if the will were there ; it will not do. The French are acting imperialistically in parts of Asia. But the fact remains that the capacity for carrying it off any longer is past. They may carry on for a year or two years, but not for very long. The Dutch may do so elsewhere and if you look at it in the historical perspective, all these things are hang-overs of something past. There may be strength behind imperialism today ; it may last even a few years and, therefore, we have to fight it and, therefore, we have to be vigilant—I do not deny that—but let us not think as if Europe or England was the same as it was 15 or 20 years ago. It is not.

I was saying about our friends who have criticized us and taken a rather negative and passive view. I mentioned at another place that their view was static. I said that, in this particular context, it was rather reactionary and I am sorry I used that word, because I do not wish to use words that hurt and I do not wish to hurt people in this way. I have certainly the capacity to use language, clever language to hurt people, and dialectical language, but I do not wish to use it, because we are up against great problems, and it is poor satisfaction just to say a word against an opponent in an argument and defeat him by a word, and not reach his heart or mind, and I want to reach the hearts and minds of our people and I feel that whatever our domestic differences may be—let there be differences honestly felt—we do not want a cold regimentation of this country.

As far as foreign affairs are concerned, there may also be differences, I do not deny that, but the fundamental things before any man who is—whatever else he may be—an Indian patriot, who wants India to progress and the world also to progress, must necessarily be Indian freedom, that is, complete freedom, India's progress, economically and otherwise, India playing a part in the freedom of the world and the preservation of peace in the world. These are the fundamental things: India must progress. India must progress internally; we can play no part unless we are strong in our country economically and otherwise. How we should do so internally may be a matter of difference of opinion. Now, I think it should be possible for people who differ considerably in regard to our internal policy, it should be possible for us to have more or less a unified foreign policy in which they agree or mostly agree. May I make myself clear? I do not wish in the slightest to stop argument or comment or criticism; it is a sign of a healthy nation, but I do wish that argument to be the argument of a friend and not of an opponent who sometimes uses that argument, not for argument's sake, but just to injure the opposite party, which is often done in the game of politics. I do not see any major difference for any person in regard to foreign policy. I do see a major difference between those individuals or groups who think in terms of other countries and not primarily of India at all. That is a basic difference and with them it is exceedingly difficult to have any common approach about anything; but where people think in terms of India's independence and progress in the near future and in the distant future and who want peace in the world, of course, there will be no great difference in our foreign policy. And I do not think there is, in fact, although it may be expressed differently. Although a Government can only speak in the language of a Government, others speak a language which we all used to speak, of opposition and agitation. So I would beg this House, and if I may say so, the country to look upon this problem not in any party spirit, not in the sense of bargaining for this little matter or that.

We have to be careful in any business deal not to lose a thing which is advantageous to the nation. At the same time, we have to look at this problem in a big way. We are a big nation. If we are a big nation in size, that will not bring bigness to us unless we are big in mind, big in heart, big in understanding and big in action also. You may lose perhaps a little here or there with your bargainers and hagglers in the market place. If you act in a big way, the response to you is very big in the world and their reaction is also big. Because good always brings good and draws good from others and a big action which shows generosity of spirit brings generosity from the other side.

Therefore, may I finish by commending this Resolution to you and trusting that the House will not only accept it, but accept it as something, as a harbinger of good relations, of our acting in a generous way towards other countries, towards the world, and thus strengthening ourselves and strengthening the cause of peace.

INDIA AND THE WORLD

ASIA FINDS HERSELF AGAIN

FRIENDS and fellow Asians, what has brought you here, men and women of Asia? Why have you come from the various countries of this mother continent of ours and gathered together in the ancient city of Delhi? Some of us, greatly daring, sent you invitations for this Conference and you gave a warm welcome to that invitation. And yet it was not merely the call from us, but some deeper urge that brought you here.

We stand at the end of an era and on the threshold of a new period of history. Standing on this watershed which divides two epochs of human history and endeavour, we can look back on our long past and look forward to the future that is taking shape before our eyes. Asia, after a long period of quiescence, has suddenly become important again in world affairs. If we view the millenia of history, this continent of Asia, with which Egypt has been so intimately connected in cultural fellowship, has played a mighty role in the evolution of humanity. It was here that civilization began and man started on his unending adventure of life. Here the mind of man searched unceasingly for truth and the spirit of man shone out like a beacon which lighted up the whole world.

This dynamic Asia from which great streams of culture flowed in all directions gradually became static and unchanging. Other peoples and other continents came to the fore and with their new dynamism spread out and took possession of great parts of the world. This mighty continent became just a field for the rival imperialisms of Europe, and Europe became the centre of history and progress in human affairs.

A change is coming over the scene now and Asia is again finding herself. We live in a tremendous age of transition and already the next stage takes shape when Asia takes her rightful place with the other continents.

It is at this great moment that we meet here and it is the pride and privilege of the people of India to welcome their fellow Asians from other countries, to confer with them about the present and

A speech inaugurating the Asian Conference delivered at New Delhi, March 23. 1947.

the future, and lay the foundation of our mutual progress, well-being and friendship.

The idea of having an Asian Conference is not new and many have thought of it. It is indeed surprising that it should not have been held many years earlier, yet perhaps the time was not ripe for it and any attempt to do so would have been superficial and not in tune with world events. It so happened that we in India convened this Conference, but the idea of such a conference arose simultaneously in many minds and in many countries of Asia. There was a widespread urge and an awareness that the time had come for us, peoples of Asia, to meet together, to hold together and to advance together. It was not only a vague desire, but the compulsion of events that forced all of us to think along these lines. Because of this, the invitation we in India sent out brought an answering echo and a magnificent response from every country of Asia.

We welcome you delegates and representatives from China, that great country to which Asia owes so much and from which so much is expected ; from Egypt and the Arab countries of Western Asia, inheritors of a proud culture which spread far and wide and influenced India greatly ; from Iran whose contacts with India go back to the dawn of history ; from Indonesia and Indo-China whose history is intertwined with India's culture, and where recently the battle of freedom has continued, a reminder to us that freedom must be won and cannot come as a gift ; from Turkey that has been rejuvenated by the genius of a great leader ; from Korea and Mongolia, Siam, Malaya and the Philippines ; from the Soviet Republics of Asia which have advanced so rapidly in our generation and which have so many lessons to teach us ; and from our neighbours Afghanistan, Tibet, Nepal, Bhutan, Burma and Ceylon to whom we look especially for co-operation and close and friendly intercourse. Asia is very well represented at this conference, and if one or two countries have been unable to send representatives, this was due to no lack of desire on their part or ours, but circumstances beyond our control came in the way. We welcome also observers from Australia and New Zealand, because we have many problems in common, especially in the Pacific and in the South-East region of Asia, and we have to co-operate together to find solutions.

As we meet here today, the long past of Asia rises up before us, the troubles of recent years fade away, and a thousand memories revive. But I shall not speak to you of these past ages with their glories and triumphs and failures, nor of more recent times which have oppressed us so much and which still pursue us in some measure. During the past two hundred years we have seen the growth of Western imperialisms and of the reduction of large parts of Asia to colonial or semi-colonial status. Much has happened during these years, but perhaps one of the notable consequences of the European domination of Asia has been the isolation of the countries of Asia from one another. India always had contacts and intercourse with her neighbour countries in the North-West, the North-East, the East and the South-East. With the coming of British rule in India these contacts were broken off and India was almost completely isolated from the rest of Asia. The old land routes almost ceased to function and our chief window to the outer world looked out on the sea route which led to England. A similar process affected other countries of Asia also. Their economy was bound up with some European imperialism or other ; even culturally they looked towards Europe and not to their own friends and neighbours from whom they had derived so much in the past.

Today this isolation is breaking down because of many reasons, political and other. The old imperialisms are fading away. The land routes have revived and air travel suddenly brings us very near to one another. This Conference itself is significant as an expression of that deeper urge of the mind and spirit of Asia which has persisted in spite of the isolationism which grew up during the years of European domination. As that domination goes, the walls that surrounded us fall down and we look at one another again and meet as old friends long parted.

In this Conference and in this work there are no leaders and no followers. All countries of Asia have to meet together on an equal basis in a common task and endeavour. It is fitting that India should play her part in this new phase of Asian development. Apart from the fact that India herself is emerging into freedom and independence, she is the natural centre and focal point of the many forces at work in Asia. Geography is a compelling factor, and geographically she is so situated as to be the meeting point of Western and Northern and Eastern and South-East Asia. Because of this, the history of India is a long history of her relations with the other countries of Asia. Streams of culture have come to India from the west and the east and been absorbed in India, producing the rich and variegated culture which is India today. At the same time, streams of culture have flowed from India to distant parts of Asia. If you would know India you have to go to Afghanistan and Western Asia, to Central Asia, to China and Japan and to the countries of South-East Asia. There you will find magnificent evidence of the vitality of India's culture which spread out and influenced vast numbers of people.

There came the great cultural stream from Iran to India in remote antiquity. And then that constant intercourse between India and the Far East, notably China. In later years South-East Asia witnessed an amazing efflorescence of Indian art and culture. The mighty stream which started from Arabia and developed as a mixed Irano-Arabic culture poured into India. All these came to us and influenced us, and yet so great was the powerful impress of India's own mind and culture that it could acccept them without being itself swept away or overwhelmed. Nevertheless, we all changed in the process and in India today all of us are mixed products of these various influences. An Indian, wherever he may go in Asia, feels a sense of kinship with the land he visits and the people he meets.

I do not wish to speak to you of the past, but rather of the present. We meet here not to discuss our past history and contacts, but to forge links for the future. And may I say here that this Conference, and the idea underlying it, is in no way aggressive or against any other continent or country? Ever since news of this Conference went abroad some people in Europe and America have viewed it with doubt imagining that this was some kind of a Pan-Asian movement directed against Europe or America. We have no designs against anybody ; ours is the great design of promoting peace and progress all over the world. Far too long have we of Asia been petitioners in western courts and chancellories. That story must now belong to the past. We propose to stand on our own feet and to co-operate with all others who are prepared to co-operate with us. We do not intend to be the playthings of others.

In this crisis in world history Asia will necessarily play a vital role. The countries of Asia can no longer be used as pawns by others ; they are bound to have their own policies in world affairs. Europe and America have contributed very greatly to human progress and for that we must yield them praise and honour, and learn from them the many lessons they have to teach. But the

West has also driven us into wars and conflicts without number and even now, the day after a terrible war, there is talk of further wars in the atomic age that is upon us. In this atomic age Asia will have to function effectively in the maintenance of peace. Indeed, there can be no peace unless Asia plays her part. There is today conflict in many countries, and all of us in Asia are full of our own troubles. Nevertheless, the whole spirit and outlook of Asia are peaceful, and the emergence of Asia in world affairs will be a powerful influence for world peace.

Peace can only come when nations are free and also when human beings everywhere have freedom and security and opportunity. Peace and freedom, therefore, have to be considered both in their political and economic aspects. The countries of Asia, we must remember, are very backward and the standards of life are appallingly low. These economic problems demand urgent solution or else crisis and disaster may overwhelm us. We have, therefore, to think in terms of the common man and fashion our political, social and economic structure so that the burdens that have crushed him may be removed, and he may have full opportunity for growth.

We have arrived at a stage in human affairs when the ideal of One World and some kind of a World Federation seem to be essential, though there are many dangers and obstacles in the way. We should work for that ideal and not for any grouping which comes in the way of this larger world group. We, therefore, support the United Nations structure which is painfully emerging from its infancy. But in order to have One World, we must also, in Asia, think of the countries of Asia co-operating together for that larger ideal.

This Conference, in a small measure, represents this bringing together of the countries of Asia. Whatever it may achieve, the mere fact of its taking place is itself of historic significance. Indeed, this occasion is unique in history, for never before has such a gathering met together at any place. So even in meeting we have achieved much and I have no doubt that out of this meeting greater things will come. When the history of our present times is written, this event may well stand out as a land-mark which divides the past of Asia from the future. And because we are participating in this making of history, something of the greatness of historic events comes to us all.

This Conference will split up into committees and groups to

discuss various problems which are of common concern to all of us. We shall not discuss the internal politics of any country, because that is rather beyond the scope of our present meeting. Naturally we are interested in these internal politics, because they act and react on each other, but we may not discuss them at this stage, for if we do so, we may lose ourselves in interminable arguments and complications. We may fail to achieve the purpose for which we have met. I hope that out of this Conference some permanent Asian Institute for the study of common problems and to bring about closer relations will emerge ; also perhaps a School of Asian Studies. Further, we might be able to organize an interchange of visits and exchanges of students and professors so that we might get to know each other better. There is much more we can do, but I shall not venture to enumerate all these subjects for it is for you to discuss them and arrive at some decisions.

We seek no narrow nationalism. Nationalism has a place in each country and should be fostered, but it must not be allowed to become aggressive and come in the way of international development. Asia stretches her hand out in friendship to Europe and America as well as to our suffering brethren in Africa. We of Asia have a special responsibility to the people of Africa. We must help them to their rightful place in the human family. The freedom that we envisage is not to be confined to this nation or that or to a particular people, but must spread out over the whole human race. That universal human freedom also cannot be based on the supremacy of any particular class. It must be the freedom of the common man everywhere and full opportunities for him to develop.

We think today of the great architects of Asian freedom—Sun Yat-Sen, Zaghlul Pasha, the Ataturk Kemal Pasha and others, whose labours have borne fruit. We think also of that great figure whose labours and whose inspiration have brought India to the threshold of her independence—Mahatma Gandhi. We miss him at this Conference and I yet hope that he may visit us before our labours end. He is engrossed in the service of the common man in India, and even this Conference could not drag him away from it.

All over Asia we are passing through trials and tribulations. In India also you will see conflict and trouble. Let us not be disheartened by this ; this is inevitable in an age of mighty transition. There are a new vitality and powerful creative impulses in all the peoples of Asia. The masses are awake and they demand their heritage. Strong winds are blowing all over Asia. Let us not be afraid of them, but rather welcome them for only with their help can we build the new Asia of our dreams. Let us have faith in these great new forces and the dream which is taking shape. Let us, above all, have faith in the human spirit which Asia has symbolized for those long ages past.

AN AGE OF CRISES

WE live in an age of crises. One crisis follows another, and even when there is peace, it is a troubled peace with fear of war and preparation for war. Tortured humanity hungers for real peace, but some evil fate pursues it and pushes it further and further away from what it desires most. It seems almost that some terrible destiny drives humanity to ever-recurring disaster. We are all entangled in the mesh of past history and cannot escape the consequences of past evil.

In the multitude of crises, political and economic, that face us, perhaps the greatest crisis of all is that of the human spirit. Till this crisis of the spirit is resolved it will be difficult to find a solution for the other crises that afflict us.

We talk of World Government and One World and millions yearn for it. Earnest efforts continue to be made to realize this ideal of the human race, which has become so imperative today. And yet those efforts have thus far proved ineffective, even though it becomes ever clearer that if there is to be no world order then there might be no order at all left in the world. Wars are fought and won or lost, and the victors suffer almost as much as the vanquished. Surely, there must be something wrong about our approach to this vital problem of the age, something essential lacking.

In India during the last quarter of a century and more, Mahatma Gandhi made an outstanding contribution not only to the freedom of India but to that of world peace. He taught us the doctrine of non-violence, not as a passive submission to evil, but as an active and positive instrument for the peaceful solution of international differences. He showed us that the human sprit is more powerful than the mightiest of armaments. He applied moral values to political action and pointed out that ends and means can never be separated, for the means ultimately govern the end. If the means are evil, then the end itself becomes distorted and at least partially evil. Any society based on injustice must necessarily have the seeds of conflict and decay within it so long as it does not get rid of that evil.

A talk broadcast to the U.S.A. from Delhi, April 3, 1948.

All this may seem fantastic and impractical in the modern world, used as it is to thinking in set grooves. And yet we have seen repeatedly the failure of other methods and nothing can be less practical than to pursue a method that has failed again and again. We may not perhaps ignore the present limitations of human nature or the immediate perils which face the statesmen. We may not, in the world as it is constituted today, even rule out war absolutely. But I have become more and more convinced that so long as we do not recognize the supremacy of the moral law in our national and international relations, we shall have no enduring peace. So long as we do not adhere to right means, the end will not be right and fresh evil will flow from it. That was the essence of Gandhiji's message and mankind will have to appreciate it in order to see and act clearly. When eyes are blood-shot vision is limited.

I have no doubt in my mind that World Government must and will come, for there is no other remedy for the world's sickness. The machinery for it is not difficult to devise. It can be an extension of the federal principle, a growth of the idea underlying the United Nations, giving each national unit freedom to fashion its destiny according to its genius, but subject always to the basic covenant of the World Government.

We talk of the rights of individuals and nations, but it must be remembered that every right carries an obligation with it. There has been far too much emphasis on rights and far too little on obligations ; if obligations were undertaken, rights would naturally flow from them. This means an approach to life different from the competitive and acquisitive approach of today.

Today fear consumes us all,—fear of the future, fear of war, fear of the people of the nations we dislike and who dislike us. That fear may be justified to some extent. But fear is an ignoble emotion and leads to blind strife. Let us try to get rid of this fear and base our thoughts and actions on what is essentially right and moral, and then gradually the crisis of the spirit will be resolved, the dark clouds that surround us may lift and the way to the evolution of world order based on freedom will be clear.

ECONOMIC FREEDOM FOR ASIA

MR. Chairman and Members of the Commission, on behalf of the Government of India, I welcome you to this country and to this place. India has long been associated with the United Nations because India has believed in the aims and purposes of the United Nations, and even though sometimes no tangible results have followed in the United Nations, nevertheless, we have believed that we must—and the world must—follow that course in the hope that tangible results will come sooner or later. We have taken part in your various Commissions, because we have felt that, quite apart from the political aspect of the United Nations, the economic aspect is at least as important, if not more important ; indeed perhaps we cannot consider the one without the other. Politically we have not met with great success so far, but I hope that if we succeed in the economic field, that will affect the political field also.

There has been talk in the past of One World in the political sense, but it is even more important to consider it in the economic sense. You are meeting here to deal with Asia and Asia's problems—problems, too, inevitably in the context of the larger world—because we cannot escape looking at almost any problem except in the global context today. Asia is big enough and the subjects you have to deal with are vast and of tremendous importance.

The Governor of Madras referred to the numerous papers and memoranda that you have before you and I feel rather over-whelmed when I look at all these files and papers and when I see all these experts, because I can only speak as a layman. But while experts are quite inevitable in the modern world, sometimes I have a feeling that they become very impersonal and look at problems as if they were mathematical and algebraic formulae. Well, we have to deal with human beings and the future of human beings and in this area under survey—Asia which has a population of at least a thousand million human beings. In India, including Pakistan, there are 40 per cent of those thousand

Inaugural address at the third session of the United Nations Economic Commission for Asia and the Far East at Ootacamund, Madras, June 1, 1948.

millions, that is four hundred millions, and we have to deal with
these vast numbers—practically half the world's population—and
if you look at the human aspect of it, these thousand millions
with their sufferings, with their wants, with their joys and sorrows,
the problem becomes something much more than a dry economic
problem which you have to solve and it assumes a tremendous
urgency.

Now, for many years past most of these problems have
been considered in the world context and I had a feeling and I
still have that feeling, that the continent of Asia is somewhat
neglected, somewhat overlooked. It is not considered important
enough for as much attention to be given to it as is given to
certain other parts of the world. Possibly that has been so, because
most of the people who were considering these problems were
themselves intimately connected with other parts of the world
and naturally they thought of them in the first instance.
Naturally also, if I have to consider these problems, I would attach
more importance to Asia, because it affects me more intimately.
But that kind of reaction apart, it is quite obvious that you cannot
consider the problem of Asia, or the problem of Europe, or the
problem of America or the problem of Africa isolated from the
problem of other countries.

It just cannot be done and if some countries which are
fortunate enough today—more fortunate than others—think
that they can lead their lives in isolation irrespective of what
happens in the rest of the world, it is obvious that they are under a
misapprehension. Today, if one part of the world goes down
economically, it has a tendency to drag others with it, just as
when unfortunately war breaks out other people are involved who
do not want war. So it is not a question of the prosperous, merely
out of the generosity of their hearts helping those that are not
prosperous, though generosity is a good thing. But it is a question
of enlightened self-interest, realizing that if some parts of the
world do not progress, remain backward, they have an adverse
effect on the whole economy of the world and they tend to drag
down those parts that are at present prosperous. Therefore, it
becomes inevitable to consider these problems in the global way
and to pay even more attention to those parts which are relatively
backward.

Now, Asia has been for generations past in a somewhat static
and backward condition. But during the last few years mighty

20

forces have been at work in Asia. These forces inevitably thought in terms of political change to begin with, because without political change it was not possible to have any far-reaching or enduring economic change. Large parts of Asia were colonial territory dominated by other countries. From that connection they have obtained some advantage sometimes. While it did undoubtedly in a sense shake up that static condition, at the same time it tended to preserve it too.

The political struggle of Asia is largely over—not entirely ; there are parts of Asia still where some kind of struggle for political freedom is still going on: and it is obvious that so long as there is that type of struggle on the political plane other activities will be ignored or will be thwarted. The sooner, therefore, it is realized that politically every country in Asia should be completely free and be in a position to follow its own genius within the larger world policy that any world organization may lay down, the better it will be. If one thing is certain, it is that there will be no peace in any part of Asia if there is a tendency for another country to dominate over an Asian country by force. I regret that some such attempts continue to be made in parts of Asia. They seem to me not only undesirable in themselves, but singularly lacking in foresight, because there can be but one end to their attempts and that is the complete elimination of any kind of foreign control.

Now, generally speaking, this political aspect of the Asian struggle is drawing to its natural and inevitable culmination. But at the same time, the economic aspect continues and is bound up with all manner of economic problems affecting the world. From the Asian point of view, it has become essentially a matter of extreme urgency to deal with these problems. From the world point of view it is equally urgent really, because unless these problems are dealt with in Asia, they affect other parts of the world. I trust that you, ladies and gentlemen, who are members of this Commission, no doubt realize the importance of what I have said, and will make it clear to the United Nations that any attempt to pay inadequate attention to Asian problems is likely to defeat the end which the United Nations have in view.

In Asia, many historical forces have been at work for many years past and many things have happened which are good and many things which are not so good as always happens when impersonal historic forces are in action. They are still in action.

We try to mould them a little, to divert them here and there, but essentially they will carry on till they fulfil their purpose and their historical destiny. That historical destiny can only be one complete political and economic freedom within certainly some kind of world framework. In Asia and the rest of the world, there are various systems at work, political and economic, in different countries. Obviously, it will not be possible to co-operate easily unless we proceed on the basis of not interfering with any system, political or economic, in any country, leaving it to that country to develop as it chooses within the larger sphere of world co-operation.

Now, you can look upon the problems of Asia from the long-term point of view and the short-term. The short-term problems demand immediate attention because of the urgency of solving some great difficulties. There is the aspect of food. It is an extraordinary state of affairs that in a country like India or similarly predominantly agricultural countries, we should lack food or that we should not have a sufficiency of food. There is something obviously wrong if that kind of thing happens.

I have no doubt in my mind that India can and will produce enough food for itself—not immediately, but in the course of a few years. But at the present moment, we have to face this problem. Other similar urgent problems will also come up for deliberation before you. Looking at these problems from a long-term point of view, it seems to me that various deficiencies have to be made good. We have to increase our productive capacity, agricultural and industrial. It is admitted now that industrialization should proceed in these countries of Asia. In the past, this has been rather held up by various problems and various interests.

The real limiting factor in industrialization is the lack of capital equipment. The difficulties are of getting the capital equipment and special experience from those countries which happen to possess it and who have a surplus of it. How far that can be obtained, it is for you to calculate and the producing countries to decide. If it is not obtained quickly, the process of industrialization may be somewhat delayed, but it will go on.

Now, if it is considered right in the larger interest of the world, that a country like India and other countries in the East should be industrialized, should increase, modernize agricultural production, it is in the interests of those countries that can help in this process to help the Asian countries with capital equipment and their special experience. But in doing so, it is to be borne in mind that no Asian countries will welcome any such assistance, if there are conditions attached to it which lead to any kind of economic domination. We would rather delay our development, industrial or otherwise, than submit to any kind of economic domination of any country.

That is an axiom which is accepted by everyone in India and I shall be surprised if any other country in Asia does not accept it. We want to co-operate in the fullest measure in any policy or programme laid down for the world's good, even though it might involve the surrender, in common with other countries, of any particular attribute of sovereignty, provided that it is a common surrender, all round. But a long age of foreign domination has made the countries of Asia very sensitive about anything which might lead to some visible or invisible form of domination. Therefore, I would beg of you to remember this and to fashion your programmes and policies so as to avoid anything savouring of the economic domination of one country by another. Political domination, it is admitted, leads to economic domination, but an invisible or semi-invisible economic domination creeps in unless you are careful ; if that creeps in, it will lead immediately to ill-will and not that atmosphere of co-operation which is so essential in this matter.

In a long-term view—I may speak of India—I suppose the most important thing is to develop our power resources. From that will flow the industrialization of the country, and an addition to our food production. As it is, you know that India has probably more in the shape of irrigation than any other country in the world. We hope to increase that very greatly. We have in view at least a score of various river valley schemes—some very big, some bigger than the Tennessey Valley scheme, some smaller, much smaller. We have to push the schemes through soon, constructing huge dams and reservoirs, and thereby adding to the irrigated parts of India large tracts which are not at present under cultivation.

May I say a word here about the population of India? A great deal has been said and written about our tremendous population and how it overwhelms us and how we cannot solve any problem till the Indian population is checked or decimated. Well, I have no desire for the population of India to go on increasing. I am all in favour of the population being checked, but I think there is a great misapprehension when so much stress is laid on this aspect. I entirely disagree with that. I think India is an under-populated country and I say this not because I want it to be much more populated. it is under populated, because large tracts of India are still unpopulated. It is true that if you go to the Gangetic plain it is thickly populated ; parts of India are thickly populated, but many parts are not populated at all.

A delegate to this Conference told me last night that coming from Karachi to Delhi, Madras and then to Ootacamund he was amazed to see the scarcity of population. Of course, he was travelling by plane ; nevertheless, the whole country-side appeared to him to be sparsely populated and after all one can judge whether the country is heavily populated or not. That is a very correct impression, because large tracts are not populated.

We are over populated, if you like, because our productive capacity is low. If we increase our production, agricultural and other, if this population is put to work for production then we are not over populated. We have these big river valley schemes which in addition to irrigating land, preventing floods, soil erosion and malaria, will produce a very great deal of hydro-electric power and at the same time we will have industrial development. If you look at the map of India, you will see the noble range of the Himalayas from the North to the North-East. I do not think there is any part of the world similar in area which has so much concentrated power—latent potential power, if only it can be tapped and used. Well, we intend tapping and using it. To some extent we have done it. The Himalayas are also full of a variety of mineral resources.

But my point is that not only India, but the whole of this Asian region is full of vast resources, human and material, and the question before us is how to yoke them together and produce results. It is not that we are lacking in men or material. We have both. In order to yoke them together the easiest way is to have certain assistance in capital equipment and experienced technical personnel from those countries which may have a surplus of it. From the world's point of view that will inevitably lead to the world's good. If that cannot be done, then naturally we have to act in a more limited way, but we shall have to go in that direction anyhow.

Apart from increasing production in this way—I mean new schemes and the rest—I think it is important for us to utilize our existing resources better. I do not think they are being utilized to the best advantage. We can get more out of what we have than we have been doing. That involves in India, as in the rest of Asia, many problems—the economic system, the relation of capital and labour and the satisfaction of labour. There is no doubt at all that in all or at any rate most of these Asian countries, there are long-standing social injustices ; and naturally where there are these social injustices you will not get proper and satisfactory work, especially now when there is an acute sense of social wrong and social injustice.

In India I have no doubt that our production has suffered because of this acute feeling of social injustice. An individual or a community may undertake to shoulder almost any burden. We have seen during the last war how nations put up with the most enormous burdens in the shape of suffering and sacrifice ; but always when there is a sense of sharing the burden inequitably, the burden being greater on some than on others, the sense of injustice becomes greater and you do not have that harmonious working and co-operation which is quite essential today, more so than in the past. Therefore, this problem has to be viewed from the human point of view, quite apart from a purely economic point of view.

If one does view it from that human point of view, if one tries to co-operate without entering into a long argument, I think one can go far in solving it and in getting that measure of co-operation even among people who may hold different theories. So I would beg this Commission to consider this problem from the human point of view of removing social injustices. The Commission, of course, is not going to dictate to each individual country about its economic structure, but any advice from the Commission will no doubt go a long way and most countries will probably follow it in the largest measure they can.

Now, to repeat what I have said, I hope this Commission will bear in mind the fact that we are dealing with hundreds of millions of human beings and not abstract countries and abstract groups. Each individual is a member of a family with children who are possibly starving, who have possibly had no education and no opportunity for growth and advancement.

I mentioned right at the beginning certain parts of Asia which have not completely solved their political problems. Some in the past year have undergone a tremendous change politically. India has—a part of India has become Pakistan ; Burma has become independent and so on. May I here especially welcome the representatives of Burma and New Zealand to this Commission? I should have also liked to see representatives here of Indonesia.

I am not going to enter into the legal or constitutional aspects of such matters, but it seems to me necessary from the practical point of view that an area like the Indonesian Republic which is one of the richest areas in Asia, obviously, cannot be ignored in any plan that you might draw up for Asia. If that area is not directly and sufficiently represented here, then your plan is inadequate. It does not meet the necessities of the situation. You cannot leave out a highly important part of Asia and then make a plan for the rest of Asia. So I regret that direct representatives of the Indonesian Republic have thus far not found a place here. I hope it may be possible for them to be invited and to take part in the Commission's deliberations in some form or other.

India, as I said, from the population point of view, forms 40 per cent of this Asian Region which you have in view. From the geographical point of view too, it is rather important, situated as it is. India proposes to take the fullest part in this co-operative effort both for Asia and for the world.

People vaguely talk of India's leadership in Asia. I deprecate such talk. I want this problem to be approached not in terms of this country or that country being the leader and pushing or pulling others, but rather in a spirit of co-operation between all the countries of Asia, big or small. If any country pulls more than its weight, well and good. If it can serve the common cause more than its share necessitates, well, I have no doubt, it will be patted on the back and it will be a good thing ; but for any country to think of its leadership of others smacks too much of a superiority complex which is not desirable in an organization working together for the common good.

We should talk only in terms of co-operation between countries, whatever they may be. It is in that spirit that I should like India to approach this problem, but at the same time I should certainly like India to play a leading part in serving the common cause, whatever the result of that may be to India.

The Commission has come here for the first time. I believe one of the points that you have to determine is the location of your temporary headquarters. Probably, there will soon be the question of locating the regional headquarters. It is for you to determine, not for me to say much. But on behalf of the Government of India, I should like to invite you to have your headquarters in India. If you so decide you will be very welcome and we shall do our utmost to meet your requirements here. We should like the regional headquarters to be here—not only the Commission. The exact location in India can be decided afterwards to suit your convenience and the convenience of the Government of India. Anyhow, I wish to put this invitation before you informally and we shall of course accept whatever decision you may take and co-operate with you, wherever your headquarters may be.

I should like now to express my welcome to you again and to wish you success in your endeavour.

WORLD HEALTH ORGANIZATION

I join the Health Minister in offering you, Delegates, a very warm welcome on behalf of our Government. I should just like to add a few words to that welcome and tell you that we not only welcome you in a formal sense, but we really attach the greatest importance to the significance of the work that this great organization is doing, more especially from the point of view of South-East Asia which compared to many other parts of the world is backward in its health conditions. Now, health is a very big word and I see it is defined in the objectives of your Charter. I am happy to read that you have defined health as " a state of complete physical, mental and social well-being and not merely the absence of disease or infirmity ". If you achieve that objective, I am sure you would have solved the whole problem in the world, because if we can achieve that nearly every problem disappears from the world. So I am happy that you too may eventually, even though perhaps we cannot achieve that end quickly, reach that goal, or something really worthwhile.

In the political sphere, the United Nations Organization has been functioning for two or three years. It is struggling hard against very great problems and not always finding it easy to make progress. Nevertheless, with all its weaknesses, which are weaknesses not so much of the organization as of the world we live in, it is making progress and it is the only thing in this world today which offers some hope of ultimate solution of the political problems of the world. Whether the world is wise enough to take advantage of that opportunity, I am not a prophet enough to say. But it appears to me that the only possibility of achieving real peace lies in greater and greater international co-operation on every plane. Therefore, it becomes the duty of us on the political plane as well as other planes to endeavour to bring about that co-operation.

On the political plane there are big conflicts, on other planes there are no such conflicts, but you must have enough

A speech delivered at New Delhi inaugurating the First Meeting of the Regional Committee of the World Health Organization for South-East Asia, October 4, 1948.

resources to tackle them. Therefore, if we have more and more international co-operation in this and like activities, not only do we do good in a sphere which is essential for the progress of the world, but indirectly we really solve the other major political and economic problems of the world. We thus create an atmosphere of international co-operation, and this is a very big thing, and I feel today, looking at the world, that there are these big conflicts and they are due to many causes and reasons, but probably the biggest cause is that there are certain psychological conditions in the world which are dominated by a sense of fear, fear of everybody, fear of one another and fear of another country. Now, if that sense of fear should go, there would be more international co-operation in every field of activity.

Therefore, if I may say so, speaking as a person who has to move largely in political field and looking at it, then, from the political field, these approaches to international co-operation in other fields are an essential preliminary to a solution of the other political and economic problems. Some people may imagine that in these times, this co-operation in other fields is somewhat isolated from the political or economic questions, but national life is ultimately an integrated whole. If there is something wrong, it upsets the whole structure. If the health of an individual goes wrong, the physical health of a nation goes wrong and it affects the world too.

Thus from every point of view, the subject of health in this World Health Conference is a most essential matter, for the future well-being of the world, both in the material sphere and in other spheres. There has been a complaint in the past, which, no doubt, many of you gentlemen have heard, perhaps voiced, that in these great international organizations special emphasis is placed on the problems, shall I say, of Europe or America or certain other parts of the world and not on parts of Asia. I complain of this, because in the nature of things the people who take a prominent part in these organizations are interested in the great problems of Europe. And yet if you look at the question of health, obviously you will have to undertake the treatment of the great tracts of Asia and some other parts of the world.

It is also well-known today that you cannot isolate the world and make part of it healthy and leave part of it unhealthy, because infection spreads: everything spreads. Today if there is war, it spreads, if there is disease, it spreads and, therefore, you have to tackle the world as a whole.   Then in tackling the world as a whole, it becomes more necessary to tackle those parts which have been backward in any particular respect. Therefore, the tackling of the health problems of South-East Asia is particularly important and I am happy that the regional system of tackling these problems is developing, so that more attention may be paid to these particular problems of particular regions. I can assure you that as far as the Government of India is concerned, they will do their utmost to help you in this organization and to carry out the decisions that you may make.

A NEW ATMOSPHERE OF
CO-OPERATION

I HAVE come to England again after many years, and I have found a welcome and friendship wherever I have been. I am deeply grateful for this.

Friends, I have spent many years here, but in the past, inevitably, there was a sense of conflict and hostility as between India and England. Fortunately, that is passing away, and we are approaching each other in new terms and in a new atmosphere of co-operation.

The old colonial empire of Britain gradually changed into a combination of free Commonwealth countries or Dominions and the relics of their colonial, non-self-governing countries. Now, those colonial countries, or many of them, have also become free. Some still remain. I hope this change over will be complete soon so that the Commonwealth of nations will become a real commonwealth of free nations.

It has been a remarkable change as far as India is concerned, because it affected not only vast numbers of people, but also because of our past conflict lasting through generations. It shows that when the right step is taken, the consequences of that right step come swiftly.

In India today there is very little ill feeling in spite of the past against England ; and I think what little might remain will also fade away soon, as we co-operate together in the great tasks that confront us.

I came here for the meeting of the Prime Ministers of the Dominions, and it was a privilege to meet many eminent statesmen who had come from the other Dominions. That meeting resulted in mutual understanding of each other ; it resulted in each person finding out some of the difficulties of the other. We may not agree about everything, but it was surprising what a large measure of unanimity there was, not only in the objectives to be aimed at, but also in the methods to be pursued.

After all, the objectives of the Commonwealth can only be the objectives so nobly stated in the Charter of the United

A talk broadcast from the B.B.C., London, October 26, 1948.

Nations—that is the establishment of peace, the prevention of conflict and the establishment of human rights all over the world.

If the Commonwealth can succeed in doing that, not only in its own sphere, but help to do that in the large sphere of the world, then the Commonwealth will have given the best possible lead to the world.

This meeting has shown me that there is great scope for the Commonwealth to function in this way, and not only to help itself but to help others also.

I should like to express again my gratitude to the people of Britain and to the Government of Britain.

TO THE UNITED NATIONS

I am grateful for the opportunity that has been given to me to address this great Assembly. I feel a little embarrassed and a little overwhelmed by this occasion, because this Assembly represents the world community, and, whether we who are present here are big men and women or small, we represent a mighty cause and something of the greatness of that cause falls upon us too, and makes us, for the moment, greater perhaps than we are.

Therefore, in venturing to address this Assembly, I feel embarrassed. You have been dealing with intricate and difficult problems, and I do not, and I would not, venture on this occasion to say anything about those great problems that confront you. You can carry the burdens and sorrows of the world. But I have often wondered whether, in dealing with those problems, the approach that is normally made to them is the right one or not. The Charter of the United Nations, in noble language, has laid down the principles and the purposes of this great organization. I do not think it would be possible to improve upon that language.

The objectives are clear ; your aim is clear ; and yet, in looking at that aim, we lose ourselves often, if I may venture to say so, in smaller matters and forget the main objective that we were looking at. Sometimes it seems that the objective itself gets a little clouded and lesser objectives are before us.

I come from a country which, after a long struggle, though that struggle was a peaceful struggle, attained her freedom and her independence. In these long years of struggle we were taught by our great leader never to forget not only the objectives we had, but also the methods whereby we should achieve those objectives. Always he laid stress on this, that it was not good enough to have a good objective, that it was equally important that the means of attaining those objectives were good ; means were always as important as ends. You will permit me to repeat that here, because I am convinced that, however good the ends,

An address to the United Nations General Assembly at Paris, November 3, 1948.

the larger ends of the United Nations, or the lesser objectives which we may from time to time have before us, either as individual nations or as groups of nations, it is important that we should remember that the best of objectives may not be reached if our eyes are bloodshot and our minds clouded with passion.

Therefore, it becomes essential for us, for a while, to think more of how we are doing things than what we are aiming at, even though we should never forget what we are aiming at. It becomes necessary for us always to remember the principles and the purposes for which this great Assembly was formed.

Now, a mere repetition of those principles and purposes would perhaps indicate to us how sometimes, with passion and prejudice, we swerve away from that path. This Assembly took shape after two mighty wars and as a consequence of those wars. What has been the lesson of those wars? Surely the lesson of those wars has been that out of hatred and violence you will not build peace. It is a contradiction in terms. The lesson of history, the long course of history, and more especially the lesson of the last two great wars which have devastated humanity, has been that out of hatred and violence only hatred and violence will come. We have got into a cycle of hatred and violence, and not the most brilliant debate will get you out of it, unless you look some other way and find some other means. It is obvious that if you continue in this cycle and have wars which this Assembly was especially meant to avoid and prevent, the result will not only be tremendous devastation all over the world, but non-achievement by any individual Power or group of its objective.

How, then, are we to proceed? It may be that it is difficult to get this hatred and prejudice and fear out of our minds. Nevertheless, unless we try to proceed in this way, to cast out this fear, we shall never succeed. Of that I am quite convinced.

You meet here, representatives of all nations of the world, or nearly all. Inevitably, you have behind you and before you the immediate great problems that confront more especially Europe, which has suffered so much.

May I say, as a representative from Asia, that we honour Europe for its culture and for the great advance in human civilization which it represents? May I say that we are equally interested in the solution of European problems ; but may I also say that the world is something bigger than Europe, and you will not solve your problems by thinking that the problems of the world are mainly European problems. There are vast tracts of the world which may not in the past, for a few generations, have taken much part in world affairs. But they are awake ; their people are moving and they have no intention whatever of being ignored or of being passed by.

It is a simple fact that I think we have to remember, because unless you have the full picture of the world before you, you will not even understand the problem, and if you isolate any single problem in the world from the rest, you do not understand the problem. Today I do venture to submit that Asia counts in world affairs. Tomorrow it will count much more than today. Asia till recently was largely a prey to imperial domination and colonialism ; a great part of it is free today, part of it still remains unfree ; and it is an astonishing thing that any country should still venture to hold and to set forth this doctrine of colonialism, whether it is under direct rule or whether it is indirectly maintained in some form or other. After all that has happened, there is going to be no mere objection to that, but active objection, an active struggle against any and every form of colonialism in any part of the world. That is the first thing to remember.

We in Asia, who have ourselves suffered all these evils of colonialism and of imperial domination, have committed ourselves inevitably to the freedom of every other colonial country. There are neighbouring countries of ours in Asia with whom we are intimately allied. We look to them with sympathy ; we look at their struggle with sympathy. Any Power, great or small. which in that way prevents the attainment of the freedom of those peoples does an ill turn to world peace.

Great countries like India who have passed out of that colonial stage do not conceive it possible that other countries should remain under the yoke of colonial rule.

We in Asia regard it as a vital problem, because it has been a vital problem for us, and it is a question to which I want to draw attention—that is the question of racial equality, which is something which is laid down in the provisions of the United Nations Charter. It is well to repeat that, because after all this question of racial equality has frequently been spoken about in the Assembly of the United Nations.

I do not think I need dwell on any particular aspect of that question, but I would remind this Assembly of the world-wide aspects of this question. Obviously there are large regions of the world which have suffered from this question of racial inequality. We also feel that there is no part of the world where it can be tolerated in the future, except perhaps because of superior force. It is obviously sowing the seeds of conflict if racial equality is not approved, and a menace to world peace and is in conflict with the principles of the United Nations Charter.

The effects of this inequality in the past have made themselves felt in Asia, Africa and other parts of the world much more than in Europe, leading towards a conflict in the future, and it is a problem which, if it is not properly understood, will not be solved.

It is a strange thing, when the world lacks so many things, food and other necessities in many parts of the world and people are dying from hunger that the attention of this Assembly of Nations is concentrated only on a number of political problems. There are economic problems also. I wonder if it would be possible for this Assembly to take a holiday for a while from some of the acute political problems which face it, and allow men's minds to settle down and look at the vital and urgent economic problems, and look at places in the world where food is lacking.

I feel that today the world is so tied up in fears, apprehensions, some of them justified no doubt, but where a person feels fear, bad consequences and evil consequences follow. Fear is not a good companion. It is surprising to see that this sense of fear is pervading great countries—fear, and grave fear of war, and fear of many things. Well, I think that it is admitted, or it will be admitted, that no aggression of any kind can be tolerated, because the very idea of aggression must upset the balance and lead to conflict. Aggression of every type must be resisted.

There are other forms of fear; there is the fear of war. In existing circumstances it is difficult for people to say that they will not defend themselves, because if there is a fear of aggression one has to defend oneself against aggression. We have to defend ourselves, but even in defending ourselves, we must not submit ourselves to this Assembly without clean hands. It is easy to condemn people. Let us not do so, for who are without blame, who cannot themselves be condemned? In a sense, all of us who are gathered here today in this continent of Europe—are there any amongst us who have not been guilty in many ways? We are all guilty men and women. While we are seeking points where error occurs, we should not forget that there is not one of us who is exempt from blame.

If we proceed to this problem, and discuss in peace the psychology of fear, if we realize the consequences of what is happening, it is possible that this atmosphere of fear may be dissipated. Why should there be this fear of war? Let us prepare ourselves against any possible aggression, let no one think that any nation, any community can misbehave. The United Nations are here to prevent any fear or hurt, but at the same time let us banish all thought of an aggressive attitude whether by word or deed. However, I feel that few of us can altogether avoid this attitude, whether it is in the course of discussions before this Assembly or elsewhere. One tries to make one's points by this sort of language. It is always easy to make one's points in the course of a discussion, but there always rests a bitterness which complicates the problem still further. As I have already said, I ask this Assembly to remember that such great problems cannot be solved if our eyes are bloodshot and our minds are obscured by passion.

I have no doubt that this Assembly is going to solve our pro-blems. I am not afraid of the future. I have no fear in my mind, and I have no fear, even though India, from a military point of view, is of no great consequence. I am not afraid of the bigness of great Powers, and their armies, their fleets and their atom bombs. That is the lesson which my Master taught me. We stood as an unarmed people against a great country and a powerful empire. We were supported and strengthened, because throughout all this period we decided not to submit to evil, and I think that is the lesson which I have before me and which is before us today. I do not know if it is possible to apply this to the problems which face the world today. It is a terrible problem, but I think if we banish this fear, if we have confidence, even though we may take risks of trust rather than risk violent language, violent actions and in the end war, I think those risks are worth taking.

In any event, there are risks—and great risks. If it is a ques-tion of taking risks why take risks which inevitably lead to greater conflict? Take the other risks, while always preparing yourself to meet any possible contingency that may arise.

It is perhaps not very proper for me to address this great Assembly in such matters, because I have not been associated with it nor with all these different problems in any intimate degree. However, there would have been no point in my addressing you merely to repeat certain pious phrases. I feel strongly about this matter, and that is why I should like to present the views and wishes of the Indian people. And the Indian people happen to be three hundred and thirty millions in number ; it is well to remember that. We have had a year of freedom and a year of difficulty. We have overcome many of those difficulties and we shall overcome the others. We propose to go ahead at a rapid pace. We propose to build and construct and be a power for peace and for the good of the world. We propose to meet every aggression, from whatever quarter it comes, in every possible way open to us.

However, we do not think that the problems of the world or of India can be solved by thinking in terms of aggression or war or violence. We are frail mortals, and we cannot always live up to the teaching of the great man who led our nation to freedom. But that lesson has sunk deep into our souls and, so long as we remember it, I am sure we shall be on the right path. And, if I may venture to suggest this to the General Assembly, I think that if the essentials of that lesson are kept in mind, perhaps our approach to the problems of today will be different ; perhaps the conflicts that always hang over us will appear a little less deep than they are and actually will gradually fade away.

I should like to state to this General Assembly, on behalf of my people and my Government, that we adhere completely and absolutely to the principles and purposes of the United Nations Charter and that we shall try, to the best of our ability, to work for the realization of those principles and purposes.

In conclusion, may I congratulate the General Assembly on the Resolution introduced by the delegation of Mexico which it has just passed? It is certainly a great Resolution. If the General Assembly follows up that Resolution, it will go a long way on the road toward peace and the solution of the problems that are before us. We may not solve those problems. No one can be optimistic enough to think that all problems will fade away simply if we feel good ; that is not what I mean to say. The problems are difficult and intricate and they will take a lot of solving. But I do feel that our approach to those problems should not be the approach of anger and passion and fear. Then, perhaps, the problems will gradually appear in a different light. Perhaps, we shall understand the other side better ; perhaps, the fear of one another will grow less in our minds, and then a solution may come. At any rate, even if the solution does not come, this pall of fear that surrounds us will grow less, and that in itself will be a partial solution of the world problem.

INTERNATIONAL CO-OPERATION

MR. Chairman and Delegates to the Asian Commission of the International Meteorological Organization, I do not quite know why I am here, that is to say, what particular qualification I possess to be present at this Conference of people who are presumed to be experts in a particular branch of science, except for a certain general interest of mine in science and scientific development, and a vague knowledge, such as possibly a semi-literate might possess. I have no expert knowledge on the subject and, therefore, I feel rather small in this gathering of experts.

However, I have come here not to talk so much about meteorology, about which you know much more than I do, but to offer you a cordial welcome on behalf of the Government of India and to express our pleasure that you have come from distant countries to meet here in Delhi and to consider the problems before you in a spirit—not of national rivalry—but of international co-operation.

In the world today, we have this very peculiar contradiction of rivalry of opposite forces. On one side, we see an inevitable development of international co-operation. The world today cannot get on without that international co-operation and one such instance is this Conference and the International Meteorological Organization, as the previous speaker mentioned. Weather conditions or such like other conditions do not take cognizance of national frontiers. They fly over them and they affect them. Something that happens in a far-off country affects us here and if we function in this field, as unfortunately most of us do in other fields, on strictly narrow lines, and think that artificial frontiers divide human beings completely, then there will be no progress in this branch of science or any other.

So, on the one hand, we have this inevitable development for international co-operation, and on the other, we have, I hope not inevitably, but unfortunately a very obvious narrowing of people's minds and their functioning strictly and narrowly on the nationalist plane. Which force will win through in the end it

A speech delivered at New Delhi inaugurating the Asian Regional Conference of the International Meteorological Organization, November 10, 1948.

is a little difficult to say, though I suppose it can be said that ultimately it is the force of international co-operation that must win through: because if it does not win through, then nothing wins through. It is not that the other force wins through, but that something which is rather negative and rather disastrous wins through. Many of the activities of the world, national or international, suffer greatly in consequence.

So it is a good thing that we take advantage of all these opportunities for international co-operation, not only because it is good in their particular field of activity, but because they affect the larger field of human relations in the world and make people realize that after all the world is being carried on today by a great measure of international co-operation. In this context, the communications system becomes more and more international and so many other branches of science can only progress internationally.

Therefore, I welcome all the delegates who have come here and I hope that your labours will bear fruit in this particular branch of science which is so important for human welfare as well as in the larger field of human relations.

THE CONQUEST OF THE AIR

MR. Chairman, Mr. President of the Council of the I.C.A.O., and representatives of Governments and International Organizations, I am here to welcome you most cordially on behalf of the Government of India to this country and to this very ancient city of Delhi. As I sat here in the last few moments, I began thinking of the vast changes that this ancient city must have seen in the course of human history. This city is one of the very few of the oldest cities of the world,—not this present city, but this site, where cities have existed from immemorial time. I wondered how many changes it had seen and what its position would be now, in this era of not only air travel but something more—of man gradually entering into the third dimension and trying to control it and utilize it both for good and for evil. So this long stretch of history came before me.

Then, if you will permit me a personal reminiscence, I remember that long, long ago, when I was a boy at school, I was exceedingly interested in the beginnings of aviation at that time and I remember writing an essay on aviation in the year 1906 at school. It was a long time ago. That was just about the time, I think, that the Wright Brothers and Latham and Bleriot and others were crossing the channel or flying somewhere. I was greatly excited by their exploits and had dreams of being an aviator or something like it myself at that time.

I remember writing to my father from school, over forty years ago, or perhaps fortytwo years ago, saying—I was then in England and he was in India—that I hoped soon to pay a week-end visit to him by air. I was a little premature about that, but the fact is, week-end visits had come into being and I do not know how many other people thought at that time in terms of week-end visits from England to India.

Soon after, I was present in Berlin when the first Zeppelin came there. That was an occasion I very well remember, and various exhibitions and flights of aeroplanes and airships took place in those early days of this century from Frankfurt to Paris,

A speech delivered at the South-East Asia Regional Air Navigation Meeting of the International Civil Aviation Organization, New Delhi, November 23, 1948.

so that, in a sense, my connection with aviation is very old and goes back to my early boyhood, and ever since then I have been intensely interested in the growth of this science and it seemed to me a most exciting thing. My own chief regret is that I pursued other avocations and professions and did not become an aviator, after all that I had hoped and dreamed that I should. Still, I hope it is not too late yet.

I come to you to offer you welcome, and because, in spite of my great interest in aviation, I do not know much about the technique or the details of the problems you are going to discuss, it would be folly on my part to talk about them and exhibit my ignorance. But apart from those details, one's imagination is fired by this major development in the history of mankind—this conquest of the air.

I am not sure myself yet whether in the ultimate analysis it is going to be good for mankind or bad. Just as every great invention can be used for good ends or evil ends, science which is the greatest thing in human history, the development of science which has advanced humanity so tremendously, has also been used for very evil purposes. But that is not the fault of science. That is the fault of the human being who uses it for evil purposes, and that is another question.

Now, I think, possibly if we look at history in long perspective, the fact of this conquest of the air will stand out as one of the really big events which change human history. I just referred to the third dimension. It is a major event that the human being crawling about on the surface of the earth, more or less in a two-dimensional way, suddenly leaps up to the third dimension. Whether his mind leapt up to it or not, I am not sure ; if it had, then all would be well, but somehow events go faster than men's minds and there is such a tremendous lag. We get the where-withal to do things. We do accomplish all manner of great deeds, and yet, we do not have the wisdom to know how to do them well. We may have the technical knowledge to do them, but not the wise man's knowledge of how to do them well and properly for the good of mankind. That subject is one for philosophers and not so much for this Conference. Nevertheless, it is good to bear that in mind, because technical excellence, important as it is, has to be allied to some other kind of mental quality if it is to be used for proper ends.

Here in India, you will learn that in a short space of time we have made considerable progress in aviation, as was natural, because this country is, in a sense, ideally suited for that purpose. You have a wide area where air travel becomes almost necessary and essential and you can hardly do without it once you get used to it, where the climate is suitable for the greater part of the year. You know what the climate is going to be in many parts of the country, and so air travel and air communications are bound to grow.

But I must say that in spite of my great enthusiasm for air travel, I did not expect the rapidity with which air services and air communications have grown in India during the last few years. I believe, a few years ago, some kind of plan was made for the development of air communications in India for the next ten years or so,—I hope I am not wrong—I believe we have already completed that ten year plan in two or three years, not very deliberately, but simply because there was this urge to grow and it grew and goes on growing. India like some other great countries is an ideal country for this purpose, and it is, if I may say so, right and proper that all of you, ladies and gentlemen, who have come from distant countries should gather here together, to take counsel together as to what we can do to develop this further, to make air travel swift, efficient, safe and otherwise serve the purpose of humanity in the future.

You represent the South-East Asia region. Now, India is curiously situated from the geographical point of view as well as from many other points of view. It belongs to South-East Asia, it belongs to South Asia, it also belongs to West Asia. It just depends on which way you look at it, because it happens to be the centre of all these. And whether you think in terms of East-Asian travel or South-Asian travel, India is there in the middle of the picture. All international routes or routes round the world have almost inevitably to pass over India.

Again, when you look at it from other points of view like trade and commerce, or when you think of it in terms of defence, India becomes the pivotal centre of South, South-East and Western Asia. Geography has given her that position, and because geography gave India that position, and also no doubt because of other factors, the course of history has shown how India has influenced all the countries around her and has been influenced by them.

Do not let any one imagine that, at any one period of India's history, she has been a country isolated from the rest of the world. She could not be so, situated as she was ; and she did not want to be so, except sometime during a period of her history when she was facing some kind of internal trouble or difficulty. Until 150 years ago, India's contacts were very largely and inevitably with her overland neighbours, and also by sea, because from the most ancient times India was a sea power and a commercial nation. In the days of ancient Greece and Rome, we had intimate trade contacts with Rome and Greece and, of course, Egypt. Our great ports on the west coast were full of people going and coming from home, carrying goods from India and bringing goods to India from the other side.

But even more intimate was the contact of India with South-East Asia. It was a very intimate contact, cultural and to some extent religious, and it is a contact which has endured for thousands of years. And if you go to any part of South-East Asia, you will find evidence of that contact,—linguistic, cultural, monumental, archaeological, architectural. So India had these contacts by sea, but in addition to that, and perhaps to some extent more important than that, were her land contacts in Asia. Her development about 150 years ago was more or less on the great sea routes. Changes took place all over the world, and changes took place in India also, which were mainly political.

The British came to India and gradually acquired domination over this country. As a result of that, partly consciously and deliberately and partly unconsciously, the contacts of India with her neighbouring nations in Asia became less and less. Our land routes languished and in fact they became almost closed except for occasional caravans or ordinary individual travellers. Our old sea trade had languished previously, and instead of all this there came into existence direct contacts by a new sea route and by new means of sea communications due to the development of steam.

The route to Europe, and more especially to England, was opened and so India became more closely connected with England and western Europe than with her neighbours in Asia who gradually became more distant and alien to her and in a sense more difficult of access to her. It is a great change that occurred and affected India very greatly. This lasted for a hundred years and more and now there has been a change again.

There was the development of aircraft and from sea travel there has been a shift to air travel in the last generation or so. Great international air liners came across the western Asian deserts, from Baghdad and Teheran and other places and went on across India to South-East Asia. It became relatively easy to go from India to China—almost a day's hop. So that these ancient contacts that had been broken in the last 150 years were revived. This development of communications has had a powerful effect on India as no doubt it has had on other countries. It has had a great effect on reviving our old contacts and no doubt the effect of air travel has been to bring the countries of the world tremendously close to one another.

Being given, to a certain extent, to looking at history in a wide perspective and somewhat imaginatively, I find my imagination fired by all these changes and, what is more, the changes that are likely to come in the future. And so any attempt to co-ordinate the activities of Asia and the world in regard to civil aviation or communications, seems to me an essential thing for the modern world to do.

And you, the representatives of groups of international organizations are, if I may say so, not only sitting here and discussing in a rather pedestrian way the technique of this business, but in a sense you are all children of the future that is taking shape. And out of your endeavours and the endeavours of the likes of you all over the world, great developments will take place which I hope will be for the good of mankind.

CRISIS IN INDONESIA

Your Excellencies, ladies and gentlemen, I bid you a warm welcome on behalf of the Government of India and on my own behalf, and I should like to express my deep gratitude to your Governments for having responded at short notice to the urgent invitation that we extended to them. That response itself is witness to the deep feelings that have been aroused all over Asia and in other parts of the world at recent happenings in Indonesia. We meet today, because the freedom of a sister country of ours has been imperilled and the dying colonialism of a past age has raised its head again and challenged all the forces that are struggling to build up a new structure of the world. That challenge has a deeper significance than might appear on the surface, for it is a challenge to a newly awakened Asia which has so long suffered under various forms of colonialism. It is also a challenge to the spirit of man and to all the progressive forces of a divided and distracted world. The United Nations—symbol of One World that has become the ideal of men of thought and goodwill—has been flouted, and its expressed will set at naught. If this challenge is not met effectively, then indeed the consequences will affect not merely Indonesia but Asia and the entire world. That would represent the triumph of the forces of destruction and disintegration and the certain sequel would be ceaseless conflict and world disorder.

Although we meet to consider a vital problem of immediate importance, my mind is filled with the historic significance of this unique gathering. Here we are, representatives of the free nations of Asia and our friends from Australia and New Zealand as well as Egypt and Ethiopia, met together for the first time to consider a matter of common concern to us. We represent, from Australia, New Zealand and the Philippines on the one side to Egypt and Ethiopia on the other, the vast area embracing half of the circumference of the globe and by far the greater part of

Presidential Speech delivered at New Delhi inaugurating the 19-nation Conference on Indonesia, January 20, 1949. The Governments of Afghanistan, Australia, Burma, Ceylon, Egypt, Ethiopia, India, Iran, the Lebanon, Pakistan, the Philippines, Saudi Arabia, Syria and Yemen were represented at this Conference by delegates at ministerial level, while China, Nepal, New Zealand and Siam sent observers.

its population. We represent the ancient civilizations of the East as well as the dynamic civilization of the West. Politically, we symbolize in particular the spirit of freedom and democracy which is so significant a feature of the new Asia. This long sweep of history passes before my eyes with all its vicissitudes for the countries of Asia, and standing on the edge of the present I look to the future that is gradually unfolding. We are the heirs of these long yesterdays of our history, but we are also the builders of the tomorrow that is shaping itself. The burden of that tomorrow has to be borne by us and we have to prove ourselves worthy of that great responsibility. If this gathering is significant today, it is still more significant in the perspective of tomorrow. Asia, too long submissive and dependent and a plaything of other countries, will no longer brook any interference with her freedom.

We meet in this Conference to consider the present situation in Indonesia and I would suggest to you that we should concentrate on that issue and not divert our attention to the many other issues which undoubtedly demand our attention. The story of Indonesia during the last three years has been a strange and revealing one. It should be remembered that Indonesia was reconquered from the Japanese by the Allied Forces and then handed over to the Dutch. Therefore, a special responsibility attaches to the Allied Nations. Many remarkable things have happened in Indonesia during these past three years and these are detailed in the papers supplied to the Conference. It is a long story of broken pledges and continuous attempts to undermine and break the Republic of Indonesia.

On the 18th December of last year, the Dutch forces launched an offensive, practically without warning, against the Republic while negotiations for a peaceful settlement were still going on. Even the dulled and jaded conscience of the world reacted to this with shock and amazement. The leaders of the Republic were imprisoned and separated from one another and treated with inhumanity. The Security Council of the United Nations passed a series of resolutions asking for the release of the Republican leaders and a cessation of hostilities as an essential preliminary to the resumption of negotiations for a peaceful and honourable settlement. The directions of the Security Council have not yet been carried out and the Dutch authorities seem to be concentrating all their efforts on the formation of a so-called interim

Government which they hope will be subservient to their will. Any person, who is acquainted with the spirit of the Indonesian people or of Asia today, knows that this attempt to suppress Indonesian nationalism and the deep urge for freedom of the Indonesian people must fail. But if open and unabashed aggression is not checked and is condoned by other Powers, then hope will vanish and people will resort to other ways and other means even though these might involve the utmost catastrophe. One thing is certain: there can be, and will be, no surrender to aggression and no acceptance or reimposition of colonial control.

It was not without deep thought and earnest consideration that we decided to hold this Conference. Believing as we do that the United Nations must be strengthened as a symbol of the New Order, we were reluctant to take any steps which might appear to weaken its authority. But when the will of the Security Council was itself flouted, then it became clear to us that we must confer together to strengthen the United Nations and to prevent further deterioration of a dangerous situation. We meet, therefore, within the framework of the United Nations and with the noble words of the Charter before us. That Charter itself recognizes regional arrangements as a means of furthering international peace and security. Ours is, therefore, a regional conference, to which we invited both Australia and New Zealand, whose interest in the tranquillity and contentment of Indonesia is as great as that of any of us. Our primary purpose is to consider how best we can help the Security Council to bring about a rapid and peaceful solution of the Indonesian problem. We meet to supplement the efforts of the Security Council, not to supplant that body. We meet in no spirit of hostility to any nation or group of nations, but in an endeavour to promote peace through the extension of freedom. It must be realized that both freedom and peace are indivisible. I should like to make it clear that we do not wish to consider this, or any other problem, in a spirit of racialism. Racialism has been, and is even today, the policy of some other countries. We, in Asia, who have suffered so much from it are not going to encourage it, but will combat it, believing as we do that it is not only a negation of democracy, but is also the seed of conflict. Our task will be threefold:

    1. To frame and submit to the Security Council proposals which would, if accepted by both parties concerned,

restore peace immediately to Indonesia and promote the
early realization of freedom by the Indonesian people ;

2. Also to suggest to the Security Council what action it should
   take if either party to the dispute fails to act according
   to its recommendations ;

3. To devise machinery and procedure by which the Governments represented here today can keep in touch with
   one another for purposes of mutual consultation and
   concerted action for the achievement of the purposes for
   which this Conference has met.

I do not think it would be proper for me at this stage to offer
any detailed proposals. That will be for the Conference to
consider. But it seems to me clear that our immediate objective
should be to restore, as far as possible, the conditions which existed
before this recent Dutch aggression, so that the Republic may be
able to function freely and to negotiate as a Free Government
without military or economic pressure. The next step should be
to aim at the elimination of colonialism. It must be appreciated
that so long as any form of colonialism exists in Asia or elsewhere, there will be conflict and a threat to peace. The situation
in Indonesia is full of dangerous possibilities and requires urgent
action. We have to aim, therefore, to complete our work as quickly as possible, so that the Security Council which is still considering this difficult problem should be in possession of our views
within the next few days. All of us who meet here have, I believe,
this community of outlook and our deliberations should bear
fruit soon.

We are living in a revolutionary age of transition. On the one
hand, we see a divided and disintegrating world, a multitude of
conflicts and an ever-present fear of world war. On the other
hand, we see creative and co-operative impulses seeking a new
integration and a new unity. New problems arise from day to
day which, in their implications, concern all of us or many of
us. The Americans have already recognized a certain community
of interest and have created machinery for the protection and
promotion of common interests. A similar movement is in
progress in Europe. Is it not natural that the free countries of
Asia should begin to think of some more permanent arrangement
than this Conference for effective mutual consultation and
concerted effort in the pursuit of common aims—not in a spirit
of selfishness or hostility to any other nation or group of nations,

but in order to strengthen and bring nearer fulfilment the aims and ideals of the Charter of the United Nations? In this world of hatred, conflict and violence, let us endeavour to work jointly and in co-operation with others of goodwill to further the cause of peace and tolerance and freedom. We shall not succeed in our mission if we follow the path of violence or seek to divide the world further, but we may well make a difference to the world if we fashion ourselves in accordance with the old spirit of Asia and hold up the torch of truth and peace to a war-distracted world. May I, in all humility but also with pride, remind this Conference of the message of the Father of our Nation who led us through the long night of our subjection to the dawn of freedom? It was not through hatred or violence or intolerance of each other, he told us, that nations grow in stature or attain their freedom. It was by following his lead in some measure that we attained our independence through peaceful methods. The world has got caught in a vicious circle of fear, hatred and violence. It will never get out of that vicious circle unless it seeks other ways and practises other means. Therefore, let us adhere to the right means with the conviction that right means will inevitably lead to right ends. Thus, we shall help in the process of integration and synthesis which is so urgently needed in the world of today.

MISCELLANEOUS

THE INTERIM NATIONAL
GOVERNMENT

FRIENDS and comrades, Jai Hind! Six days ago my colleagues and I sat on the chairs of high office in the Government of India. A new Government came into being in this ancient land, the Interim or Provisional Government we called it, the stepping stone to the full independence of India. Many thousands of messages of greeting and good wishes came to us from all parts of the world and from every nook and corner of India. And yet we asked for no celebration of this historic event and even restrained our people's enthusiasm. For we wanted them to realize that we were yet on the march and the goal had still to be reached. There were many difficulties and obstacles on the way and our journey's end might not be so near as people thought. Any weakness now, any complacency would be fatal to our cause.

Our hearts were heavy also with the terrible tragedy of Calcutta and because of the insensate strife of brother against brother. The freedom we had envisaged and for which we had laboured, through generations of trial and suffering, was for all the people of India, and not for one group or class or the followers of one religion. We aimed at a co-operative commonwealth in which all would be equal sharers in opportunity and in all things that give meaning and value to life. Why then this strife, this fear and suspicion of each other?

I speak to you today not much of high policy or our programme for the future—that will have to wait a while—but to thank you for the love and affection which you have sent us in such abundant measure. That affection and spirit of co-operation are always welcome, but they will be needed more than ever in the difficult days ahead of us. A friend sent me the following message: "May you weather every storm, first pilot of the ship of State, *bon voyage!*" A cheering message, but there are many storms ahead and our ship of State is old and battered and slow-moving and unsuited to this age of swift change. It will have to be scrapped and give place to another. But however old the ship and however feeble the pilot, when there are so many millions of

A talk broadcast from New Delhi, September 7, 1946.

willing hearts and hands to help, we can brave the high seas and face the future with confidence.

That future is already taking shape and India, this old and dear land of ours, is finding herself again through travail and suffering. She is youthful again with the bright eyes of adventure, and with faith in herself and her mission. For long years she had been narrowly confined and had lost herself in brooding. But now she looks out on the wide world and holds out her hands in friendship to the other peoples of the world, even though that world may still be full of conflict and thoughts of war.

The Interim National Government is part of a larger scheme which includes the Constituent Assembly which will meet soon to give shape to the Constitution of free and independent India. It is because of this expectation of an early realization of full independence that we have entered this Government, and we propose to function so as progressively to achieve that independence in action both in our domestic affairs and our foreign relations. We shall take full part in international conferences as a free nation with our own policy and not merely as a satellite of another nation. We hope to develop close and direct contacts with other nations and to co-operate with them in the furtherance of world peace and freedom.

We propose, as far as possible, to keep away from the power politics of groups, aligned against one another, which have led in the past to world wars and which may again lead to disasters on an even vaster scale. We believe that peace and freedom are indivisible and the denial of freedom anywhere must endanger freedom elsewhere and lead to conflict and war. We are particularly interested in the emancipation of colonial and dependent countries and peoples, and in the recognition in theory and practice of equal opportunities for all races. We repudiate utterly the Nazi doctrine of racialism, wheresoever and in whatever form it may be practised. We seek no dominion over others and we claim no privileged position over other peoples. But we do claim equal and honourable treatment for our people wherever they may go, and we cannot accept any discrimination against them.

The world, in spite of its rivalries and hatreds and inner conflicts, moves inevitably towards closer co-operation and the building up of a world commonwealth. It is for this One World that free India will work, a world in which there is the free co-operation of free peoples, and no class or group exploits another.

In spite of our past history of conflict, we hope that an independent India will have friendly and co-operative relations with England and the countries of the British Commonwealth. But it is well to remember what is happening in one part of the Commonwealth today. In South Africa racialism is the State doctrine and our people are putting up a heroic struggle against the tyranny of a racial minority. If this racial doctrine is going to be tolerated it must inevitably lead to vast conflicts and world disaster.

We send our greetings to the people of the United States of America to whom destiny has given a major role in international affairs. We trust that this tremendous responsibility will be utilized for the furtherance of peace and human freedom everywhere.

To that other great nation of the modern world, the Soviet Union, which also carries a vast responsibility for shaping world events, we send greeting. They are our neighbours in Asia and inevitably we shall have to undertake many common tasks and have much to do with each other.

We are of Asia and the peoples of Asia are nearer and closer to us than others. India is so situated that she is the pivot of Western, Southern and South-East Asia. In the past her culture flowed to all these countries and they came to her in many ways. Those contacts are being renewed and the future is bound to see a closer union between India and South-East Asia on the one side, and Afghanistan, Iran, and the Arab world on the other. To the furtherance of that close association of free countries we must devote ourselves. India has followed with anxious interest the struggle of the Indonesians for freedom and to them we send our good wishes.

China, that mighty country with a mighty past, our neighbour, has been our friend through the ages and that friendship will endure and grow. We earnestly hope that her present troubles will end soon and a united and democratic China will emerge, playing a great part in the furtherance of world peace and progress.

I have not said anything about our domestic policy, nor at this stage do I wish to do so. But that policy will inevitably have to be governed by the principles by which we have stood all these years. We shall look to the common and forgotten man in

India and seek to bring him relief and raise his standard of living. We shall continue our fight against the curse of untouchability and other forms of enforced inequality, and shall especially try to help those who are economically or otherwise backward. Today millions lack food and clothing and houses, and many are on the verge of starvation. To meet this immediate need is an urgent and difficult task and we hope other countries will help us by sending foodgrains.

An equally urgent and vital task for us is to conquer the spirit of discord that is abroad in India. Out of mutual conflict we shall never build the House of India's freedom of which we have dreamt so long. All of us in this land have to live and work together, whatever political developments might take place. Hatred and violence will not alter this basic fact, nor will they stop the changes that are taking place in India.

There has been much heated argument about sections and groupings in the Constituent Assembly. We are perfectly prepared to, and have accepted, the position of sitting in sections, which will consider the question of formation of groups. I should like to make it clear, on behalf of my colleagues and myself, that we do not look upon the Constituent Assembly as an arena for conflict or for the forcible imposition of one viewpoint over another. That would not be the way to build up a contented and united India. We seek agreed and integrated solutions with the largest measure of goodwill behind them. We shall go to the Constituent Assembly with the fixed determination of finding a common basis for agreement on all controversial issues. And so, in spite of all that has happened and the hard words that have been said, we have kept the path of co-operation open and we invite even those who differ from us to enter the Constituent Assembly as equals and partners with us with no binding commitments. It may well be that when we meet and face common tasks, our present difficulties will fade away.

India is on the move and the old order passes. Too long have we been passive spectators of events, the playthings of others. The initiative comes to our people now and we shall make the history of our choice. Let us all join in this mighty task and make India, the pride of our heart, great among nations, foremost in the arts of peace and progress. The door is open and destiny beckons to all. There is no question of who wins and who loses, for we have to go forward and together as comrades and either all of us win or we all go down together. But there is going to be no failure. We go forward to success, to independence and to the freedom and well-being of the four hundred millions of India. JAI HIND!

AN INDEPENDENT SOVEREIGN REPUBLIC

I BEG to move that:

(1) This Constituent Assembly declares its firm and solemn resolve to proclaim India as an Independent Sovereign Republic and to draw up for her future governance a Constitution ;

(2) WHEREIN the territories that now comprise British India, the territories that now form the Indian States, and such other parts of India as are outside British India and the States as well as such other territories as are willing to be constituted into the Independent Sovereign India, shall be a Union of them all ; and

(3) WHEREIN the said territories, whether with their present boundaries or with such others as may be determined by the Constituent Assembly and thereafter according to the Law of the Constitution, shall possess and retain the status of autonomous Units, together with residuary powers, and exercise all powers and functions of government and administration, save and except such powers and functions as are vested in or assigned to the Union, or as are inherent or implied in the Union or resulting therefrom ; and

(4) WHEREIN all power and authority of the Sovereign Independent India, its constituent parts and organs of government, are derived from the people ; and

(5) WHEREIN shall be guaranteed and secured to all the people of India justice, social, economic and political: equality of status, of opportunity, and before the law ; freedom of thought, expression, belief, faith, worship, vocation, association and action, subject to law and public morality ; and

(6) WHEREIN adequate safeguards shall be provided for minorities, backward and tribal areas, and depressed and other backward classes ; and

(7) WHEREBY shall be maintained the integrity of the territory of the Republic and its sovereign rights on land, sea and air according to justice and the law of civilized nations ; and

---

A speech moving the Objectives Resolution delivered at the Constituent Assembly, New Delhi, December 13, 1946.

(8)   This ancient land attain its rightful and honoured place in the world and make its full and willing contribution to the promotion of world peace and the welfare of mankind.

Sir, this is the fifth day of this first session of the Constituent Assembly. Thus far we have laboured on certain provisional and procedural matters which are essential. We have a clear field to work upon ; we have to prepare the ground and we have been doing that these few days. We have still much to do. We have to pass our Rules of Procedure and to appoint Committees and the like, before we can proceed to the real step, to the real work of this Constituent Assembly, that is, the high adventure of giving shape, in the printed and written word, to a nation's dream and aspiration. But even now, at this stage, it is surely desirable that we should give some indication to ourselves, to those who look to this Assembly, to those millions in this country who are looking up to us and to the world at large, as to what we may do, what we seek to achieve, whither we are going. It is with this purpose that I have placed this Resolution before this House. It is a Resolution and yet it is something much more than a resolution. It is a Declaration. It is a firm resolve. It is a pledge and an undertaking and it is for all of us, I hope, a dedication. And I wish that this House, if I may say so respectfully, should consider this Resolution not in a spirit of narrow legal wording, but rather look at the spirit behind the Resolution. Words are magic things often enough, but even the magic of words sometimes cannot convey the magic of the human spirit and of a nation's passion. And so, I cannot say that this Resolution at all conveys the passion that lies in the hearts and the minds of the Indian people today. It seeks very feebly to tell the world what we have thought or dreamt of so long, and what we now hope to achieve in the near future.   It is in that spirit that I venture to place this Resolution before the House and it is in that spirit that I trust the House will receive it and ultimately pass it. And may I, Sir, also, with all respect, suggest to you and to the House that, when the time comes for the passing of this Resolution, let it not be done in the formal way by the raising of hands, but much more solemnly, by all of us standing up and thus taking this pledge anew.

The House knows that there are many absentees here and many members who have a right to come here have not come. We regret that fact, because we should have liked to associate with ourselves as many people, as many representatives from the different parts of India and different groups as possible. We have undertaken a tremendous task and we seek the co-operation of all people in that task ; because the future of India that we have envisaged is not confined to any group or section or province, but it comprises all the four hundred million people of India, and it is with deep regret that we find some benches empty and some colleagues, who might have been here, absent. I do feel that they ought to come, I do hope that they will come and that this House, in its future stages, will have the benefit of the co-operation of all. Meanwhile, there is a duty cast upon us and that is to bear the absentees in mind, to remember always that we are here not to act for one party or one group, but always to think of India as a whole and always to think of the welfare of the four hundred millions that comprise India. We are all now, in our respective spheres, party men, belonging to this or that group and presumably we shall continue to act in our respective parties. Nevertheless, a time comes when we have to rise above party and think of the nation, think sometimes even of the world at large of which our nation is a great part. And when I think of the work of this Constituent Assembly, it seems to me the time has come when we should, so far as we are capable of it, rise above our ordinary selves and party disputes and think of the great problem before us in the widest and most tolerant and most effective manner so that, whatever we may produce, will be worthy of India as a whole and will be such that the world will recognize that we have functioned, as we should have functioned, in this high adventure.

There is another person who is absent here and who must be in the minds of many of us today—the great leader of our people, the Father of our Nation—who has been the architect of this Assembly and all that has gone before it and possibly of much that will follow. He is not here because, in pursuit of his ideals, he is ceaselessly working in a far corner of India. But I have no doubt that his spirit hovers over this place and blesses our undertaking.

As I stand here, Sir, I feel the weight of all manner of things crowding upon me. We are at the end of an era and possibly very soon we shall embark upon a new age ; and my mind goes back to the great past of India, to the 5,000 years of India's history, from the very dawn of that history which might be considered almost the dawn of human history, till today. All that past crowds upon me and exhilarates me and, at the same time, somewhat oppresses me. Am I worthy of that past? When I think also of the future, the greater future I hope, standing on this sword's edge of the present between the mighty past and the mightier future, I tremble a little and feel overwhelmed by this mighty task. We have come here at a strange moment in India's history. I do not know, but I do feel that there is some magic in this moment of transition from the old to the new, something of that magic which one sees when the night turns into day and even though the day may be a cloudy one, it is day after all, for when the clouds move away, we can see the sun again. Because of all this I find a little difficulty in addressing this House and putting all my ideas before it and I feel also that in this long succession of thousands of years, I see the mighty figures that have come and gone and I see also the long succession of our comrades who have laboured for the freedom of India. And now we stand on the verge of this passing age, trying, labouring, to usher in the new. I am sure the House will feel the solemnity of this moment and will endeavour to treat this Resolution which it is my proud privilege to place before it in a correspondingly solemn manner. I believe there are a large number of amendments coming before the House. I have not seen most of them. It is open to the House, to any member of this House, to move any amendment and it is for the House to accept it or reject it, but I would, with all respect, suggest that this is not the moment for us to be technical and legal about small matters when we have big things to face, big things to say and big things to do, and, therefore, I hope that the House will consider this Resolution in a broad-minded manner and not lose itself in wordy quarrels and squabbles.

I think also of the various Constituent Assemblies that have gone before and of what took place at the making of the great American nation when the fathers of that nation met and fashioned a Constitution which has stood the test of so many years, more than a century and a half, and of the great nation which has resulted, which has been built up on the basis of that Constitution. My mind goes back to that mighty revolution which took place also over 150 years ago and the Constituent Assembly that met in that gracious and lovely city of Paris which has fought so many battles for freedom. My mind goes back to the difficulties that that Constituent Assembly had to face from the King and other authorities, and still it continued. The House will remember that when these difficulties came and even the room for a meeting was denied to that Constituent Assembly, they betook themselves to an open tennis court and met there and took the oath, which is called the Oath of the Tennis Court. They continued meeting in spite of Kings, in spite of the others, and did not disperse till they had finished the task they had undertaken. Well, I trust that it is in that solemn spirit that we too are meeting here and that we too whether we meet in this chamber or in other chambers, or in the fields or in the market place, will go on meeting and continue our work till we have finished it.

Then my mind goes back to a more recent revolution which gave rise to a new type of State, the revolution that took place in Russia and out of which has arisen the Union of the Soviet Socialist Republics, another mighty country which is playing a tremendous part in the world, not only a mighty country, but for us in India, a neighbouring country.

So our mind goes back to these great examples and we seek to learn from their success and to avoid their failures. Perhaps we may not be able to avoid failures, because some measure of failure is inherent in human effort. Nevertheless, we shall advance, I am certain, in spite of obstructions and difficulties, and achieve and realize the dream that we have dreamt so long. In this Resolution which the House knows has been drafted with exceeding care we have tried to avoid saying too much or too little. It is difficult to frame a resolution of this kind. If you say too little, it becomes just a pious resolution and nothing more. If you say too much, it encroaches on the functions of those who are going to draw up a Constitution, that is, on the functions of this House. This Resolution is not a part of the Constitution we are going to draw up, and it must not be looked upon as such. This House has perfect freedom to draw up that Constitution and when others come into this House, they will have perfect freedom too to fashion that Constitution. This Resolution, therefore, steers between these two extremes and lays down only certain fundamentals which, I do believe, no group or party and hardly any individual in India can dispute. We say that it is our firm and solemn resolve to have an Independent Sovereign Republic. India is bound to be sovereign, it is bound to be independent and it is bound to be a Republic. I will not go into the arguments about monarchy and the rest, but obviously we cannot produce monarchy in India out of nothing. It is not there. If it is to be an independent and sovereign State, we are not going to have an external monarchy and we cannot begin a search for a legal heir from among local monarchies. It must inevitably be a Republic. Now, some friends have raised the question: "Why have you not put in the word 'democratic' here?" Well, I told them that it is conceivable, of course, that a Republic may not be democratic, but the whole of our past is witness to the fact that we stand for democratic institutions. Obviously, we are aiming at democracy and nothing less than a democracy. What form of democracy, what shape it may take is another matter. The democracies of the present day, many of them in Europe and some elsewhere, have played a great part in the world's progress. Yet it may be doubtful if those democracies may not have to change their shape somewhat before long if they have to remain completely democratic. We are not going just to copy, I hope, a certain democratic procedure or an institution of a so-called democratic country. We may improve upon it. In any event, whatever system of government we may establish here must fit in with the temper of our people and be acceptable to them. We stand for democracy. It will be for this House to determine what shape to give to that democracy, the fullest democracy, I hope. The House will notice that in this Resolution, although we have not used the word 'democratic', because we thought it obvious that the word 'republic' contains the meaning of that word and we did not want to use unnecessary words and redundant words, but we have done something much more than using the word. We have given the content of democracy in this Resolution and not only the content of democracy but the content, if I may say so, of economic democracy in this Resolution. Others might take objection to this Resolution on the ground that we have not said that it should be a Socialist State. Well, I stand for socialism and, I hope, India will stand for socialism and that India will go towards the constitution of a Socialist State and I do believe that the whole world will have to go that way. What form of socialism again is another matter for your consideration. But the main thing is that in such a Resolution, if, in accordance with my own desire, I had put in that we wanted a Socialist State, we would have put in something which might be agreeable to many and might not be agreeable to some and we wanted this Resolution not to be controversial in regard to such matters. Therefore, we have laid down, not theoretical words and formulas, but rather the content of the thing we desire. This is important and I take it there can be no dispute about it. Some people have pointed out to me that our mentioning a Republic may somewhat displease the rulers of Indian States. It is possible that this may displease them. But I want to make it clear personally, and the House knows, that I do not believe in the monarchical system anywhere, and that in the world today monarchy is a fast disappearing institution. Nevertheless, it is not a question of my personal belief in this matter. Our view in regard to the Indian States has been, for many years, first of all that the people of those States must share completely in the freedom to come. It is quite inconceivable to me that there should be different standards and degrees of freedom as between the people of the States and the people outside the States. In what manner the States will be parts of that Union is a matter for this House to consider with the representatives of the States. And I hope that, in all matters relating to the States, this House will deal with the real representatives of the States. We are perfectly willing, I take it, to deal in such matters as appertain to them, with the rulers or their representatives also, but finally when we make a Constitution for India, it must be through the representatives of the people of the States as with the rest of India, who are present here. In any event, we may lay down or agree that the measure of freedom must be the same in the States as elsewhere. It is a possibility and personally I should like a measure of uniformity too in regard to the apparatus and machinery of Government. Nevertheless, this is a point to be considered in co-operation and in consultation with the States. I do not wish, and I imagine this Constituent Assembly will not like to impose anything on the States against their will. If the people of a particular State desire to have a certain form of administration, even though it might be monarchical, it is open to them to have it. The House will remember that even in the British Commonwealth of Nations today, Eire is a Republic and yet in many ways it is a member of the British Commonwealth. So it is a conceivable thing. What will happen, I do not know, because that is partly for this House and partly for others to decide. There is no incongruity or impossibility about a certain definite form of administration in the States, provided there is complete freedom and responsible government there and the people really are in charge. If monarchical figure-heads are approved of by the people of the State, of a particular State, whether I like it or not, I certainly would not interfere. So I wish to make it clear that so far as this Resolution or Declaration is concerned, it does not interfere in any way with any future work that this Constituent Assembly may do, with any future negotiations that it may undertake. Only in one sense, if you like, it limits our work, if you call that a limitation, i.e., we adhere to certain fundamental propositions which are laid down in this Declaration. These fundamental propositions, I submit, are not controversial in any real sense of the word. Nobody challenges them in India and nobody ought to challenge them, but if anybody should challenge them, well, we shall accept that challenge and hold our position.

Well, Sir, we are going to make a Constitution for India and it is obvious that what we are going to do in India, is going to have a powerful effect on the rest of the world, not only because a new free independent nation comes out into the arena of the world, but because of the very fact that India is such a country that by virtue, not only of her large size and population, but of her enormous resources and her ability to exploit those resources, she can immediately play an important and a vital part in world affairs. Even today, on the verge of freedom as we are today, India has begun to play an important part in world affairs. Therefore, it is right that the framers of our Constitution should always bear this larger international aspect in mind.

We approach the world in a friendly way. We want to make friends with all countries. We want to make friends, in spite of the long history of conflict in the past, with England also. The House knows that recently I paid a visit to England. I was reluctant to go for reasons which the House knows well. But I went because of a personal request from the Prime Minister of Great Britain. I went and I met with courtesy everywhere. And yet at this psychological moment in India's history when we wanted, when we hungered for messages of cheer, friendship and cooperation from all over the world, and more especially from England, because of the past contact and conflict between us, unfortunately, I came back without any message of cheer, but with a large measure of disappointment. I hope that the new difficulties that have arisen, as every one knows, because of the recent statements made by the British Cabinet and by others in authority

there, will not come in our way and that we shall succeed yet in
going ahead with the co-operation of all of us here and those who
have not come. It has been a blow to me, and it has hurt me that
just at the moment when we were going to stride ahead, obstructions were placed in our way, new limitations were mentioned
which had not been mentioned previously and new methods of
procedure were suggested. I do not wish to challenge the *bona
fides* of any person, but I wish to say that whatever the legal
aspect of the thing might be, there are moments when law is a
very feeble reed to rely upon, when we have to deal with a nation
which is full of the passion for freedom. Most of us here during
many years past, for a generation or more, have often taken
part in the struggle for India's freedom. We have gone through
the valley of the shadow. We are used to it, and if necessity arises,
we shall go through it again. Nevertheless, through all this long
period, we have thought of the time when we should have an
opportunity, not merely to struggle, not merely to destroy, but to
construct and create. And now, when it appeared that the time
had come for constructive effort in a free India to which we looked
forward with joy, fresh difficulties were placed in our way at such
a moment. It shows that, whatever force might be behind all this,
people who are able and clever and very intelligent, somehow
lack the imaginative daring which should accompany great offices.
For, if you have to deal with any people, you have to understand
them imaginatively ; you should understand them emotionally ;
and, of course, you have also to understand them intellectually.
One of the unfortunate legacies of the past has been that there
has been no imagination in the understanding of the Indian
problem. People have often indulged in, or have presumed to give
us advice, not realizing that India, as she is constituted today,
wants no one's advice and no one's imposition upon her. The only
way to influence India is through friendship and co-operation and
goodwill. Any attempt at imposition, the slightest trace of patron-
age, is resented and will be resented. We have tried, I think
honestly, in the last few months, in spite of the difficulties that
have faced us, to create an atmosphere of co-operation. We shall
continue that endeavour. But I do very much fear that that atmosphere will be impaired if there is not sufficient and adequate
response from others. Nevertheless, because we are bent on great
tasks, I hope and trust that we shall continue that endeavour and
I do hope that, if we continue, we shall succeed. Where we have

to deal with our own countrymen, we must continue that endeavour even though in our opinion some of our countrymen take a wrong path. For, after all, we have to work together in this country and we have inevitably to co-operate, if not today, tomorrow or the day after. Therefore, we have to avoid in the present anything which might introduce a new difficulty in the creation of that future which we are working for. Therefore, as far as our own countrymen are concerned, we must try our utmost to gain their co-operation in the largest measure. But co-operation cannot mean the giving up of the fundamental ideals on which we have stood and on which we should stand. It is not co-operation to surrender everything that has given meaning to our lives. Apart from that, as I said, we seek the co-operation of England even at this stage even when we are full of suspicion of each other. We feel that if that co-operation is denied, it will be injurious to India, certainly to some extent, probably more so to England, and, to some extent, to the world at large. We have just come out of a world war and people talk vaguely and rather wildly of new wars to come. At such a moment is this New India taking birth—renascent, vital, fearless. Perhaps it is a suitable moment for this new birth to take place out of this turmoil in the world. But we have to be clear-eyed at this moment, —we, who have the heavy task of constitution-building. We have to think of this tremendous prospect of the present and the greater prospect of the future and not get lost in seeking small gains for this group or that. In this Constituent Assembly we are functioning on a world stage and the eyes of the world are upon us and the eyes of our entire past are upon us. Our past is witness to what we are doing here and though the future is still unborn, the future too somehow looks at us, I think, and so I would beg of this House to consider this Resolution in the mighty perspective of our past, of the turmoil of the present and of the great and unborn future that is going to take place soon.

THE RESOLUTION ABOUT OBJECTIVES

IT was my proud privilege, Sir, six weeks ago, to move this Resolution before this Honourable House. I felt the weight and solemnity of that occasion. It was not a mere form of words that I placed before the House, carefully chosen as those words were. But these words and the Resolution represented the agony and hopes of the nation coming at last to fruition.

As I stood here on that occasion I felt the past crowding round me, and I felt also the future taking shape. We stand on the razor's edge of the present, and as I was addressing not only this Honourable House but the millions of India who were vastly interested in our work and because I felt that we were coming to the end of an age, I had a sense of our forbears watching this undertaking of ours and possibly blessing it, if we moved aright, and the future of which we became trustees, became almost a living thing taking shape and moving before our eyes. It was a great responsibility to be trustees of the future, and it was some responsibility also to be inheritors of our great past. And between the great past and the great future which we envisage, we stood on the edge of the present and the weight of that occasion, I have no doubt, impressed itself upon this Honourable House.

So I placed this Resolution before the House, and I had hoped that it could be passed in a day or two and we could start our other work immediately. But after a long debate this House decided to postpone further consideration of this Resolution. May I confess that I was a little disappointed, because I was impatient that we should go forward? I felt that, by lingering on the road we were not true to the pledges that we had taken. It was a bad beginning that we should postpone such an important Resolution about objectives. Would that imply that our future work would go along slowly and be postponed from time to time? Nevertheless, I have no doubt that the decision this House took in its wisdom in postponing this Resolution was a right decision,

---

A speech winding up the debate on the Objectives Resolution delivered at the Constituent Assembly, January 22, 1947.

because we have always balanced two factors, one, the urgent necessity of reaching our goal, and the other, that we should reach it in proper time and with as great a unanimity as possible. It was right, therefore, if I may say with all respect, that this House decided to adjourn consideration of this motion and thus has not only demonstrated before the world our earnest desire to have all those people here who have not so far come, but also to assure the country and everyone else how anxious we were to have the co-operation of all. Since then six weeks have passed, and during these weeks there has been plenty of opportunity for those who wanted to come. Unfortunately, they have not yet decided to come and they still hover in a state of indecision. I regret that, and all I can say is this, that we shall welcome them at any future time when they may wish to come. But it should be made clear without any possibility of misunderstanding that no work will be held up in future, whether any one comes or not. There has been waiting enough. Not only of six weeks' waiting but many in this country have waited for years and years, and the country has waited for some generations now. How long are we to wait? And if we, some of us, who are more prosperous can afford to wait, what about the waiting of the hungry and the starving? This Resolution will not feed the hungry or the starving, but it brings a promise of many things—it brings the promise of freedom, it brings the promise of food and opportunity for all. Therefore, the sooner we set about our task the better. We waited for six weeks, and during these six weeks the country thought about it, pondered over it, and other countries also and other people who are interested have thought about it. Now, we have come back here to take up the further consideration of this Resolution. We have had a long debate and we stand on the verge of passing it. I am grateful to Dr. Jayakar and Mr. Sahaya for having withdrawn their amendments. Dr. Jayakar's purpose was served by the postponing of the Resolution, and it appears now that there is no one in this House who does not fully accept this Resolution as it is. It may be that some would like it to be slightly differently worded or the emphasis placed more on this part or on that part. But taking it as a whole, it is a Resolution which has already received the full assent of this House, and there is little doubt that it has received the full assent of the country.

There have been some criticisms of it, notably from some of

the Princes. Their first criticism was that such a Resolution should not be passed in the absence of the representatives of the States. In part I agree with that criticism, that is to say, I should have liked all the States to be properly represented here, the whole of India, every part of India to be properly represented here when we pass this Resolution. But if they are not here it is not our fault. It is largely the fault of the scheme under which we are working, and we have this choice before us: are we to postpone our work, because some people cannot be here? That would be a dreadful thing if we stopped not only this Resolution, but possibly so much else, because representatives of the States are not here. As far as we are concerned, they can come in at the earliest possible moment ; we shall welcome them if they send proper representatives of the States. As far as we are concerned, even during the last six weeks or a month we have made some effort to get into touch with the Committee representing the States rulers to find a way for their proper representation here. It is not our fault that there has been delay. We are anxious to get every one in, whether it is the representatives of the Muslim League or the States or anyone else. We shall continue to persevere in this endeavour so that this House may be as fully representative of the country as it is possible to be. So we cannot postpone this Resolution or anything else, because some people are not here.

Another point has been raised: the idea of the sovereignty of the people which is enshrined in this Resolution does not commend itself to certain rulers of the Indian States. This is a surprising objection and, if I may say so, if that objection is raised in all seriousness by anybody, be he a ruler or a minister, it is enough to condemn the Indian States system that exists in India. It is a scandalous thing for any man to say, however highly placed he may be, that he is here by special divine dispensation to rule over human beings today. That is a thing which is an intolerable presumption on any man's part, and it is a thing which this House will never allow and will repudiate if it is put before it. We have heard a lot about this Divine Right of Kings ; we have read a lot about it in past histories and we thought that we had heard the last of it and that it had been put an end to and buried deep down in the earth long ages ago. If any individual in India or elsewhere claims it today, he will be doing so without any relation to the present in India

So I would suggest to such persons in all seriousness that, if they want to be respected or considered with any measure of friendliness, no such idea should even be hinted at, much less said. On this there is going to be no compromise.

But, as I made plain on the previous occasion when I spoke, this Resolution makes it clear that we are not interfering in the internal affairs of the States. I even said that we are not interfering with the system of monarchy in the States, if the people of the States want it. I gave the example of the Irish Republic in the British Commonwealth and it is conceivable to me that, within the Indian Republic, there might be monarchies if the people so desire. That is entirely for them to determine. This Resolution, and presumably, the Constitution that we make, will not interfere with that matter. Inevitably, it will be necessary to bring about uniformity in the freedom of the various parts of India, because it is inconceivable to me that certain parts of India should have democratic freedom and certain others should be denied it. That cannot be. That will give rise to trouble, just as in the wide world today there is trouble, because some countries are free and some are not. There will be much more trouble if there is freedom in parts of India and lack of freedom in other parts.

But we are not laying down in this Resolution any strict system in regard to the governance of the Indian States. All that we say is this: that they, or such of them as are big enough to form unions or group themselves into small unions, will be autonomous units with a very large measure of freedom to do as they choose, subject no doubt to certain central functions in which they will co-operate with the Centre, in which they will be represented at the Centre and in which the Centre will have control. So that, in a sense, this Resolution does not interfere with the inner working of those Units. They will be autonomous and, as I have said, if those Units choose to have some kind of constitutional monarchy at their head, they will be welcome to do so. For my part, I am for a Republic in India as anywhere else. But, whatever my views may be on that subject, it is not my desire to impose my will on others : whatever the views of this House may be on this subject, I imagine that it is not the desire of this House to impose its will in these matters.

So the objection of the ruler of an Indian State to this Resolution becomes an objection in theory to the theoretical implications and the practical implications of the doctrine of the sovereignty of the people. To nothing else does any one object. That is an objection which cannot stand for an instant. We claim in this Resolution the right to frame a Constitution for a Sovereign Independent Indian Republic—necessarily Republic. What else can we have in India? Whatever the State may have or may not have, it is impossible and inconceivable and undesirable to think in any terms but those of a Republic in India.

Now, what relation will that Republic bear to the other countries of the world, to England and to the British Commonwealth and the rest? For a long time past we have taken a pledge on Independence Day that India must sever her connection with Great Britain, because that connection had become an emblem of British domination. At no time have we ever thought in terms of isolating ourselves in this part of the world from other countries or of being hostile to countries which have dominated over us. On the eve of this great occasion, when we stand on the threshold of freedom, we do not wish to carry a trail of hostility with us against any other country. We want to be friendly to all. We want to be friendly with the British people and the British Commonwealth of Nations.

But what I would like this House to consider is this: when these words and these labels are fast changing their meaning—and in the world today there is no isolation—you cannot live apart from the others. You must co-operate or you must fight. There is no middle way. We wish for peace. We do not want to fight any nation if we can help it. The only possible real objective that we, in common with other nations, can have is the objective of co-operating in building up some kind of world structure, call it One World, call it what you like. The beginnings of this world structure have been laid in the United Nations Organization. It is still feeble ; it has many defects ; nevertheless, it is the beginning of the world structure. And India has pledged herself to co-operate in its work.

Now, if we think of that structure and our co-operation with other countries in achieving it, where does the question come of our being tied up with this group of nations or that group? Indeed, the more groups and blocs are formed, the weaker will that great structure become.

Therefore, in order to strengthen this big structure, it is desirable for all countries not to insist, not to lay stress on separate groups and separate blocs. I know that there are such separate groups and blocs today, and because they exist today, there is hostility between them, and there is even talk of war among them. I do not know what the future will bring us, whether peace or war. We stand on the edge of a precipice and there are various forces which pull us on one side in favour of co-operation and peace, and on the other, push us towards the precipice of war and disintegration. I am not enough of a prophet to know what will happen, but I do know that those who desire peace must deprecate separate blocs which necessarily become hostile to other blocs. Therefore, India, in so far as it has a foreign policy, has declared that it wants to remain independent and free of all these blocs and that it wants to co-operate on equal terms with all countries. It is a difficult position, because, when people are full of fear of one another, any person who tries to be neutral is suspected of sympathy with the other party. We can see that in India and we can see that in the wider sphere of world politics. Recently an American statesman criticized India in words which show how lacking in knowledge and understanding even the statesmen of America are. Because we follow our own policy, this group of nations thinks that we are siding with the other and that group of nations thinks that we are siding with this. That is bound to happen. If we seek to be a free, independent, democratic Republic, it is not to dissociate ourselves from other countries, but rather as a free nation to co-operate in the fullest measure with other countries for peace and freedom, to co-operate with Britain, with the British Commonwealth of Nations, with the United States of America, with the Soviet Union, and with all other countries, big and small. But real co-operation would only come between us and these other nations when we know that we are free to co-operate and are not imposed upon and forced to co-operate. As long as there is the slightest trace of compulsion, there can be no co-operation.

Therefore, I commend this Resolution to the House and I commend this Resolution, if I may say so, not only to this House but to the world at large so that it can be perfectly clear that it is a gesture of friendship to all and that behind it there lies no hostility. We have suffered enough in the past. We have struggled sufficiently, we may have to struggle again, but under the leadership of a very great personality we have sought always to think in terms of friendship and goodwill towards others, even those who opposed us. How far we have succeeded, we do not know, because we are weak human beings. Nevertheless, the impress of that message has found a place in the hearts of millions of people of this country, and even when we err and go astray, we cannot forget it. Some of us may be little men, some may be big, but whether we are small men or big, for the moment we represent a great cause and therefore something of the shadow of greatness falls upon us. Today in this Assembly we represent a mighty cause and this Resolution that I have placed before you gives some semblance of that cause. We shall pass this Resolution, and I hope that this Resolution will lead us to a Constitution on the lines suggested by this Resolution. I trust that the Constitution itself will lead us to the real freedom that we have clamoured for and that real freedom in turn will bring food to our starving people, clothing for them, housing for them and all manner of opportunities for progress; that it will lead also to the freedom of the other countries of Asia, because in a sense, however unworthy we may be, we have become—let us recognize it—the leaders of the freedom movement of Asia, and whatever we do, we should think of ourselves in these larger terms. When some petty matter divides us and we have difficulties and conflicts amongst ourselves over these small matters, let us remember not only this Resolution, but this great responsibility that we shoulder, the responsibility of the freedom of 400 million people of India, the responsibility of the leadership of a large part of Asia, the responsibility of being some kind of guide to vast numbers of people all over the world. It is a tremendous responsibility. If we remember it, perhaps we may not bicker so much over this seat or that post, over some small gain for this group or that. The one thing that should be obvious to all of us is this, that there is no group in India, no party, no religious community, which can prosper if India does not prosper. If India goes down, we go down, all of us, whether we have a few seats more or less, whether we get a slight advantage or we do not. But if it is well with India, if India lives as a vital, free country then it is well with all of us to whatever community or religion we may belong.

We shall frame the Constitution, and I hope it will be a good Constitution, but does anyone in this House imagine that, when a free India emerges, it will be bound down by anything that even this House might lay down for it? A free India will see the bursting forth of the energy of a mighty nation. What it will do and what it will not, I do not know, but I do know that it will not consent to be bound down by anything. Some people imagine that what we do now may not be touched for 10 years or 20 years : if we do not do it today, we shall not be able to do it later. That seems to me a complete misapprehension. I am not placing before the House what I want done and what I do not want done, but I should like the House to consider that we are on the eve of revolutionary changes, revolutionary in every sense of the word, because when the spirit of a nation breaks its bonds, it functions in peculiar ways and it should function in strange ways. It may be that the Constitution this House frames may not satisfy an India that is free. This House cannot bind down the next generation or the people who will duly succeed us in this task. Therefore, let us not trouble ourselves too much about the petty details of what we do, these details will not survive for long, if they are achieved in conflict. What we achieve in unanimity, what we achieve by co-operation is likely to survive. What we gain here and there by conflict and by overbearing manners and by threats will not survive long. It will only leave a trail of bad blood. And so now I commend this Resolution to the House and may I read the last paragraph of this Resolution? But, one word more, Sir, before I read it.

India is a great country, great in her resources, great in man-power, great in her potential, in every way. I have little doubt that a free India on every plane will play a big part on the world stage, even on the narrowest plane of material power, and I should like India to play that great part on that plane. Nevertheless, today there is a conflict in the world between forces in different planes. We hear a lot about the atom bomb and the various kinds of energy that it represents and in essence today there is a conflict in the world between two things, the atom bomb and what it represents and the spirit of humanity. I hope that while India will no doubt play a great part in all the material spheres, she will always lay stress on the spirit of humanity and I have no doubt in my mind that ultimately in this conflict that is confronting the world the human spirit will prevail over the atom bomb. May this Resolution bear fruit and the time may come when in the words of this Resolution, this ancient land will attain its rightful and honoured place in the world and make its full and willing contribution to the promotion of world peace and the welfare of mankind.

TO THE DEFENCE SERVICES

SOLDIERS of Free India, JAI HIND! Some months ago, I told the Commander-in-Chief that it was my desire to meet as frequently as possible the officers and men of the Indian armed forces, to visit units and to see them at work and at play and particularly to talk to them. I wanted to know you and speak to you, because it is very necessary that we should understand each other. It is very necessary in an independent country for those in authority, who represent the people, to know what is in the minds of the men of the armed forces. There should be no distance between the people generally and the armed services ; they are all one, because recruitment to the armed forces is made from the masses. The old idea that the army was a separate entity does not now hold good. It therefore becomes essential that we should understand each other. However, owing to extreme pressure of work and the many vital problems requiring immediate attention, I could not meet most of you, although I have had occasion to meet and talk to some. Therefore, I decided to say a few words to you this evening over the radio.

Our country has become free. What is the meaning of freedom? It means that we are free to do things without outside interference. It does not mean that anyone is free to do what he likes, because such licence would lead to chaos. If everyone takes the law into his own hands, it becomes jungle law. That sort of freedom does not become civilized people.

Ours is an ancient land with an ancient civilization dating back to thousands of years. Our new-born freedom has brought us great responsibilities. If anything goes wrong, it will be our fault, we cannot blame others. If we do good we reap the benefits ; if we do evil we suffer. Therefore, it behoves you, men of the armed forces especially, to realize these responsibilities. Your duty is to serve your country and your countrymen.

They call me the Prime Minister of India, but it would be more appropriate if I were called the first servant of India. In this age, it is not titles and positions that matter but service. You,

A talk broadcast to the men of the Armed Services from New Delhi, December 1, 1947, inaugurating the New Forces Programme on the A. I. R.

in particular, have a great opportunity to serve, because you have the armed power of the State in your hands. You must take care not to abuse it.

You know that our forces are operating in Kashmir to drive out those who invaded that State. Why did our forces go to Kashmir? We do not want to invade other countries and enslave people. As we have wanted freedom for our country, so do we desire freedom for other countries, especially those in Asia. Kashmir, of course, is a part of this land. Our forces went there not to oppress or conquer. They went there because the people of Kashmir were in peril, and their country was being overrun by forces of aggression. When Kashmir was being ravaged by the raiders, the people asked us for help. It was thus our duty to go and help. We sent our forces who performed their task speedily and courageously. Much has been accomplished, but more difficult work lies ahead and I am confident that they will succeed.

I went there and spoke to our men. I told them that they were there as guests and friends and as servants of the people of Kashmir and that on their actions depended the fair name of India. Any ill-considered action by our men in Kashmir would bring discredit to India. I am glad that while performing their duty they have established cordial relations with the Kashmir people. We must constantly remind ourselves that whatever our religion or creed, we are all one people.

I regret that the recent disturbances have given us a bad name. Many have acquiesced in the prevailing spirit. This is not citizenship. Citizenship consists in the service of the country. We must prevail on the evil-doers to stop their activities. If you, men of the Navy, the Army and the Air Force, serve your country-men without distinction of class or religion, you will bring honour to yourselves and to your country. JAI HIND!

LAUNCHING A SHIP

In launching this ship all manner of thoughts come to us, especially on such an occasion when the first Indian ship of this size has been built and launched after centuries. Inevitably one thinks of the ages when ship-building was the premier industry of India. Somehow, we come to appreciate the past ages and the Middle Ages which did much good and yet much ill to our country and which have formed part of our history. In doing so, one thinks partly of the ship-building industry, but more so the good of the country itself. Somehow, the launching of a ship brings to mind the analogy of the ship of State which was also launched a few months ago in India and which has gone through stormy weather. We have survived and are surviving the storms, but we have plenty of storms to face in India. Indeed, all over the world more storms are continuing and there are many ahead. But I think we have shown that we are strong enough and are resolved to face them. As I was watching this good ship "Jala-Usha" launched into the sea, I thought of the ship of State entering the sea.

India is an old country and I have always thought of India as the offspring of mountains and seas, the Himalayas and the Indian Ocean embracing her on two sides. So I have always thought of India not as a country isolated from the rest of the world, but a country eminently suited for the closest and widest intercourse with the other countries of the world. Unfortunately, in recent years—200 years, more especially during the last 150 years—it has become isolated both by mountain and by sea. All our contacts with the western countries of the world, chiefly England, have been only by sea. But other contacts were ended and cut off. We lost touch with the highland of Central Asia and eastern and western Asia. Indian history tells us of greater enterprises across the seas and across mountains and we were not an isolated people in those days. We looked forward as we ventured across the seas and took our metal and culture to far off countries.

A speech delivered at Vizagapatam, Madras, on the launching of S.S. Jala-Usha, the first ocean-going steamer made in India, March 14, 1948.

Narrow-mindedness was unheard of in those days. But with
the passage of time we have developed narrow-mindedness in the
name of religion. What kind of religion is it that prevents
man from meeting man? In the name of religion, it has been
called a sin to undertake a sea voyage. What kind of religion is
it that prevents a man from going to his mother and trusting
his mother? If one is not to trust his mother, father, and brother
how can one live and progress? We have had enough of this
religion and narrow-mindedness in outlook. We grow afraid of
the sea, our mother. If we grow afraid of our mother and distrust
her, where can we rest and take shelter in times of danger?
Now, we must go back to the sea, our mother, and send our
ships fearlessly. Let that sea be a symbol for us in the future.
Let us send the ship of State, that is India, into the sea with a
stout heart and in this way not only develop India, but enhance
her stature and co-operate with other nations and venture with
a stout heart more and more in future.

Isolation means, in future, death and ruin of the country.
To every great country, however big, isolation means standing
apart from the world. It means falling behind in the progress of
the world. We are not looking forward to interfering with the
lives of other countries. We seek no dominion over others. We
seek the friendship of all and co-operation with all. At the same
time we brook no interference from outside. So it is in this spirit
that I launched this ship and let this spirit of adventure,
mercantile or naval enterprise be carried on.

In this port of Vizagapatam, we are not only building up the
ship-building industry, but it is also an important naval base. It
is the most important port on the eastern coast of India, and
I should like the naval base to develop and I should like our
young men, bright young men, to join the Navy. Personally, I
would have liked to join the Navy myself had I been young. If
there is anything I am more attracted to than the Navy it is the
Air. But unfortunately life has dealt with me very badly and I
am at an office desk which is the thing I hate most. I understand fishermen from Orissa are applying to join the Navy. I
welcome these applications, but before they can be recruited
they will have to acquire some required standards. It is, therefore,
our duty to facilitate their attaining the standards that are
required.

In your speech, Mr. Chairman, there is a strange and rather

astounding phrase used ; that is about harmonious relations between the Government and Industry. Is industry a rival of our Government? The Government will help industry in every way. If industry does not function efficiently, the Government interferes and takes it over. The Government is going to encourage industry. Industry will become one hundred per cent Government if it does not function efficiently. Shipping will not suffer and will go on at all costs and at every cost. How it is going on is another matter. Rest assured, the Government is immensely interested in encouraging this industry. We are beholden to the Scindia Company for the enterprise it has shown in the past. Enterprise will always be encouraged. It has waged a ceaseless struggle against foreign vested interests. Inevitably this vital enterprise must come more and more under the control of the State. After all, people who build ships—from the top men sitting in your office to the workmen who actually do the job— do not really matter. Whatever happens, take it from me, the technical personnel and managerial personnel who contribute to the making of magnificent things will not undergo any change. They remain the same. It is only that somewhere at the top certain changes affecting policy and profits will come about. I am glad to learn that in your dockyard there prevails a feeling of amity and comradeship between employers and employees and that you are following the principle of industrial truce that we laid down some time ago. I think one of the most important things for us to realize today is that industrial warfare injures and weakens the nation at any time, of course, but more especially today, when we have just launched our ship of State. If the crew of the ship starts non-co-operation how will the ship start its voyage?

I have a feeling that things are not well in the Madras Presidency. Not here, of course, but in some other places. Without going into the merits and demerits of this uneasiness, I want to tell you that that kind of thing cannot be tolerated. It will be up to the Madras Government and the Government of India, in so far as they are concerned, to prevent this strife. I have been watching from a distance and seen that some strikes are organized just for the sake of striking without its ever resulting in any good to the worker. This sort of strike, merely for the sake of striking without any good being done to anybody cannot be tolerated. There is a spirit of violence abroad

That, too, cannot be tolerated. We are a democratic country and we want to give the largest measure of freedom of opinion, of action and of expression to each group, even though we may differ from it. Freedom does not mean violence or instigation to violence. If there is instigation to violence, as there is in this Presidency, it will have to be dealt with seriously. We are living in critical times, not only in this country, but in the world. None knows what the morrow will bring. At times swift action, wherever necessary, will have to be taken to keep the ship of State moving even though the waters may be stormy. All the world over, things are becoming rougher and rougher. Therefore, we must not entangle ourselves with the world's difficulties and problems. Yet we cannot escape them either. We have to look at things in their proper perspective.

We have to keep an effective eye on the maintenance of peace in the country. If we lead a disciplined life and solve our own problems, industrial and other, I hope industry will prosper. Industry will have above all to seek and solve its own problems, certainly with the help of the Government. I hope the workers, too, will realize, if there is ever a time for striking, certainly this is not the time for it. There are too many perils and dangers ahead. The weapon of strike is a precious and valuable one and it should not be used haphazardly. We must evolve proper and sane alternatives to strike in order to govern industrial relations if we are to progress as a nation. Any system that depends on periodical conflicts is not sane or reasonable. So I congratulate you again on this venture. May this ship that we have launched today be the beginning of many other ships, big and small, and may they carry the message of India to all corners of the world!

TO THE MOUNTBATTENS

YOUR Excellencies, Your Highnesses, ladies and gentlemen—Fifteen months ago, almost to the day, some of us went to Palam airfield to welcome the new Viceroy and his wife. Some of us will go again to Palam airfield tomorrow morning to bid them good-bye. Fifteen months have passed and these fifteen months seem a long time, and yet it seems but yesterday that Lord and Lady Mountbatten and Pamela Mountbatten came here, and yet if you look again it seems that an age has gone by because of the accumulation of sensation and experience, of joy and sorrow that has come to us during these fifteen months.

I find it a little difficult to speak on this occasion, because the people about whom I am going to speak have become during this period very dear and intimate friends of ours, and it is always difficult to speak of those who are friends and who are dear to us. One may overdo it or one may, on the other hand, guard oneself unduly and underdo it. In any event, I do not know that any words of mine are needed here to say much about Lord and Lady Mountbatten. In the past few days, there have been numerous parties where they received words of praise and friendship and welcome I suppose, but they did not affect me very much. They were rather formal on the whole.

I do feel that any words of mine this evening, after the demonstration in the City of Delhi three or four hours ago, will be in the nature of an anti-climax, because three or four hours ago, the City of Delhi, that is the common people of Delhi, gathered together to welcome or rather to bid goodbye to them, and that was such a wonderful demonstration of friendship and affection that any words or phrases can hardly be suited to an occasion after that event. I do not know—at the most I can only guess—how Lord and Lady Mountbatten felt on that occasion : but used as I am to these vast demonstrations here, I was much affected and I wondered how it was that an Englishman and an Englishwoman could become so popular in India during this brief period of time ; and that brief period being a period certainly of

A speech delivered in New Delhi at a banquet given to Lord and Lady Mountbatten on the eve of their departure from India, June 20, 1948.

achievement and success in some measure. but also a period of sorrow and disaster.

In fact, I have often wondered why the people of India put up with people like me who are connected with the governing of India after all that has happened during the last few months. I am not quite sure that if I had not been in the Government, I would put up with my Government. Quite apart from the merits or demerits, the fact is that a government should and must be responsible for everything that happens, and if everything that happens is not right, then the government ought to be held responsible. I think that is a good maxim, generally speaking. It may perhaps be possible to find sufficient excuses. So it surprised me all the more that after this period of storm and stress and difficulty, the Governor-General and his wife, who were in some sense associated with all this, should still be able to win the affection of the people to such a tremendous degree.

Obviously, this was not connected so much with what had happened, but rather with the good faith, the friendship and the love of India that these two possessed. They saw them working hard with indomitable energy, with perseverance, with optimism, which defied everything, they felt even more than they saw the friendship which they had for India and they saw that they were serving India to the best of their ability.

We have many failings and many weaknesses in India, but when we see friendship for India and service for India, our hearts go out and those who are friends of India and those who serve India are our comrades, whoever they might be or wherever they might be. And so the people of India, realizing that Lord and Lady Mountbatten undoubtedly were friendly to India and the Indian people, undoubtedly were serving them, gave you their affection and love. They could not give very much else. You may have many gifts and presents, but there is nothing more rare or precious than the love and affection of the people. You have seen yourself, Sir and Madam, how that love and affection work. If I may say so, they are the most precious of gifts. So when you have seen all this, I have little to add except to say a few words, rather personal perhaps, and also impersonal.

You have been here, in your individual capacity and in a great public capacity. We have become friends with you, many of us, and we have been thrown together at a strange moment in history, and we have been actors also in this historic scene. It is difficult for me or for anyone to judge of what we have done during the last year or so. We are too near it and too intimately connected with events. Maybe we have made many mistakes, you and we. Historians a generation or two hence will perhaps be able to judge whether we have done right and whether we have done wrong. Nevertheless, whether we did right or wrong, the test, perhaps the right test, is whether we tried to do right or did not, for if we did try to do right with all our might and main, then it does not very much matter, although it does matter in the sense that it turned out to be a wrong thing. I cannot judge our own motives, but I do believe that we did try to do right and I am convinced that you tried to do the right thing by India, and, therefore, many of our sins will be forgiven us and many of our errors also.

You came here, Sir, with a high reputation, but many a reputation has foundered in India. You lived here during a period of great difficulty and crisis, and yet your reputation has not foundered. That is a remarkable feat. Many of us who came in contact with you from day to day in these days of crisis learnt much from you, we gathered confidence when sometimes we were rather shaken, and I have no doubt that the many lessons we have learnt from you will endure and will help us in our work in the future.

To you, Madam, I should like to address myself also. The gods or some good fairy gave you beauty and high intelligence, and grace and charm and vitality, great gifts, and she who possesses them is a great lady wherever she goes. But unto those that have, even more shall be given, and they gave you something which was even rarer than those gifts, the human touch, the love of humanity, the urge to serve those who suffer and who are in distress, and this amazing mixture of qualities resulted in a radiant personality and in the healer's touch. Wherever you have gone, you have brought solace, you have brought hope and encouragement. Is it surprising, therefore, that the people of India should love you and look up to you as one of themselves and should grieve that you are going? .... Hundreds of thousands have seen you personally in various camps and hospitals and other places, and hundreds of thousands will be sorrowful at the news that you have gone.

May I say a word of Pamela Mountbatten? She came here straight from school, and possessing all the charm she does, she did a grown-up person's work in this troubled scene of India. I do not know if all of you who are present here know the work she has done, but those who do, know well how splendid that has been and how much it has been appreciated.

I do not wish to say more, but to repeat what many no doubt have told you, that while we say good-bye to you, we do not look upon this as a good-bye and farewell.

The bonds that tie the Mountbattens to us are too strong to be broken and we hope to meet here or elsewhere from time to time, and whether we meet you or not, we shall remember you always. We cannot give you anything more precious or more valuable a gift than you have received from the people of Delhi—from the people of India—but as a small souvenir my colleagues in the Cabinet and the Governors of all the provinces of India have joined together in presenting you with this small gift which I shall have the privilege to hand to you.

This, as you see, is a kind of plate or tray. It has inscribed upon it the engraved signatures of all the members of the Cabinet and all the Governors in India, and the inscription upon it is this:

"To the Mountbattens
On the eve of their departure from India
With affection and good wishes and as a token of
friendship."

Your Excellencies, Your Highnesses, ladies and gentlemen, may I ask you to drink to the health and good fortune of the Mountbattens?

THE TUNE FOR THE NATIONAL ANTHEM

THIS question was addressed to my colleague, the Home Minister. But as I have been largely concerned with this matter, I am taking the liberty of answering it myself. I am grateful to the Hon'ble Member who has put this question as this enables the Government to remove certain misapprehensions on the subject.

The question of having a National Anthem to be played by orchestras and bands became an urgent one for us immediately after the 15th August, 1947. It was as important as having a National Flag. It was important from the point of view of our Defence Services, and our Foreign Embassies and Legations and other establishments. It was obviously not suitable for " God Save the King " to be played by our Army Bands, or abroad, after the change over to independence. We were constantly being asked what tune should be played on such occasions. We could not give an answer, because the decision could only be made ultimately by the Constituent Assembly.

The matter came to a head on the occasion of the General Assembly of the United Nations in New York in 1947. Our delegation was asked for our National Anthem for the orchestra to play on a particular occasion. The delegation possessed a record of ' Janaganamana ' and they gave this to the orchestra who practised it. When they played it before a large gathering it was very greatly appreciated, and representatives of many nations asked for a musical score of this new tune which struck them as distinctive and dignified. This orchestral rendering of ' Janaganamana ' was recorded and sent to India. The practice grew for our Defence Services bands to play this tune, and Foreign Embassies and Legations also used it whenever occasion required. From various countries we received messages of appreciation and congratulation on this tune, which was considered by experts and others as superior to most of the National Anthems which they had heard. Many expert musicians in India and abroad, as well as many bands and orchestras

A statement made in reply to a short notice question in the Constituent Assembly (Legislative), New Delhi, August 25, 1948.

practised it, and sometimes slightly varied it, with the result that the All India Radio collected quite a number of renderings.

Apart from the general appreciation with which this tune was received, there was at the time not much choice for us, as there was no proper musical rendering available to us of any other national song which we could send abroad. At that stage, I wrote to all the Provincial Governors and asked their views about our adopting 'Janaganamana', or any other song as the National Anthem. I asked them to consult their Premiers before replying. I made it perfectly clear to them that the final decision rested with the Constituent Assembly, but owing to the necessity of sending directions to Foreign Embassies and the Defence Services, a provisional decision had become essential. Every-one of these Governors, except one (the Governor of the Central Provinces), signified their approval of 'Janaganamana'. Thereupon the Cabinet considered the matter and came to the decision that provisionally 'Janaganamana' should be used as the tune for the National Anthem, till such time as the Constituent Assembly came to a final decision. Instructions were issued accordingly to the Provincial Governors. It was very clear that the wording of 'Janaganamana' was not wholly appropriate and some changes would be necessary. What was important was the tune to be played by bands and orchestras, and not the wording. Subsequently the new Premier of West Bengal informed us that he and his Government preferred 'Vande Mataram'.

That is the position at present. It is unfortunate that some kind of argument has arisen as between 'Vande Mataram' and 'Janaganamana'. 'Vande Mataram' is obviously and indisput-ably the premier national song of India, with a great historical tradition, and intimately connected with our struggle for freedom. That position it is bound to retain and no other song can displace it. It represents the passion and the poignancy of that struggle, but perhaps not so much the culmination of it. In regard to the National Anthem tune, it was felt that the tune was more important than the words, and that this tune should be such as to represent the Indian musical genius as well as to some extent the Western, so that it might be equally adaptable to orchestra and band music, and to being played abroad. The real signi-ficance of the National Anthem is perhaps more abroad than in the home country. Past experience has shown us that 'Janagana-mana' tune has been greatly appreciated and admired abroad.

It is very distinctive and there is a certain life and movement in it. It was thought by some people that the 'Vande Mataram' tune with all its very great attraction and historical background, was not easily suitable for orchestras in foreign countries, and there was not enough movement in it. It seemed therefore that while 'Vande Mataram' should continue to be the national song *par excellence* in India, the National Anthem tune should be that of 'Janaganamana', the wording of 'Janaganamana' to be altered suitably to fit in with the existing circumstances.

This question has to be considered by the Constituent Assembly, and it is open to that Assembly to decide as it chooses. It may decide on a completely new song or tune if such is available.

THE LAST LAP OF OUR LONG
JOURNEY

MR. Vice-President, Sir, we are on the last lap of our long journey. Nearly two years ago, we met in this hall and on that solemn occasion it was my high privilege to move a Resolution which has come to be known as the Objectives Resolution. That is rather a prosaic description of that Resolution, because it embodied something more than mere objectives, although objectives are big things in the life of a nation. It tried to embody, in so far as it is possible in cold print to embody, the spirit that lay behind the Indian people at the time. It is difficult to maintain the spirit of a nation or a people at a high level all the time and I do not know if we have succeeded in doing that. Nevertheless, I hope that it is in that spirit that we have to approach the framing of this Constitution and it is in that spirit that we shall consider it in detail, always using that Objectives Resolution as the yard measure with which to test every clause and phrase in this Constitution. It may be, of course, that we can improve even on that Resolution ; if so, certainly we should do it, but I think that Resolution in some of its clauses laid down the fundamental and basic content of what our Constitution should he. The Constitution is after all some kind of legal body given to the ways of Governments and the life of a people. A Constitution if it is out of touch with the people's life, aims and aspirations, becomes rather empty : if it falls behind those aims, it drags the people down. It should be something ahead to keep people's eyes and minds up to a certain high mark. I think that the Objectives Resolution did that. Inevitably since then in the course of numerous discussions, passions have been roused about what I would beg to say are relatively unimportant matters in this larger context of giving shape to a nation's aspirations and will. Not that they were unimportant, because each thing in a nation's life is important, but still there is a question of priority, there is a question of relative importance, there is a question also of what comes first and what comes second. After all there may

A speech on the motion moved by the Hon'ble Dr. B. R. Ambedkar that the Draft Constitution as framed by the Drafting Committee be taken into consideration, delivered at the Constituent Assembly, New Delhi, November 8,. 1948.

be many truths, but it is important to know what is the first truth. It is important to know what in a particular context of events is the first thing to be done, to be thought of and to be put down, and it is the test of a nation and a people to be able to distinguish between the first things and the second things. If we put the second things first, then inevitably the first and the most important things suffer a certain eclipse.

Now, I have ventured with your permission, Sir, to take part in this initial debate on this Draft Constitution, but it is not my intention to deal with any particular part of it, either in commendation of it or in criticism, because a great deal of that kind has already been said and will no doubt be said. But in view of that perhaps I could make some useful contribution to this debate by drawing attention to certain fundamental factors again. I had thought that I could do this even more, because in recent days and weeks, I have been beyond the shores of India, have visited foreign lands, met eminent people and statesmen of other countries and had the advantage of looking at this beloved country of ours from a distance. That is some advantage. It is true that those who look from a distance do not see many things that exist in this country. But it is equally true that those who live in this country and are surrounded all the time with our numerous difficulties and problems sometimes fail to see the picture as a whole. We have to do both ; to see our problems in their intricate detail in order to understand them and also to see them in some perspective so that we may have that picture as a whole before our eyes.

Now, this is even more important during a period of swift transition such as we have gone through. We who have lived through this period of transition with all its triumphs and glories and sorrows and bitterness, we are affected by all these changes ; we are changing ourselves ; we do not notice ourselves changing or the country changing so much and it is quite helpful to be out of this turmoil for a while and to look at it from a distance and to look at it also to some extent with the eyes of other people. I have had that opportunity. I am glad of that opportunity, because for the moment I was rid of the tremendous burden of responsibility which all of us carry and which in a measure some of us who have to shoulder the burden of Government have to carry more. For a moment I was rid of those immediate responsibilities and with a freer mind

I could look at that picture and I saw from that distance the rising star of India far above the horizon and casting its soothing light, in spite of all that has happened, over many countries of the world, who looked up to it with hope, who considered that out of this new Free India would come various forces which would help Asia, which would help the world some-what to right itself, which would co-operate with other similar forces elsewhere, because the world is in a bad way, because this great continent of Asia or Europe and the rest of the world are in a bad way and are faced with problems which might almost appear to be insurmountable. And sometimes one has the feeling that we were all actors in some terrible Greek tragedy which was moving on to its inevitable climax of disaster. Yet when I looked at this picture again from afar and from here, I had a feeling of hope and optimism not merely because of India, but because also of other things that I saw that the tragedy which seemed inevitable was not necessarily inevitable, that there were many other forces at work, that there were innumerable men and women of goodwill in the world who wanted to avoid this disaster and tragedy, and there was certainly a possibility that they would succeed in avoiding it.

But to come back to India, we have, ever since I moved this Objectives Resolution before this House—a year and eleven months ago almost exactly—passed through strange transitions and changes. We function here far more independently than we did at that time. We function as a sovereign independent nation, but we have also gone through a great deal of sorrow and bitter grief during this period and all of us have been powerfully affected by it. The country for which we were going to frame this Constitution was partitioned and split into two. And what happened afterwards is fresh in our minds and will remain fresh with all its horrors for a very long time to come. All that has happened, and yet, in spite of all this, India has grown in strength and in freedom, and undoubtedly this growth of India, this emergence of India as a free country, is one of the significant facts of this generation, significant for us and for the vast numbers of our brothers and sisters who live in this country, significant for Asia, and significant for the world, and the world is beginning to realize—chiefly I think and I am glad to find this—that India's role in Asia and the world will be a beneficent role ; sometimes it may be with a measure of apprehension,

because India may play some part which some people, some
countries, with other interests may not particularly like. All that
is happening, but the main thing is this great significant factor
that India after being dominated for a long period has
emerged as a free sovereign democratic independent country, and
that is a fact which changes and is changing history. How far
it will change history will depend upon us, this House in the
present and other Houses like this coming in the future who
represent the organized will of the Indian people.

That is a tremendous responsibility. Freedom brings
responsibility; of course, there is no such thing as freedom without
responsibility. Irresponsibility itself means lack of freedom.
Therefore, we have to be conscious of this tremendous burden of
responsibility which freedom has brought: the discipline of
freedom and the organized way of working freedom. But there
is something even more than that. The freedom that has come
to India by virtue of many things, history, tradition, resources,
our geographical position, our great potential and all that, inevitably leads India to play an important part in world affairs.
It is not a question of our choosing this or that ; it is an inevitable
consequence of what India is and what a free India must be.
And because we have to play that inevitable part in world affairs,
that brings another and greater responsibility. Sometimes, with
all my hope and optimism and confidence in my nation, I rather
quake at the great responsibilities that are being thrust upon us,
and which we cannot escape. If we get tied up in our narrow
controversies, we may forget this. Whether we forget it or not,
that responsibility is there. If we forget it, we fail in that measure.
Therefore, I would beg of this House to consider these great
responsibilities that have been thrust upon India, and because we
represent India in this as in many other spheres, on us in this
House, and to work together in the framing of the Constitution
always keeping that in view, because the eyes of the world
are upon us and the hopes and aspirations of a great part
of the world are also upon us. We dare not be little ; if we do
so, we do an ill service to our country and to those hopes
and aspirations of other countries that surround us. It is in
this way that I would like this House to consider this Constitution: first of all to keep the Objectives Resolution before us and
to see how far we are going to act up to it, how far we are going
to build up, as we said in that Resolution: "an Independent

Sovereign Republic, wherein all power and authority of the Sovereign Independent India, its constituent parts and organs of Government, are derived from the people, and wherein shall be guaranteed and secured to all of the people of India justice, social, economic and political ; equality of status, of opportunity, and before the law ; freedom of thought and expression, belief, faith, worship, vocation, association and action, subject to law and public morality ; and this ancient land attain its rightful and honoured place in the world and make its full and willing contribution to the promotion of world peace and the welfare of mankind ".

I read that last clause in particular, because that brings to our mind India's duty to the world. I should like this House when it considers the various controversies—there are bound to be controversies and there should be controversies, because we are a living and vital nation, and it is right that people should think differently—to realize that it is also right that, thinking differently when they come to decisions, they should act unitedly in further-ance of those decisions. There are various problems, some very im-portant problems, on which there is very little controversy and we pass them—they are of the greatest importance—with a certain unanimity. There are other problems, important no doubt, poss-ibly of a lesser importance, on which we spend a great deal of time and energy and passion also, and do not arrive at agreements in the spirit with which we should arrive at agreements. In the country today, reference has been made—I will mention one or two matters—to linguistic provinces and to the question of language in this Assembly and for the country. I do not propose to say much about these questions, except to say that it seems to me and it has long seemed to me inevitable that in India some kind of reorganization of the provinces should take place to fit in more with the cultural, geographical and economic condition of the people and with their desires. We have long been committed to this. I do not think it is good enough just to say linguistic provinces ; that is a major factor to be considered, no doubt. But there are more important factors to be considered, and you have, therefore, to consider the whole picture before you proceed to break up what we have and refashion it into something new. What I would like to place before the House is that, important from the point of view of our future life and govern-ment as this question is, I would not have thought that this was a question of such primary importance that it must be settled here and now today. It is eminently a question which should be settled in an atmosphere of goodwill and calm and by scholarly discussion of the various factors of the case. I find, unfortunately, that it has raised a considerable degree of heat and passion and when heat and passion are there, the mind is clouded. Therefore, I would beg of this House to take these matters into consideration when it thinks fit, and to treat it as a thing which should be settled not in a hurry when passions are roused, but at a suitable moment when the time is ripe for it.

The same argument, if I may say so, applies to the question of language. Now, it is an obvious thing and a vital thing that any country, much more so a free and independent country, must function in its own language. Unfortunately, the mere fact that I am speaking to this House in a foreign language and so many of our colleagues here have to address the House in a foreign language itself shows that something is lacking. It is lacking, let us recognize it ; we shall get rid of that lacuna undoubtedly. But, if in trying to press for a change, an immediate change, we get wrapped up in numerous controversies and possibly even delay the whole Constitution, I submit to this House it is not a very wise step to take. Language is and has been a vital factor in an individual's and a nation's life and because it is vital, we have to give it every thought and consideration. Because it is vital, it is also an urgent matter ; and because it is vital, it is also a matter in which urgency may ill-serve our purpose. There is a slight contradiction. Because, if we proceed in an urgent matter to impose something, maybe by a majority, on an unwilling minority in parts of the country or even in this House, we do not really succeed in what we have started to achieve. Powerful forces are at work in the country which will inevitably lead to the substitution of the English language by an Indian language or Indian languages in so far as the different parts of the country are concerned ; but there will always be one all-India language. Powerful forces are also at work in the formation of that all-India language. A language ultimately grows from the people ; it is seldom that it can be imposed. Any attempt to impose a particular form of language on an unwilling people has usually met with the strongest opposition and has actually resulted in something the very reverse of what the promoters thought. I would beg this House to consider the fact and to realize, if it agrees with me, that the surest way of developing a natural all-India language is not so much to pass resolutions and laws on the subject, but to work to that end in other ways. For my part I have a certain conception of what an all-India language should be. Other people's conception may not be quite the same as mine. I cannot impose my conception on this House or on the country just as any other person will not be able to impose his or her conception unless the country accepts it. I would much rather avoid trying to impose my or anyone else's conception and instead work to that end in co-operation and amity and see how, after we have settled these major things about the Constitution, after we have attained an even greater measure of stability, we can take up each one of these separate questions and dispose of them in a much better atmosphere.

The House will remember that when I brought the motion of the Objectives Resolution before this House, I referred to the fact that we were asking for or rather we were laying down that our Constitution should be framed for an Independent Sovereign Republic. I stated at that time and I have stated subsequently that this business of our being a Republic is entirely a matter for us to determine, of course. It has nothing or little to do with what relations we should have with other countries, notably the United Kingdom or the Commonwealth that used to be called the British Commonwealth of Nations. That was a question which had to be determined again by this House and by no one else, independently of what our Constitution was going to be. I want to inform the House that in recent weeks when I was in the United Kingdom, whenever this subject or any allied subject came up for private discussion—there was no public discussion or decision, because the Commonwealth Conference which I attended did not consider it at all in its sessions—inevitably these were private discussions, because it is a matter of high moment not only for us, but also for other countries as to what, if any, relation we should have, what contacts, what links we should bear with these other countries, inevitably the first thing that I had to say in all these discussions was that I could not as an individual—even though I had been honoured with the high office of Prime Ministership—I could not in any way or in any sense commit the country—nor even the Government which I had the honour to represent. This was essentially a matter which the Constituent Assembly of India alone could decide. That I made perfectly

clear. Having made that clear, I further drew their attention
to the Objectives Resolution of the Constituent Assembly.
I said it was, of course, open to the Constituent Assembly to vary
that Resolution as it could vary everything else, because it was
sovereign in this and other matters. That was the direction
which the Constituent Assembly had given itself and to its
Drafting Committee for Constitution, and as long as it remained
as it was, and I added that, as far as I knew, it would remain as it
was that Constitution would be in terms of the Objectives
Resolution. Having made that clear, Sir, I said that it had
often been said on our behalf that we desired to be associated
in friendly relationship with other countries, with the United
Kingdom and the Commonwealth. How in this context it can be
done or it should be done is a matter for careful consideration
and ultimate decision, naturally, on our part by the Constituent
Assembly, on their part by their respective Governments or
peoples. That is all I wish to say about this matter at this stage,
because in the course of this session this matter no doubt
will come up before the House in more concrete form. But in
whatever form it may come up whether now or later, the point I
should like to stress is this, that it is something apart from and
in a sense independent of the Constitution that we are considering. We pass the Constitution for an Independent Sovereign
Democratic India, for a Republic as we choose, and the second
question is to be considered separately at whatever time it suits
this House. It does not in any sense fetter our Constitution or
limit it, because this Constitution coming from the people of
India through their representatives represents their free will with
regard to the future government of India.

Now, may I beg again to repeat what I said earlier? Destiny
has cast a certain role on this country. Whether anyone of
us present here can be called men or women of destiny or
not I do not know. That is a big word which does not
apply to average human beings, but whether we are men or
women of destiny or not, India is a country of destiny and
so far as we represent this great country with a great destiny
stretching out in front of her, we also have to act as men
and women of destiny, viewing all our problems in that long
perspective of destiny and of the world and of Asia, never forgetting the great responsibility that freedom, that this great
destiny of our country has cast upon us, not losing ourselves in

petty controversies and debates which might be useful, but which would in this context be either out of place or out of tune. Vast numbers of minds and eyes look in this direction. We have to remember them. Hundreds of millions of our own people look to us and hundreds of millions of others also look to us; and remember this that while we want this Constitution to be as solid and as permanent a structure as we can make it, nevertheless, there is no permanence in constitutions. There should be a certain flexibility. If you make a thing rigid and permanent, you stop a nation's growth, the growth of a living, vital, organic people. Therefore, it has to be flexible. So also, when you pass this Constitution you will, and I think it is so proposed, lay down a period of years—whatever that period may be—during which changes to that Constitution can easily be made without any difficulty. That is a very necessary proviso for a number of reasons. One is this: that while we, who are assembled in this House, undoubtedly represent the people of India, nevertheless, I think it can be said, and truthfully, that when a new House, by whatever name it goes, is elected in terms of this Constitution, and every adult in India has the right to vote—man and woman—the House that emerges then will certainly be fully representative of every section of the Indian people. It is right that the House so elected—under this Constitution, of course, it will have the right to do anything—should have an easy opportunity to make such changes as it wants easily. But in any event, we should not, as some other great countries have, make a Constitution so rigid that it cannot be easily adapted to changing conditions. Today especially, when the world is in turmoil and we are passing through a very swift period of transition, what we do today may not be wholly applicable tomorrow. Therefore, while we make a Constitution which is sound and as basic as we can make it, it should also be flexible and for a period we should be in a position to change it with relative facility.

May I say one word again about certain tendencies in the country which still think in terms of separatist existence or separate privileges and the like? This very Objectives Resolution has set out adequate safeguards to be provided for minorities, for tribal areas, depressed and other backward classes. Of course, that must be done, and it is the duty and responsibility of the majority to see that this is done and to see that they win over all minorities which may have suspicions against them, which may suffer from fear. It is right and important that we should raise the level of the backward groups in India and bring them up to the level of the rest. But it is not right that in trying to do this we create further barriers, or even keep existing barriers, because the ultimate objective is not separatism, but building up an organic nation, not necessarily a uniform nation, because we have a varied culture, and in this country, ways of living differ in various parts of the country, habits differ and cultural traditions differ. I have no grievance against that. Ultimately in the modern world there is a strong tendency for the prevailing culture to influence others. That may be a natural influence. But I think the glory of India has been the way in which it has managed to keep two things going at the same time: that is, its infinite variety and at the same time its unity in that variety. Both have to be kept, because if we have only variety, then that means separatism and going to pieces. If we seek to impose some kind of regimented unity that makes a living organism rather lifeless. Therefore, while it is our bounden duty to do everything we can to give full opportunity to every minority or group and to raise every backward group or class, I do not think it will be the right thing to go the way this country has gone in the past by creating barriers and by calling for protection. As a matter of fact, nothing can protect such a minority or a group less than a barrier which separates it from the majority. It makes it a permanently isolated group and it prevents it from coming closer to the other groups in the country.

I trust, Sir, that what I have ventured to submit to the House will be borne in mind when these various clauses are considered and that ultimately we shall pass this Constitution in the spirit of the solemn moment when we started this great endeavour.

THIS GENERATION IS SENTENCED TO HARD LABOUR

Mr. Khosla, members of the Central Board of Irrigation, Your Excellencies and gentlemen,

I am happy to associate myself with this meeting of yours and I am thankful to you for inviting me on this occasion. I have been interested in many types of activities during the past few years and in the position I occupy now, I have to cultivate a many-sided interest in many things. Life itself is rather an intri cate and complicated affair for the individual and for the nation and it is sometimes difficult to say which of any two things is more important, for each depends upon the other. Nevertheless, it is true, as I have said many times before and as you, Sir, have said in the course of your address, that the development of river valleys in India is of the most basic and fundamental importance. For a number of years past, I have been very greatly interested in this matter not as an engineer, because I am not an engineer, but in its wider public aspect, in a sense, in its aspect of the foundation of very large scale planning in India. I have been interested in planning, because it seems such an extraordinary and such an unfortunate fact that all the potential resources avail able in India—and in a way it applies to the whole world—that all these enormous resources have not been utilized to raise the standard of living of our people and our nation.

There was a time in the past—in the long distant past—when it might have been said with some correctness that the world's resources were not really enough to raise the standard of living of the population of the world to the extent desired. Now, I suppose it must be clear to the meanest intelligence that with the proper utilization of the present resources of the world,—leaving out further development, or even leaving out the world if you like, we can raise the standard of India. This can be shown with a pencil and paper. Nevertheless, the fact remains, not only that we did not utilize them to the best advantage, but we wasted these resources in destructive activities. That is the tragedy of the pre-

A speech delivered at the Nineteenth Annual Meeting of the Central Board of Irrigation, New Delhi, December 5, 1948.

sent generation, even more so than it has been of past generations.

Always found in history, we find to an even acuter degree today this conflict between the forces of contructive effort and those of destruction. We find this conflict in the attitude of nations to one another, of groups and ultimately perhaps in the spirit of man himself. Now, no man can be a prophet enough to say what is going to happen. Nevertheless' any man can work effectively with the faith in him that the forces of constructive and creative effort shall win. I have no doubt that they will win, but I do not know what damage the other forces might bring about by delaying the process of planning and raising the standard of humanity.

Well, we have to convert this vast potential into actuality. Look at the map of Asia and of India. It stares at me in my room and in my office, and whenever I look at it, all kinds of pictures come into my mind ; pictures of the long past of our history, of the gradual development of man from the earliest stages, of great caravan routes, of the early beginnings of culture, civilization and agriculture, and of the early days when perhaps the first canals and irrigation works were constructed and all that flows from them. Then I think of the future. My attention is concentrated on that huge block of massive mountains called the Himalayas which guard our north-eastern frontier. Look at them. Think of them. Can you think of any other part of the world similar to it in extent, which is as great a reservoir of power, of potential strength and power? I know of no other place in the world which has as much tremendous power locked up in it as the Himalayas and the water which comes to the rivers from them. How are we to utilize it? There are many ways. Essentially, it is the job of the engineers to tap this tremendous reserve of power for the benefit of the people. It falls to the lot of you engineers to play a very effective and vitally important role in this work. Looked at from that point of view, the profession and work of an engineer in India is of the highest importance and significance.

You can judge of the growth of a nation by finding out which class of that nation, in a particular period of history, is held in honour and repute more than the others. At one time, you may find that the landholder, the proprietor of the land, is a nobleman and he is held in the greatest esteem. From that you can judge the nature of the society of that period. So you will find various occupations occupying the forefront at different periods and you can come to some conclusion as to the nature of the social background of the society of the time ; whether it is static, whether it is creative or whether its growth is dynamically constructive.

A short while ago, not to go back to the long past of history,— it is very interesting to consider that a short while ago, in the last generation or two in India, there were two avenues to which Indians looked forward. One was Government service, more especially the administrative Government service. Of course, a state should have good administration. It is important. But the administrative service in India was rather of an unusual variety. It was good in so far as it went, in so far as it served the purpose for which it was meant. It was not meant for other purposes. It was not really meant to cultivate a social outlook in the Government or the people, but in so far as it went it did its work well. Perhaps, it may have been said so 30, 40 or 50 years ago,—that the ambition of an Indian was to belong to that administrative service in India, because that brought respect and a certain measure of power, considerable emoluments in office and prestige. About the same time there was another branch. To those people who did not take up Government service, the law provided the greatest opportunities of distinction, of money-making and the like. So we find that in the past two or three generations in India, there were two peaks of ambition for young Indians: to rise in the superior administrative service or to rise in the profession of law. This, of course, has happened in other countries too. Now, both of these, the profession of law and administrative service, useful I suppose as they are in their own way (though I rather have some doubts about the profession of the law), yet both of them represented what might be called a static view of society, not essentially changing nor dynamic. The lawyer always talks about precedents. The administrator carries on with the aid of conventional practice. Of course, there may have been a dynamic administrator and a dynamic lawyer, but they represented a static unchanging view of society. No country can, however, be completely unchanging. You find that the same lawyer played a very important part in the national movements. That again might be the same in other countries too. At a certain stage in the national movement, the lawyer played a great part in other countries also. Today you will find that the lawyer has progressively ceased to play that part in the national movement or other varieties of national endeavour. He is still

important in his own particular field of activity, but that
importance, looked at from a wider viewpoint, is infinitely less
than it used to be. The civil administrator in India is still important as an administrator always is. But his importance is much less
than it used to be.

What is a young man's ambition today? There may be
varieties of ambitions, but I rather doubt if there are quite so
many people who think in terms of law or administrative service.
They think in other terms. They think of the politician's life or of
going to the assemblies and then becoming ministers, secretaries,
etc. Not a very happy training for anybody, but still people do
look that way. They think of joining our Defence Services, the
Army, the Air Force and the Navy. They think of becoming
economists, because an economist plays a big part in the modern
world. They think of becoming engineers, because engineers are
playing and will play an important part. You see the static nature
of our society gradually changing into something dynamic and
that will reflect in the people's and individual's urge as to what
profession he should take up.

The world as it is constituted today is tremendously dynamic.
That is right, of course, and that is inevitable, even if somehow we
have failed in this respect. The world as it is constituted
today is in a stage of revolutionary change so that you just
cannot help trying to change yourself ; otherwise you get into
trouble. We have passed through a period, a fairly long one,
though it was very short in terms of India's long history, a period
which though undoubtedly changing was, nevertheless, in another
sense unchanging—this British period in our history. Changes
worked consciously and unconsciously, but when the superior
outside power dominates a certain situation, the various forces
that are working inside the country are curbed by that power and
they cannot easily find balance and adjustment between themselves. Finding a balance is achieved by the evolutionary
process or by a revolutionary process either by peaceful or violent
means. In any human society there is always an attempt to find
a balance and for as long as it does not succeed there is trouble.
Now, when some outside agency prevents the achievement of
that balance the result, for the moment, may be even good
if you like, but the result is that problems accumulate—
problems which history solves in its own way, sometimes peacefully, sometimes with bloodshed. If you do not solve it, you solve

the problem by killing it. Thus it is with nations and communities. But when an extraordinary agency prevents such a solution, problems accumulate. So in India problems accumulated. The problem of the Indian States has no doubt been solved. Our agrarian problems which ought to have been solved long ago dragged on and on till we have to face them now immediately and to solve them in a hurry whereas this should have been solved gradually and in a much better way. Now, because problems have accumulated, we have today to face not one problem, but a multitude of problems. It is very difficult to decide that you will set aside all these problems and take up one or two first. We just cannot, because if we slacken our attempt to solve some problems and merely concentrate on one or another, the other problems tend to overwhelm us. Let us take the problem of the refugees. There are millions of them. It is not a fundamental problem as problems go. It is a temporary problem, but it is of exceeding importance. It is important, because a large number of human beings and their lives are involved, and where human lives in large numbers are involved, it is of vital significance to the nation. We cannot allow that human material to deteriorate and simply to go to pieces, but apart from that, apart from the human aspect of it, if we try to ignore it, the problem becomes worse and comes in the way of other problems.

These accumulated problems have to be faced to some extent together. One has to proceed on various fronts and one has to see that the progress is more or less co-ordinated on each front or else you go ahead on one front and there is a bottle-neck on another and you have to stop. That is where planning comes in, planning becomes essential.

We have talked about planning for a considerable time in India. I myself have been associated with the planning scheme and the like. I must confess to a feeling of exceeding disappointment that all our effort has not yielded better results. I expected much better results and better results there should have been. When you know what happened in the past and our difficulties and our failings in the matter, it is well, if I may say so, for each one of us, whether he happens to occupy a very responsibe position such as that of a Prime Minister or other Minister or any other important officer of the State, it is well always to think of any problem that we are entrusted with, not as if failure was somebody else's responsibility or somebody else's fault, but that we are ourselves responsible for any failure that may occur. There is too great a tendency for each one of us—and again I say I include the Prime Minister and other Ministers in this category,—always to think in terms of somebody else having failed. If each person thought of his own job and that he had failed in it, we should get on better with the problem. The fact is that each major job requires the co-operation and the hard work of a large number of people from top to bottom and if that co-operation is lacking, this spirit of working together is lacking—then that job is not done properly or is delayed and then it serves no useful purpose for us to go on finding fault with each other, though sometimes that may be necessary. We have various jobs to do in this country in every field. Somebody said once that we had been born in a period of world history which was both changing and revolutionary and very inconceivable things were happening. Now, it is no good complaining of these inconceivable happenings. Since we are born, we have to face them. We cannot escape them. Not being able to escape, we have to face them like men and conquer the difficulties. I am afraid in our generation (I do not know about succeeding generations) there is going to be little rest or real peace. There are going to be no dividends of leisure and repose brought about for our generation. The prospect before us is work, hard labour. This generation is sentenced to hard labour. That hard labour can be of the type of constructive activity which, however hard, is something that raises the community and the nation, or it may be in fruitless labour, or even evil labour, but hard labour you cannot escape. Therefore let us divert that hard labour into constructive and creative channels so that at least it may be said of this generation that we helped to build up our country to the extent possible so that the next generation and succeeding generations may have leisure—greater leisure, though I am not myself keen on too much leisure for any individual, but some leisure there ought to be. Perhaps, it is not leisure that is so much required. It is the type of work that is better than the leisure itself. However, I am afraid I am just meandering in my thoughts and ideas.

I listened to Mr. Khosla's address with interest. I might say that I agree with almost everything that he said in his address. I like the approach and I hope it is going to be the approach of this Board and of engineers as a whole in India and of the Government. I do wish you to realize, engineers who are present here, that the burden on the engineers today and the responsibility for constructive effort is tremendous and a great deal depends on how they discharge their duties and in what spirit they discharge them. We want you to be first-rate and competent in your jobs, because second-rateness is never good. It is bad for the nation. But in addition to that, we also want you to infuse your work with something, some higher spirit of doing a fine creative job, with the fulfilment of certain objectives and ideals that immediately infuse into your work something which is bigger than you. To go back to the Middle Ages or even to older times, you still see the remains of ancient buildings, ancient structures, temples, cathedrals, mosques and the like. No one knows who built them, but any man who sees them knows that the people who built them were not only fine builders, fine engineers, but they were men of faith in their work. No man can build or construct anything beautiful unless he has faith. See the magnificent cathedrals of Europe. People seldom know who their builders were, but we do know, because the evidence is there for our eyes to see, that the embodiment of the faith of the builder is the engineer. So also with our great temples and mosques and other buildings. Now, we live in a different age. We do not spend much time and energy so much on mosques, cathedrals and temples, but in other types of public works. But those public works should also be fine and beautiful, because there is that faith. So I would like you to work in that faith and you will find that if you work with that faith and that spirit, that will itself be a joy to you.

On a smaller matter, Mr. Khosla mentioned something about the dictionary of technical terms in Hindi. I am glad to hear that. But may I warn you that in evolving terms, technical terms, you do not evolve something which the common man does not understand. There is too much of a tendency today to do that. For my part, I think that words from foreign languages which have become current coin in this country should be retained, retained partly because they are current coin, partly because the more common words you have with the rest of the world the better for scientific and technical subjects. Science and technology know no frontiers. Nobody talks or ought to talk about English science, French science, American science, Chinese science. Science is something bigger than the countries. There ought to be no such thing as Indian science. So also with technology. This great business of looking at these questions in a narrow nationalist way will ultimately lead to the narrowing of your science and the narrowing of your technology and your work itself. This business of evolving special terms which are known neither to the general public nor to anybody else in the wide world really means that you are isolating yourself from the general drift of knowledge and at the same time dissociating yourself from your own people who do not understand your technical terms and thus you convert yourself into something which nobody understands and nobody cares for.

Gentlemen, I have great pleasure in declaring open the annual meeting of the Central Board of Irrigation.

A RECORD OF THE MARTYRDOM
OF MAN

I have come here to offer you a cordial welcome on behalf of the Government of India. As a Government we are naturally interested in many activities and as a Prime Minister I have to function on many stages and to say something on a variety of subjects. But I rather doubt if any subject would interest me more to listen to and sometimes even to speak on than the subject of history. I confess that being myself an amateur I feel a little overwhelmed when I meet a multitude of experts. Nevertheless, perhaps even an amateur has a place in the scheme of things and sometimes perhaps he may see the wood a little more and not be lost in the individual trees which an expert is apt to do.

Now, we talk of history, and people, I suppose, have numerous ways of thinking and looking at history. But whatever way you may have, whatever approach you may have, whether it is the old and completely out-of-date approach of a record of the doings of kings and battles and the like, or of social and economic progress, or of cultural progress, or the development of humanity as a whole, whether it is the history of a single country or a nation or it is viewed in the context of world history as it naturally must be, inevitably the basis of all that is an accumulation of facts and records and data. Otherwise, one simply builds one's idea of history on improvised knowledge without any accurate data. Therefore, a Historical Records Commission is most essential for the building up of a proper history. This Historical Records Commission which is celebrating its Silver Jubilee this year is to be congratulated on this occasion on the work it has done in the past and on the work which I hope it is going to do with even greater fervour in the future.

Now, I do not know what many of you feel when you think about a historical subject. For my part I feel tremendously fascinated by and interested in the subject of history and my mind begins to wander a little trying to think of this long sweep and trying to draw not only interest, but inspiration of knowledge or

An address delivered at New Delhi inaugurating the Silver Jubilee Session of the Indian Historical Records Commission, December 23, 1948.

understanding or all of them. I do not know if one always succeeds in getting that inspiration from it as a whole ; one does sometimes find other aspects of it which are far from inspiring. In any event, one has to go back to it to understand the present and to try to understand what the future ought to be. They say that history never repeats itself. I suppose that is true. Nevertheless, to understand anything you have to go back to the roots of the forces and the various other happenings that are taking place today and that is the only possible data which you can have ; otherwise you have to trust to your imagination only.

History, as a famous writer has described it, is a record of the martyrdom of man. Perhaps so. It is also a record of repeated re-surrections after every crucifixion. So you see this process of martyrdom and crucifixion of man, and resurrection following it, in interminable succession. You may consider history as the onward march of humanity, of the human spirit, and yet sometimes we are pulled back by seeing how that onward march is suddenly arrested and thrown back.

Now, every age, I suppose, thinks that it is an age of transition. Nevertheless, I suppose there is an element of truth in our thinking that the present age we live in is peculiarly an age of transition and change: at any rate the problems we have to face appear to be far bigger and acuter than any other problems, partly because of the extent of the problems. Because every problem now becomes a world problem. It is quite impossible today to think of current events or of history in the making in terms of any one nation or country or patch of territory ; you have inevitably to think in terms of the world as a whole. You may, of course, and you should, think of each of the smaller aspects of that larger picture ; you may examine them more closely. But the whole conception of the history of a particular country and our learning by heart the names of a large number of kings and emperors, I suppose, is long dead. I am not quite sure whether in the schools and colleges of India it has ceased to exist or not, but I hope at any rate that it is dead, because anything more futile than children's study of the record of kings' reigns and battles I cannot imagine.

The other aspect of history which has come much more to the forefront—the social aspect of history, the development of the social organism—involves much closer research into the daily lives of the common man. Maybe in family budgets a hundred or a thousand years ago, there were a hundred and a thousand and one things which make us realize something of what the life of humanity was in the past age. It is only then that we can really clothe the dry bones of history with life, flesh and blood. I must confess that even now, in spite of this acknowledged new approach, most of the books on history and papers on history that appear, interesting though the subject-matter may be, appear to me to be quite singularly lifeless and dead. They are just the dry bones ; there is no flesh and blood in them. And I suppose the only way really to read, write or understand history is to evoke in the mind a picture of a living society functioning, thinking and having all the virtues and failings which the human being has possessed, and gradually changing whether it is in the direction of progress or something else. For that too, I suppose, two things are necessary : one, of course, a much more intimate knowledge of detail which this Commission should collect and supply, and the other is a co-ordinating type of mind which is capable of clothing that detail in proper garb and give it some semblance of life. I hope that this Historical Records Commission and the eminent historians associated with it who will collect material or write papers and essays and books on it will always try to think of two things. One is that they should not always write only for their brother historians. There are other people also outside their charmed circle who ought to be approached. I say this, because the average technical or scientific paper is so very much meant, or at any rate it looks as if it were meant, for the charmed circle of people who are interested in a specifically narrow aspect of a particular question that it loses all interest for the wider public. Now, surely a Commission like this, as all other Commissions, should try to function in a larger atmosphere and try to appeal to the minds of the larger public—the intelligent or semi-intelligent public. It appears to be a different species of approach and a different species of writing to go on with popularization which means a deviation from scholarship. I do not think there is any necessary conflict between real scholarship and a popular approach. I find in such papers and articles that I sometimes see rather an attempt at unconsciously forgetting the fact that a larger public has to be or should be addressed. I do not think that is good, because you isolate yourself from that larger public. You do not get their backing, and that larger public cannot benefit by your labours. Secondly, any subject that you may investigate—although necessarily you investigate a particular subject—might generally be viewed in relation to a larger whole. Otherwise, it has no real meaning except as some odd incident which might interest you. Because, if there is to be an understanding, there must be an understanding of every subject in that relationship. It has no meaning otherwise. Now, once you start on this question of the relationship of events to one another it opens out an enormous field, because everything is related to everything else: nothing is isolated. Every aspect of life is related in some way or other to another aspect, and every aspect of life in one nation is related to other national lives. It was so to some extent even in the past. But in the present age that is so obvious, because of all kinds of factors which bring nations close to one another even though they might not love one another. So that, it is in relation to that that each small item should be viewed ; also I would say, though perhaps that involves a much more difficult undertaking, how far this can be related to, shall I say, an integrated view of history. Whether history can be considered in that sense or not I do not know. But the human mind always tries to understand things in an integrated way. Otherwise, they have no significance and we have to arrive at the conclusion that things that happen have no connection with each other and happen in an odd, haphazard way. Looking at it in that integrated way, one has to think what is history—a record of human progress, a record of, shall I say, the struggle of the advancement of the human mind, of the human spirit, towards some known or unknown objective. It becomes a very fascinating study. Whether it is ultimately true or not,, nevertheless, it does give some string to connect all the separate incidents. Originally history was taught, I suppose, purely on political lines. And with that were associated, of course, many other aspects, religious, and to some extent cultural also.

Then a great deal of stress was laid on the economic aspect which undoubtedly is exceedingly important. Nobody has ever said that the economic aspect is the sole aspect—that would be absurd—but it is an important aspect, and in the larger sense it would cover the cultural aspect too. But quite apart from these individual and separate aspects of history, I suppose there is something which I cannot define, some attempt to understand what all this sweep of history means, where possibly it is leading to, or whether it has any meaning at all or not. Ultimately, I suppose, practically all the problems we have to face in the world can be put in a sentence or two. They are problems of relationships: the relationship of the individual with the individual, the relationship of the individual with the group, and the relationship of groups. Almost every political, cultural or personal problem can be brought within that sentence, and it is these gradually changing relationships that give meaning to the social organism and ultimately to the national and international life that we see around us.

I am rather casually throwing out ideas before this very learned audience so that this Historical Records Commission may try to relate their work, in so far as it is possible, to those wider vistas of mind and thought in history, because without that it narrows its scope and it cannot evoke very much response from the average mind. All of us in a greater or lesser measure make history. History ultimately is some kind of a resultant of millions and millions of human lives, but it is true that some individuals perhaps play a greater part in the making of history. It has been given to us in the present age to play some part in the making of history, and for a person who does that it becomes an even more important thing to understand the processes of history so that he might not lose himself in trivial details and forget the main sweep. Because fate and circumstance placed me in a position to be an actor in the saga, or the drama of India, if you like, in the last twenty or thirty years in common with many others, my interest in history became not an academic interest in things of the past and of long ago, but an intense personal interest. I wanted to understand those events in relation to today and to understand today in relation to what had been, and try to peep into the future, however dimly, with the help of that understanding. Now, I do not know if that quest helped me very much or not in any real understanding, because events have happened, which I can only say are past all understanding, in the last few years—great wars and the like—and all one's conceptions of an ordered progress of humanity have been shaken. Well, whether these studies have helped to understand or not, they have been a very fascinating pursuit and I sometimes feel how delightful it must be to carry on that pursuit in the calmer atmosphere of a University or some Institute, cut away from the provocations and disturbances of the type of life that I lead. But that is merely a kind of nostalgia from which I suppose many of us suffer who do not like the particular job they are placed in.

I welcome you all here, and I hope your labours will bear fruit not only in building up true history which is something much more than dates and events, but will also I hope help, shall I say, in binding together people. History shows us both the binding process and the disrupting process and today in the world as always I suppose—today a little more obviously— the binding or the constructive forces are at work, as also the disruptive or the fissiparous forces, and in any activity that we are indulging in, we have the choice of laying emphasis on the binding and constructive aspect or the other. We must not, of course, give way to wishful thinking and emphasize something which we want to emphasize and which has no relation to fact. Nevertheless, I think it is possible within the terms of scholarship and preciseness and truth to emphasize the binding and constructive aspect rather than the other, and I hope the activities of historians and of this Commission will be directed to that end. I welcome you again.

SAROJINI NAIDU

It has been my painful duty, Sir, as Leader of this House, to refer from time to time to the passing away of the illustrious sons and daughters of India. Recently I referred to the passing away of a very eminent son of India, Sir Tej Bahadur Sapru. Then the Governor of a province suddenly died. He was a very distinguished servant of the State. When we refer to these distinguished sons or daughters of the country, we say often enough that it will be difficult to replace them, that they are irreplaceable, which may be true enough in a partial manner. But, today, I, with your leave, would like to refer to the passing away early yesterday morning of one about whom it can be said with absolute truth that it is impossible to replace her or to find her like.

She was for the last year and a half or a little more the Governor of a great province with many problems and she acted as Governor with exceeding ability and exceeding success as can be judged from the fact that every one in that province, from the Premier and his Ministers and Government to the various groups and classes and religious communities down to the worker and the peasant in the field, had been drawn to her and had found a welcome in her heart. She had succeeded very greatly as a Governor and as a great servant of the State in an exalted position. But it is not as a Governor that I should speak much of her, for she was a much greater person than Governors are normally supposed to be. What she was exactly it is a little difficult for me to say, because she had become almost a part of us, a part of our national heritage of today and a part of us individuals who had the great privilege of being associated with her for a multitude of years in our struggle for freedom and in our work.

Sir, it is a little difficult to see persons, with whom you have been so closely associated, in proper perspective, and yet one can feel that to some extent. And thinking of her one sees a person to whom any number of epithets and adjectives might be applied.

A commemorative speech on Her Excellency Srimati Sarojini Naidu, delivered at the Constituent Assembly (Legislative), New Delhi, March 3, 1949.

Here was a person of great brilliance. Here was a person, vital and vivid. Here was a person with so many gifts, but above all with some gifts which made her unique. She began life as a poetess. In later years, when the compulsion of events drew her into the national struggle and she threw herself into it with all the zest and fire that she possessed, she did not write much poetry with pen and paper, but her whole life became a poem and a song. And she did that amazing thing ; she infused artistry and poetry to our national struggle. Just as the Father of the Nation had infused moral grandeur and greatness to the struggle, Mrs. Sarojini Naidu gave it artistry and poetry and that zest for life and indomitable spirit which not only faced disaster and catastrophe, but faced them with a light heart and with a song on her lips and smile on her face. Now, I do not think, being myself a politician which most of us are, that hardly any other gift was more valuable to our national life than this lifting it out of the plane of pure politics to a higher artistic sphere, which she succeeded in doing in some measure.

Looking back upon her life, one sees an astonishing combination of gifts. One, here is a life full of vitality ; one, here are 50 years of existence—not merely existence but a vital, dynamic existence—touching many aspects of our life, cultural and political. And whatever she touched, she infused with something of her fire. She was indeed a pillar of fire. And then again, she was like cool running water, soothing and uplifting and bringing down the passion of her politics to the cooler levels of human beings. So it is difficult for one to speak about her except that one realizes that here was a magnificence of spirit and it is gone.

We shall, no doubt, for generations to come remember her, but perhaps those who come after us and those who have not been associated with her so closely will not realize fully the richness of that personality which could not easily be translated into spoken words or records. She worked for India. She knew how to work and she knew how to play. And that was a wonderful combination. She knew how to sacrifice herself for great causes. She knew also to do that so gracefully and so graciously that it appeared an easy thing to do and not anything entailing travail of spirit. If a sensitive person like her must suffer from the tremendous travail of spirit, no doubt she did, but she did it so graciously that it appeared that that too was easy for her. So she lifted our struggle to a higher plane and gave it a certain touch which I cannot think anybody else can give or is likely to give it in future.

Sir, I said she was a curious combination of so many things ; she represented in herself a rich culture into which flowed various currents which have made Indian culture as great as it is. She herself was a composite both of various currents of culture in India as well as various currents of culture both in the East and the West. And so she was, while being a very great national figure, also truly an internationalist, and wherever she might go in the wide world she was recognized as such and as one of the great ones of the earth. It is well to remember that, especially today, when through stress of circumstances we may occasionally drift into a narrow nationalism and forget the larger objectives that inspired the great ones who laid the foundations of our national movement.

The great Father of the Nation and this great woman have shaped our national movement so powerfully, not so much on the direct political plane, although she was active there and adequately functioned, but in those invisible planes, which are so very important, because they shape the nation's character ; because they mould ultimately its mental and aesthetic and artistic outlook ; and without that mental, moral, aesthetic and artistic outlook, any success that we may gain may well be an empty success ; because, after all, we seek freedom to gain which is good in itself, but we seek freedom to achieve something else. We seek freedom to achieve a good life for our people. What is a good life? Can you imagine any good life which does not have an artistic and an aesthetic element in it, and a moral element in it? That would not be a good life ; it would be some temporary phase of existence, which would be rather dry and harsh, and unfortunately, the world grows drier and harsher and more cruel. In our own experience of the last two years, political life has become a little more harsh, cruel, intolerant and suspicious and in the world today we see suspicion and fear all round, fear of one another. How are we to get over this? It is only through some experience of moral heights that we might overcome it, and that was the way shown to us by the Father of the Nation, or else the other way is to approach it from the human point of view, from the artistic and aesthetic point of view, and the human point of view is the forgiving point of view, is the point of view full of compassion and understanding of humanity and its failings as well as its virtues. And so Sarojini brought that human point of view, full of understanding, full of compassion for all who are in India or outside.

The House knows that she stood more than any single human being in India for the unity of India in all its phases, for the unity of its cultural content, the unity of its geographical areas. It was a passion with her. It was the very texture of her life. It is well to remember, when we sometimes fall into narrower grooves, that greatness has never come from the narrowness of mind, or again, greatness for a nation as for an individual comes from a wide vision, a wide perspective, an inclusive outlook and a human approach to life. So she became an interpreter in India of the various phases of our rich cultural inheritance. She became an interpreter in India of the many great things that the West had produced, and she became an interpreter in other parts of India of India's rich culture. She became the ideal ambassador and the ideal link between the East and the West, and between various parts and groups in India. I do not myself see how we are to find the like of her now or in the future. We shall, no doubt, have great men and women in the future, because India, even when she was low in the political scale, had never failed to produce greatness in her children. And now that India is free, I have no doubt that India will produce great men and women in the future, as she has done in the past and in the present ; before our very eyes, we have seen these great figures, and yet I doubt, while India produces great men and women, whether she will or can produce just another like Sarojini. So we think of her as a brightness, as a certain vitality and vividness, as poetry infused into life and activity, as something tremendously important and rich, and yet something which in terms of the material world is rather insubstantial, difficult to grasp and difficult to describe, as something which you can only feel, as you can feel beauty, as you can feel the other higher things of life. Maybe some memory of this will reach other generations who have not seen her and inspire them. I think it will, but I do not think they will ever feel it as we poor mortals have felt who had the privilege of being associated with her.

So, in making this reference to this House, I can only recount various ideas that come into my mind, and perhaps I recount them in a somewhat confused way, because my mind feels afflicted and confused as if an intimate part of it were cut off from it and because it is difficult to speak or to judge people for whom one has a great deal of affection. It was the affection of unity. It was the affection of one who even in his younger days was tremendously inspired by her speech and action and who during the succeeding decades grew more and more to love her and to admire her and to think of her as a rich and rare being. That rich and precious being is no more and that is sorrow for us, inevitably, and yet it is something more than sorrow. It is, if we view it in another light, a joy and triumph for us that the India of our generation produced such rare spirits as have inspired us and as will inspire us in the future.

Sir, it is customary when making such a reference to say that the sympathy and condolence of this House might be conveyed to the relatives of the person who has passed away. I say so and yet really the bond that held Sarojini to all of us here and to thousands and tens of thousands in this country was as close and great as the bond that held her to her own children or to her other relatives and so we send this message of condolence on behalf of this House. All of us really require that message ourselves to soothe our hearts.